Assemble
Building Collective

Aaron Betsky

Assemble
Building Collective

Aaron Betsky

With over 500 illustrations

Contents

INTRODUCTION 006

Putting On The Show

024

The Cineroleum
Folly for a Flyover
Theatre on the Fly

OTOProjects
Big Slide
School of Narrative Dance

The Playing Field
Horst Festival

Making a Home

084

Sugarhouse Studios Stratford
Yardhouse
Sugarhouse Studios Bermondsey

Make, Don't Make Do
Blackhorse Workshop

Domeview Yard
The Blue

Going Public

126

New Addington
Bell Square Pavilion
Art on the Underground
Skating Situations

Baltic Street Adventure
Playground
The Voice of Children
Play KX

The Brutalist Playground
Bramcote Park

Building Community

168

Granby Four Streets
10 Houses on Cairns Street

Granby Workshop
Granby Winter Garden

Stille Strasse
St Anne's College

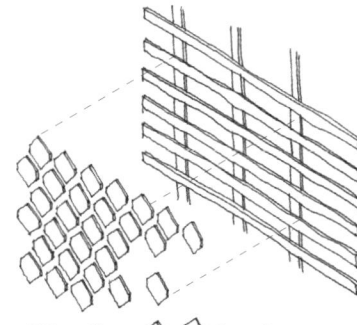

Workshop(ing) Architecture 208

Goldsmiths CCA
Kunstacademie Zwevegem
Design Museum Gent
Kaaitheater

Bill Brown Creative Workshops
Kamikatz Brewery
Material Institute
Fabric Floor

D. H. Chen Foundation Gallery
Atelier LUMA
Armitage Shanks

Showing Off 270

Lina Bo Bardi: Together
Triangle Chairs
Harrow Lowlands
Turner Prize Exhibition
Robin Day
How We Build

A Factory As It Might Be
The Factory Floor
Laguna Viva
The Rules of Production
Tufting Gun Tapestries
Ways of Listening

Charlotte Perriand:
    Design Museum
Being Human
The Sympathy of Things

Still Assembling 314

Dairy Road Industrious
    Neighbourhood
House of Annetta

Open School East
Totteridge Academy Quad
GROW Totteridge Farm

Art in Hovinbyen

ASSEMBLE MEMBERS	344
ENDNOTES	345
PROJECT DIRECTORY	346
IMAGE CREDITS	348
INDEX	349

An Assemble group working session at Tavistock Square. The early members were there to develop the design for Folly for a Flyover.

INTRODUCTION

It started, as so much in art and design does, in a pub. That, at least, is part of Assemble's foundation myth. As best as the various participants' memories align, the idea to work together came up at a birthday party in London for original member Giles Smith in 2009. A mixture of Cambridge University students and recent graduates, the group of friends thought it a better way to pursue architecture than going to work for a firm, as most of them had already done or were pondering doing. The suggestion was then made (by whom is not completely clear) that all of those interested meet the following week at the George and Vulture in Hoxton. Those who showed up on that day in January 2010 formed the crew that would become Assemble. The group coalesced around a single project of their own devising, conceived to occupy a disused petrol station lot that they had discovered in Clerkenwell. They gathered together a group of designers, artists, builders and enthusiasts to build and operate a pop-up cinema, named The Cineroleum. This project was the start of their journey as a design collective – one that has gone on to complete dozens of projects around the world.

Although both the origins and structure of Assemble are unusual, like all design organizations, they emerged from a particular set of circumstances. First and foremost was their shared experience at Cambridge University, which most of them attended. As one of the oldest and most prestigious educational institutions in the world, it is suffused by a particular culture. Many of Assemble's members were students there when a like-minded set of teachers fostered a culture of experimentation with materials and ways of addressing larger social issues. Beyond the confines of the university, Assemble also emerged at a time when new ways of making architecture, deeply rooted in British traditions but also addressing global issues, were emerging.

The Cambridge School of Architecture as it appears today. It is located on the edge of the university's historic core.

The School's rear, showing the new studio designed by Mole Architects in 2008.

Architecture has held a particular place at Cambridge. A relative latecomer to the university, the architecture department has never gained the prestige, either within the institution or in the larger discipline, that many of the older departments have attained. The field of architecture in the UK has remained strongly focused on London, where most larger and more influential design firms are based, providing examples of built work, a stream of teachers for the local institutions and employment opportunities for those schools' students. Press and exhibition venues are also largely based in London.[1]

The atmosphere at the Cambridge School of Architecture during the period many of the original Assemble members studied there was one in which the design part of the curriculum exhibited a certain tension. Many professors saw the discipline very much as part of history and a stylistic and formal continuum. Others were part of a movement to open traditions and existing social fabric to new participants. The resolution of this tension came with a focus on the vernacular as a means to invigorate building practices in a critical manner. Under the guidance of historians such as Dalibor Vesely, and within the traditions set by writer J. M. Richards, students were steered towards everyday structures as much as they were the grand monuments of traditional architectural history. They participated in studies that looked towards the revitalization of neglected neighbourhoods and social structures, using tactics such as direct participation in social activism and community construction; they documented existing conditions through photography and

INTRODUCTION

The exterior of the William Morris & Co. workshop at Merton Abbey.

Block printing chintzes at William Morris's Merton Abbey workshop.

statistics, then translated this material as directly as possible into theoretical proposals. This emphasis was especially strong under the leadership of Mary Ann Steane, who ran the undergraduate programme there for two decades.[2]

The work of such cultural historians as Raymond Williams and Richard Hoggart is evident in these efforts, but there was also a particular architectural history in which Cambridge was operating at the time. Architecture critic Irénée Scalbert traces this lineage back to the Arts & Crafts tradition of the middle of the 19th century, through the work of Alison and Peter Smithson after the Second World War, and then into the neo-vernacular efforts of such firms and designers as Sergison Bates, Tony Fretton, Caruso St John and David Adjaye.[3]

The genesis of this strand of thinking was an economic critique that took the form of a cultural project. John Ruskin, the art critic and philosopher who laid the groundwork for the Arts & Crafts movement, argued for the importance of an organic form of art as a way of conventionalizing and communicating nature, rooted in the idea that the person making artefacts and images according to this method was himself (rarely herself) attuned to their body and their surroundings, whether human-made or natural. The political and economic corollary to this argument was not only a profound nativism and conservatism (in every sense of that phrase), but also a call to break up the large, abstract systems of the Industrial Revolution into small communities based on craft and agriculture that would trade among themselves. This Ruskinian notion of a kind of anarcho-syndicalism was then developed by the next generation of Arts & Crafts makers, such as William Morris and C. R. Ashbee, into groupings that drew on medieval

Hunstanton Secondary Modern School in Hunstanton, Norfolk, designed by Alison and Peter Smithson (1949–54).

guilds, but also on contemporary utopian theories, to create communities of craft and commerce.

Although such efforts had largely either failed or been subsumed into capitalist modes of production by the beginning of the 20th century, the traditions persisted in academic and artistic circles and small crafts communities around England. For Raymond Williams, these efforts (though he thought them misguided) and the definitions of art that justified them, as outlined in his book *Culture & Society 1780–1950* (1958), provided a potential manner in which the remnants of what he defined as a working-class culture could be activated: by preserving or 'tending' to them and continuing aspects of their formal expressions.

For architects, the obvious direction for a critical 'tendency' was protecting, preserving, studying and elaborating those aspects of the built environment that could be seen as being outside of capitalism. That work was accomplished historically through the documentation of vernacular buildings such as pubs by the likes of Nikolaus Pevsner. At the same time, the preservation movement, galvanized by the continual destruction inherent in then-modern notions of urban growth and the architecture that made it up, shifted from calling for the protection of individual structures to a more holistic approach. They realized that it was essential to take into account the whole context or human-made landscape in order to preserve forms that could contain and protect communities and modes of economic organization resistive to capitalism.

Of equal importance was the tradition of looking seriously at the built environment – not by the standards of architecture reserved for the making of the central institutions of the state and culture, or the houses and office buildings in the central city – but as it existed in the vernacular Richards and Pevsner were fond of documenting. It is important to point out that these authors did not reject Modernism as a whole, but rather tried to find ways in which simple structures, especially those of the rural and suburban

INTRODUCTION

Another view of Hunstanton, showing the simple but clear order established by the visible steel frame with its brick and glass infill.

Hunstanton's interior, also composed of simple materials and filled with light, with circulation elements such as the stairs clearly expressed.

A collage the Smithsons made to show the outdoor 'streets' at the Golden Lane Estate as they were envisioning it in 1952.

environment, could provide alternate models better suited to the realities of both building production and the daily life of the inhabitants of those structures. As Richards pointed out in his analysis of the English suburb, *Castles on the Ground* (1946), there was a particular quality to what had been built in the 19th century that also needed to be understood:

> These, then, are the special qualities the observant pilgrim is able to distinguish in the suburban style: it is an ad hoc world, created rather than evolved; it concerns itself first of all with scenic effects, which outweigh strictly architectural considerations; these scenic effects depend on depth as well as breadth, and on a sense in the observer of being within the dense suburban jungle, not outside it; and it relies much on the romantic technique of concealment and surprise, of charms enhanced because they are grudgingly revealed. Finally, to counterbalance the suburb's instinct for panoramic effect, there is also a more conscious and personal interest in detail of every kind.[4]

Although texts such as these were not addressed primarily to architects but to the general public, in the late 1950s architects began to propose ways of designing new structures that would strengthen and elaborate, rather than stand against or contradict, such organic landscapes. The recapturing of the 'vernacular' forms developed in the 19th century to house workers and their places of gathering, using an aesthetic dominated by brick and other local materials and marked by the necessarily minimal amount of decoration, detailing, or other added elements that could not be afforded when building for working class environments, brought with it certain crafts that aligned with the Arts & Crafts tradition. At the same time, the acceptance of chance, ad hoc conditions and existing ornamental traditions also became part of the proposals these designers made.

Alison and Peter Smithson in particular showed a way of designing in this manner that was evolutionary and incremental, offering an alternative to the radical rejection of modernity that countries such as Italy or the Netherlands developed in the 1960s, by trying to resurrect what they saw as native traditions. The Smithsons' practice veered between a fascination with new technology and the radical forms it made

The Smithsons' Robin Hood Gardens housing estate in Poplar, London (1972) built out of precast concrete units stacked up to utilize mass-production techniques.

The housing estate contained 213 flats arranged in a tower and a lower section that together defined a sheltered green area. The building was an attempt to build community and place.

possible, as in the various exhibition pavilions and theoretical projects they designed (House of the Future in 1956 and Appliance House in various versions also starting in 1956), and an adoption and adaptation of traditional brick construction with sloped, tiled roofs and standard windows in projects such as Sugden House in Watford (1956).

In between these two extremes they developed a manner of combining industrial imagery and mass production methods with more traditional materials such as brick, tile and wood, as seen at Hunstanton School (1954). They also helped set the tone for an alternative to both the large-scale reproduction of vernacular housing forms in commercial estates and the production of even larger-scale housing objects in the form of modernist flats and their horizontal equivalent of rowhouses. Their undulating, terraced and at times fragmented housing designs, such as their unbuilt competition entry for the Golden Lane Estate in London (1952) and their realized design for Robin Hood Gardens, also in London (1972), aimed to create communities around shared courtyards and other social spaces, embodying their search for an architecture that continued familiar forms with modern methods.[5]

It was out of those attempts that the work and theory of the strongest influences on the early members of Assemble developed. While these kinds of modes and approaches had been kept alive by some architects (the Smithsons themselves practiced into the 1980s), it was certainly not part of the mainstream by the 1990s, and designers and firms such as Tony Fretton, Sergison Bates and Caruso St John set about recapturing that trajectory.

INTRODUCTION

The Smithsons provided balconies for as many units as possible at Robin Hood Gardens, and manipulated the structure to create a breakdown of scale from the large to the individual flat.

A view of one of the estate's 'streets in the air', which acted as circulation spaces but were also intended for social gathering.

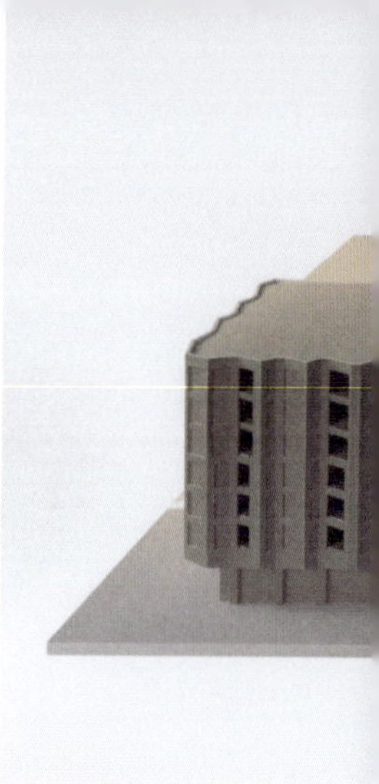

Of these, it was Fretton who first made the connection to a European form of reduced and restrained expression that was to become an important part of the British approach to neo-vernacular Minimalism. A professor of architecture in Delft, the Netherlands, between 1993 and 2003, he also maintained an active practice in London that produced mainly housing projects in the Netherlands. The facades of these buildings were often vertically elongated in their proportions and the structure usually consisted of a thin layer of brick manipulated into planes broken up by thin accent lines. He used this technique at many different scales, suppressing most other details and leaving glass or metal infill panels as the only other salient aspect of his compositions.

Fretton first become known in the UK not for this housing, but for his building for the Lisson Gallery in London. Starting work in 1986, the first phase was completed in 1990 and featured a deft arrangement of glass and stucco elements creating a largely open facade. He also created structures that followed what he believed to be local vernacular traditions, abstracting these into houses with pitched, skewed roofs or small blocks of rowhouses. Particularly notable in this mode was the Molenplein housing project in Den Helder, the Netherlands (2013), a large assembly of different modes of housing broken up to resemble structures that have appeared over the years.[6]

The work of Sergison Bates is similar to that of Fretton in several aspects: a fondness for simple geometric blocks clad in brick or other traditional materials, a distortion of proportions within this reduced palette (though it is here less pronounced) and a concentration on housing. This is not surprising since Jonathan Sergison, who founded the firm with Stephen Bates in 1996, worked for Fretton as well as the godfather of current British Minimalism, David Chipperfield. Sergison Bates's work is, to put it simply, thicker than that of Fretton, displaying a stronger tendency towards solidity and monumentality. It is also less wary of acute angles, using them to break up larger volumes in recent projects such as its Hampstead mansion block in London (2022) or its harbour building in Antwerp,

A model for the Cadix harbour building (2021), an eighty-unit apartment building Sergison Bates designed in Antwerp with a facade that responds to the nearby historic warehouses.

The Lisson Gallery in London (1992) designed by Tony Fretton as a combination of open and closed volumes that echo the mixed array of buildings around the new structure.

The gallery seen straight on, with the individual galleries visible from the street.

Belgium (2021). Sergison Bates has a fondness for forms that recall industrial buildings and greenhouses, making its work somewhat closer to that of the Smithsons.[7]

Neither of these firms' architecture, however, has many distinguishing characteristics that clearly defines that work in either a formal or a spatial sense, and that is a part of how they present themselves: as architects who do not impose alien forms on a urban situation, but rather mine their sites for clues, translating them with as little effort as possible into mute and, they believe, elegant forms. They share that approach with many firms working in the Flanders area and in Switzerland, where Bates now teaches and works (the Swiss office of Sergison Bates was opened in 2010). Their work can thus be seen as part of a European reaction against the expressive forms of both Postmodernism and Deconstructivism (understanding that both are umbrella terms, covering many different approaches) closely associated with the ideas of Aldo Rossi, in which memory and history are thought to have eroded individual expression or specificity out of buildings, leaving structures that are close to archetypes.

It was Adam Caruso and Peter St John who, starting in 1990, began to develop a form of this mode of Minimalism that was tied more closely both to British architectural history and to socially critical approaches. They also brought a keen eye for the ad hoc, anarchic and yet very real practices that the theoreticians of the 1950s had noted in the British vernacular. Their practice began with studies of vernacular building types, concentrating on the quirkiness of structures, claddings and spaces that accumulate over time. For inspiration, they looked first to theoreticians such as Robert Venturi, adopting his call for a more diverse and multivalent architecture, but also one that would delight in the full repertoire of formal tricks architecture has up its sleeves. Instead of following him in his preference for the classical

INTRODUCTION

A collage by the Smithsons of the Golden Lane Estate project (1952) showing how they envisioned the decks of the project looking through to what they called the 'yard-gardens'.

forms that elevated monuments and buildings to the powerful, Caruso and St John sought to apply his ideas to what they call the 'aesthetics of poverty' and the use of cast-offs pioneered by artists such as Joseph Beuys and Robert Smithson. They saw this approach both as a critique of liberal capitalism, which was especially potent during the Thatcher and Major governments in which they started working and which continued in the guise of a more socially oriented neoliberalism in the Blair era, as well as an alternative way to find work in a field dominated by commissions for large corporations, prestigious cultural institutions and self-aggrandizing public institutions.[8]

In Caruso St John's early work, which remains its most influential on the Assemble generation, it is sometimes difficult to find the architecture. Its Pleasant Place Doctors' Surgery in Hersham (1991) appears at first to be only a minimal renovation and abstraction of the existing rowhouse, fitting in with its neighbour with little effort. It is only in the replacement of some cladding, the sliding of new elements through the existing fabric and a few carefully considered construction details that its craft becomes visible. Its first urban project, Studio House in London (1994), makes use of an existing warehouse building, adding only a few walls and windows. A private house in Lincolnshire that the duo completed at the same time presents itself as an off-kilter version of the surrounding, much older buildings, and coalesces into forms and spaces that are by no means normative, but still simple. However, it is The Stable in Wroxall (1992) that exemplifies what to some of their followers became the essence of their work. Here Caruso St John left as much of the original

The Cadix harbour building in Antwerp by Sergison Bates seen from the front.

A view from the building's rear court through to the street, showing the experimentation with different types and patterns of bricks Sergison Bates uses as decoration in its restrained material palette.

building alone and visible, making careful incisions and additions whose form is minimal in both finish and form.

In the 2000s, the firm developed a more eye-catching approach to forms, partly a result of many of its later commissions being for public institutions like museums. Though this brought the firm considerable fame, by then the next generation of architects, most notably the group that calls itself 6a, was pushing the wilful minimalism of action and effect and the maximum composition of existing with new in a 'dirty' or vernacular manner much further.[9]

Tom Emerson, founding member of 6a, who also taught at Cambridge when some of the original Assemble members were in attendance, teaching several of them directly, studied with Tony Fretton and both Caruso and St John. Along with Sergison Bates, Mark Pimlott, Jonathan Woolf and David Adjaye they were known as 'The Whisperers' (a term coined by Sir Peter Cook), a group of architects who attempted to develop a quiet, difficult-to-discern architecture.[10] What these designers had in common, according to Emerson and Scalbert, was that they combined a minimalist and abstract style and an interest in the vernacular, much as described above, but in a manner that sought to do as little as possible, creating minor incisions and improvements in the existing building and urban fabrics. The Whisperers may have failed to follow their own precepts, at least as soon as they received larger commissions, but 6a tried to stay true to them and even push these ideas further.[11]

In this, Emerson's friendship with the artist Richard Wentworth was particularly important. In his photographic work, which he pursued after starting his career as a sculptor, Wentworth seeks chance compositions on the street: the way a repair has been made to a road; a bottle sitting on a stoop; a kluged addition to a hinge; the contrast of different paint

Caruso St John's Pleasant Place Doctors' Surgery (1991) seen from the adjacent graveyard. The view emphasizes the continuity the architects created with the adjacent rowhouses.

colours on a housefront. Through his lens, these all turn into found compositions. His attitude is radical in its refusal to 'do' anything to what he finds or to tune his lens and printing techniques to heighten aesthetic effects. In this way his work is unlike, for instance, his contemporary Wolfgang Tillmans. It is exactly the not-quite-pretty and completely unadorned manner of what he finds that is Wentworth's art.

According to Scalbert, from their teachers and artists such as Wentworth, 6a developed an architecture marked by a distinct aesthetic of nonchalance that is nonetheless highly studied:

> ...what distinguishes 6a's sensibility is less a sense of the virtuous than a forensic curiosity, a frame of mind that is specifically historical. Architecture involves some detective work. You look at things, you look under and through things because they are sources of knowledge, signs of a momentary resourcefulness.[12]

Scalbert describes 6a's approach as 'anthropological', connecting the firm to the legacy of the Smithsons and Williams, and notes that they work through bricolage. She also cites the Greek notion of metis:

> Metis goes back and forth between the intelligible and the sensible, a quality that commends it to architects and to 6a in particular who can be said to practice it. Unlike engineering, it does not lend itself to precise measurement, to exact calculations and rigorous logic. It is instead an attitude that combines 'flair, wisdom, forethought, subtlety of mind, deception, resourcefulness, vigilance, opportunism, varied skills, and experience'.[13]

The most complete early work that embodies these attitudes is 6a's renovation of a gallery space called Raven Row in London (2009). The design accepts many of the conditions of the structure as found, including the marks of a fire outbreak but also more substantive inheritances such as the presence of occupants in an upstairs apartment. What 6a did design is even more minimalist than the work of its predecessors. It eschews fetishized details and carefully composed

The Stable in Wroxall (1992), an early project by Caruso St John in which minimal elements were inserted into an old stone building.

A view of The Stable from the outside. The architects emphasized where they inserted new windows by colouring the stucco.

planes in favour of plain white surfaces whose assembly and placement are purely convenient.

When 6a builds entirely new structures, such as the extension to the South London Gallery (2010), the firm emphasizes not just abstraction, but a tension and elongation of proportions with the elements of the existing building, whether walls, windows or whole facades. Even larger projects, such as Cowan Court residence hall at Churchill College, Cambridge University (2016), convey a sense that 6a has emerged from both the immediate and general context. The dark brick and light wood elements of the exterior are designed to resemble late 20th-century housing projects as well as Churchill's original buildings, while on the interior, structural wood elements impose themselves on spaces and exist in close proximity but distinct scales to demonstrate their functions.

While 6a had not yet completed many projects when Emerson was teaching at Cambridge, its members were active participants in the informal gatherings of The Whisperers and took their students to see their work, as well as making the version of British architectural history that interested them (which was very much in line with what I have described above) available to their charges. More importantly, Emerson also led design/build studios in which students were tasked with creating pavilions on the grounds of the school. Despite the lack of an adequate shop, or perhaps because of that, the students were able to construct inventive objects that used a wide variety of often found or reused materials. The early members of Assemble cite the combination of exploring the rougher aspects of construction, combined with their field trips to London, as a major influence on the development of their work.

INTRODUCTION

Richard Wentworth, *London 1976/England 1976, Making Do and Getting By* (1995).

Richard Wentworth, *South West France* (2007).

According to both Scalbert and several of the Assemble members' former tutor Ingrid Schroder (now Director of the Architectural Association), these constructions also resembled the theatrics Cambridge students put on.[14] Assembled without direct institutional control or support, these performances help those students with interests in drama further their career by proving their abilities in a public manner, while forming a strong bonding and networking opportunity for those whose careers go in other directions. They become both calling cards and ways of making shared values and beliefs concrete.

What underlays much of the work of Emerson and other tutors at Cambridge was a strong interest in the social aspects of architecture. According to architectural historian Joseph Bedford, if the formal interests visible in Assemble's work can be traced back through the work of the Smithsons into an Arts & Crafts tradition, their theoretical pursuits come from the focus on 'the discourse on the richness of the cultural life of the city' and 'urban phenomenology' articulated by sociologists Richard Sennett and Jane Jacobs, which resonated with the older British interest in the culture of the working class. Bedford points to other contemporary entities – part design agencies, part research groups – with similar interests, such as EXYZT and Spatial Agency, with their 'collages filled with old people walking down the street, fishmongers in the market, and seagulls picking up trash'.[15]

Those theoretical concerns were tied to social activism, which saw the architect's role as visualizing the fullness of urban life and facilitating the extension of its richness, rather than its extinguishment through planning and new buildings. At most, designers should add bulwarks against commercialization and appropriation through gentrification. These efforts were channelled through a visual style that eschewed abstraction, data representation and other difficult-to-understand images. Instead, the architects in The Whisperers

Richard Wentworth, *Nicosia* (2001).

and those in this larger ecosystem of experimental groups were concerned with acting to preserve and protect working-class urban life. They learned from advertising (and its power to convince and sell), but also from cartoons, zines and action movies that transformed zeros into heroes and trash into the home of an alternate power structure.

Collected in such volumes as Shumon Basar and Markus Miessen's *Did Someone Say Participate? An Atlas of Spatial Practices* (2006), these attempts to make images out of and for the street scenes they encountered, and to strengthen the ability of communities to survive and thrive using documentation, analysis and communication in a graphically striking manner, cropped up after the turn of the millennium.[16] Particularly in Switzerland, Belgium and the Netherlands where they connected to traditions that paralleled and overlapped with those generated by the Smithsons, in particular those of the loosely organized Team X group (of which the Smithsons were an important part), whose work was assembled, exhibited and published in Rotterdam the year before the *Atlas* came out. These approaches were embedded in a socially democratic practice that emphasized the collective urban (and later suburban) scene as the anchor not only of political but also cultural and educational systems. Designing and building primary schools, community centres and satellite cultural facilities along with social housing was understood to be the proper activity of architecture – not the making of monuments.

Just as important to this focus on community action through research, documentation and acceptance of the vernacular, and direct participation in the making of social activators, was the emergence of 'tactical urbanism', in which architects saw their role as supporting neighbourhood coalescence and power and acting through non-building modes. Founded in 1998 in Caracas, Venezuela, the architecture and urbanism firm Urban-Think Tank was a pioneer in this field.

INTRODUCTION

Interior view of 6a's Raven Row Gallery in London (2009).

The upstairs room of the gallery was preserved as a semi-ruin.

Urban-Think Tank first set up a card table in a favela in Caracas to offer its services (the members were briefly kidnapped for their efforts) and progressed to designing an urban tramway through the city that combined affordable urban transportation with community buildings within the stations.[17] The firm also documented the informal public takeover of the Torre David, an unfinished forty-storey office tower in the city and victim of the country's 1994 economic crisis.

These urban tacticians worked with local community groups and politicians to produce interventions, performances and temporary structures that transformed the lack of resources in poorer neighbourhoods into advantages. These acts of architecture could install themselves quickly, mobilizing and demobilizing as necessary, connecting to cultural and political acts and disappearing before they could be either commercialized or destroyed by the powers that be. These structures also stretched the notion of what architecture might be, disappearing into the assembly of available materials as needed at one end and transforming into urban infrastructure and public landscaping at the other.[18]

Taken together, these movements sought to expand the definition of what it was that an architect does, while retaining a focus on accepting the vernacular and a desire to work in space. As Basar and Miessen said:

> [We argue] for a re-evaluation of architecture beyond the traditional definitions of built substance into the possibility of an architecture of knowledge that is built up, importantly, by architects eschewing conventional practice and non-architects participating in space; thus becoming what is termed here 'spatial practitioners'. They share an essential interest: the understanding, production, and altering of spatial conditions as a pre-requisite of identifying the broader reaches of political reality.[19]

Miessen went on to explain how such an attitude could work its way into a form of practice:

6a used charred timber to evoke the fire that partially destroyed the existing building in 1972.

Another view of the gallery from the outside, showing a new cast iron facade molded on original timbers from the site.

> Within contemporary discourse, a strong resistance towards pure object lust forms the backbone of an increasing amount of projects that are often self-initiated. They are likely to be temporary and informal, contingent and ephemeral in nature, and most often imply a particular local, political interest.[20]

He also placed this attitude – which seems like a blueprint for Assemble's structure and aims – in a larger historical tradition that:

> object[s] to the idea that there are such terms as high and low culture. The social ambition of these practices is rooted in a much more heterogeneous understanding of society and consequently the city. The protagonists of such socio-political urban practice take popular and marginal cultures into account. They base their work on an urban sociology… While propelling a practice that goes beyond mere representation, they also start to create positions of their own personal freedom. Rather than understanding themselves as a singular character within the infrastructure of an office, they situate themselves in networks of aware practitioners that – as part of collaborative frameworks – broaden their collective horizon by self-initiated discursive platforms and collaborative projects.[21]

The *Atlas* and the websites devoted to this sort of tactical urbanism that proliferated at that time assembled many of these tactics and outlined the possibilities, making them readily available to Assemble's future members. Some of them recall seeing and discussing the Caracas tramway and other examples in their early discussions.

Mostly, however, those who assembled at that pub in 2010 concentrated on local examples, taking frequent day trips to London to see the built work of The Whisperers and related designers, attending lectures and exhibitions, and observing the self-generated changes in historically working-class neighbourhoods under threat of gentrification such as Brixton and Hoxton. It was within these movements and constructions, and with the tools and sensibilities they gained at Cambridge, that they then created their own tactical insertions into the urban realm.

INTRODUCTION

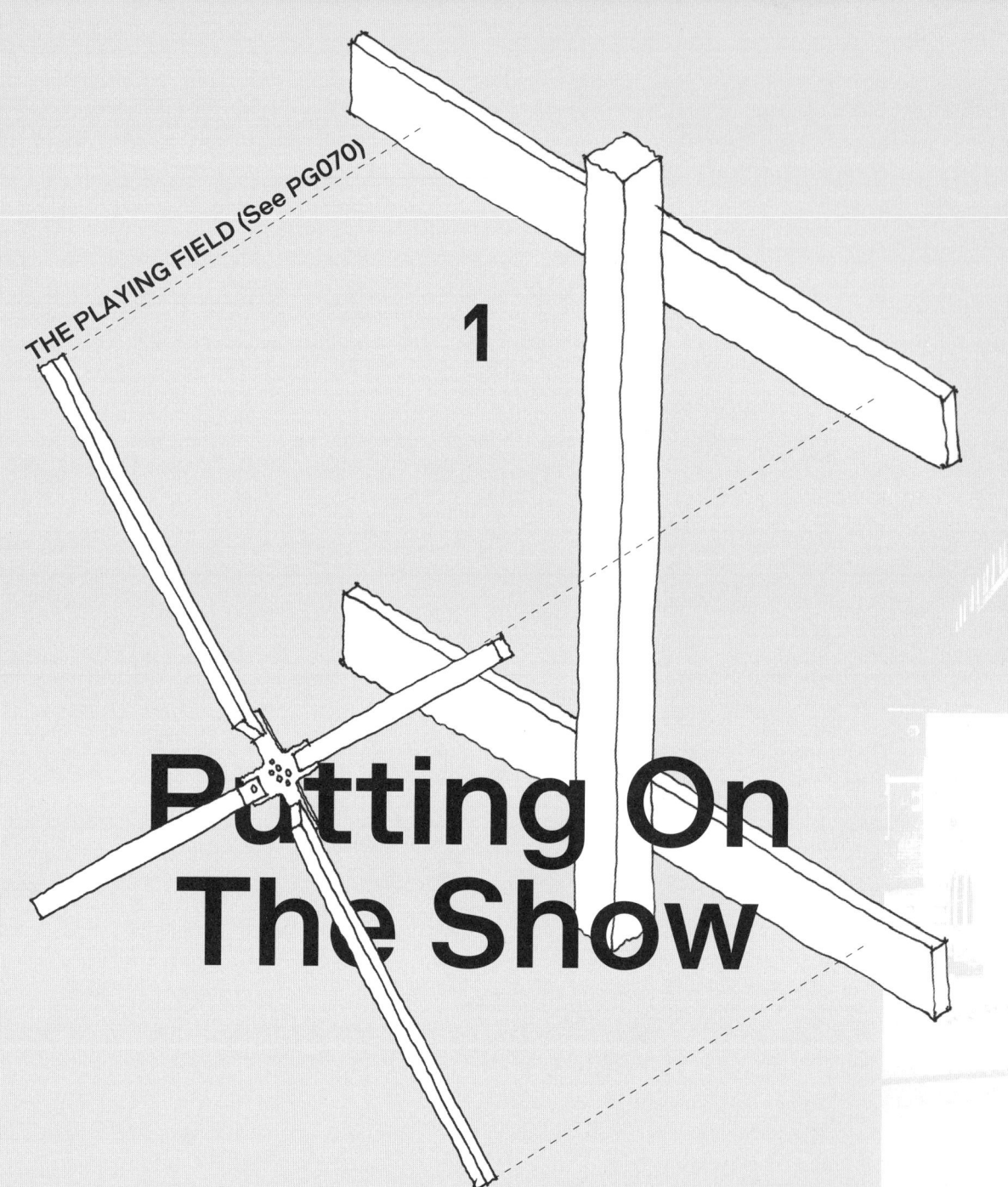

THE PLAYING FIELD (See PG070)

1

Putting On The Show

THE CINEROLEUM The project around which Assemble formed in 2010 was self-initiated. The group found the site (a disused petrol station in Clerkenwell, central London), came up with the idea that it should be occupied by a temporary cinema, came up with a name (The Cineroleum, combining cinema and petroleum) and designed the installation. They then sought out the necessary permissions and expertise required to construct and run a short-term cinema: how to assemble the scaffolding, rig the curtains and put together the chairs; how to manage a large group of volunteers and actually run the events; and finally, how to make sure people knew about what they were doing. In learning how to build what they had imagined in this way, they set the tone for what was to become Assemble's modus operandi: discover opportunities, reimagine places, acquire skills and knowledge and come together

The Cineroleum right before a performance, showing the structure, the combination of handmade and borrowed chairs, and the Tyvek curtain.

The disused petrol station Assemble found in Clerkenwell. The structure had been designed by Arup. The garage to the rear of the site still remained.

025

Assemble set up a production line for putting together the chairs for The Cineroleum out of salvaged scaffolding boards, according to a jig they devised for the purpose.

The Tyvek material used for the curtains came in 50-metre (54-yard) rolls. Assemble came up with a method to crimp the material together with strings so that it became pleated and could be lowered and raised.

with a variety of perspectives, aesthetics and craft approaches to put on a really good show.

The Cineroleum's theatrical aspect proved to be central not only to its success, but to the group's approach to this and many of their projects. From the very beginning, Assemble, as they came to be called while applying for funding for Folly for a Flyover (see p. 040), was a group of individuals who wanted to gain hands-on experience on their own terms and produce architecture with a theatrical bent in the process. The origins of this approach can be traced back to their time at Cambridge University, where theatrics were central to much of the university's cultural life, from the May Week festivities to the plays students staged on a regular basis. There was an entrepreneurial approach to everything from publications to art exhibitions, and a tradition of students coming up with an idea, putting together the resources and garnering the skills required to realize it independently. This became Assemble's way of doing things, which was enhanced even further through persistent inquiry, study and networking.

Several of the first Assemble members had previously experienced – some even participating in – other experiments in self-generated projects. In 2008, future Assemble member Maria Lisogorskaya worked on the Southwark Lido project, which was designed, curated and mounted by the French collective EXYZT in collaboration with filmmaker Sara Muzio. Built as part of the London Festival of Architecture, it was designed to bring people together during the hot summer months. A set of pavilions erected out of metal scaffolding, off-the-shelf tents, tent material and wood provided various ways

For the marquetry-style decoration of the doors and tables in the lobby, Assemble made a set of laser-cut Formica elements that fit together in a repeating pattern.

To adapt the ceiling tiles in the garage, Assemble handmade a vacuum former.

for the public to enjoy bathing, cleansing and simple lounging around water. EXYZT's form of organization and its approach to architecture and its construction served as a concrete model for these students trying to figure out what they wanted to make of themselves and their careers.

The original members of Assemble also cite Frank's Cafe as inspiration. Run every summer since 2009 on the roof of a multi-storey car park in Peckham, it consists of little more than a blood-red canopy strung between timber posts. The outer rows of posts lean back in an expressive and structurally logical mode and the canopy partially covers some rough timber furniture. It was conceived, designed and built by Practice Architecture, a firm that pioneered some of the tactics and modes of presentation Assemble carried on.

Practice Architecture, for which Frank's Cafe was as much a founding moment as The Cineroleum was for Assemble, made small residential and commercial renovation projects. They developed a specialty in small amphitheatres, created both as pure furniture (Big Bench, first constructed for the New Art Centre in Salisbury in 2010) and as interior retrofits (the Yard Theatre, London, 2011). Both of these projects were intended to be flexible and, to a certain extent, modular accommodations for play and performance. Of special note is the presentation technique Practice often employed to demonstrate their ideas; using some of the simplest software programs available, they combined perspectives and rendered them with in-built filters or 'layers' of light and washed-out colours to embue the image with a soft aura-like quality. Rather

Testing the raising of the curtains; Assemble borrowed stage weights to anchor the drapes in place.

The MDF 'Cineroleum' sign being hoisted onto the petrol station's roof.

A team meeting on site during construction to assess the sample of the curtain and other elements going into the project.

Sewing the curtains; Assemble members taught themselves pleating techniques to obtain the desired effect.

The cinema space right before the opening, with lighting designed by collaborators Studio Dekka, used to emphasize aspects of both the existing structure and new elements.

than the human models and high-art artefacts strewn around slicker renderings, the scenes are populated with recognizable people and objects. The firm is no longer active.

It is unclear how exactly these influences and models merged to spark the idea for The Cineroleum, but several members cite as crucial a session in which all of the original members ('in a rolling manner, although we didn't keep roll,' says Owen Lacey) gathered at the guardianship occupied by Paloma Strelitz, Jane Hall and Lewis Jones in Tavistock Square. After several more or less social discussions to exchange ideas, they all decided to lie on the floor and silently think about what they wanted to do. Soon after that, the project emerged. This story, which was told to me by several participants, typifies Assemble's personal narrative and the aura that surrounds it. Although they are not shy about claiming individual authorship for aspects of work and readily acknowledge different perspectives, they are adamant in preserving a sense of the collective in the production of their projects, from inception to completion: a slightly mysterious process of talking, criticism and seemingly unrelated activities. Never does any of them say: 'I came up with the idea, and then we developed it,' or 'I suggested using this material.' At most, they acknowledge that one person either notices an opportunity and checks it out, or subsequently takes the (usually co-) lead on a project. They do point out that different members trained themselves from the beginning in particular skills, such as curtain-making or how to run a bar, but the overall ideation and installation remains, in their memories and projections, a collective artefact.

However it was that The Cineroleum came to be, the site and programme turned out to be a fortuitous

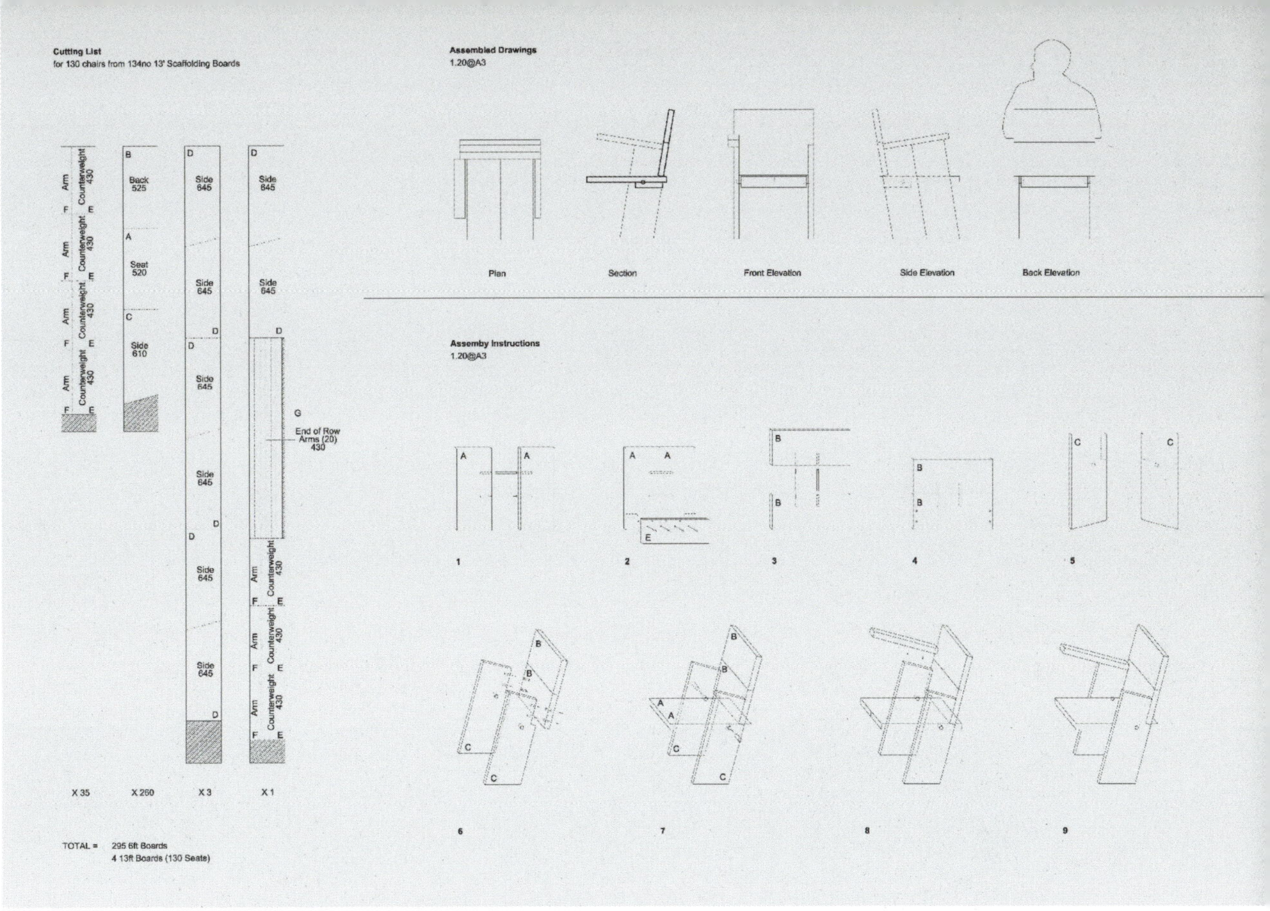

The drawings for the chairs, including a diagram of how they could be put together as efficiently as possible out of 1.8 by 3.6 metre (6 by 12 feet) boards.

confluence. What was left of the petrol station had an expressive structure (originally designed by Arup), including a canopy supported by steel struts that the designers could appropriate. Clerkenwell was by then the home of both adventurous and established members of London's creative class; Zaha Hadid's studio occupied parts of a former school building nearby. Developers were, as they always are, hoping to build on the pioneering activities of these creatives, although the site of The Cineroleum was replaced by a rather nondescript hotel building soon after the run of the event.

To Assemble, an essential part of the design process was and is working with stakeholders, obtaining permissions and acquiring expertise. For The Cineroleum, this involved finding and going to the site's owners and acquiring a license to operate a temporary building, a projection site and a licensed bar. Each of these activities involved bureaucratic and technical hurdles that for the group became not an obstacle, but a chance to learn. While undertaking a work placement at the National Theatre, Alice Edgerley was introduced to nearby Flints Theatrical Chandlers, the UK's major supplier of specialist theatrical hardware, and curtain maker Ken Creasey who was based nextdoor to them in Elephant & Castle at the time. Both took care of theatrical rigging and the making of curtains and sets

The Cineroleum during a performance, with the curtains lowered.

THE CINEROLEUM

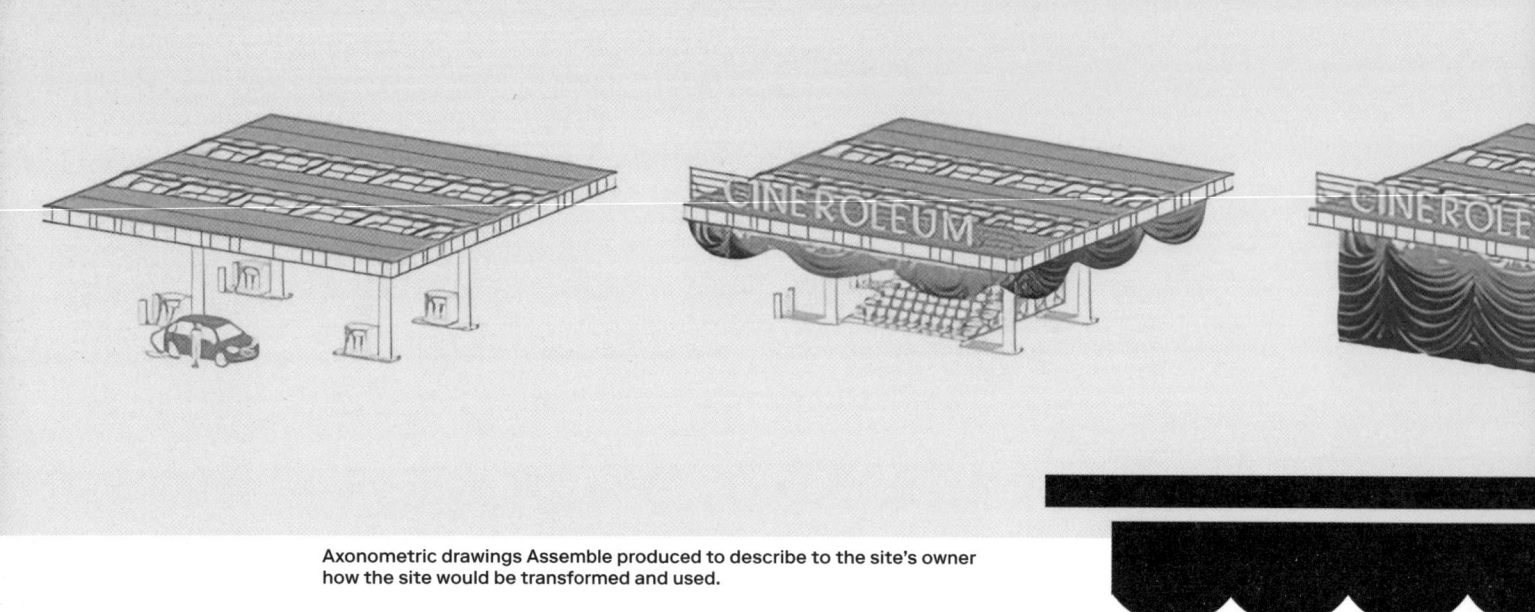

Axonometric drawings Assemble produced to describe to the site's owner how the site would be transformed and used.

THE CINER

for the West End and the movie industry, as well as all the other details that go into setting the scene for performance. They were generous with their time and information. In addition, Edgerley, Hall and Strelitz visited the Duke of York theatre on Drury Lane to understand how boat rigging is used in fly systems.

What turned out to be The Cineroleum's most remarkable aspect, at least to those driving by the former petrol station that summer it was in operation and, more importantly, to the press, were the curtains that surrounded the whole space. This was, if you will, the 'big idea' into which the silent session on the floor translated: a raising of the curtain on the box in which the show usually operates. The curtain and its operation made the essence of the cinema as public spectacle into the architecture itself, shedding all of the steps that usually come between the advertisement of an event and the viewing of a spectacle, while adding a few theatrical moments of its own.

The designers fabricated the curtain collectively in a British version of the American quilting bee. They acquired the cheapest material they could find – roofing membrane – and then figured out a way to gather it together into swags that evoked not only the kind of theatre curtains that were pulled up to the top (as opposed to parting in the middle), but also the window swags and elaborate women's dresses of the Victorian era. The combination of nostalgia with roughness of construction was thus sewn into The Cineroleum's main element.

None of the Assemble members knew much more than rudimentary sewing techniques. Just as they had to learn how to operate a cinema and a bar, they also had to acquire

A rear view of The Cineroleum from a side street during a performance.

the craft of working with their hands and small machines to make the curtains. In the end, the labour involved stitching three kilometres (1.9 miles) of seams. In many ways, that collective effort became as much the founding deed of Assemble as the design itself. Members recall the many hours spent learning and sewing, teaching each other and socializing over the work and enlisting friends, families and even passersby for either a few minutes or many days of collaboration. 'We became a family there,' recalls Hall. 'It turned out we all balanced each other,' adds James Binning, 'with different outlooks and skills.' That idea of becoming skilled in a craft together, working together and being together, with the group expanding and contracting around a core number of stalwarts, remains as central to how Assemble operates as the idea of putting on a show. 'It was an all-encompassing period,' recalls Joe Halligan, 'it had the atmosphere of both a theatre we were acting out and a ritual.' 'It was when we lived up to our name by putting people and pieces together, assembling them,' says Lisogorskaya.

Within the world created by the curtains, Assemble pursued another strategy that remains key to how they operate: reuse. Almost everything that made up The Cineroleum beyond the curtains was found and then upcycled or repurposed. For the foyer, they used salvaged furniture from schools, including square-section metal-framed tables with timber laminate (for which the group made new tops) and circle-section metal

THE CINEROLEUM 035

A view out from the lobby, which was located in what had been the petrol station's shop, showing the neon sign Assemble made alongside the schedule board.

chair legs that they made into stools and benches. The Cinema Museum, which had become a key collaborator, lent them some of their plusher seats to provide a premium viewing opportunity, while the group made the remainder of the chairs, as well as the risers on which they sat, out of recycled scaffold boards. The same was true for most of the implements they used in the bar. And, of course, the films themselves – classics that the group picked collectively, with advice from friends who knew cinema history such as Assemble member Amica Dall (who had worked for the London Film Festival), and The Cinema Museum (who knew what was available) – were in a sense reused.

The Cineroleum was a success by any standard. First, it turned out to be a beautiful, highly impactful design that, like all good architecture, showed off its structure and material in a way that made it attractive to users and viewers, exhibiting itself and its craft and working effectively at the same time. It did so – again, like much good design – by combining, abstracting and further developing a set of sources into new forms. And it did so with a sense of composition and spatial and temporal sequencing that was all the more remarkable because it was the result of collective design.

Second, the pavilion and its construction and operation became the generator for Assemble, both in terms of working methods and fascinations as well as its

Another view of the lobby, with old school furniture transformed through the application of Formica marquetry. The bulbous ceiling tiles are also visible.

A detailed view of one of the reconditioned stools with its inlay top.

nature as a peculiar body of skills and knowledge: a working organization (and later professional entity) and a flexible sociality all rolled into one. In working together, Assemble found that they could do so, enjoyed doing so and could have success doing so. It was a true collaboration.

Third, The Cineroleum was popular. Every screening was sold out and the parties into which these events evolved often extended long after the movie was over. The Cineroleum, both through its success and its location, but also through the networking and publicity skills the Assemble members (despite their oft-repeated disavowals of using them consciously) brought with them, made a big splash in the media. Its image appeared in almost all of the major British newspapers, as well as in professional journals and on websites. I saw it on several of those sites while I was living in America's Midwest, and was so struck by them that I was tempted to get on an airplane to try to attend one of the screenings myself. It was astonishing how much publicity such a small, temporary building received. It also made fans out of critics such as *The Observer*'s Rowan Moore, who then recommended Assemble for crucial subsequent commissions.

THE CINEROLEUM

At the end of each performance, the curtains would be raised and the audience would find themselves viewing and being viewed by the theatre of the street.

Perhaps the final important aspect of The Cineroleum was that it was temporary. It was as much an event as it was an object in a period when architecture critics, using a phrase Bernard Tschumi had coined over a decade earlier, were calling for 'event architecture'.[22] Such temporary designs could counter those tendencies of the discipline to be monumental, which served to alienate its intended users, turning vital social functions into solidified and grand structures that did not respond to changing needs or perspectives. The idea of architecture as a social flywheel that stood as the generator, rather than the endpoint or burial, of critical change in a community (as both the Southwark Lido project and Frank's Cafe were), was becoming central to the thinking of those architects who wanted a more responsive, socially active and sustainable design strategy. The Cineroleum became one of the most successful and most playful instances of event architecture. Being temporary meant that its reputation grew in memory, and it quickly acquired a mythic status as being even more joyful and inventive than it might have been during its brief reality.

The Cineroleum viewed from the street, with a screening in process inside.

  The Cineroleum might have remained a singularly successful flash put on with an extraordinary effort by a bunch of students barely out of school, as many other such structures have turned out to be throughout the history of architecture. However, it turned out to have legs that leapt forwards in repeats and extensions of the original idea: the following year, Assemble was able to build on its achievements and use what they had learned for their next project, Folly for a Flyover.

THE CINEROLEUM

The site for the Folly for a Flyover as Assemble found it, including overgrown vegetation and graffiti.

FOLLY FOR A FLYOVER

Assemble's second project was the result of an injection of both funding and attention into some of London's eastern districts – in particular Hackney, Stratford and surrounding areas – that came with the preparations for the 2012 Olympic Games. Large infrastructure, landscaping and sporting facilities around the River Lea were the most visible part of this endeavour, but the city and the UK government also set up funds (through a programme called Create London, which also attracted corporate funding) to support smaller artworks, neighbourhood improvements and festivals in the areas in and around the Olympic Games site itself. Assemble applied for and received a public art commission from Create London, towards which they had been pointed by the Barbican Centre, who had wanted them to participate in an animation festival that summer.

Hackney Wick would reap the rewards. In the 1960s, the neighbourhood found itself bisected by the flyover of the A12 highway, which had created a dead zone underneath its concrete ceiling and next to the Lee Navigation (the portion of the River Lea that has been made into a canal). By the 2010s, the area had evolved and was continuing to evolve both socially and economically, and the London Legacy Development Corporation (LLDC) commissioned the architecture firm muf to develop a public realm strategy for the neighbourhood. The result was a feasibility study, on which Assemble member Lewis Jones worked.

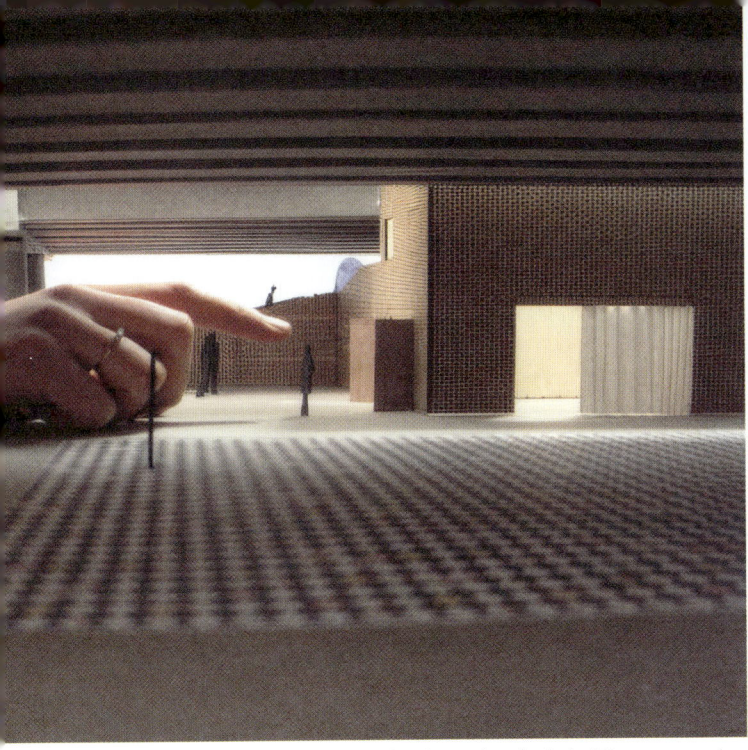

The model for the project included the proposed brick 'curtains' and terrazzo floor.

In the drawing Assemble used to propose the project, they evoked the 'invented history' of the Folly as the ruins of a 'nail house' that pre-existed the flyover.

      muf, founded in 1995 by Katherine Clarke, Liza Fior, Juliet Bidgood and Kath Shonfield, proudly proclaims that it has never had less than eighty percent female employees, and that it concentrates on 'the design of public spaces, and in making spaces public' with a strong emphasis on public engagement. In 2010, the firm had been responsible for the British Pavilion at the Venice Biennale of Architecture, which involved a great deal of hands-on, on-site construction to create a plywood theatre and reading room inside the Pavilion's central space. Like Assemble, muf was adamant about making as little as possible, instead concentrating on how to insert small, tactical objects, changes to the landscape, or renovations to existing buildings in such a way as to open the space up to the community that used these sites. They also utilized some of the same presentation techniques as both Practice and Assemble.

      Building on the feasibility work muf had undertaken, Assemble spent time in the neighbourhood talking to locals and activists and trying to understand both the human-made and the natural setting in greater depth in order to produce something truly beneficial. As part of the Barbican Centre's animation festival, Assemble would make another temporary cinema and performance site and hopefully jumpstart more general improvements to this long-neglected area of Hackney Wick. The team turned to models in the Netherlands, where NL Architects had revitalized a similar flyover in Zaandam with A8ernA project (2006) and the landscape architects West 8 had done the same with Carrascoplein in Amsterdam (1998).

FOLLY FOR A FLYOVER

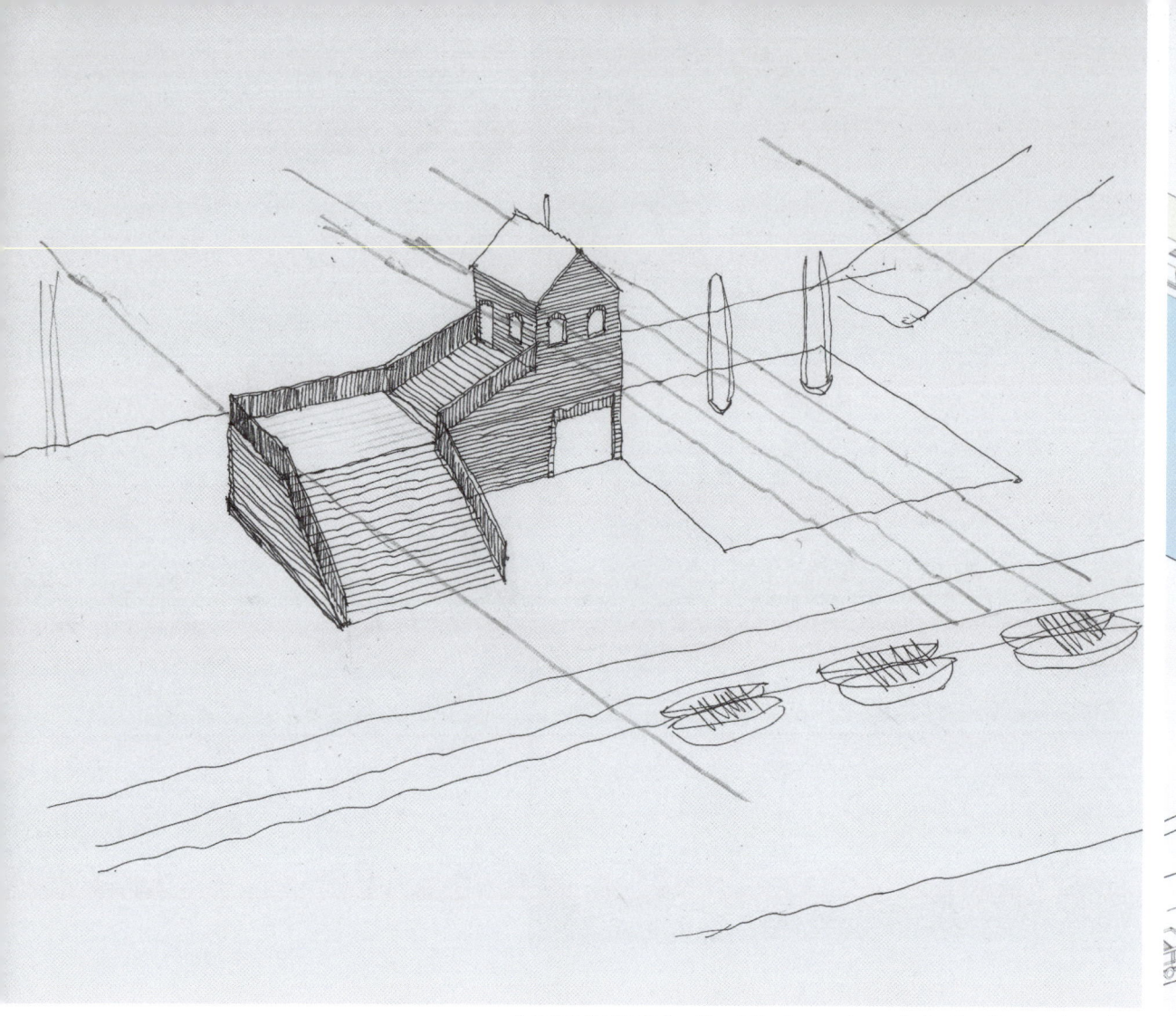

A sketch for the Folly without the flyover shown, indicating the mooring point for rowboats that visitors could rent to explore the canal.

The Folly was much more than a cinema. In addition to showing films, the venue hosted theatrical performances and lectures, as well as workshops for both adults and children. Local entrepreneurs set up a canalside launch so that you could board canoes or boats and tour the nearby Olympic Games site from the water. A cafe provided sustenance. For Assemble, the collection of activities was meant to activate the site for as much of the time as possible during the nine weeks that the Folly was open.

The designers embedded the Folly's operations in an imagined past and future. They developed a story in which the building, with its peaked roof rising over a facade made from recycled bricks, was actually a holdover from before the flyover was built: a house once owned by an inhabitant who refused to sell to the government, so that the roads were built around and over his structure. The open ruin could now, after Assemble's intervention, be reinhabited. By telling this story,

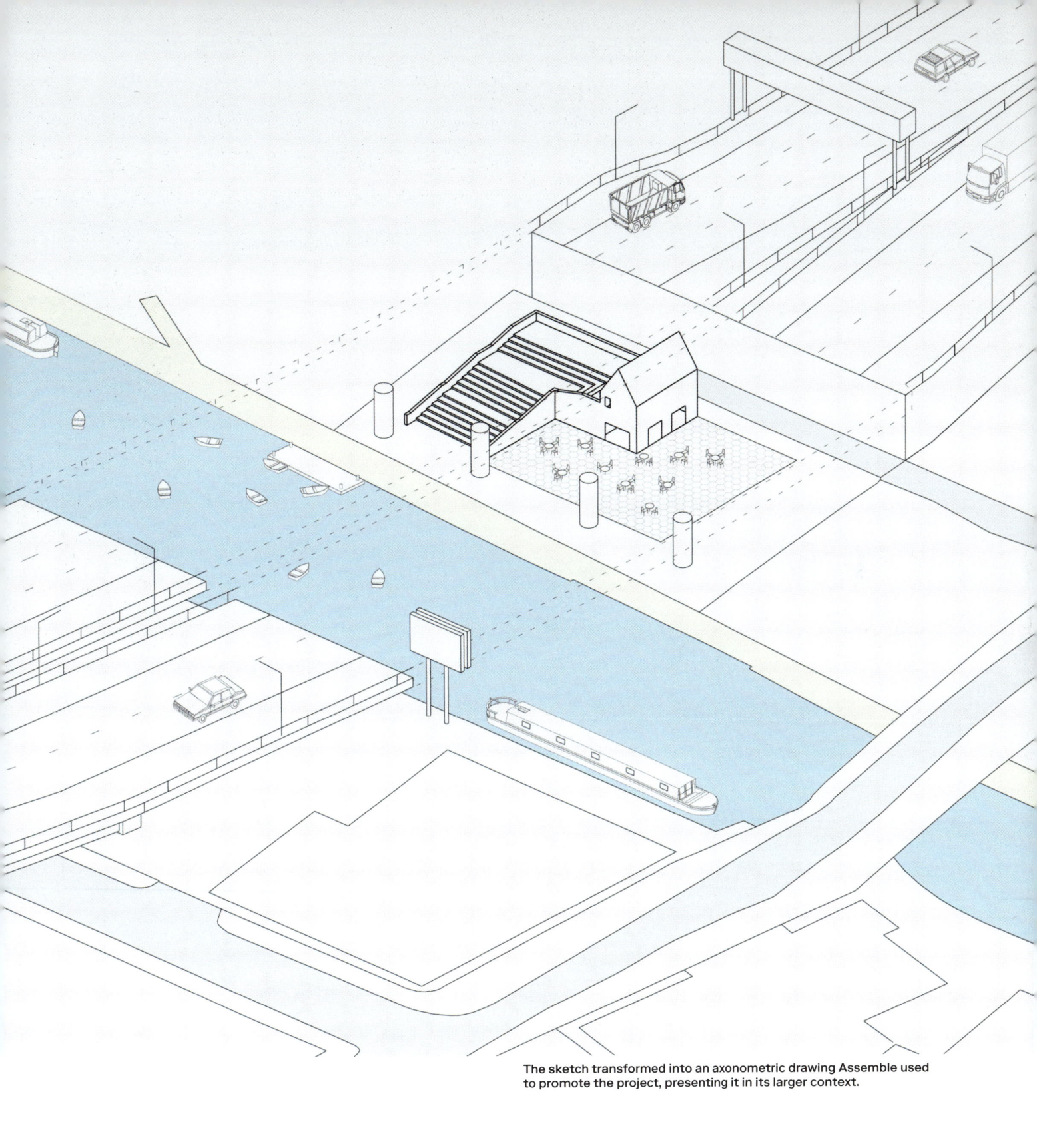

The sketch transformed into an axonometric drawing Assemble used to promote the project, presenting it in its larger context.

FOLLY FOR A FLYOVER

043

Assemble made custom stools for the project out of reclaimed wood and broom handles that served as legs. Each piece was different.

the designers hoped to show the continuity of the past into a more open present. They also hoped that what had been a dead spot in Hackney Wick would now become a place that would attract similar cultural, educational and sporting events, even after their structure was torn down. Following the project, muf installed permanent power on the site and skateboarders are frequent visitors. In the years since 2012, the canal and its adjacent walkway have benefited from investments made in these waterways as an extension of Queen Elizabeth Olympic Park although in a less socially focused direction; the area has sprouted many new residential and office blocks.

  The Folly itself was a remarkable structure because its form, whatever the story the designers told about it, served as a strong counterpoint to the concrete masses all around it. The gabled peak rose up in the gap between the flyover's two bridges, making it (barely) visible to the vehicles racing above, but also emphasizing the opening itself, suggesting the ability to crack open the space. The facade then extended to one side under the highway lanes, sloping down under the overpass until it turned to both announce itself to the walkway and create a defined space. That area became the theatre where movies and performances took place, while a raised, tiled patio provided space for cafe seating.

  Assemble built the main structure out of wood pieces, made to look like bricks, stacked loosely on top

044

To make the 'curtain', each brick was drilled in two places to thread the rope through and connect every brick together. The curtain was then tied back to the scaffolding frame at multiple points.

Top: Threading the bricks, which were then tied back to a scaffolding behind.

Bottom: Assembly members hauling the cables for the electricity power that had to be run across the canal from the opposite bank.

FOLLY FOR A FLYOVER

Surplus sand from the construction process was left on site for children to play with. They could also have fun with the rowing boats when they were not in use.

of each other and strung together with rope tied to scaffolding so that, according to the group, it resembled an 'interwoven bead curtain'. The walls' mottled appearance mimicked the appearance of the surrounding houses and industrial buildings, while the gaps between the pieces reinforced the ruin story and made the whole structure appear light and ephemeral even as it sat underneath the perennial gloom of the flyover. The elements used for construction were all recycled, sourced in Essex from Ashwell's Recycle Timber and put together by Assemble and a team of close to 200 volunteers. Similarly, the furniture was built out of recycled wood pieces, and the designers accepted and even accentuated the varied textures and rough forms that were the combined result. Amy Perkins, a member of Assemble who was working at Caruso St John at the time, helped them obtain wood panelling that the firm was stripping out during their renovation of the Tate Britain building. They also made the chairs, tables and benches into abstractions of their types, giving the chairs elongated and tapered backs that resembled children's drawings of furniture by Charles Rennie Mackintosh. The tiles on which they sat were similarly repurposed.

      The act of reuse did not stop with the generation of the form. After the Folly was dismantled, as per the terms of the contract with the London Borough of Hackney, most of its

Assemble also provided mini versions of the bricks used on the project and helped the children make fantasy structures with them.

A view from the south-east side showing the sand, boats, terrazzo deck with the handmade chairs and the main Folly structure.

pieces and furniture were reused in local schools and community centres. For Assemble, the aim was to have the built architecture be an event that appeared as if out of nowhere, by a force of evocative magic (and the work of all those volunteers), be vivid and present for nine weeks and then disappear again. What they constructed was, they hoped, not just that concentration in time and place of activities, but also new experiences and stories that would have an effect in Hackney Wick and beyond.

For the members of Assemble, the Folly was also another step in the process of becoming a viable group that could extend its own life and activities. They were able to use some of the skills they had learned in making The Cineroleum – not only the craft aspects of the work, but also the organizational ones. They proved themselves able to not only marshal their own forces, but also a much larger group of friends, family and community members than had helped on the first project. They also found themselves putting the research skills they had learned at university to more diverse purposes. Not only did the members of Assemble familiarize themselves with the nature and history of Hackney Wick, but local authorities and agencies also forced them to prove the project's viability well beyond its structure and function. For instance, they had to perform a bat survey to make sure they would not disturb these existing inhabitants of the flyover. What was just as important to Assemble's future development was

Looking out from the window on the second floor of the Folly to a brass band performing under the flyover.

The cafe was serviced from the Folly and spread out over the terrazzo terrace.

that the members had to generate the idea not just by lying on their backs in a flat, but by building on the analysis muf had done, and then working with the local community to come up with and implement the array of performance, education and social events that took place during the run of the Folly.

While this event architecture would be as ephemeral as The Cineroleum, it also received as much, if not more, publicity and attention, again appearing in both the popular press and in professional outlets. Assemble showed themselves once again especially adept at condensing the message they wanted to give by the selection of photographs they released, and drawings that were simpler and clearer than some of their more evocative renderings.

After the Folly, similar projects started to appear on their doorstep and in their inboxes, even as the original group was in flux. Several members went back to school to obtain the education necessary in the UK to work as an architect, while others continued to work full time for other firms to keep themselves fed. Other members joined, bringing

The Folly's roof peaking up between the two sides of the flyover.

in fresh perspectives: Fran Edgerley (cousin of Assemble member, Alice), who had a background in philosophy and an interest in social activism, had become a mainstay of the group early on and stayed for over a decade.
The projects that kept this amorphous group coherent focused on performance and temporary construction. The first of these followed in 2012, the year after the Folly, in Chichester, completing a triad of temporary performance places built in three successive years.

A child playing with some of the mini bricks and a view into the Folly.

Looking back at the Folly from across the canal. The scaffolding holding up the brick curtains is visible through the double doors.

The Folly during an evening performance.

FOLLY FOR A FLYOVER

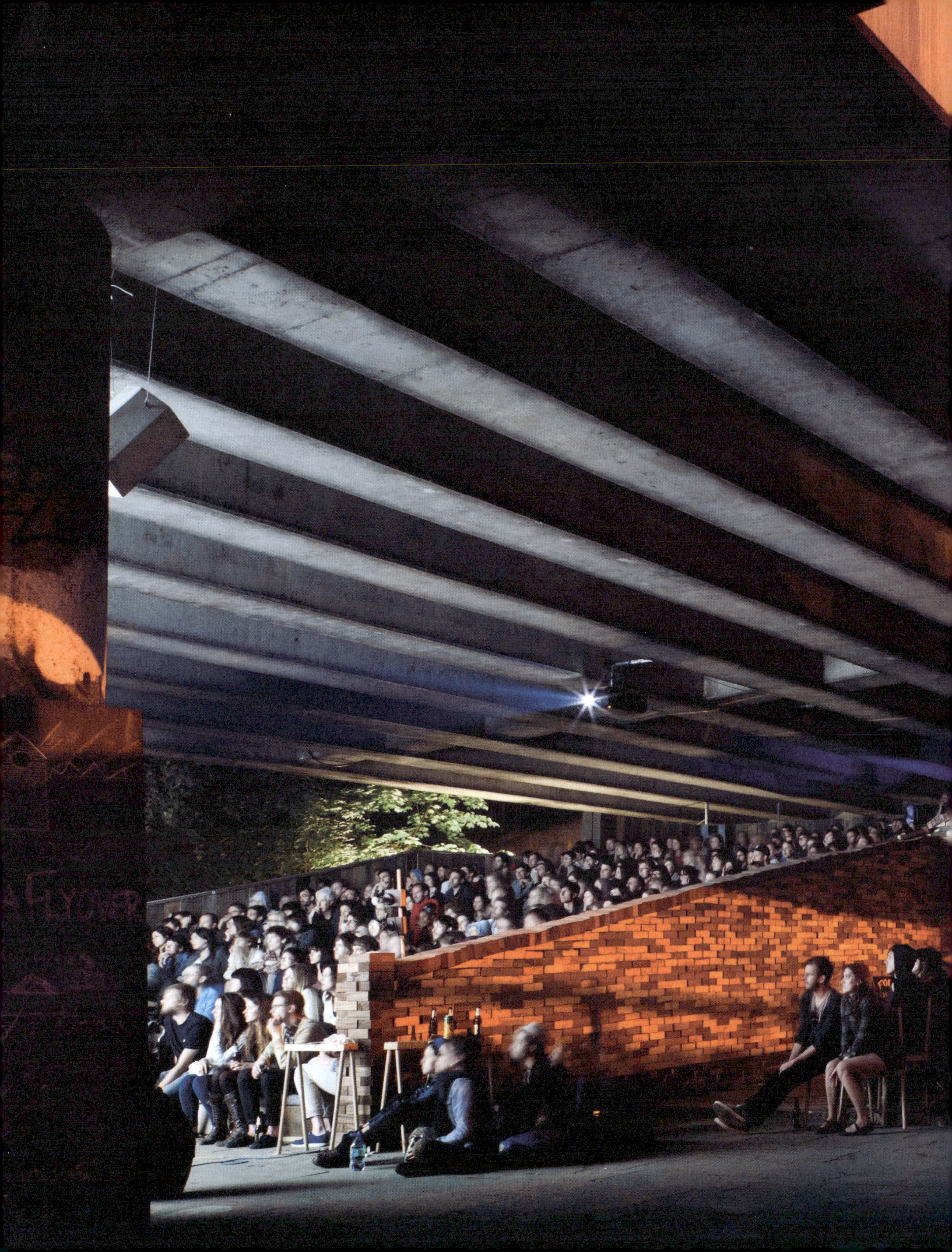

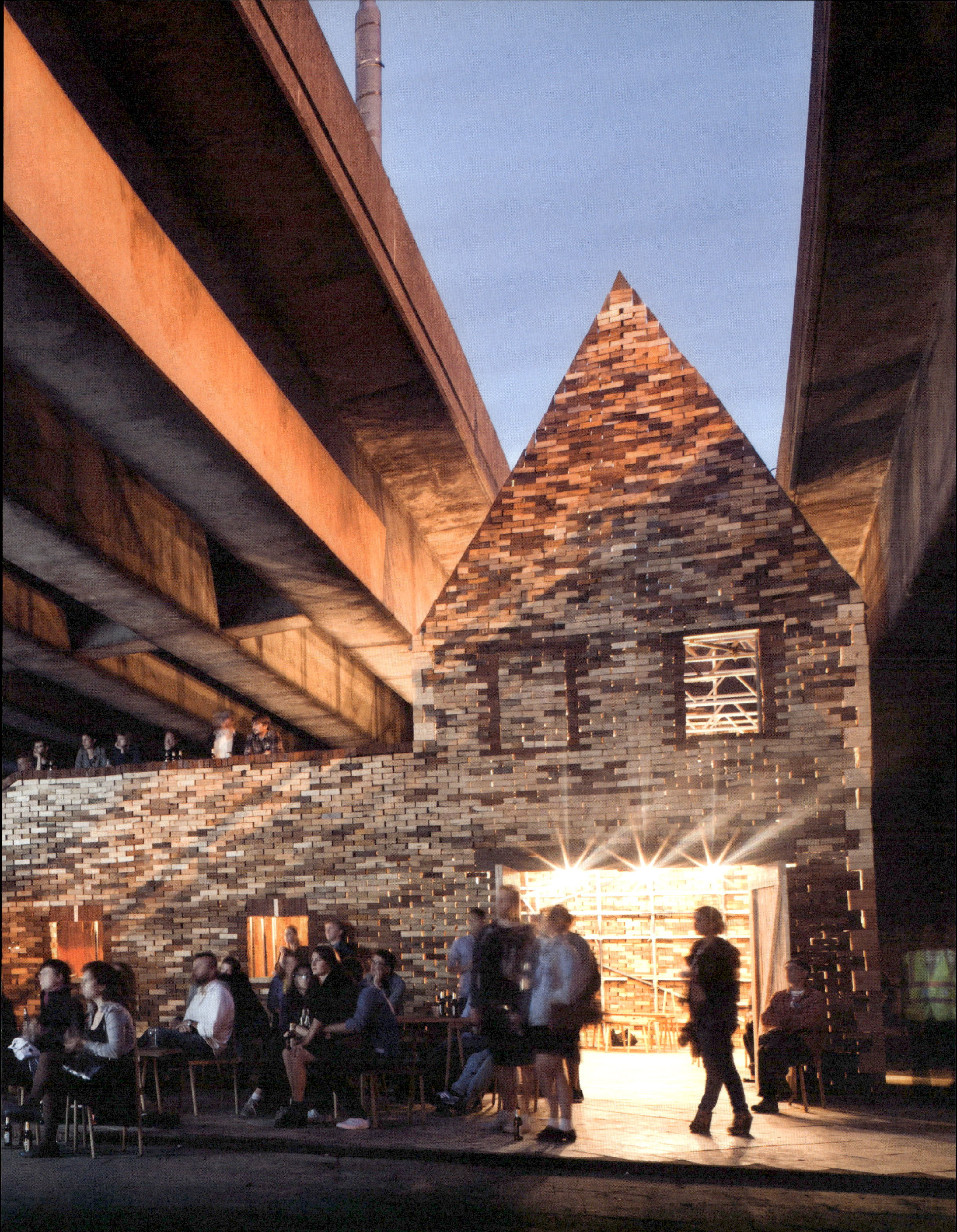

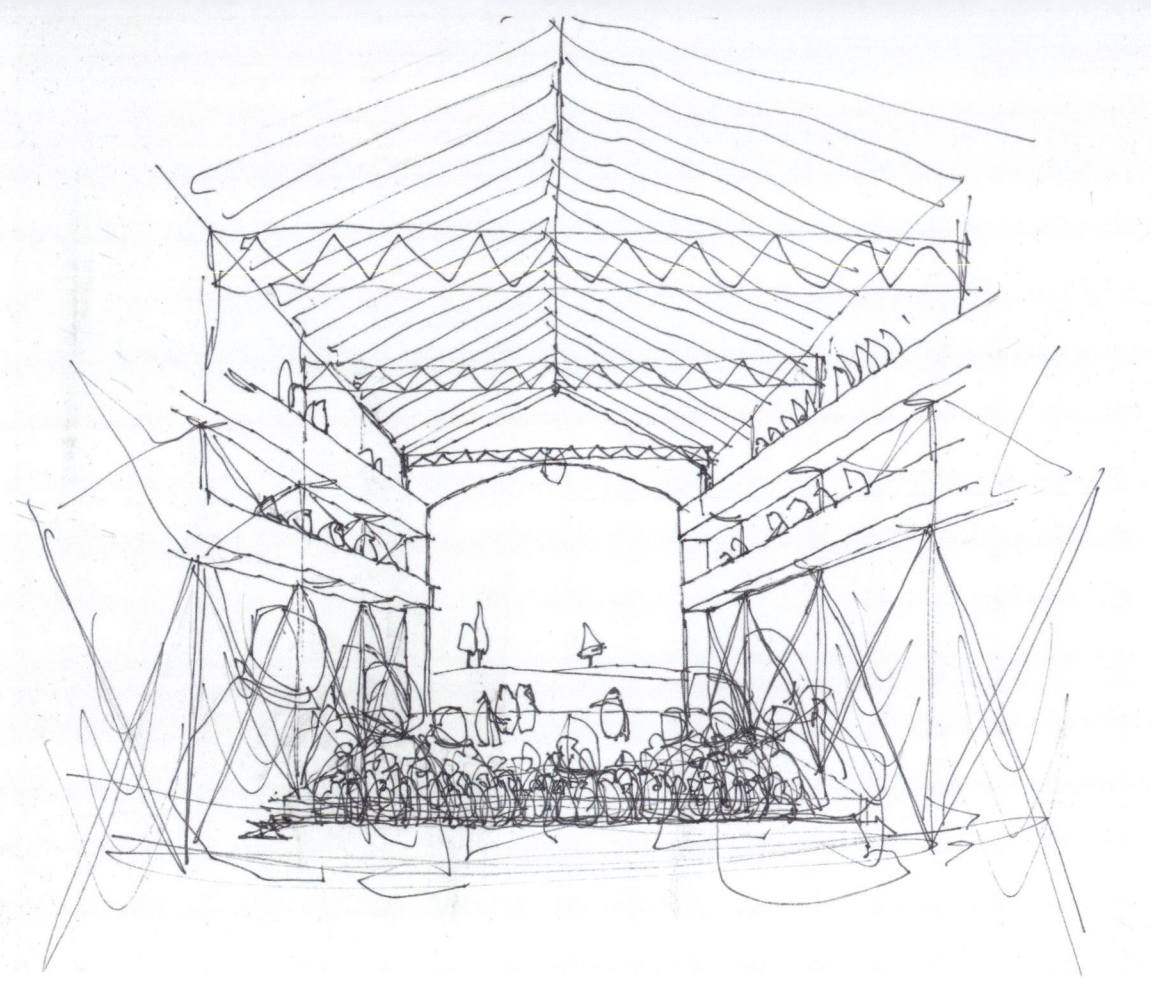

A sketch Assemble made of Theatre on the Fly to show to the client. You can see the idea of the theatre opening out to the parkland beyond.

THEATRE ON THE FLY

Chichester Festival Theatre was inaugurated in 1962. The brutalist structure was designed by architects Powell & Moya and its first artistic director was none other than Hollywood royalty Laurence Olivier. For their 50th anniversary in 2012, the theatre commissioned a temporary structure that would occupy the grounds of Oakland Park adjacent to the theatre, which was soon to be closed for renovations (undertaken by Haworth Tompkins). The team of apprentice directors including Tim Hoare, Anna Ledwich and Michael Oakley were keen to showcase their work as well as that of the organization's youth theatre. The theatre turned to Assemble on the basis of the collective's previous two projects, asking them to build something economical and flexible that would accommodate experimental theatre productions.

The team got to work using recycled materials, supplementing found lumber with off-the-shelf timber and components. As in The Cineroleum, the most startling and effective of these materials was a large-scale Fiberweb geotextile that covered both the facades and the roofs. It turned the structure into a hybrid of a tent (in material) and barn (in shape). Assemble described the cheap plastic geotextile (that cost just £300 in total) as changeable; depending on the theatrical lighting

Top: During construction, props supported the structure. Here the floor is being smoothed out before the laying of the wood flooring.

Bottom: Fixing the MDF sign cut with a jigsaw. The Fiberweb geotextile made by Terram is visible behind the signage.

Children seen through the geotextile. In front you can see the scaffolding that formed the theatre structure.

THEATRE ON THE FLY

The theatre's front entrance. The Fiberweb geotextile covering is draped over a scaffolding base.

and the time of day, it could be opaque or translucent. The material was ordinarily used as a waterproof lining for applications such as roadbeds or ornamental ponds. Using their experience from The Cineroleum project, Assemble members sewed, pleated and gathered the lining and attached it to a scaffolding-like frame that became the overall building.

   The ambiguous structure both sat naturally within its parkland surroundings while evoking the notion of the circus coming to town; at times glowing from the inside and at others mimicking the theatre structure itself as a dark monolith among the trees. Inside, Assemble created flexible stacks of seating, leaving the stage as an open and only partially defined space. They exposed everything: not only the structure and the underside of the Fiberweb draping, but also all the show mechanisms usually hidden from the audience in a space above the stage called the fly tower. The lighting, rigging, pulleys and elements of the scenery not in use were visible above and around the audience. It was both this exposure, as well as the quick manner in which Assemble put together and later dismantled the structure, that gave the facility its name: Theatre on the Fly.

   The building's appearance, its textile facade, the spiderweb of equipment and the shows performed inside formed a continuous whole. And it did not stop there. At the back of the stage, barn doors opened up the rear facade so that building and performance could spill out into the park.

The theatre during a performance, in which the fly tower is being used for scenery. The seating is made from recycled foam covered with dust sheets.

THEATRE ON THE FLY

A performance with children based on Noah's ark, showing how, with open doors, both the theatre and the lawn become places for performance. The Chichester Festival Theatre building is visible to the left.

A view at night as the theatre prepares for a performance. The boards at the base of the structure are recycled scaffolding hoarding.

The theatre during an evening performance with the barn doors closed. The ramps were added by Chichester Festival Theatre for this performance.

▶

THEATRE ON THE FLY 059

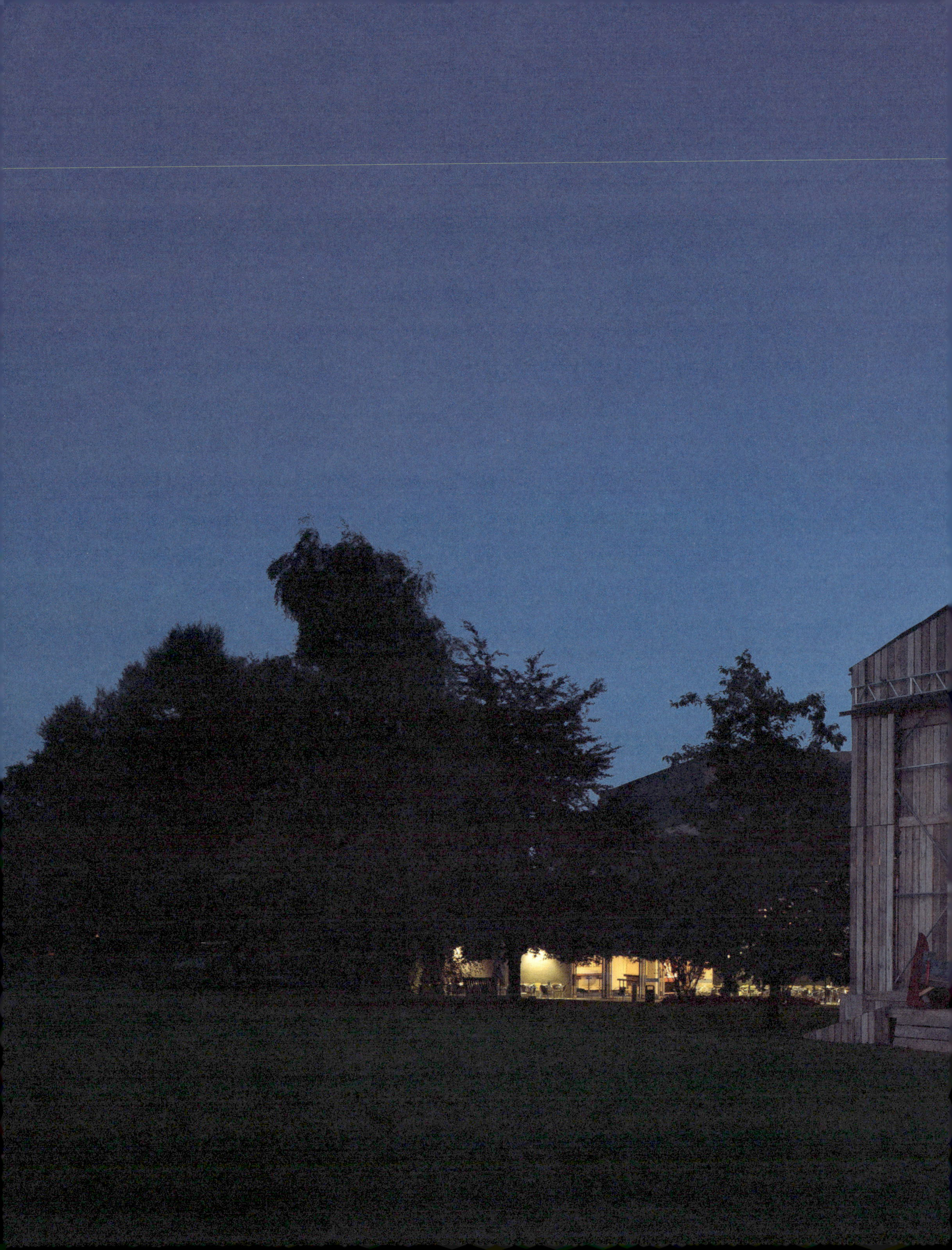

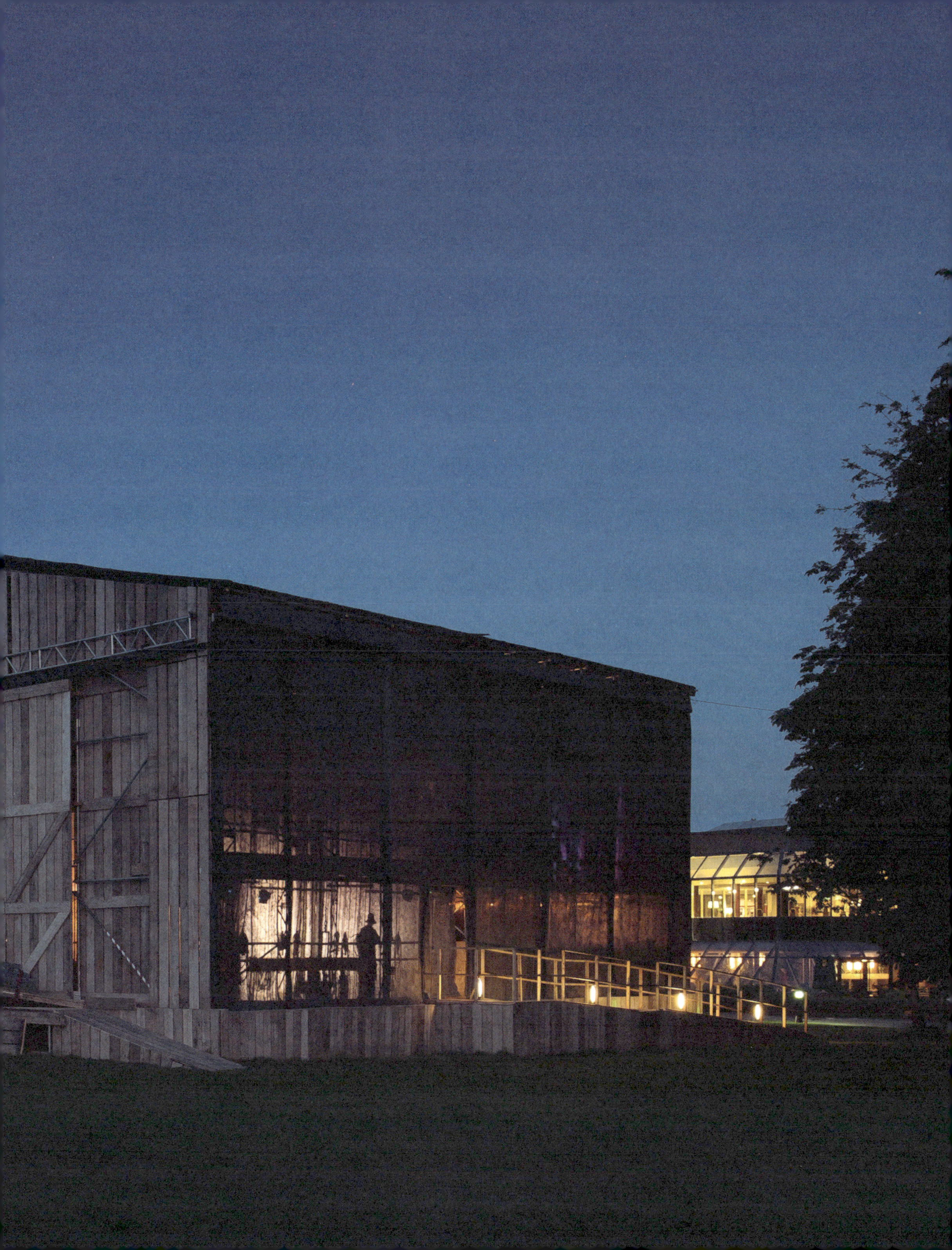

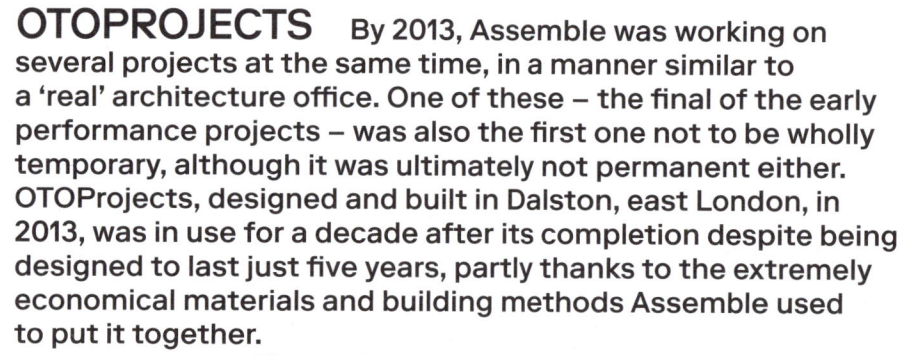

Volunteers stamping down rice sacks filled with earth and rubble from the site for OTOProjects. The metal poles were used to compress the layers; the buttresses supported the walls.

OTOPROJECTS By 2013, Assemble was working on several projects at the same time, in a manner similar to a 'real' architecture office. One of these – the final of the early performance projects – was also the first one not to be wholly temporary, although it was ultimately not permanent either. OTOProjects, designed and built in Dalston, east London, in 2013, was in use for a decade after its completion despite being designed to last just five years, partly thanks to the extremely economical materials and building methods Assemble used to put it together.

The project was commissioned by the experimental music venue Cafe OTO, which already hosted musical performances in a small space across the road from an empty lot filled with rubble. The organization had little funding, but was able to obtain permission from the local council to use the lot for a temporary performance venue. Assemble had a single client and a more-or-less commercial function with which to contend, but once again an almost non-existent budget.

Their reaction was to work with what they found on site, which was largely rubble from the buildings that had stood there previously, some of which had been destroyed as long ago as the Second World War. Recruiting the help of sixty or so volunteers (including many of the local and international musicians for whom OTO was an important venue) as well as technical advice from Eva MacNamara of Expedition Engineering, the team sifted what they could of rubble and soil and put it into end-of-line

Top: The premade Trussform roof trusses being lifted onto the wall. In the foreground you can see the mixer used to combine lime, water, sand and ground rubble into the 'rubbledash' render that covered the building.

Bottom: Volunteers attaching the rubbledash to the outside walls by hand; larger pieces of rubble were pressed in afterwards as decoration.

The finished space with its stacked rice sacks and plywood floors, made from leftover plywood pieces donated by the Barbican. The skylights are made out of twinwall polycarbonate sheets.

A performance in the finished space. Chairs were provided by Cafe OTO.

Getting ready for an evening performance. The lighting consists of bare lightbulbs.

woven plastic rice sacks. Then they stacked these sacks on top of each other to form the building's perimeter walls. Compressing them and tying them together for stability, they covered them on the outside with their own version of a light adobe they termed 'rubbledash'. The effect was a monolithic coherence, as if the structure had indeed been pushed out of the earth itself as one. On the inside, they left the stacks of rubble-filled bags as is with the effect of an oversized kind of masonry.

On top of these walls Assemble then placed off-the-shelf timber trusses of the sort used for small residential structures, framing them with a plywood cornice that gave the building the vague appearance of a Greek temple. Wooden doors, plywood floors and exposed equipment were the only other structural elements of the design. The inside, shot through with off-the-shelf skylights, became a luminous space during the day and a highly defined one at night.

As it turned out, the combination of the rubble sacks and the plywood created wonderful acoustics, and OTOProjects became such a popular venue that it remained standing and in use until 2023, despite the roughness and seemingly slapdash quality of the construction.

Over the next few years, Assemble continued to create temporary theatre and performance constructions for various occasions, although they seemed to abandon such projects after their incorporation in 2018 (see Chapter 2). The 'let's put on a show' character of these events fits well with their limited and loose structure during the early years, when members came and went, much of the work was done by volunteers and the group was still busy learning the skills necessary to make buildings.

Top: A view of the finished space from the outside. The cap was made from plywood, while the door was made out of Featherboard fencing panels assembled on a diagonal.

Bottom: A view from the street. The gate was also made with Featherboard. The protruding cap covers the trusses and protects the walls from weather.

OTOPROJECTS 065

The step side of the Big Slide, showing the mismatched plywood Assemble found, along with the rough timber railings. The steps were purposefully high to make climbing them an adventure.

BIG SLIDE

At the same time that they were building Theatre on the Fly, Assemble produced a much simpler structure for the Stratford Rising Festival, a temporary event in front of the Theatre Royal Stratford East in London. The emphasis of the festival was on children and on play, which has also become a recurring focus for Assemble, who have continued to build both temporary and more permanent play structures (see Chapter 4).

The Big Slide was a two-sided construction made from custom-made roof trusses and studding timber, plywood and angle brackets found at a local hardware store. For the slide, Assemble used marble-effect laminate, a greenish linoleum-like product used for worktops and furniture. To reach the top of the slide, the children had to climb up a series of oversized steps on the other side, making the journey up as much of an adventure as the journey down. In keeping with Assemble's approach by that point, the steps also served as seating platforms from which the children could watch some of the performances put on in the square during the three days the slide was in place.

Top: Children sliding down the front of the slide. The structure consisted of pre-made roof trusses.

Bottom: The underside of the slide could also be used as a portal and as a space for children to play.

The slide was wide enough for children and adults to slide down simultaneously.

BIG SLIDE

Blue foam mats placed in the shade of the sweeping roof of the MAXXI museum in Rome provide a performance space for the School of Narrative Dance.

Performers sit on the painted plywood circle that defines the stage.

SCHOOL OF NARRATIVE DANCE

In 2014, the group branched out geographically with their first project outside of London. For the School of Narrative Dance, an ongoing project by the artist Marinella Senatore, Assemble created an installation in the courtyard of the MAXXI museum in Rome, Italy: a circus without walls. Reflecting the goals of Senatore's nomadic school, where anyone can be a student, Assemble produced an inclusive art installation in which professional dancers could mix with their audience.

The central object was inspired by travelling circuses, where a temporary sand or sawdust pit would be installed as a stage for the main show. A glorified sandbox encircled by red-painted plywood hosted dance performances and children's play. Around it, Assemble constructed scaffolding units to support lighting and other technical equipment; one of these pieces sported a bright yellow curtain that turned the sandpit into a proper stage, inviting anyone to make a grand entrance and perform. Blue mats laid under the sweeping canopy of the museum provided another impromptu performance space.

Here, Assemble established a way of thinking that they would carry into several other public space interventions. They asked what was the minimum they could do that would afford

A view from above, showing the sand performance and play space, plus the scaffolding defining the stage and backdrops.

the maximum number of activities. Although the motive for this strategy was usually budgetary, it was also a way to minimize the imposition of objects, and design in general, on a community. Instead of deciding what people would need to perform, play or gather, they came up with what is commonly referred to as 'urban acupuncture', which releases energy in public space. Interventions in this vein can be as simple as changing the texture of the pavement or slightly modulating how you enter or sit in a space. It can extend to objects that inevitably take on the character of a kind of scaffolding, rather than simply the objects themselves. In later projects, Assemble would undertake simple landscaping 'moves' that could help clarify or suggest how otherwise undesigned spaces might be used or enjoyed.

SCHOOL OF NARRATIVE DANCE

A view before a performance of a play based on a fan's relation to the local football team.

Top: A computer rendering of an early stage of the design for The Playing Field showing the construction and colour; the latter a reference to the colours of the local football team's kit.

Bottom: The solid Douglas fir timber frame in construction with its red painted struts for levelling bases.

THE PLAYING FIELD

Much more elaborate, and perhaps the grandest of Assemble's early temporary performance structures, was The Playing Field. Built in 2014 in the central square of Southampton and in place for seventeen days, the structure was designed to draw new audiences to the local Nuffield Theatre. The structure was much larger than anything else they had done, with space for 450 spectators.

Confronting that jump in scale, Assemble turned to England's largest spectator events: football matches. As Binning said at the time: 'The ambition was to create a dramatic new typology of theatre space – drawing on the architecture, crowd dynamic and match day ritual of football culture. Utilizing the aesthetic and architectural language of Britain's football stadia, the auditorium creates a spectacle that occupies an area between theatre and football.' Hence the name, which brought together the two performance types.

The cast of a production preparing for the performance. The red chairs were hired from a local scaffolding company and went back to them afterwards.

The tunnel entrances either side of the performance space, where the plywood is painted a rich red.

Assemble's design was successful in evoking the scale of stadia. Working with engineers Structure Workshop, a timber grid was created that rose up to the equivalent of four storeys. The massive posts and beams formed a colonnaded structure that remained largely open, inviting the public in while embodying a structural expressionism common in football stadia. The metal bracing Structure Workshop felt was necessary for stability was painted red, matching the red plastic seats (later recycled) on which the audience sat.

In the centre of the facade, Assemble and Structure Workshop had removed several of the posts at the ground level to create an entryway. Plywood volumes both supported the seats and contained scenery and technical equipment when the stage was not in formal use (the structure itself remained open to the public at all times). Audience members entered via two red tunnels on the left- and right-hand sides of the structure, which sported two steep tiers of seating partially shaded by a flat plywood roof. During performances, all the rigging and scenery was on display. Fittingly, the Nuffield's most popular performance during its short run was a dramatization of the wells and woes of Southampton's football fans.

THE PLAYING FIELD

A detail view of the structure showing the laser-cut painted metal sign and the technical gantry, as well as the red steel bracing.

A performance of a play about a fan's relation to the city and its football club, and how their fortunes mirror the ups and downs in his own life.

The entrance structure being prepared for an evening performance. By leaving out three columns in the centre, Assemble created an entrance supported by the timber frame, which acted as a truss.

THE PLAYING FIELD 073

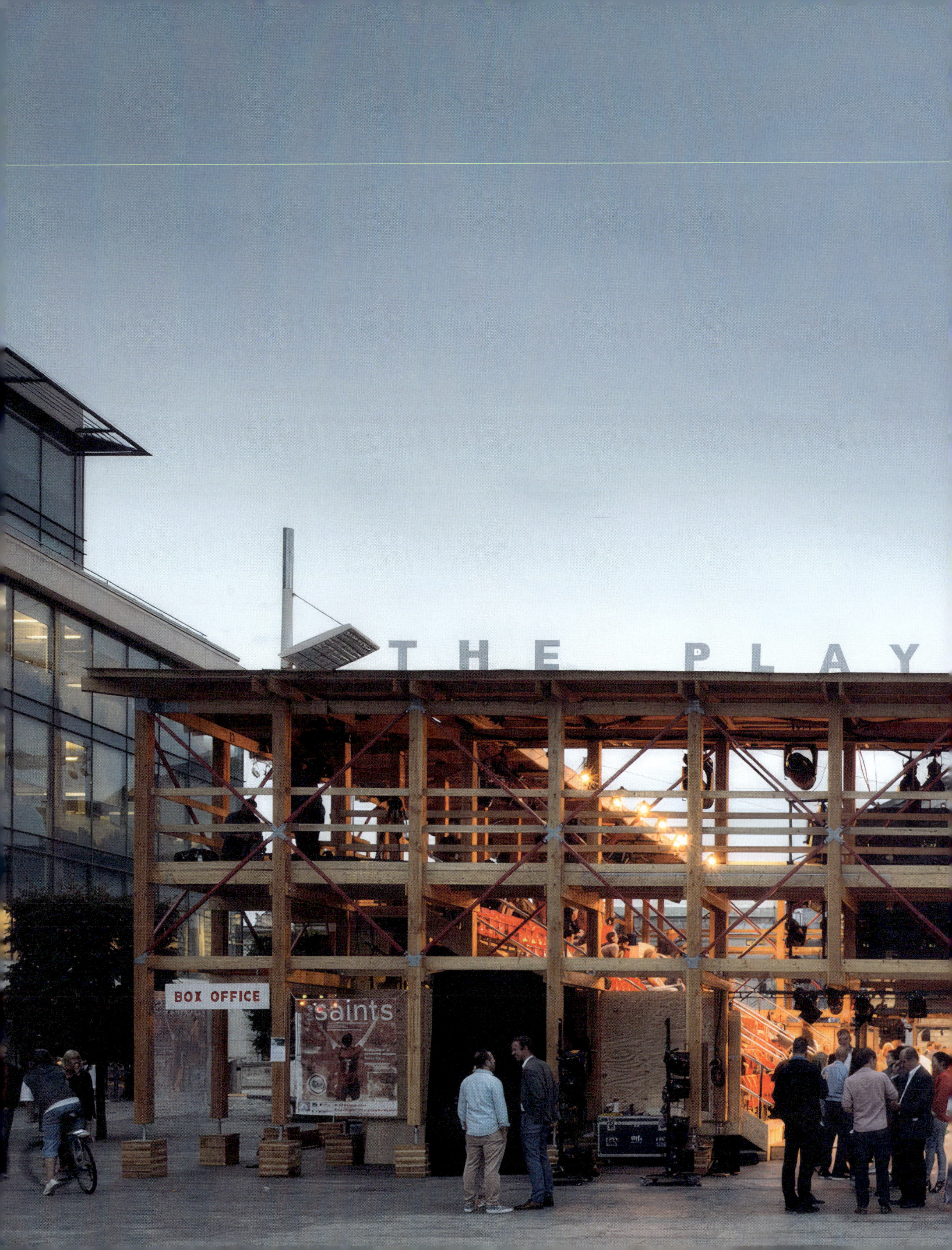
THE PLAY
BOX OFFICE
saints

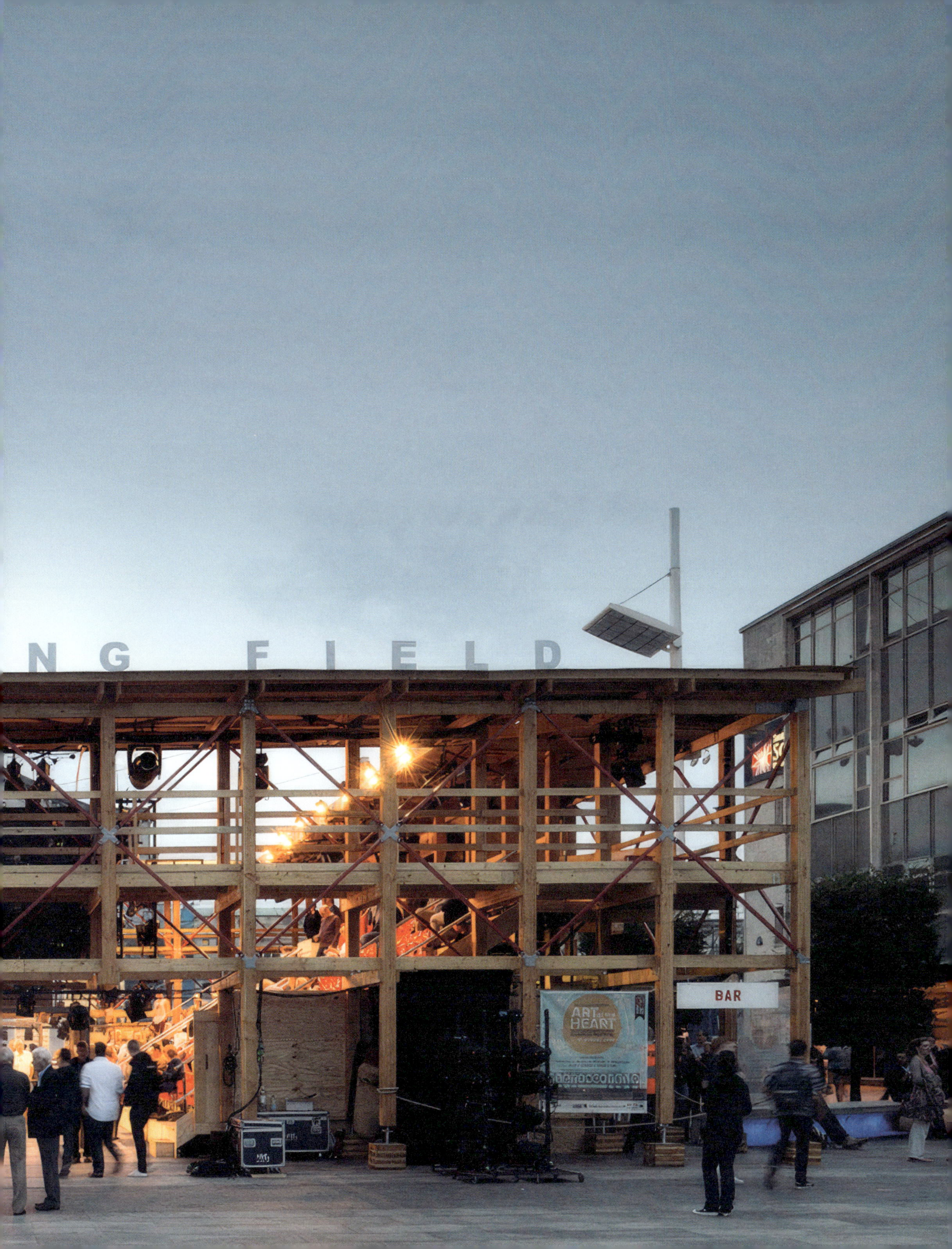
NG FIELD
BAR
ART
HEART

Horst Castle standing in the Belgian countryside.

A conceptual rendering of how the temporary structure, the Newcastle, would evoke the geometry, tower and buttresses of the castle.

HORST FESTIVAL

The last of the series of temporary performance structures Assemble designed (though they continued a line in play spaces and public square interventions) was a pavilion for the 2017 Horst Arts and Music Festival in Belgium. The two-day dance music event and two-month art exposition was held on the site of a medieval castle that was undergoing renovation at the time. Assemble designed what they called – in a continuation of their playful way with words – the Newcastle. The scaffold form was an abstraction of the adjacent castle, skewed and angled to accommodate the dancers inside, both in a mosh pit and in two levels of balconies surrounding the open space. Assemble wanted the arrangement to evoke a Shakespearian theatre, but its most obvious reference was to the urban nightclubs that such music more regularly calls home.

The designers emphasized and enlarged the form of the castle's buttresses to indicate an entrance between sloping volumes and added a stage staircase that could also be used to access the upper levels. They covered the whole structure with blue construction netting so that, like the Theatre on the Fly, it could appear either solid or translucent depending on your viewpoint, the time of day and the organizer's lighting schemes. The structure appears to have been a more ephemeral version of The Playing Field, devoid of heavy structures and filled with heaving and spectating crowds when fully in use.

In the first years Assemble were designing, they concentrated on performance. They 'performed buildings', which is to say that the act of coming up with the ideas, the developing of those concepts, the research and networking necessary to implement them, the acquisition of skills and the collaborative construction were as much part of what they produced as the structures themselves. The designers made true event

The dance and performance space under construction, showing the scaffolding and blue mesh covering.

The completed space during the day, with some audience members watching a performance from the balcony levels.

architecture, avoiding the monumentality and imposition of static form that they and many of their peers felt was the most alienating aspect of architecture. Building on the work of their teachers, employers and other architects, designers and activists, they developed the most complete proof of concept of this approach to architecture that anyone had seen at the time.

That this event architecture was geared to performance and play was essential to its success. Rather than serving a function that was definable – and defined by whomever organized and commissioned the structure – these spaces invited and even demanded participation. They also transformed continually, depending on whether an organized activity was taking place, and on the nature of that play or performance. The influential British sociologist and philosopher Anthony Giddens, building on the work of Erving Goffman and others, emphasized that one of the essential acts of sociality – perhaps even the most important – was staging performances that allowed individuals, in relationship to others and the scenery of public space, to act out the roles into which they would like to grow.[23] The idea that architecture could be a scaffolding for the development of collective performance and individual self-definition seemed like a natural antidote to the then-reigning architecture culture of high-tech, minimalist or parametric forms.

What Assemble needed now was a place and format in which they could act out their own transformation into a more permanent organization with the skills and knowledge necessary to expand their field of operation. Assemble found that structure in the manner in which they built their own home, an act which has been repeated several times as they have moved offices, and which they have performed for others in a manner that has become not only a professional but also an economic foundation for the emerging practice.

HORST FESTIVAL

The temporary structure from the outside during the day, when its geometry and basic elements, including the notional buttresses and the stairs to the upstairs gallery, are visible.

078

The same structure at night, when it becomes a glowing and ethereal counter to the solid castle.

The inside of the structure during an evening dance event.

Viewers on one of the balconies looking over the dancing crowd below.

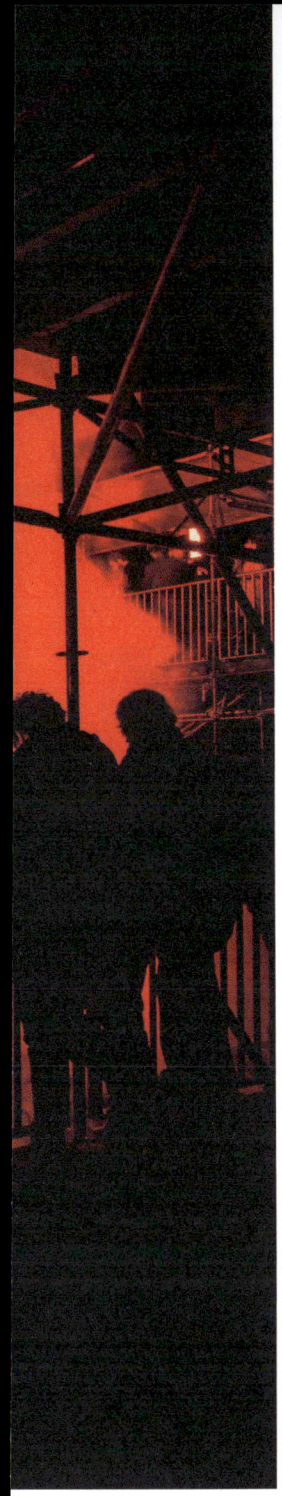

The lighting and music together transformed the basic structure Assemble designed into a spectral environment.

HORST FESTIVAL 081

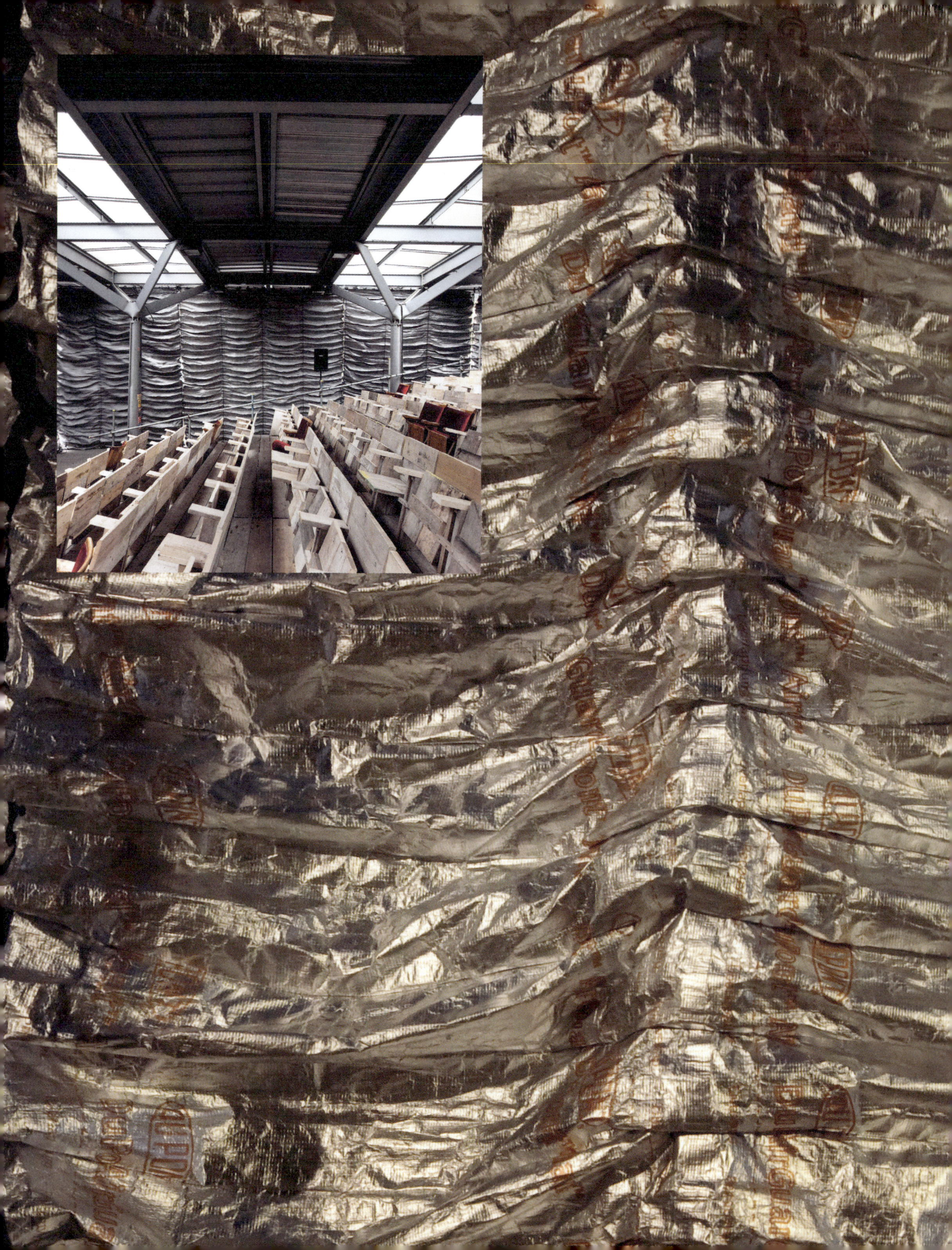

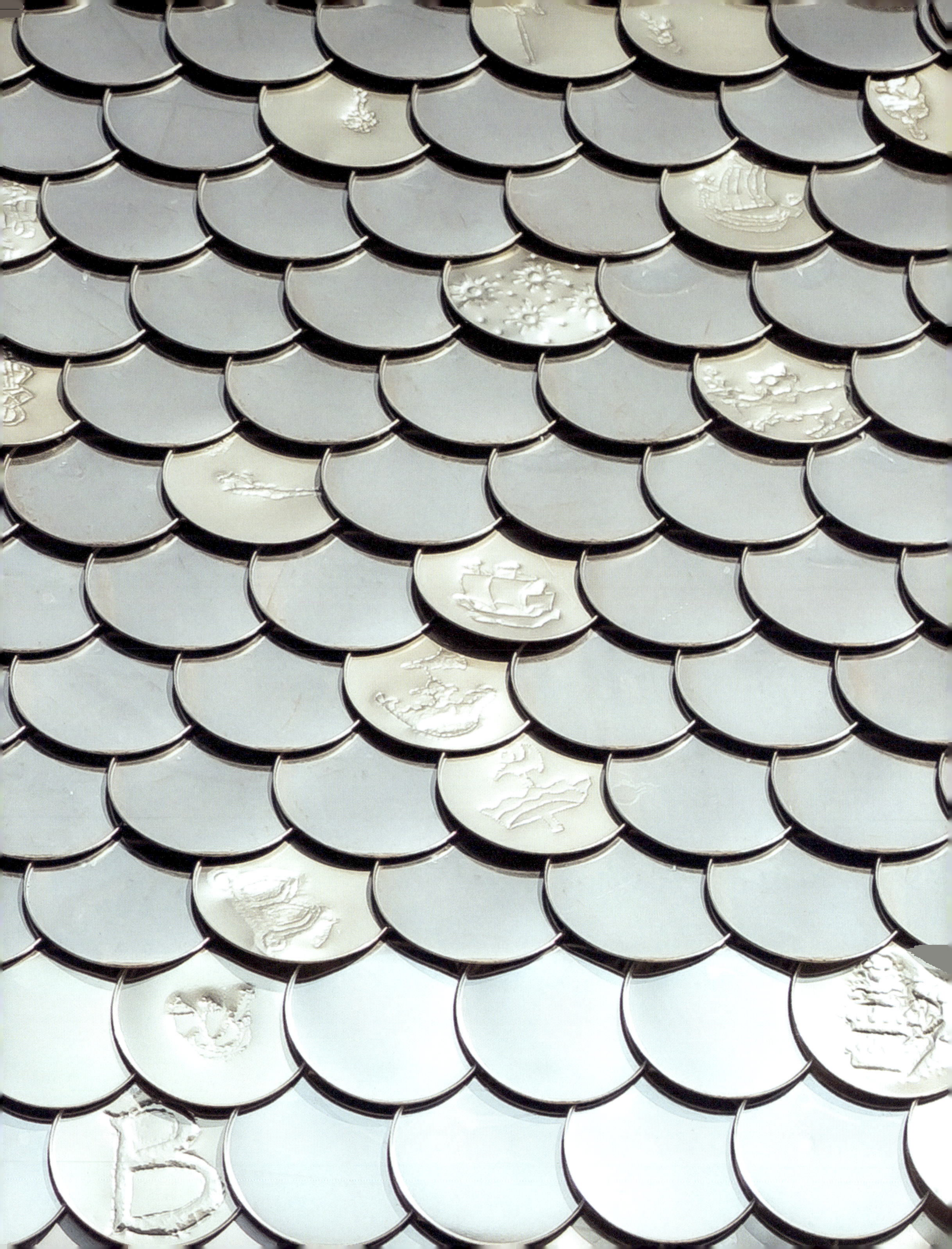

YARDHOUSE (See PG094)

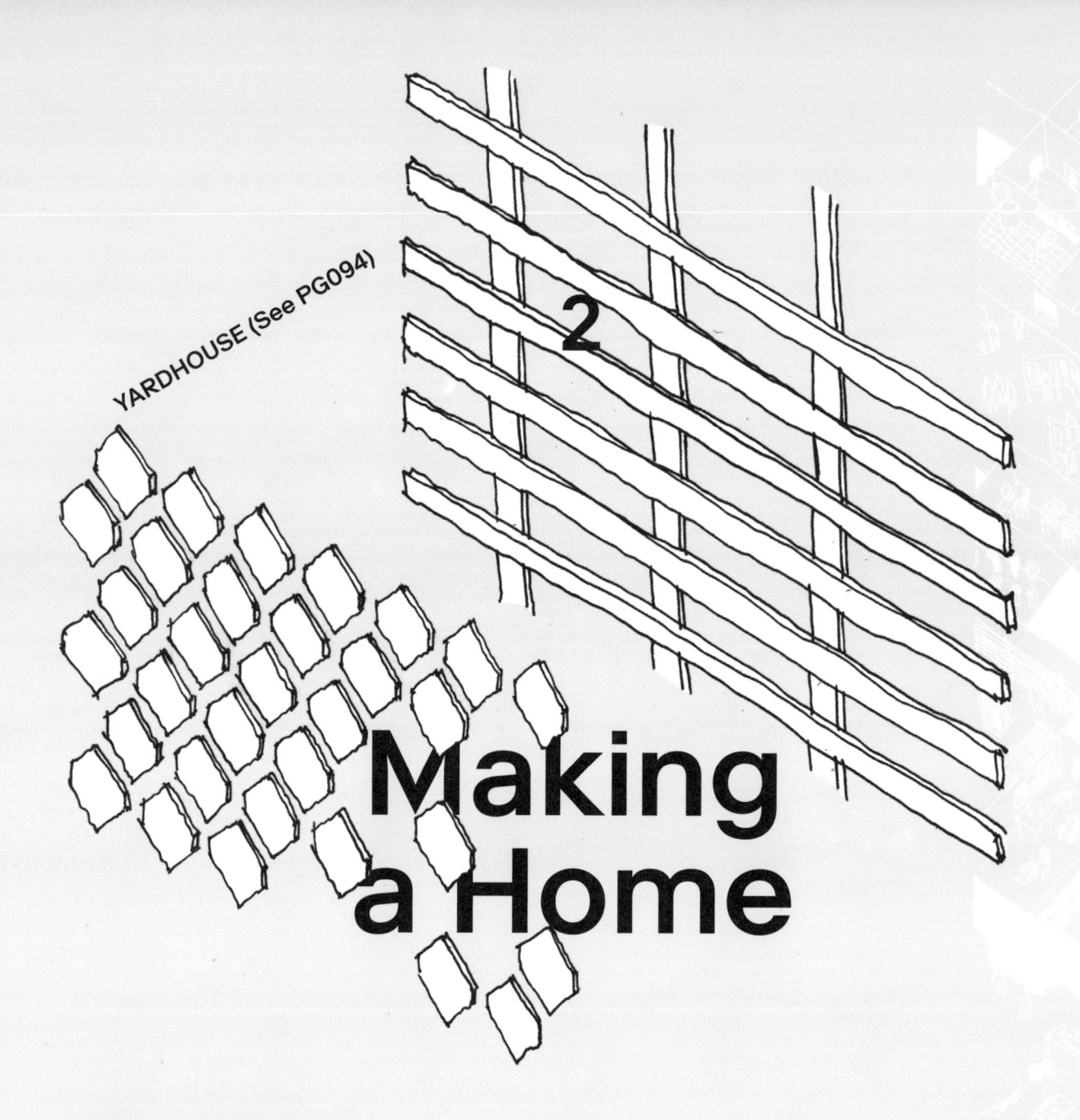

2

Making a Home

SUGARHOUSE STUDIOS STRATFORD As Assemble began to expand and regularize its activities in the years after 2011, it became clear that operating out of various homes and gathering for work sessions at different locations was not going to be viable much longer. The group needed a place in which to not only design together, but also to do the research, development and, crucially, the fabrication that was integral to what they saw as their task. They wanted a place to store the materials they were collecting, which included things they wanted to reuse from current or just finished projects, as well as pieces of wood, scaffolding, fabric and other fragments they thought could be useful for the next endeavour. Finally, they also wanted a place to be, sensing that their existence as a group depended on being together, but also on their ability to connect with volunteers and experts in various crafts and techniques with whom they could collaborate. Assemble found the solution in a former factory on

A concept drawing Assemble made to show their notion of Sugarhouse as a collection of 'open studios'.

The door of the Sugarhouse Studios Stratford with the self-designed and fabricated Assemble name in place.

085

A view of the studio's front area taken from above, with members working on the materials for the Goldsmiths CCA commission (see p. 208).

Sugar House Island in Stratford, east London. They dubbed their new home – and the subsequent iterations of their headquarters in other locations – Sugarhouse Studios.

The site was a historic grouping of former factories and warehouses along the River Lea, just south of the area soon to be occupied by the Olympic Games. Tidal mills had operated in the area as early as the 11th century, producing flour and later gin. The island itself is named after a 19th-century sugar refinery that still stands on the site. By 2011, however, most of the facilities were no longer in use, both because factories had moved to areas with better logistics and because the city and UK government envisioned redeveloping the area into housing after the Olympic Games. Although this goal has largely been accomplished, in the years leading up to and during the Olympic Games they were banking their holdings; Assemble managed to obtain permission from the London Legacy Development Corporation (LLDC) – the planning authority for all five Olympic Boroughs – to establish residence. During their tenure, ownership was transferred to the Swedish developer Vastint who would go on to execute the planned residential transformation, but Assemble still managed to stretch their planned two years residence closer to five.

The availability of Sugarhouse Studios' Stratford site highlights the large extent to which Assemble's growth was made possible by the 2012 Olympic Games. The redevelopment of east London around the River Lea opened up the area for use, in some cases temporarily, making much of Assemble's early work and their first home possible. Just as important was the fact that various levels of government made funding available to celebrate and extend the sporting activities, as well as to revitalize and make presentable the still mainly industrial area that millions of people would turn their attention to that summer. The situation in which Assemble found itself thriving was to a certain extent a result of lucky timing, but it also reflected a sea-change in architecture and planning taking place at the time.

086

Top: The front gate and part of the front facade of the Sugarhouse building. The sequin sign mirrored that of some of the local businesses in the area.

Bottom: A diagram Assemble made to advertise the first Sugarhouse, highlighting it as a workshop where many modes of fabrication were possible.

A full-height storage wall separated the 'front of the house', which was originally public, from the rear studio and workshop areas.

SUGARHOUSE STUDIOS STRATFORD

A stone mason built out her studio in Sugarhouse Studios Stratford; the surrounding architecture was as Assemble and she found it when they moved in.

London was not the first city to see the huge investment required to stage an Olympic Games as an opportunity for large-scale urban revitalization, but it was the one that executed it most thoroughly and successfully. The plan started with a landscape project by the American firm Hargreaves Associates (now Hargreaves Jones, who had also planned the open area of the Sydney Olympic Games on a similar type of site). It focused on the River Lea, the easternmost of a series of tributaries running from the northern uplands down to the River Thames. These waterways influenced the development of London into a set of distinct communities that harnessed both the water's power and the direct routes it provided to riverine trading opportunities. In the 18th century, the lower River Lea was canalized, attracting small industry, but in the 19th and 20th centuries many of those enterprises moved elsewhere and the area became marked by emptiness, pollution and economic hardship. By concentrating on restoring the river landscape, the designers sought to turn the waterway into the area's main asset.

The development of the Queen Elizabeth Olympic Park was successful in revitalizing the neighbourhood and it has since attracted a series of cultural institutions. That this then led to a gentrification of the area, which pushed out the original inhabitants as well as some of those that helped pioneer the area's changes (such as Assemble), is unfortunately par for the course in our capitalist system. Nevertheless, Assemble and other architects worked with and continue to collaborate with neighbourhood groups all around the area, as we saw in the first chapter, to elicit life and community activity.

A studio in Yardhouse, which Assemble built at Sugarhouse Studios Stratford (see p. 094). The large timber structure for the building is visible to the rear.

Woodworker Emma Leslie using the shared workshop.

The area Assemble were given was large ('I don't think anybody bothered counting how many square metres it actually was,' says James Binning) and they soon realized that it gave them an opportunity to attract more than their own members to Sugar House Island. The site at their disposal consisted of two warehouses and a large yard facing Stratford High Street. Part of their initial agreement with the LLDC when they arrived in 2011 was the creation of a public-facing venue. They created a cinema and cafe with a workspace attached to it. Neighbours were invited over for meals, they held parties and organized concerts and performances. Such events have, although at a less frequent pace, remained part of life at Sugarhouse.

The team then set up a workshop with tools amassed during The Cineroleum build, creating spaces for individuals and organizations to occupy. Pretty soon, Sugarhouse was home not just to Assemble, but to carpenters, ironworkers, fabric artists and other creative types. Those craftspeople brought their own equipment and material, which then could be used by others at Sugarhouse, while the work of the carpenters or metalworkers could inspire Assemble when they were looking for techniques or building elements for one of their projects – and vice versa. The team would go on to establish a more formal workshop with the brains behind the centre for making, Workshop East, who they had met during a research trip for Blackhorse Workshop (see p. 103) at the nearby Building Crafts College.

The end of the studio spaces, where the previous owner had torn down part of the building; Assemble installed a new door opening and stabilized the covering, making the inside weathertight.

To manage the space, Assemble developed a model that became crucial for their own survival. The collective charged occupiers a reasonable rent and collected funds to cover management fees, the cost of the minimal renovations and shared services. This became a steady source of income that helped offset some of the then-inchoate group's fixed expenses, smoothing over the times when they were not receiving funds from grants, design fees or other architecture-related sources. Over time, the group developed more expertise in this kind of facility management, while outsourcing some of its aspects to appropriate experts. As we shall see on later pages, they then extended this model to other sites around London, as well as to subsequent Sugarhouse sites. This tactic was an alternative to the kind of side hustles (such as teaching or doing work-for-hire for other firms, both of which Assemble members have done at times) and small-scale construction and development work that most small architecture firms have to undertake in order to keep themselves operating while receiving almost always insufficient fees. It also supported the development of the kind of skills the group sought, while allowing them to maintain and keep close the network of makers, builders and consultants that they needed to realize projects with the minimal training and experience most of the members of Assemble had at that point.

Loading the kiln; larger kilns were later added.

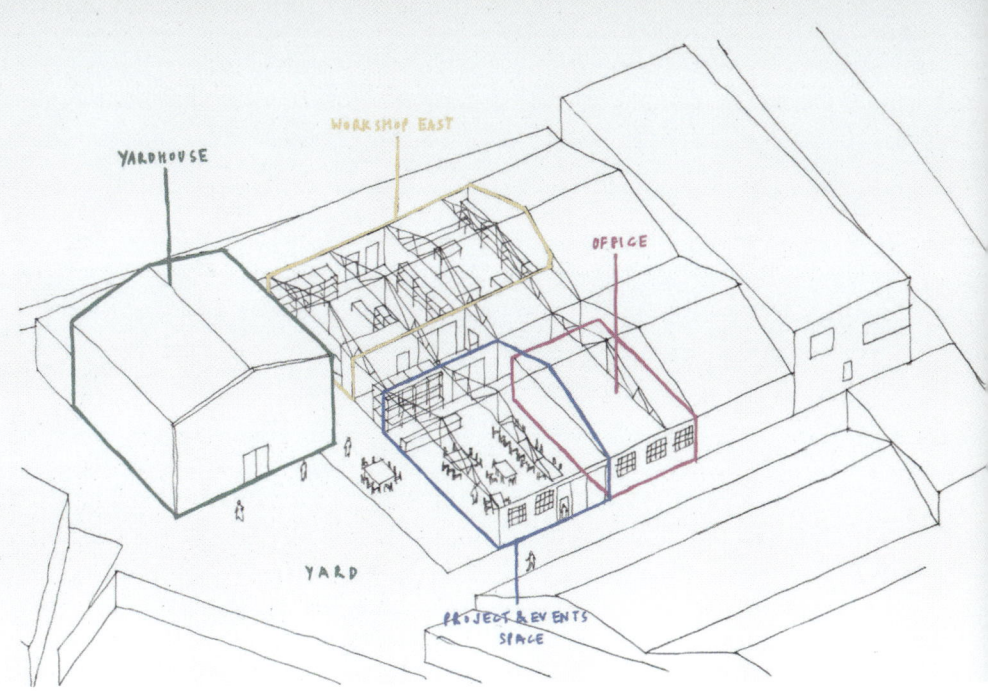

A diagram showing the layout of Sugarhouse Studios Stratford as it was towards the end of Assemble's occupation of the site.

Sugarhouse's interior became a rabbit warren, albeit an open and skylit one, of different offices and workshops. Here and in other such facilities, Assemble kept the visible design of the spaces to a minimum. Most construction consisted either of plywood or salvaged building materials. Sugarhouse's organization took priority over its looks, and much of the furniture and some of the wall and flooring material was gathered from around the area. A drawing Assemble produced during this period shows an idealized version of this messy reality, filled with people working, crafting, learning and browsing exhibitions in an array of rooms that far exceeds Sugarhouse's actual size – although it obviously corresponded to how Assemble saw their own home.

The cafe, despite having to be closed soon after opening due to lack of footfall, soon came to function as a canteen for the local music school, and Assemble and its friends conducted construction classes for students at local schools. The site became a venue for parties and, inevitably, film showings. These events reinforced the Assemble brand, so to speak, enhanced their network and continued to keep the group in the mind of a wider audience of potential collaborators, clients and critics. Whether Assemble intended it or not, it also worked towards the goals of the island's new owners, by transforming this forgotten part of London into an attractive spot on the creative class's mind map of London.

The cafe that originally occupied the front space at Sugarhouse Studios Stratford. Assemble designed and built the walls and scaffolding board doors, as well as some of the furniture.

Top: The front space tidied up before one of the parties Assemble holds regularly to engage their communities.

Bottom: A summer party held during Assemble's time in Stratford.

SUGARHOUSE STUDIOS STRATFORD

The heavy timber structure for the Yardhouse at Sugarhouse Studios Stratford going up.

YARDHOUSE In 2014, Assemble expanded the Sugarhouse Studios Stratford space by building a temporary, freestanding structure in the yard, called Yardhouse. The building was the result of a grant from the LLDC that sought to encourage new creative workplaces in the aftermath of the Olympic Games, which Assemble then matched with their own funds. Assemble proposed the structure as a pilot of what could be built on interim use sites. The total cost was less than £300 per square metre.

The facade, or way in which the building appeared – especially when seen from the nearby road – was, as in all the early Assemble projects, its main point. To make it, the team worked in close collaboration with artist Mollie Anna King, who would later become a tenant of the building. Together they produced lightweight concrete tiles, each with a different pigment. These tiles were then hung from horizontal timber battens in an overlapping fish-scale pattern, displaying a seemingly random array of colours that served to break up the overall facade. The gabled expanse drew on the motley appearance of the red and yellow brick, concrete and metal buildings in the surrounding area, as well as on the nearby River Lea, creating an image that both stood out from and fitted in with its context.

The making of the fibre cement concrete tiles used to cover Yardhouse.

The finished facade of Yardhouse, showing the decorative pattern of different coloured tiles; they were planned in a design drawing, but in the end assembled more by the order they were ready to be attached.

Yardhouse's main structure consisted of heavy timbers, similar to The Playing Field in Southampton. However, unlike in the theatre – and perhaps as a demonstration of their growing expertise – Assemble was careful to detail the elements to ensure their joinery was articulated, their proportions followed classical triads (dividing the space into thirds in height and volume) and their relationship to each one another were carefully considered. Nevertheless, they acknowledge that, in reality, the design was largely dictated by the spans they could achieve with lumber construction. The building consisted of three two-storey high bays; the outer bays housed individual studios and the central bay was left open for the kind of communal activities Assemble had discovered were central to their character.

Even if the individual tenants almost immediately filled in their spaces with partitions and all the equipment they needed to do their work, the overall structure was clear enough to provide the kind of order that was largely absent in the rest of Sugarhouse. The central space also became a showplace for Assemble where they could exhibit their architecture chops to prospective collaborators and clients. Although not made out of recycled materials, the building was designed to be taken apart and re-erected.

The tiles going onto the front facade. The finished, but still unoccupied and undivided interior, is visible through the door.

The finished Yardhouse before it was subdivided. The timbers were left exposed in the finished building.

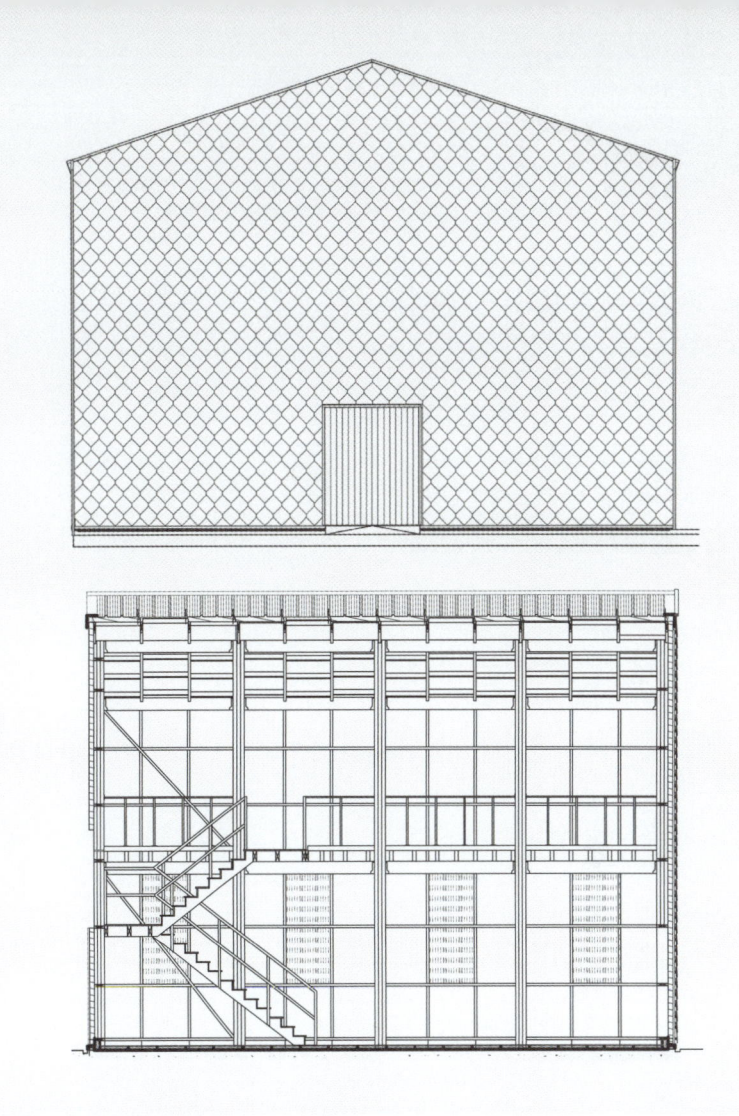

Top: Assemble's computer drawings for the facade, showing the tile pattern and the scaffolding board door; the section shows the structure.

Bottom: The finished building during the day.

YARDHOUSE 097

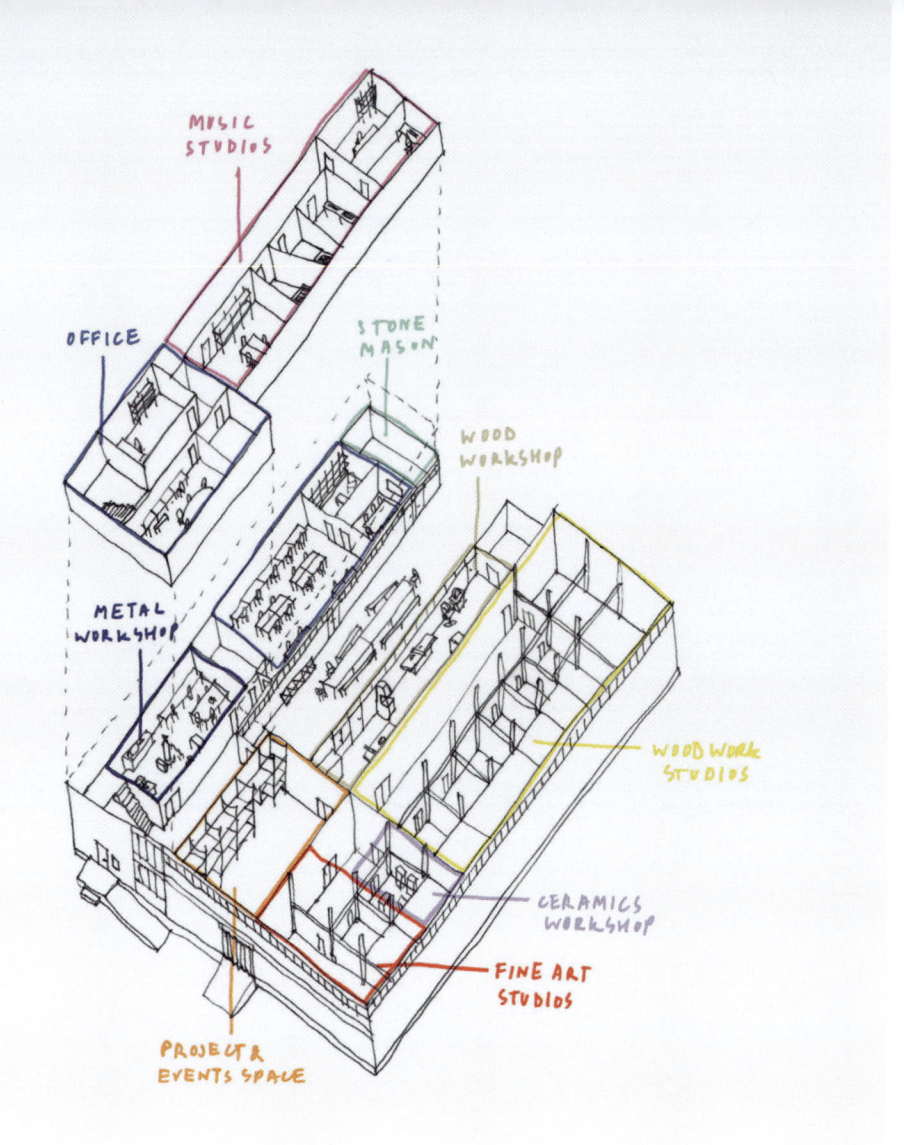

A drawing Assemble made to show the arrangement of spaces at Sugarhouse Studios Bermondsey.

SUGARHOUSE STUDIOS BERMONDSEY

In 2016, Assemble had finally overstayed their welcome on Sugar House Island and moved to a similar site in Bermondsey. Although the second Sugarhouse did not have as much visibility or open space as the original one, this iteration was more convenient to central London and soon filled up with collaborators and craftspeople. In 2023, the Bermondsey location was in turn redeveloped as gentrification reached the neighbourhood, and so Assemble moved to a third location close to the original one on the River Lea.

On Sugar House Island, the team developed a process of rigorous research to ensure the most suitable interventions in the area, a method that they would take with them to each new location. 'We were fascinated by what was going on there, but we were also interested in the idea of open-ended design and realistic research,' recalls Lewis Jones. By 'open-ended

The central swimming pool space at the Bermondsey site as Assemble found it; it was turned into studio spaces.

A view into the ceramics studio.

design', he was referring to the idea that architecture could (in the manner of the event-orientated work the group had done before) not lead to a solution or endpoint, but rather suggest ideas that could be developed in different directions, either by whomever made the proposal or by others. The architecture would have an open-ended character, somewhere between a planning guideline and an actual design. For instance, it could suggest the reuse of a site for retail or arts centres and show what that might look like in a rough drawing, without defining the actual dimensions, materials, structure or client.

By 'realistic research', the group meant that they went out into the neighbourhood where they worked and documented what they saw, while also taking note of the broader reality of the place, from the state of the roads to the roar of a highway overpass. They supplemented these images with historical research, which they collected not as simply pure data or narratives, but as historical photographs, maps and other drawings that helped show the reality of the place.

Through this work, Assemble noted that the area was full of historical fabric similar to their own site, but that these assets were often hidden from the public and thus potential use behind walls and other barriers that factories and

The woodworking shop being used by a student at the East London School of Furniture Making.

The front-of-house and storage space. Assemble installed the off-the-shelf structure, as well as the table in the foreground.

workshops had put up over the years to protect themselves. They also noted the rapid transformation about to occur there, digging up both developer brochures and more fanciful depictions of Sugar House Island's and Stratford's future (including a collage by Oliver Wainwright, architecture critic for *The Guardian* newspaper). 'We were inspired by muf's approach,' notes Maria Lisogorskaya, 'but also by the *Pet Architecture* book by the [Tokyo-based architecture firm] Atelier Bow Wow.' The work of both these firms was part of a larger movement around the world towards tactical urbanism, which saw similar bodies of work performed by urbanists and designers such as Crimson Historians & Urbanists and ZUS in Rotterdam in the Netherlands and Urban-Think Tank in Caracas, Venezuela, and Cape Town, South Africa. This kind of 'urban acupuncture' became one of Assemble's specialties.

A metalworker's studio with a view into an adjacent workshop.

SUGARHOUSE STUDIOS BERMONDSEY 101

A view from the second floor of the ceramics studio at Sugarhouse Studios Bermondsey looking into the collective making space.

MAKE, DON'T MAKE DO

The group collected their research and proposal for Sugar House Island into a booklet they both printed and published online. Entitled *Make, Don't Make Do*, it proposed ten guiding principles for the area's development. These included some basic planning suggestions, such as 'Make better links to Bromley-by-Bow', as well as obvious suggestions, such as 'Make use of vacant spaces' and 'Make more affordable workspace', that would be dependent on economic forces over which the designers had no direct control. Yet other ideas veered towards concrete proposals, such as 'Make uses visible on High Street'. All of the ideas together were illustrated with diagrams that showed how the study site could become more active, more integrated and more pleasant to occupy, while eschewing the large-scale new structures that were due to replace the factories, workshops and open lots.

Assemble also had more specific ideas. They wanted to close down the overpass that cut through the site, first temporarily for the kind of festival they were now becoming specialists at putting together, and later permanently, to be replaced by small-scale development (which was slated to happen in the planning documents they unearthed). They identified not only where trees could be planted, but what kind to use. They also wanted to preserve some of the 'legacy' billboards and add new ones as art projects.

Make, Don't Make Do helped train Assemble in how to analyze sites and make proposals that were open enough that they could be further developed in collaboration

The second-floor studio of one of the tenants at Sugarhouse Studios Bermondsey.

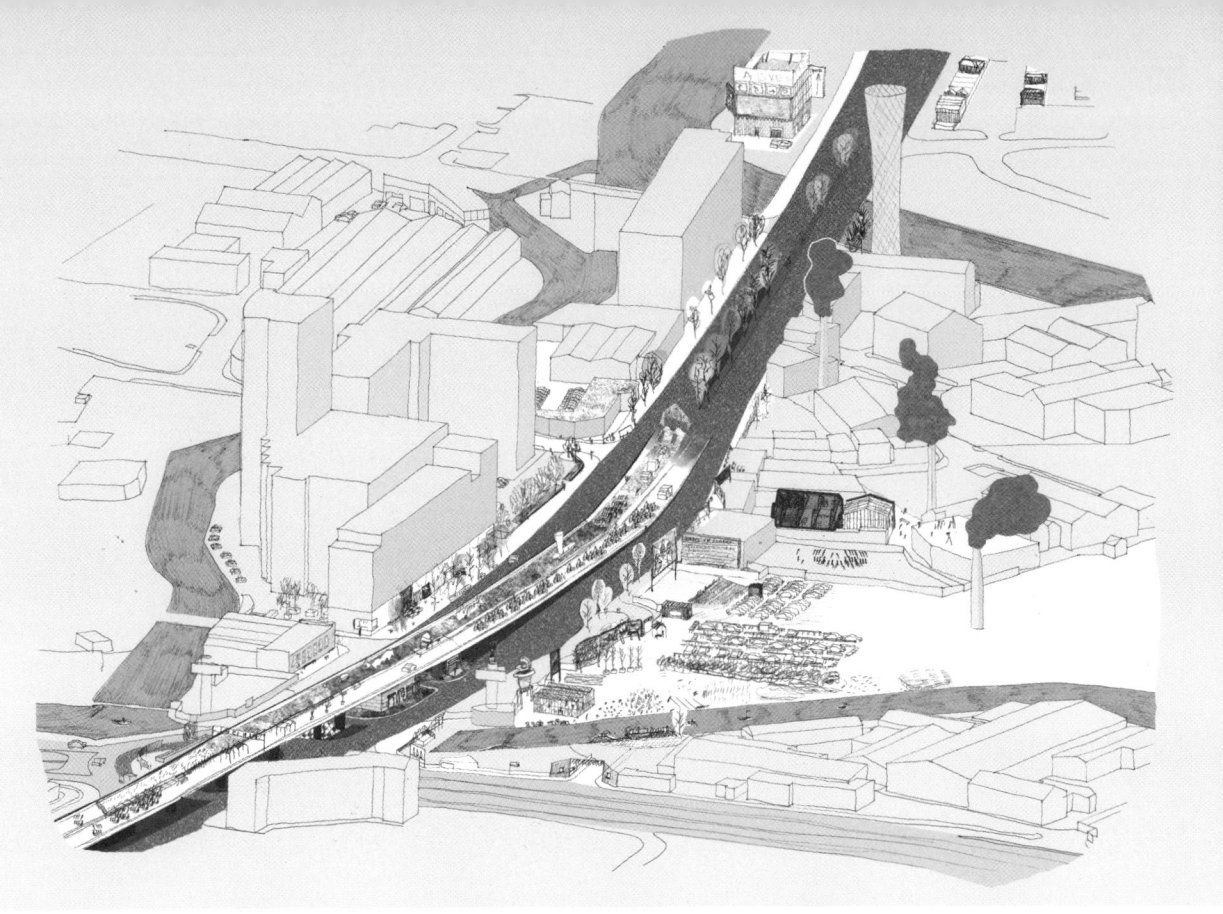

One of the drawings for *Make, Don't Make Do*, showing Assemble's proposals for the area around Sugarhouse Studios Stratford.

with future users or clients. It was also a test for what Lisogorskaya called 'ideas for enterprises': self-generated proposals that would bring work to the group. The little booklet became a model for how Assemble organized and presented their research and ideas, and some of the proposals became part of projects in subsequent years.

BLACKHORSE WORKSHOP

In 2014, Assemble had the opportunity to test this method of working and to expand on what they had developed at Sugarhouse Studios within Blackhorse Workshop – a 'maker space' of the type then just emerging around the world. Located in Walthamstow, just a few miles to the north of Sugar House Island in Stratford, it gave them a chance to think about their studio as a transferable idea.

The idea of the workshop, recalls Jane Hall, was inspired by the Men's Shed's movement, which started in Australia in the 1980s and was by then well-established in the UK. The sheds started out as places where mainly retired men could share facilities for making things, extending their sense of purpose while fostering a sense of community. The Men's Shed movement had spread across the world by the beginning of the millennium and resonated with many, including Assemble, who were interested in the social side of the movement for how it brought people who were isolated together through the act of making. The name for

BLACKHORSE WORKSHOP

Blackhorse Workshop's original outdoor sign designed by graphic design studio Europa. Its perforated metal echoes the pegboard used on the interior.

this collection of shared spaces, some collectively owned, some built as for-profit enterprises and some started by institutions such as research universities, comes from American tech publisher Dale Dougherty's *Make: Magazine*, which he started in 2005. However, it traces back a few years before that.

At the core of the idea was the notion that, with the increased automation and miniaturization of mass production, as well as its disappearance from major Western cities into the hinterlands or far-off countries, a space had opened up for more specialized, made-to-order and DIY production. The revival of specialized craft (highlighted, for instance, when Daniel Day-Lewis took a break from acting to learn how to make shoes in Florence, Italy, but also and more prosaically through the rise of marketplaces such as Etsy) fed the need for tools that were often too expensive for one person to purchase and maintain. The internet made it not only easier to sell specialized products, but also to research the availability of facilities. Soon schools and universities, especially those with a vocational mission, began to realize that their students needed to learn particular crafts rather than the skills necessary for factory production, as that was where human power was needed. Sites such as, perhaps most famously, the Bushwick and Williamsburg sections of Brooklyn, New York in the USA became large-scale incubators for the maker movement.

In 2013, Assemble won a tender to develop the idea for a public workshop, which eventually grew into a brief that included research and business planning, as well as the identification of potential sites. They found a warehouse of a somewhat less glamorous nature than the

Front door of the workshop's first phase. The logo is by Europa and was hand-painted by artist Sean Thomas.

A computer-based illustration by Joe Prytherch showing the workshop about four years after the opening.

Olympic Games-adjacent site that was capacious enough to be repurposed and suggested that craft be at the heart of the enterprise. They conducted local research, met with local businesses, artists and other stakeholders and held consultation events at a range of spaces, from the local shopping mall to a community centre. Their most 'inspired find' was arts manager Harriet Warden who applied for and became Blackhorse's Creative Director and guiding spirit.

What Assemble actually did in a manner that is physically visible at Blackhorse is minimal, both in the sense that it is relatively difficult to identify, blending seamlessly into its context, and because what is present is extremely simple in its design. Even when the workshop became successful enough to warrant an expansion, Assemble accommodated that space with a combination of simple shed constructions and off-the-shelf cabins. New fencing was designed to double up as a metal pegboard for use as a community noticeboard.

Design is evident at Blackhorse in the way windows and doors have been picked out in bright red paint, sometimes with contrasting yellow and green borders, in the

View into the shared bench space. The bench was designed and made by Workshop East. The concrete floor was painted to demarcate the work area.

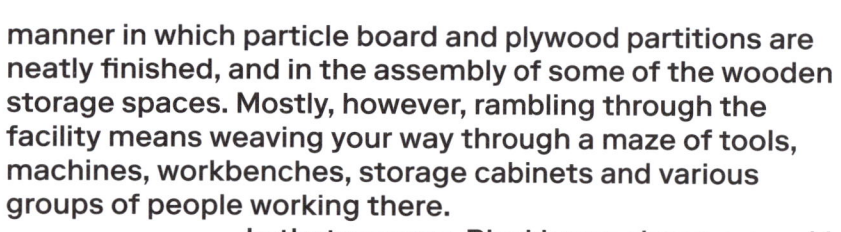

manner in which particle board and plywood partitions are neatly finished, and in the assembly of some of the wooden storage spaces. Mostly, however, rambling through the facility means weaving your way through a maze of tools, machines, workbenches, storage cabinets and various groups of people working there.

In that manner, Blackhorse shows a new kind of discipline Assemble was developing, one which became crucial to their success, even if it made their achievements difficult to identify. Having put on a show and shown off their inventive minds in their early projects, they now concentrated more on what, to them, was the heart of what they wanted to accomplish: to use all the skills and knowledge embedded in architecture to make social change, education, performance and even play possible. Every decision they made collectively and logically on projects from this point on asked the question, whether consciously or not, what, if anything, was physically necessary in any given situation. Often the answer was not much. What the architects provided was, first of all, organization: of information, whether historical, statistical, contextual or economic; of resources, whether institutional, human or economic; of the process to make all of this come together; and of the structures and spaces that resulted.

Top: The chop saw used for constructing the workshop. Behind is the new partition to create the workshop manager's office, made from off-the-shelf materials.

Bottom: The same space looking from the other direction, also showing the metal pegboard used to organize the shared tools.

Looking from the cafe to the bench space and workshop in the distance. The wood burner takes all the waste wood and is the primary heating source for the ground floor.

BLACKHORSE WORKSHOP

The cafe; the hatch to the kitchen was used by bakers to sell their own bread. The cafe was relocated to a new extension during the second phase of the project.

The trestle tables were designed in the Blackhorse Workshop, while the blue bent metal stools were designed by Assemble and built at Blackhorse.

BLACKHORSE WORKSHOP

A section drawing by Assemble of the Domeview Yard building showing the new concrete block partitions; the ceiling was originally intended to be left exposed.

As Joe Halligan says, remarking on the early projects: 'We became less interested in aesthetics or, rather, we became interested in the tool as directly producing the aesthetic. We found joy in ingenuity, in reflecting the process.' 'To a certain extent,' he continued, 'that was a result of the group process, as there was little opportunity for artistic license. We wound up debating other, mainly social issues.' Binning agrees. 'We were less interested in precisely how things looked and more interested in how a process produced a particular appearance and how to make use of that. That did not mean that we wanted to make things ugly, or that we weren't exercising care, but that we accepted the constraints of the materials and tools we had access to.' 'Ultimately,' he concludes, 'we had to be quite pragmatic. We were working with limited materials and tight budgets, but we could use simple tools in inventive ways and, by keeping the overall forms simple, lend those materials a quality that is distinctive and in its own kind of way skillful.'

The group found models for this approach in the work of their former employers, such as muf, and their teachers, such as 6a architects. 'We learned from them, perhaps not in a conscious way, but then we made things even simpler and clearer,' remembers Halligan. 'In the end,' says Binning, 'the working culture adopted aspects of quite a varied set of different ideas that all had in common a detailed interest in the way that you put things together.'

DOMEVIEW YARD

In addition to applying that approach to later projects, and in particular to the next two Sugarhouse Studios they developed, Assemble also created another workshop. This one was to be completely commercial, as a way to both provide space for makers in London and to support the office. Called Domeview Yard, it is housed in two warehouses tucked between the access road to the tunnel under the River Thames and the Greenwich Peninsula Golf Driving Range, within sight of the O2 dome.

The space under construction. New skylights were added and metal columns stabilize the concrete block partitions.

The former pie factory transformed into a raw and divisible workshop collective.

Even more simple than Blackhorse Workshop, these facilities are also temporary, as the whole area is being developed into luxury housing and office buildings, many of which were already finished or under construction even as Domeview Yard opened. One of the Domeview Yard's two buildings also has larger spaces, which means even less evident design, but allows for manufacturing at a scale not possible in the other facilities. The other building, by contrast, provides compact spaces and has become a favourite among musicians, animators and special effects artists who can ply their craft there with no complaints from neighbours. 'It is a bulwark of craft and creativity in a London where it is becoming almost impossible to work at a small scale,' says Hall, rather grandly. She also acknowledges that it will be difficult to find a replacement for Domeview Yard once the developers take the space over. 'We built these places up at a particular time in London,' states Lisogorskaya. Now the group is creating maker spaces far away from their original home, in places such as Hong Kong (the D. H. Chen Foundation Gallery [2019], an exhibition space inside a former textile mill that hosts textile workshops) and New Orleans, Louisiana, USA (the Material Institute [2018], a fashion school and community workshop inside a warehouse) – see Chapter 5 for more details.

One of Assemble's aims in developing these workshops was to create anchors for community development as an alternative to the gentrification that eventually wiped out the original Sugarhouse in Stratford and – despite *Make, Don't Make Do*'s proposals – have turned the area into a grid of soulless mid-rise blocks. The same fate probably awaits the area of Bermondsey where the second Sugarhouse was located, as well as that of Domeview Yard. Only Blackhorse, which has a long-term agreement with the local council and is a public sector project, seems to have been able to avoid that fate for the foreseeable future.

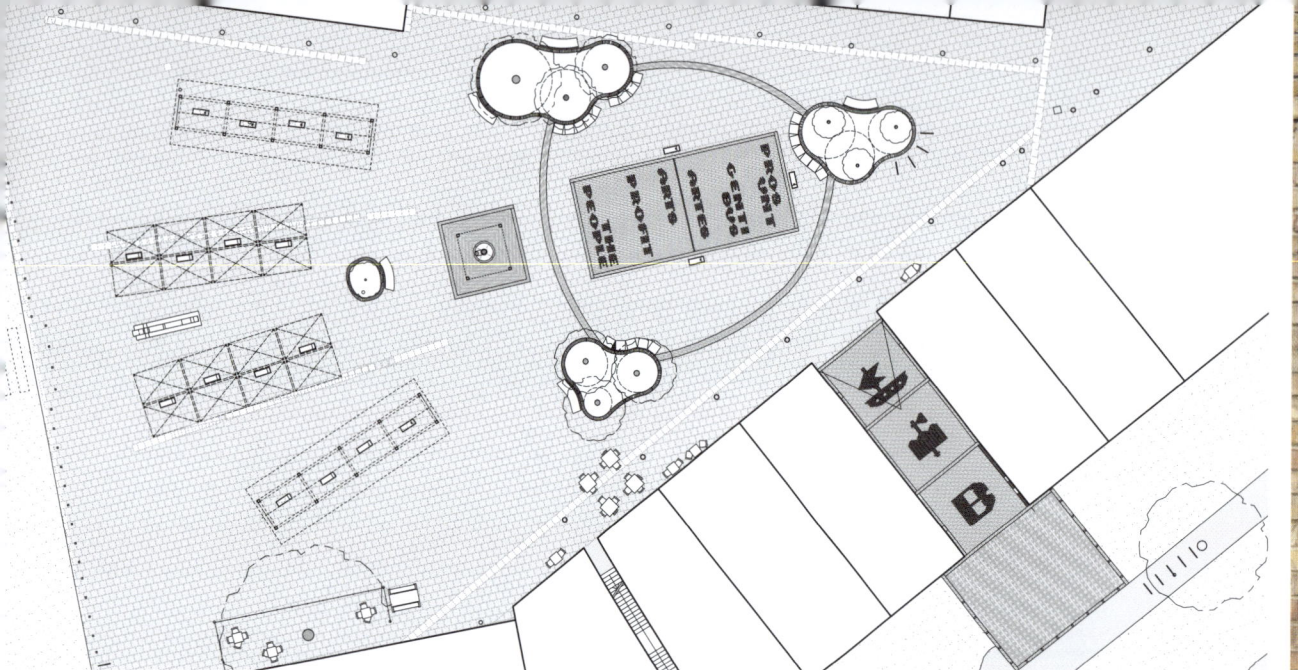

Hayatsu Architects' plan for the redesign of The Blue, showing the new paving, the location of the permanent market stalls, the central clocktower and the cut-through to the rear street.

THE BLUE

Assemble was able to install one project in Bermondsey that will stand as their legacy, and which embodies some of the principles they developed in analyzing Stratford: the redevelopment of The Blue, the community's traditional market square. A second project, for Bramcote Park in South Bermondsey, developed in collaboration with some of the activists Assemble encountered at The Blue in response to an open tender from the council, is currently awaiting planning approval (see p. 160).

The Blue is located just a few blocks away from the second Sugarhouse Studios. Members of Assemble were familiar with the area – a chaotic crossing of roads where market stalls vied with traffic in an only vaguely defined area – from shopping there for the lunches they collectively cooked and shared most days in their offices. What they saw, however, was a shadow of the market's former self. In the Bermondsey's dockyard days, The Blue spread out to over two hundred stalls. Redevelopment in the 1960s cut into that space, and the decline of industry lessened The Blue's economic viability.

Local activists, most notably several of the more vocal stall holders, began arguing for the area's revival. Meanwhile, immigration made the population more diverse, and brought cultures more used to traditional markets back into the area. Assemble worked as part of a team that included Hayatsu Architects and graphic designers Stinsensqueeze, all of whom were working out of Sugarhouse at the time, to develop responses to the activists starting in 2019. Most of their work was completed in 2022.

Design is more evident here than in some of Assemble's other projects, although much of what is visible

A member of graphic design group Stinsensqueeze laying out the proposed sign over the alleyway cut-through.

A view into the new cut-through. The new steel structured, rendered arch hides the services to the flats above. New brick sheets also hide the original walls.

is the work of Stinsensqueeze. The designers developed a typeface that recalls the signage that might have been found on 19th-century factories and deployed it on portals, bike racks and other pieces of urban furniture that took the form of metal arches, some with abstracted pictures of heraldic emblems or of the kind of implements you might have once found in the market, all of which contributed to the largely nostalgic character of the design.

    Assemble's and Hayatsu Architects' contributions also had, unusually for the latter's designs, a certain nostalgic air. The main structure is a pavilion and a clocktower that also serves as a gathering point and marker for the market's centre. Constructed using a plane-oaked frame, the building is clad in metal medallions. Each medallion is stamped with an abstracted image of the kinds of goods, such as fish or meat, that you might buy at The Blue, or with heraldic signs, ranging from lions to anchors, that might have been historically present there in various forms. The modernist typeface of the cubic clock is placed on top of the elongated pyramid covered by these scales (see p. 119), which were finished in various textures so that they have weathered in a variegated manner.

THE BLUE

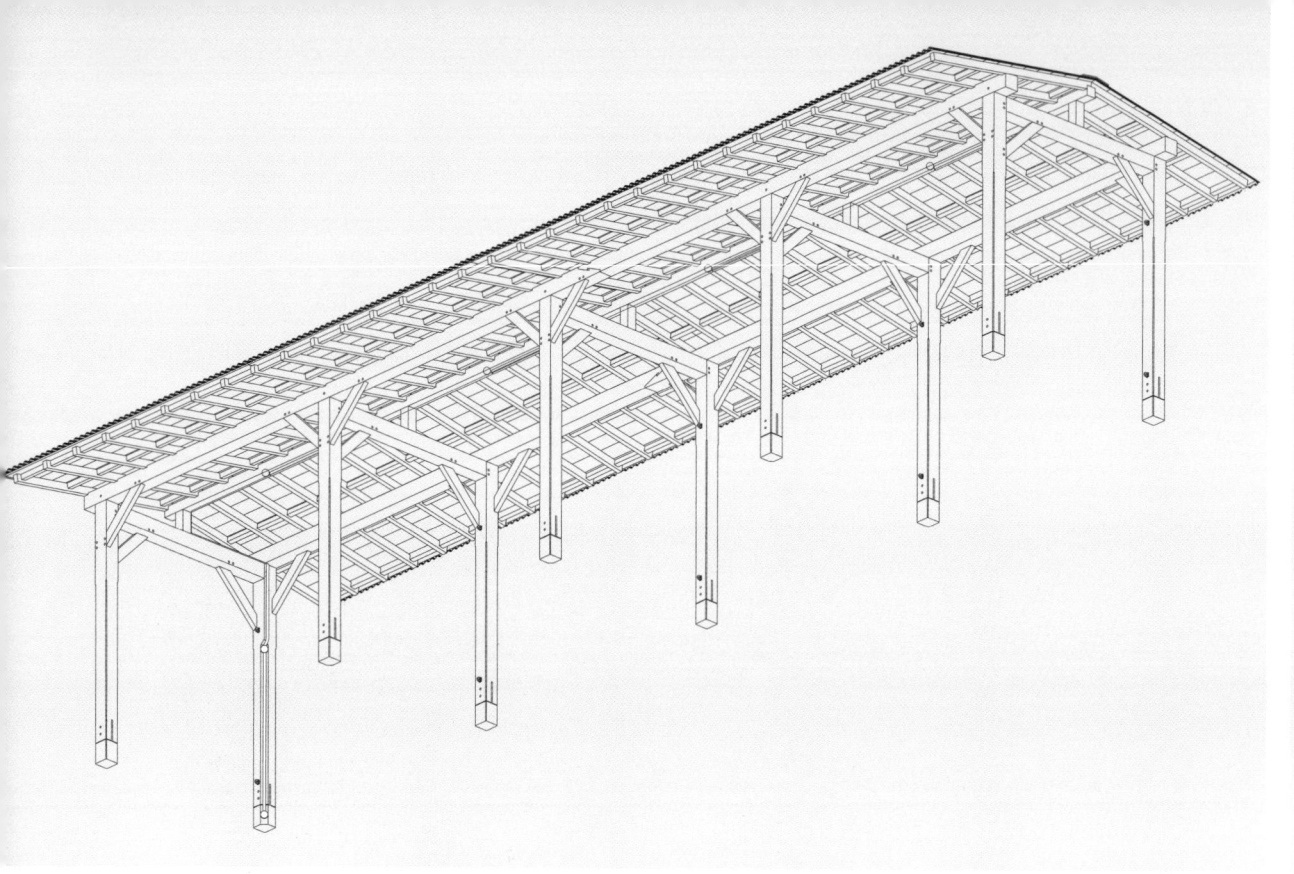

A drawing Hayatsu made providing a 'worm's eye view' of the heavy timber pavilions designed to cover the market stalls. You can also see the concrete 'feet' and the off-the-shelf galvanized metal roof.

    The clocktower gazebo's bottom is completely open, inviting people to wait or gather there. A drinking fountain built from terrazzo gestures in various directions. The design evokes the grand urban fountains that, originating as outgrowths of wells, once anchored (and were the genesis of) many such market squares.
    At The Blue, Hayatsu Architects and Assemble also designed permanent canopies for traders that on busy market days are supplemented by temporary stalls, the latter housed in adjacent storage facilities also improved as part of the project. In addition, the designers collaborated on benches, some in wood and some in a combination of red-pigmented concrete blocks and recycled terrazzo, that surround new plantings dotted around the square. These direct traffic and indicate gathering places, as well as introduce a bit of green in the otherwise rather barren environment. The remainder of the design – made from existing concrete slabs and clay pavers – consists of the manipulation of the pavement in a manner that helps organize where the stalls are set up during market days, breaks up the expanse and helps guide movement across its amorphous expanse. Equally important was the cut-through created in one of the adjacent residential structures, which improved circulation and visibility while providing a dramatic entrance from the rear of The Blue.
    Today, The Blue has become a lively and well-used space (at least when weather permits) and is a focal point for the diverse community that currently calls Bermondsey

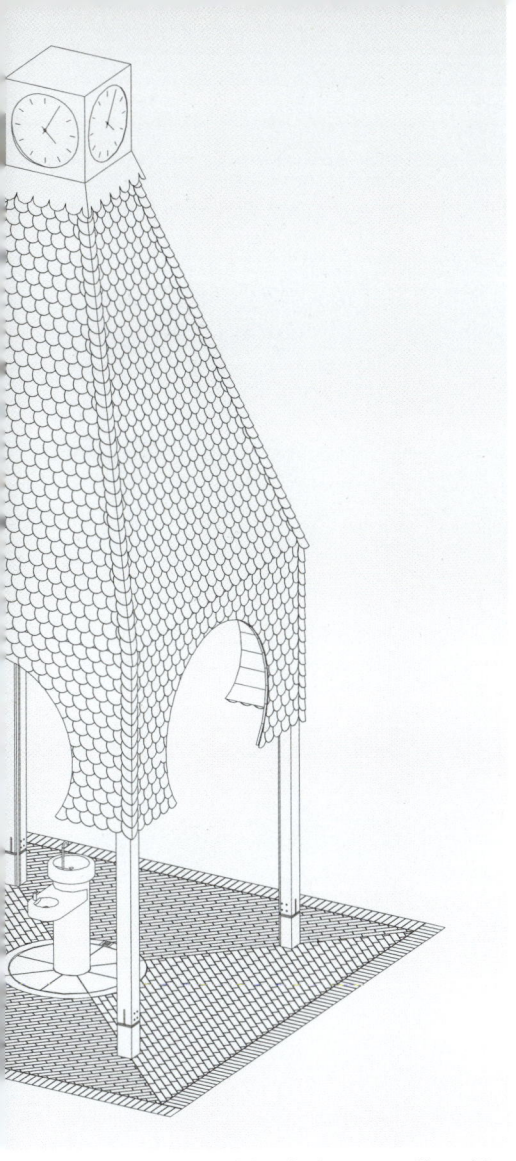

Hayatsu's drawing of the clocktower pavilion with the drinking fountain in the middle and the clock above.

Hayatsu also made a 1:50 scale model of the proposed square to try out different locations for the market pavilions. The clocktower was meant to be visible from trains passing nearby.

home. Whether it will survive the forces of gentrification that have already wiped out the second Sugarhouse, and which are for now somewhat constrained by an elevated train line just to the north of The Blue, remains to be seen.

This is a quandary Assemble has confronted in almost all of their early work, and continues to find at many of the sites where they are asked to consult or intervene. Having started by staging events at places that were either being temporarily revived as part of a civic showcase (Folly for a Flyover; Theatre on the Fly; The Playing Field) or that were slated for redevelopment soon after the installation was torn down (The Cineroleum and the Sugarhouse Studios), they have found their efforts aiding the kind of activity that they, in their theoretical stances, have sought to avoid. *Make, Don't Make Do* and The Blue and several other early public space projects (see Chapter 3) in fact proposed ways

THE BLUE

The site for The Blue as Assemble and their collaborators found it, with the continuous paving and isolated trees.

in which neighbourhoods could retain their existing character (and, by implication, communities). Assemble did so by gathering resources spread throughout the area, providing cultural and small-scale manufacturing ('making') facilities and thoughtful, pinprick improvements in the area ranging from changes in pavements or planting to the removal of barriers or the reuse of signs. Yet the effect of all this thinking and making was, essentially, wiped out by the larger realities of urban growth. In these early years, Assemble found themselves fighting a rear-guard battle against gentrification, winning many early battles by establishing sites such as the Sugarhouse Studios that attracted not only attention, but also users. In the end, however, they lost the war. As Lisogorskaya points out: 'There are few sites in London left where you can make at a small scale, and I am afraid that artists and artisans are getting wiped out here completely.' The same can be said of most other large cities, such as New York, San Francisco and even Shenzhen and Shanghai.

Assemble, of course, realized this situation even when they were working on these early projects. Their response was to invest as minimally as possible, designing their interventions for the largest possible impact in the time they knew would be given for the projects to be on site. They also saw their attitude as going, to a certain extent, with the flow, continually finding new opportunities where they felt both that they could make a difference and operate as a collective. They keep doing so even today, in their third Sugarhouse, while projects such as Blackhorse Workshop continue to survive.

The Blue being used during a market day, with both temporary stalls and those contained in the timber structures. The trees have been surrounded by low planting and seating.

The Blue on opening day, with craftspeople demonstrating their techniques.

      The other achievements of these early projects were to learn and to demonstrate. To create them, Assemble taught themselves a wide array of skills beyond the ones they had learned on The Cineroleum and other temporary structures, not only in making buildings, but also in working with other craftspeople and designers as well as with communities. They also developed an economic model for the studio that has allowed them to survive without having recourse to the kind of commercial projects for well-paying (and thus wealthy or institutionally entrenched) clients that support most other firms. In showing how this could be done, a significant aspect of Assemble is its function as a kind of model and training academy that has been inspirational for at least two generations of young designers.

      This is not to say that all of Assemble's early work has vanished, and in the series of public space and collective institution projects that remain and continue to operate, Assemble have integrated fully into communities, their lives and their futures.

THE BLUE

The clocktower's timber structure before it was clad. The frame was made by one of Sugarhouse Studios Bermondsey tenants, woodworker William Floyd-Maclean.

118

A detail of the scales, showing the various heraldic devices and references to local businesses designed by Stinsensqueeze.

The finished clocktower with its cladding of embossed tin can lids that were meant to patina and were laid like fish scales.

A view of the clocktower from above, showing the water fountain fabricated by Granby Workshop and the new wood benches made by Sugarhouse Studios Bermondsey tenant Emma Leslie.

THE BLUE

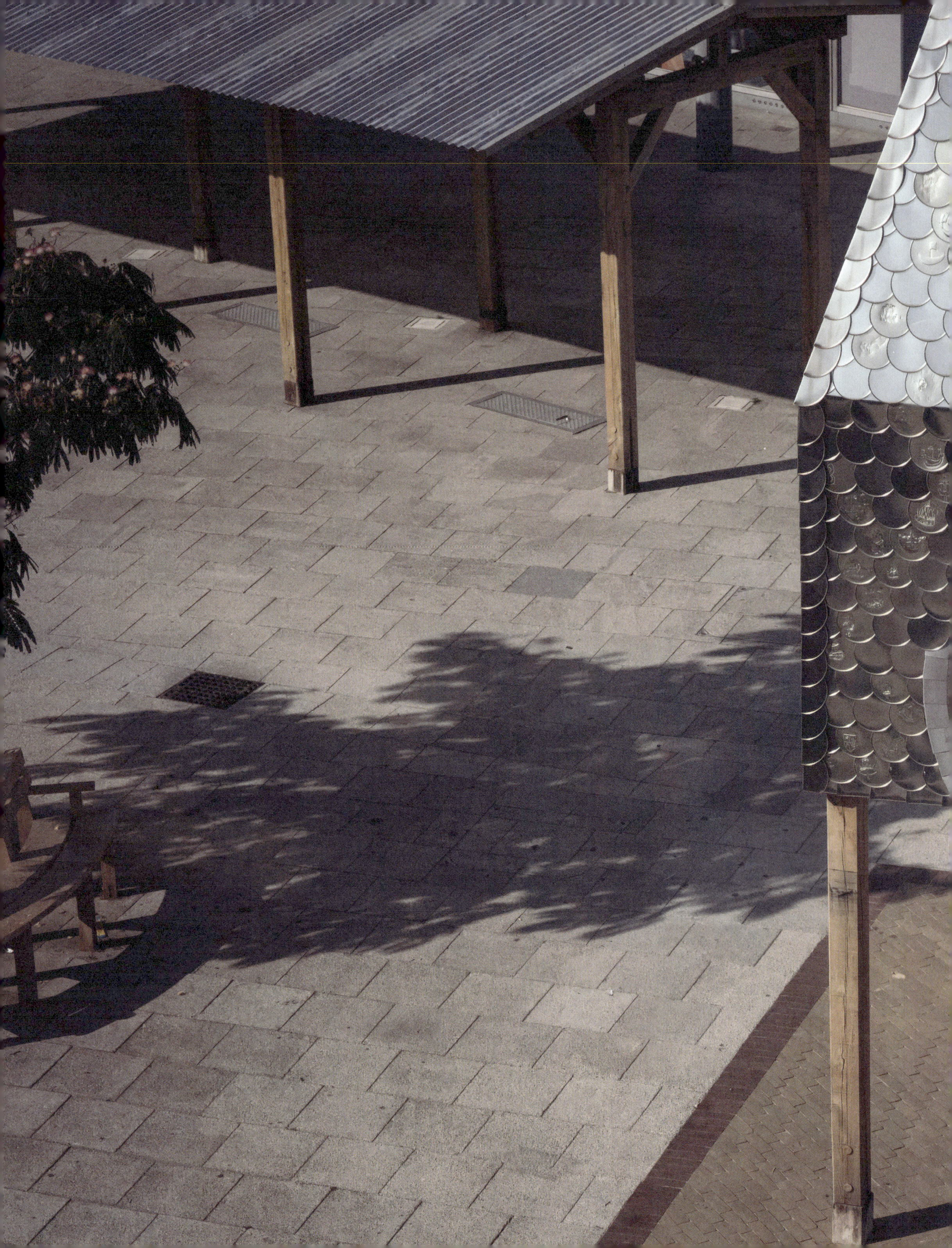

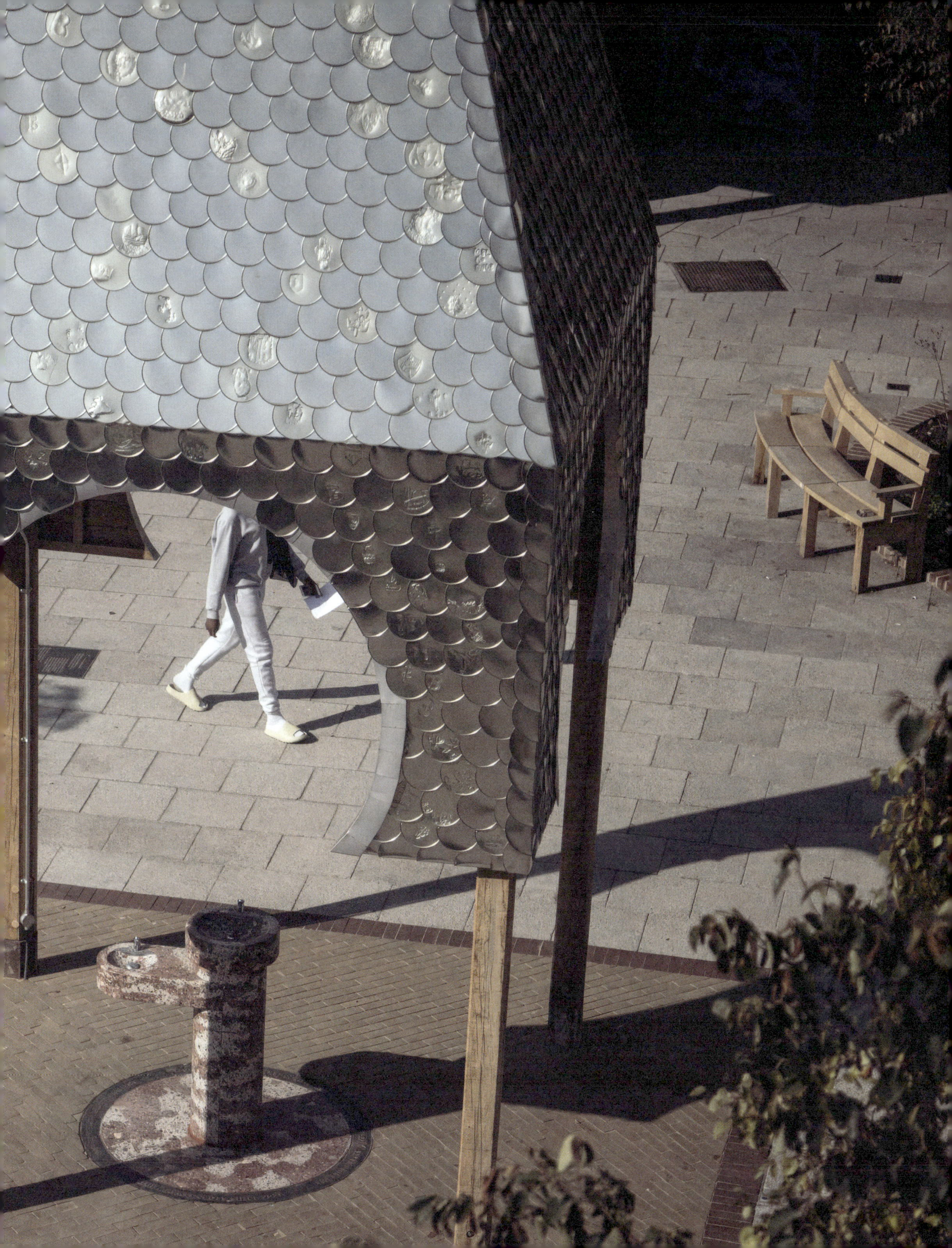

The Blue soon after its opening, with the existing stores and flats visible in the background.

122

One of the market stall pavilion structures on a non-market day with the new planting areas around the existing trees visible in the background.

Top: The terrazzo water fountain uses a method Assemble developed for making mantelpieces at Granby Workshop. The brick paving is also new.

Bottom: A detail of the post-and-beam wood structure of the market stall, with no visible pegs or screws.

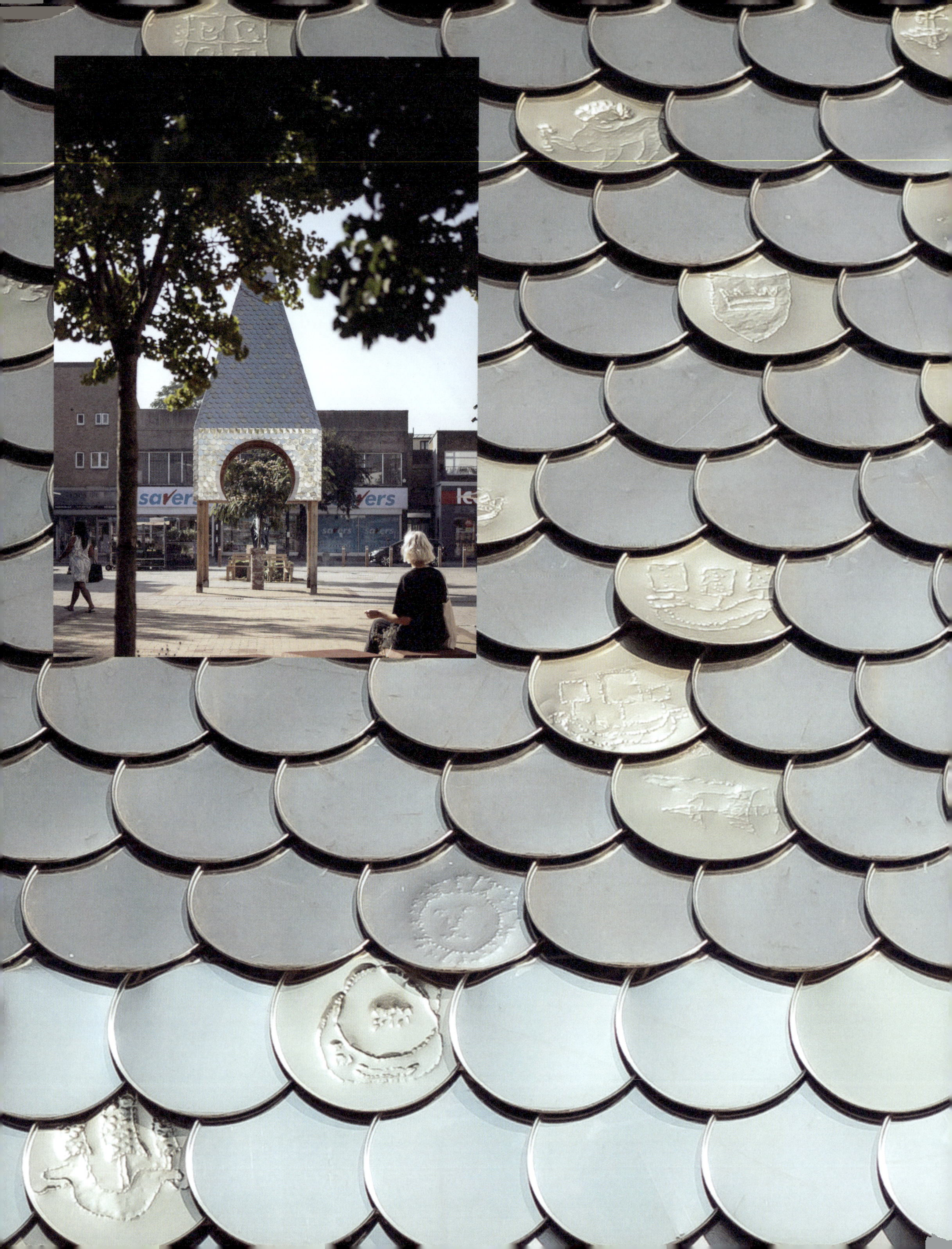
savers

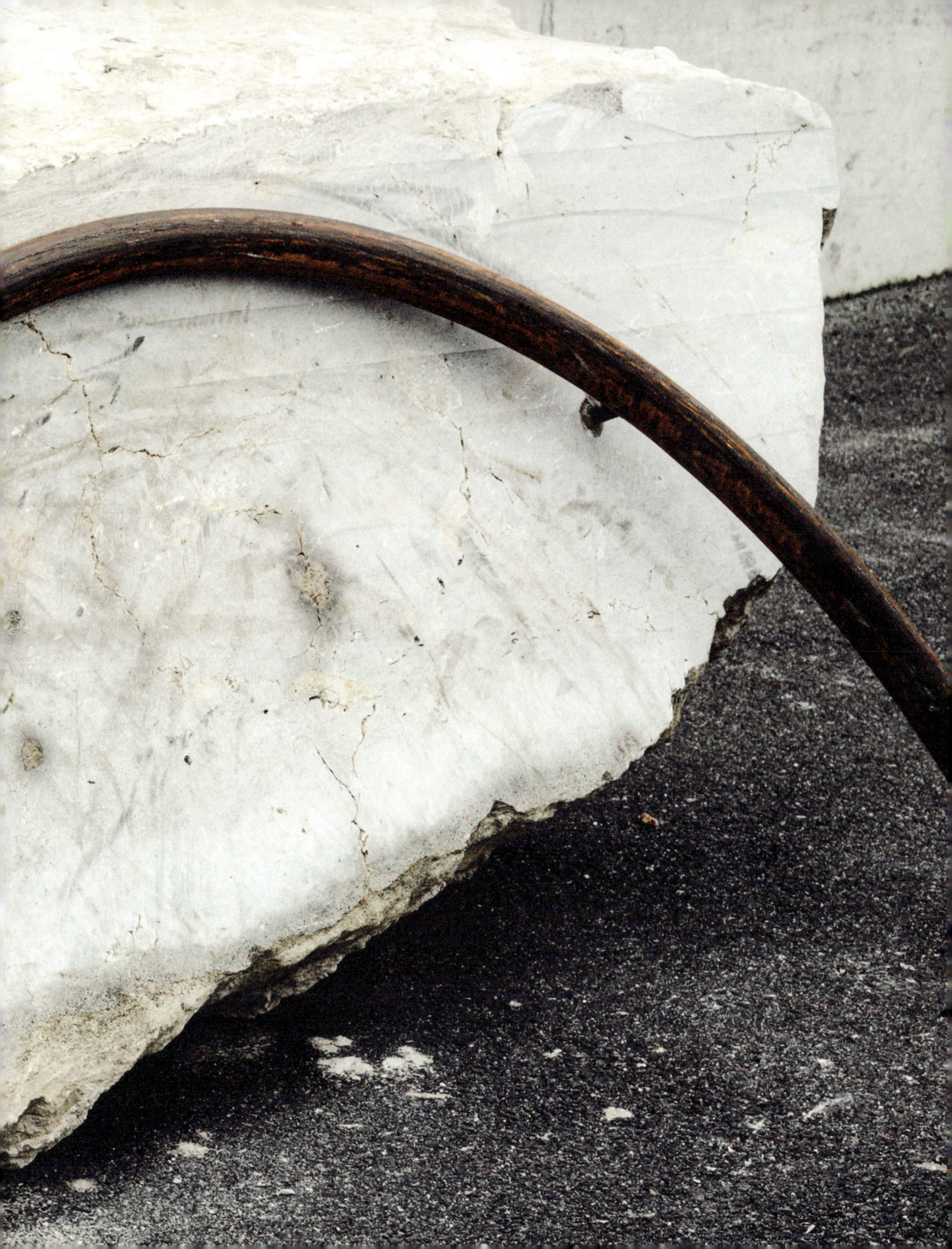

3

Going Public

THE BRUTALIST PLAYGROUND (See PG152)

NEW ADDINGTON A mainstay of Assemble's work from the beginning has been the design of public space. This concentration is deeply rooted in the education the members received and in the work of many of their tutors and employers. In seeking out and designing these kinds of projects, the group has worked closely and intensely with the local communities that these squares, event spaces and, in an important subset, play areas were meant to activate and bring together. At times, this focus has led to results in which it is difficult at first to see what the group has accomplished. The built elements are often minimal, at times messy and sometimes meant to disappear into the activities that take place there. That does not make them any less powerful in achieving their goals.

The project that enabled Assemble to put many of their ideas about on making public space into practice was the redesign of New Addington, a market square in a

The brick-covered raised area in the Central Parade of New Addington that can act as a stage. Its hardwood floor mirrors the one in the existing community hall next to the square.

A poster designed by motion designer Linus Kraemer that lists the activities to be found in New Addington during an event staged by Assemble as part of the design process; the idea was to show how the Central Parade could attract and give room to these events.

127

During the design, Assemble organized a tea dance in the existing community hall.

The Central Parade as Assemble found it, showing the housing and commons behind. Assemble's work took place on the other side of the road.

somewhat isolated part of Croydon on the fringes of south London. Assemble's interventions here were minimal, but they developed new approaches and techniques towards the organization and opening up of public space.

New Addington was developed in 1935 as a bedroom community (residential suburb) in the 'garden city' mode of meandering roads and semi-detached homes. The Second World War halted construction before the plan was complete and, by the time it resumed, the buildings were more regularized and larger in scale (like many other housing estates of the time).[24] Few amenities followed this mass production of homes. This monotonous, low-quality housing stock and lack of schools, public space or other accoutrements, combined with New Addington's relative isolation – removed from other population centres and served only by a single tramline – led to urban decay and violence.

At the area's core, both geographically and in terms of its problems, was the Central Parade – a strip of public space in an ovoid shape intended as the heart of the garden city community. Business and park space lined the core of the Parade. The central area was used for markets but had also become a site for young people and even gangs to congregate. In the 2010s, the city and UK government was making funds available through its Outer London Fund to help revitalize neglected or economically challenged communities at the edges of the metropolis, and New Addington received a relatively small amount of funding – a little less than a million pounds – to improve the Parade.

Assemble received the commission to work on the Parade's core through a limited design competition at the end of 2011. They were wary of the situation, however, as the site had already been through several rounds of planning. 'We definitely encountered consultant fatigue when we first went there,' recalls Maria Lisogorskaya. In response, Assemble

128

The 'skateable' raised area Assemble designed with its sloped brick surfaces framed in concrete. The main stage is visible in the background.

decided not to start with abstract analysis of local data, nor to come with ideas and plans, but as James Binning recalls, 'to be there, present and available'.

They convened numerous meetings starting in December of 2011, first with local community leaders and officials and then with as varied a group of inhabitants as they could. They reached out to the public with flyers and through the internet, and visited schools and community centres. The hub of their activities became the disused brick toilet building in the centre of the Parade, which they repurposed as a place where they not only worked but also, at times, lived. They also invited Alison Crawshaw, who had worked with muf and had tutored several of the members at Cambridge, to bring in her expertise with design for community spaces.

'What we heard,' says Binning, 'was, on the whole, negative.' The community members were not only sceptical that anybody from the outside could bring real change, but also that anything was needed beyond ways to deter crime – or people gathering in the space, which some local shopowners equated with loitering or more dangerous activities: 'The early discussions were just about security, crime, and vandalism…'

Digging deeper, the members of the Assemble team began questioning what could help transform not so much the physical space as the perception of the Parade. Not surprisingly, given the other designs they were working on at the time, they decided to throw a party. 'The total amount of money available at first was £500,000, so not an inconsiderable sum,' recalls Binning. 'We decided to spend £20,000 of that on an event that would, more than anything else, show people what

A dance event for local youth at the opening of the redesigned Parade.

the positive possibilities of the Parade were.' A series of events were held during December 2011. They designed a temporary stage – a very simple version of the structures that were a mainstay of their activities at the time – and sought out the participation of a wide variety of clubs and associations. There was a local 'Man of Steel' body building competition, dancing and amateur theatrics. There were also meetings in the square. Local skateboarders were made welcome, as were older people playing cards. They tried not to exclude anyone. 'We were a mirror, rather than a motor,' says Binning.

Based on how the event packed out, and the subsequent uses of the Parade's temporary facilities, as well as Assemble's observations and conversations with those who occupied the Parade, the designers started to make a few elemental changes to the square's arrangement. The most effective and controversial of these was the placement of stones that prevented cars from parking on the square. 'A "meteor" storm: Anti-parking boulders which cost £7,000 spark fury', the *Evening Standard* headlined in October of 2012.[25] The newspaper found an inhabitant who thought they were not just a waste of money, but also ugly and dangerous for children who might play on them. In reality, the stones were not only well-enough accepted to allow Assemble to continue with full community support, but also effective in defining the beginning of a new kind of Parade that was more than a crime-ridden parking area.

People gathered in the Parade during a market day. The limestone boulders are a traffic calming measure that double up as seating.

A new, low brick wall defines the Parade's edge and separates it from the parking area. Tree species found in the neighbouring streets and estates were introduced here.

Assemble spent most of the remainder of the funds on paving. They spent time looking at and documenting the surrounding housing estates, choosing bricks and stone that continued the vernacular they found there. To define the usable space, they developed a herringbone pattern that set this brick apart from the regular houses and streets around it. At-grade crossings were defined by similar distinctive arrangements of pavement.

The only three-dimensional elements Assemble built on the square were slightly raised areas, some filled with new planting, and others that defined places to sit or gather around existing trees and other features. A small concrete raised area in the otherwise flat surface indicated where a stage or a playing court could be, while also being useful for bike and skateboard tricks. Taking what was there, emphasizing it and doing the least possible amount to accommodate different uses without dictating anything became Assemble's strategy. As Lisogorskaya recalls: 'There we learned how little you can do and how effective it can be'.

The only other element Assemble introduced was a version of the repurposed billboards they had proposed for Stratford in *Make, Don't Make Do*. It consisted of a programmable reader board mounted on one of the commercial buildings next to the Parade. The designers envisioned the screen as a place for community messages and art projects, and it functioned as such, although now its technology is outdated and the board is no longer in use. Assemble built a website for it and for the Parade (no longer operative), gaining another skill they were able to repurpose in

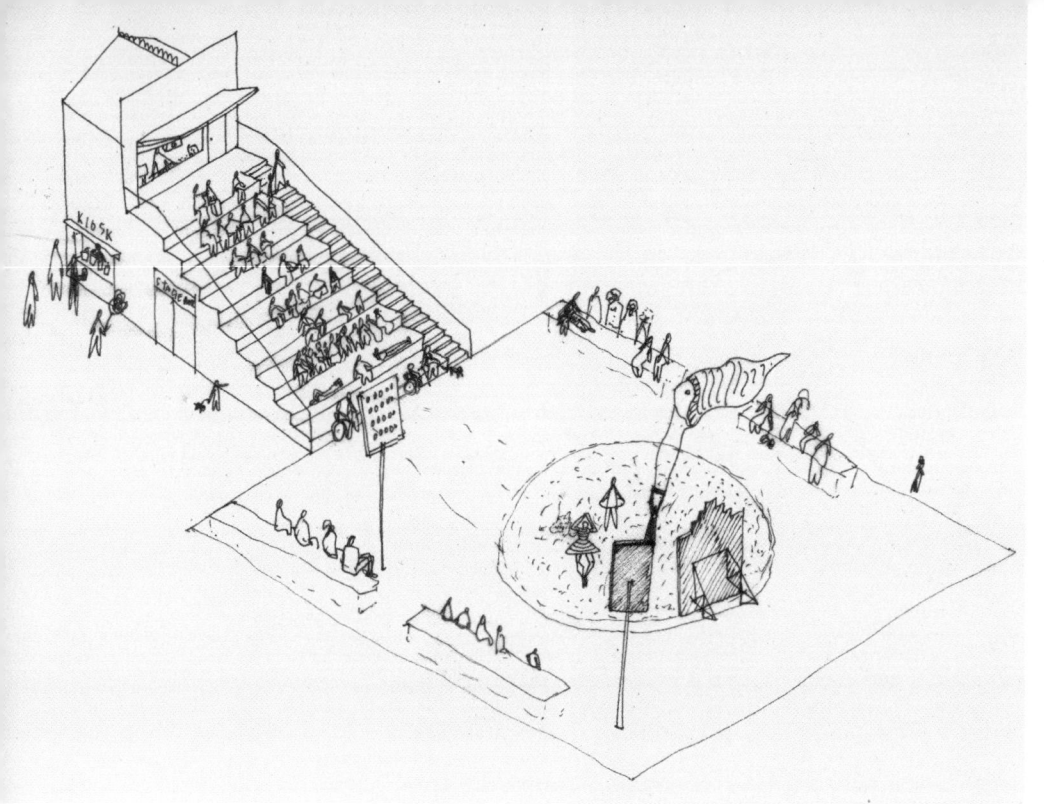

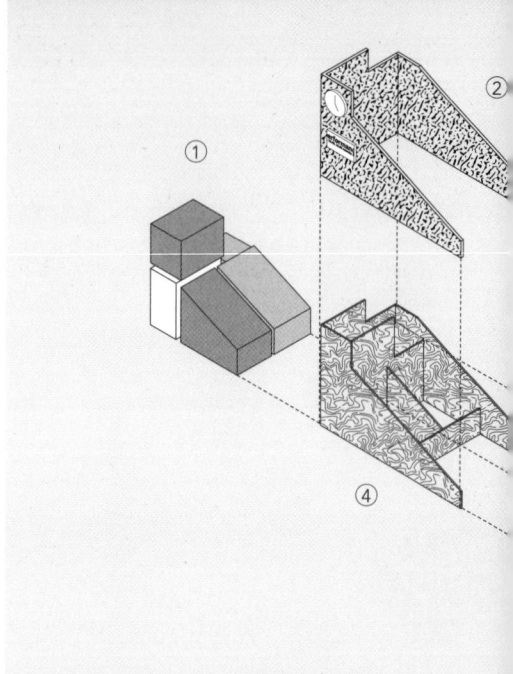

A sketch Assemble drew to show how the new pavilion would work during an event as a seating area for the audience.

subsequent projects. 'We also learned how to do spreadsheets and organize the project flow in a professional manner there,' says Binning. 'It really was where we began to operate for the first time in a professional manner.' 'But it also taught us,' adds Lisogorskaya, 'how to take our theatrical bent and make it part of what we could offer to a community.'

New Addington was the first of a series of public space renovations in which Assemble engaged that came out of observation, discussion and collaboration, that used physically minimal means and that were meant to be activators of, rather than containers for, public activities. Although the Parade is by now, a decade after its construction, well-worn, it continues to operate in that manner in the middle of New Addington.

BELL SQUARE PAVILION

The project Assemble designed in Hounslow, west London in 2014 had as much if not more success as New Addington in terms of instigating events, although it never led to any permanent construction. The group won this commission in a public tender in which the aim was – much as in New Addington – to improve the quality of life in the community's central square. Once again, members of the group went to the site and spent considerable time with all the users and potential

An axonometric drawing that describes how the seating would fit over the storage and information booth, with a technical area above.

Top: A digital drawing in which Assemble explain to the client how the public could use the pavilion during the day in a casual manner.

Bottom: Another view of the proposal, here seen at night from Stones Road.

A photo montage illustrating the blue concrete steps and ceramic tiles Assemble wanted to use to clad the pavilion.

occupants they could find. They organized events and showed how the square could be used. They installed a temporary performance booth on the pavilion painted in bright colours.

They also proposed a permanent building, which had much in common with the theatre pavilions they had previously designed. It would have combined the large steps of which the group is so fond with a stage front that could be alternatively the proscenium when seen from Bell Square, and a backdrop for the auditorium steps. Behind that rectangular front was a gabled container, much like the implied volume of the ruined house in Folly for a Flyover, that would store equipment for Watermans, a local theatre group. When not in use, the structure could remind inhabitants of the potential for performance and act as a site for advertisements.

The whole structure was meant to be covered in deep blue tiles placed over a structure made out of concrete blocks. Assemble researched various colours and patterns to etch onto the tiles, intended to break down its scale while giving it enough presence to stand confidently in the middle of a large space surrounded by a hodgepodge of commercial buildings at different scales clad in various materials. Although the design was welcomed by the community and could have been built for the available budget, changes in local administration meant that the project, though still officially active a decade later, was never completed.

BELL SQUARE PAVILION

The abandoned commercial unit at Seven Sisters tube stop as Assemble found it upon receiving the commission.

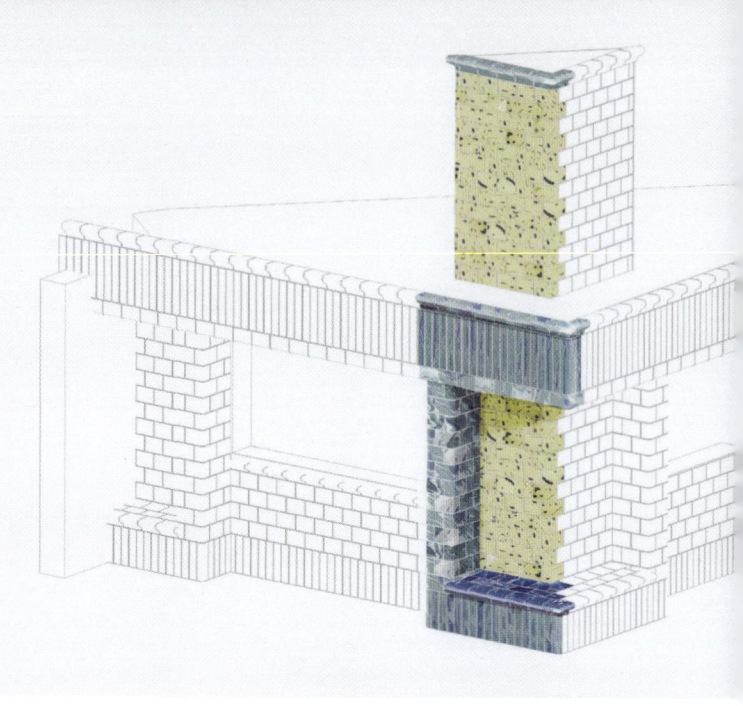

A design development drawing Assemble used to test out different coloured tiles, how they would be assembled and how they would clad new pillars and seating elements.

ART ON THE UNDERGROUND

One project that echoes proposals such as New Addington and Bell Square Pavilion in its approach, and that is also one of the oldest permanent Assemble designs, is a remodelled commercial unit at the entrance of London Underground's Seven Sisters stop. Assemble collaborated with Matthew Raw, a ceramic artist, to reclad the disused structure with over a thousand new handmade tiles in blues, greens and yellows. Raw and Assemble also facilitated two paid apprenticeships in collaboration with the youth arts and education organization A New Direction's Create Jobs training programme, and together they experimented with different ways to colour and shape the tiles. They also added a small tower to mark the reopened structure, and fashioned a bench for people to sit on.

The result is a composition of intersecting geometries punctuated by an open vending window, which gives the structure an unexpected complexity. The building more than holds its own among the surrounding urban chaos, partially because it abstracts and condenses the shapes of the buildings around it. The form of this marker and urban activator harks back to the commercial Modernism of the 1920s and 1930s, while the ceramics signal the extensive tile works in the tube stations themselves. The experiments also strengthened Assemble's interest in the material, which has become a constant motif in much of their work.

One thing both the Bell Square Pavilion and Art on the Underground designs made clear was the fascination some members of Assemble had with the kind of vivid condensation and abstraction of vernacular forms into blocks that communicate their function and nature. They accomplished this through an appeal to the archetypes that fit into the postmodern traditions first documented by Charles Jencks in the 1970s and continue

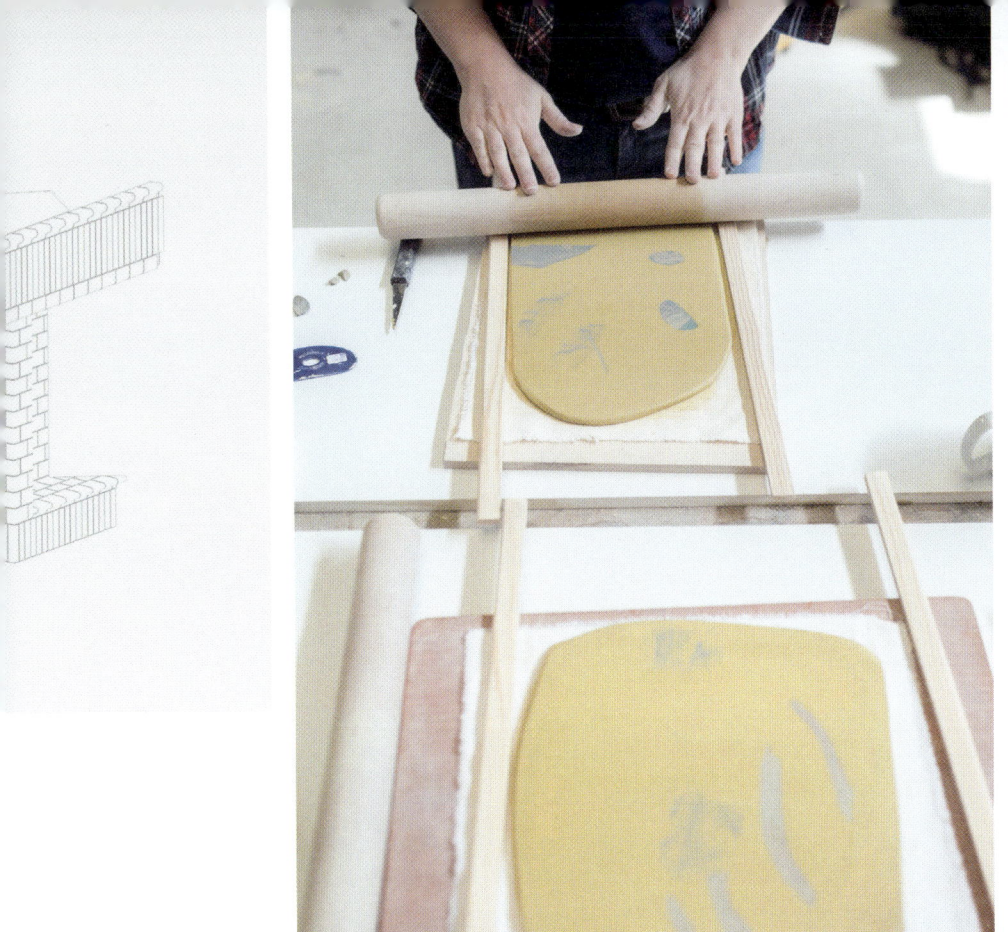

Rolling out one of the tiles at Sugarhouse Studios Bermondsey. Different colours were pressed in during the process to produce the marbling effect.

A batch of the tiles being fired by ceramicist Matthew Raw in a rented kiln at Sugarhouse Studios Bermondsey.

to this day through the work of several generations of London-based designers. The members of Assemble all eschew this association, seeing it as being linked to a kind of commercially oriented, 'easy' solution to how architecture can communicate to different communities, but the unconscious links are too clear to ignore. There is an evident relation between the facade-oriented, signage-focused and easily recognizable character of structures such as the Bell Square Pavilion and the early work of American architect Robert Venturi and British Postmodernists such as Terry Farrell, James Stirling and James Outram.

What Assemble was able to do was pick up on the notion of making an architecture that took what people using or seeing it might easily recognize and then making it both more theatrically effective and up-to-date. At the same time they worked to lose the intensity of materials, structure, composition and costs that came with the elaborate designs often associated with Postmodernism, and which made many of those structures expensive, confusing and difficult to maintain. Assemble's fascination with these methods, however, is sporadic, and most of their subsequent public space projects were rougher and simpler, picking up on what they had learned from New Addington: less is more.

The testing of colour glazes and patterns. The marbling effect was produced in the clay itself rather than in the matte, semigloss and gloss glazes.

A detail of one of the benches and pillars with bespoke curved tiles for the seats and wall edges.

Assemble used the contrast between the yellow and blue tiles to pull out the unit's different structural pieces, creating a relationship between the new tower and the existing structure.

The finished unit in use as a coffee shop. The new soffit provides shelter for the seating, while the tower announces both it and the tube entrance.

ART ON THE UNDERGROUND

137

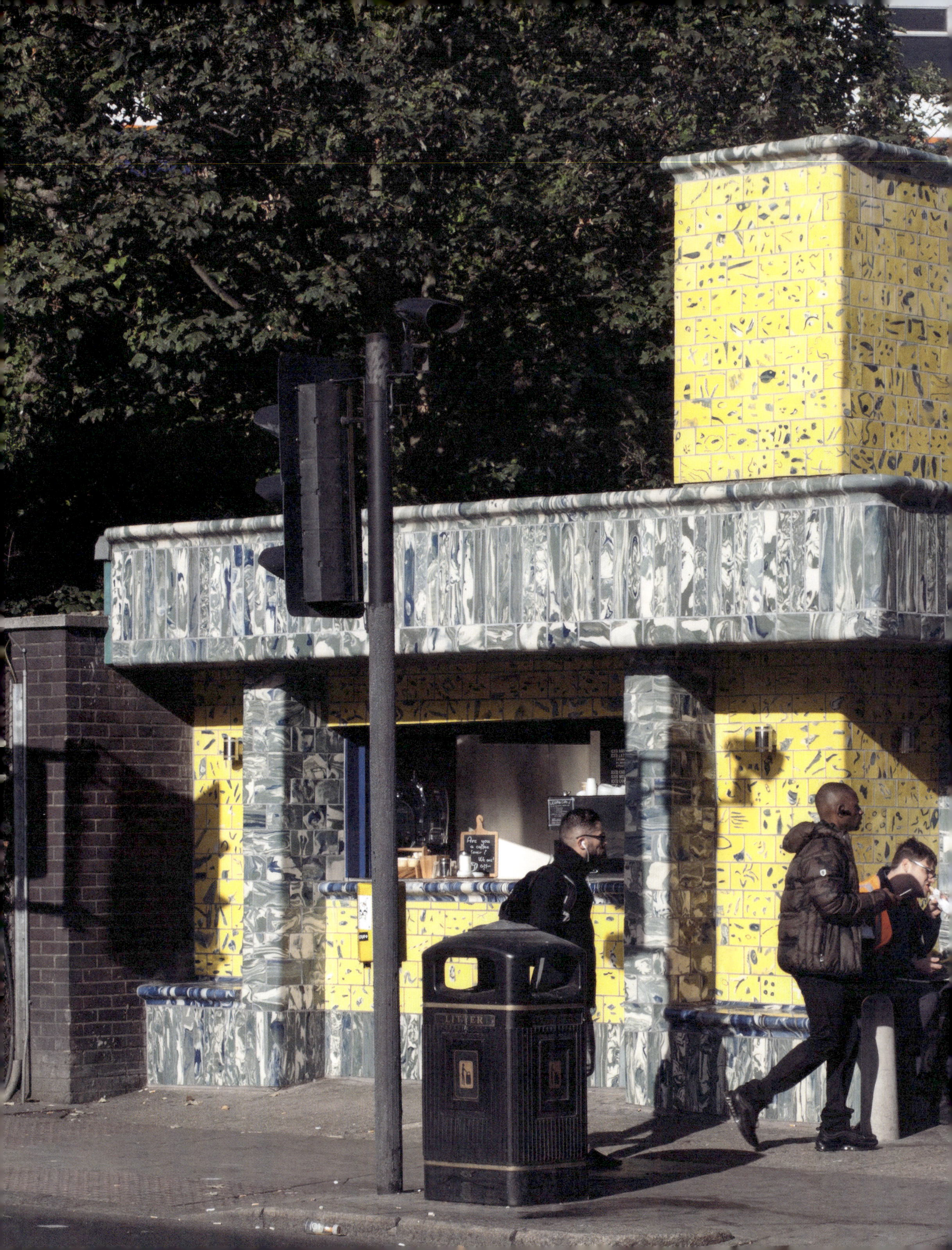
LITTER

UNDERGROUND

OVERGROUND

London Overground
planned closures

Planned closures

Monday 24 until
Sunday 30 September

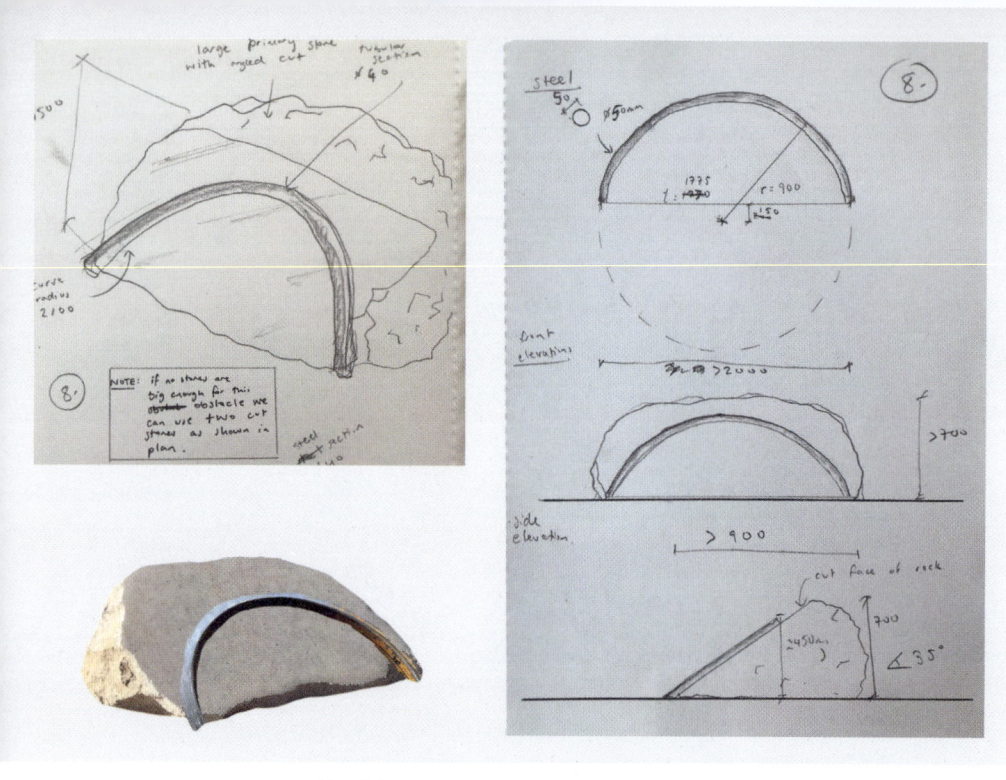

Hand-drawn sketches and a computer collage Assemble made to figure out the dimensions of some 'skating situations'. Steel would be inserted into stone to realize them.

Bringing one of the Kentish Ragstone boulders on to the site on Folkestone harbour arm.

SKATING SITUATIONS

Typical of such work is Skating Situations, installed in Folkestone, Kent in 2021 as part of the Folkestone Triennale. Assemble started from the perspective of the local skaters who used the site and for whom the project was being developed. Rather than engaging in their usual process of reaching out to a wider community, they concentrated on these potential users. That decision and the project's development was aided by the knowledge of Assemble member Mark Gavigan, an avid skater himself.

In writing about Skating Situations on their website, Assemble mused on the larger implication skating has for understanding one's urban environment:

> Skateboarders are obsessed with the fabric of the city. Though a skateboarder primarily sees the city not for the spectacle of its architecture, or the historical, symbolic and authorial content that comes along with it. Architecture is encountered in relation to surface plane, edge, angle, and texture.

As a result, they continued:

> The city is no longer buildings but a set of concrete benches, paving slabs, public litter bins, granite curbs, and slanted walls. Through this lens, the city is a series of micro-spaces, where value is measured only in the challenge afforded to the skateboarder's skill. This interest being described in movement, angle, texture, and edge condition.

Although they authored that analysis for one particular project, it is part and parcel of how the group sees the environment in which they work, at least since their minimal intervention in New Addington. What they work on, or have concentrated on after the theatricality of their early projects, is indeed the city as 'plane, edge, angle and texture'. They see their most

One of the nine skating situations: a boulder paired with a simple steel arch embedded in the existing tarmac.

effective actions, at least as they pertain to public space, as manipulating those conditions in such a way that different forms of public use become possible, while also changing the perception of these spaces by highlighting these easy-to-change aspects of how they are constituted. That tactic is efficient and cost-effective, while also avoiding the problem of forms imposed on space by one particular set of individuals – to wit, architects and their clients.

That this produces 'micro-spaces', rather than monumental ones, is essential to the outcome Assemble seeks. Neither Skating Situations nor any of their other public space designs produce anything larger than a local effect. They refuse to come together into grand statements or even (with the possible exception of the central pavilion on The Blue, whose aedicula-like pretensions are diffused by the placement of a water fountain in its centre) into any kind of focal point.

In Skating Situations, the objects were a bit less 'micro' than the barely visible platforms that were installed at New Addington's Central Parade. In Folkestone, Assemble also used boulders, in this case local Kentish Ragstone rocks of various sizes. Some were piled together on the edge of an existing concrete wall, while others were left standing alone in the space. These placements were dictated by what tricks local skaters thought they could perform with them. Assemble 'grafted' steel pieces on to some of these stones: a pipe leaning on a small rock, a square element next to the pile and a small arch rising over

SKATING SITUATIONS

Top: Assemble member Mark Gavigan testing another one of the situations: a rusted steel pipe resting on a small boulder.

Bottom: Local skater Joe Snowman testing out another skating situation.

142

A skater grinding on the same situation seen on the opposite page (bottom).

Snowman trying out another situation, with the harbour walkway in view behind.

All nine of the skating situations on the tarmac of the harbour arm. The design explicitly avoided the traditional language of skateboarding venues. ▶

SKATING SITUATIONS

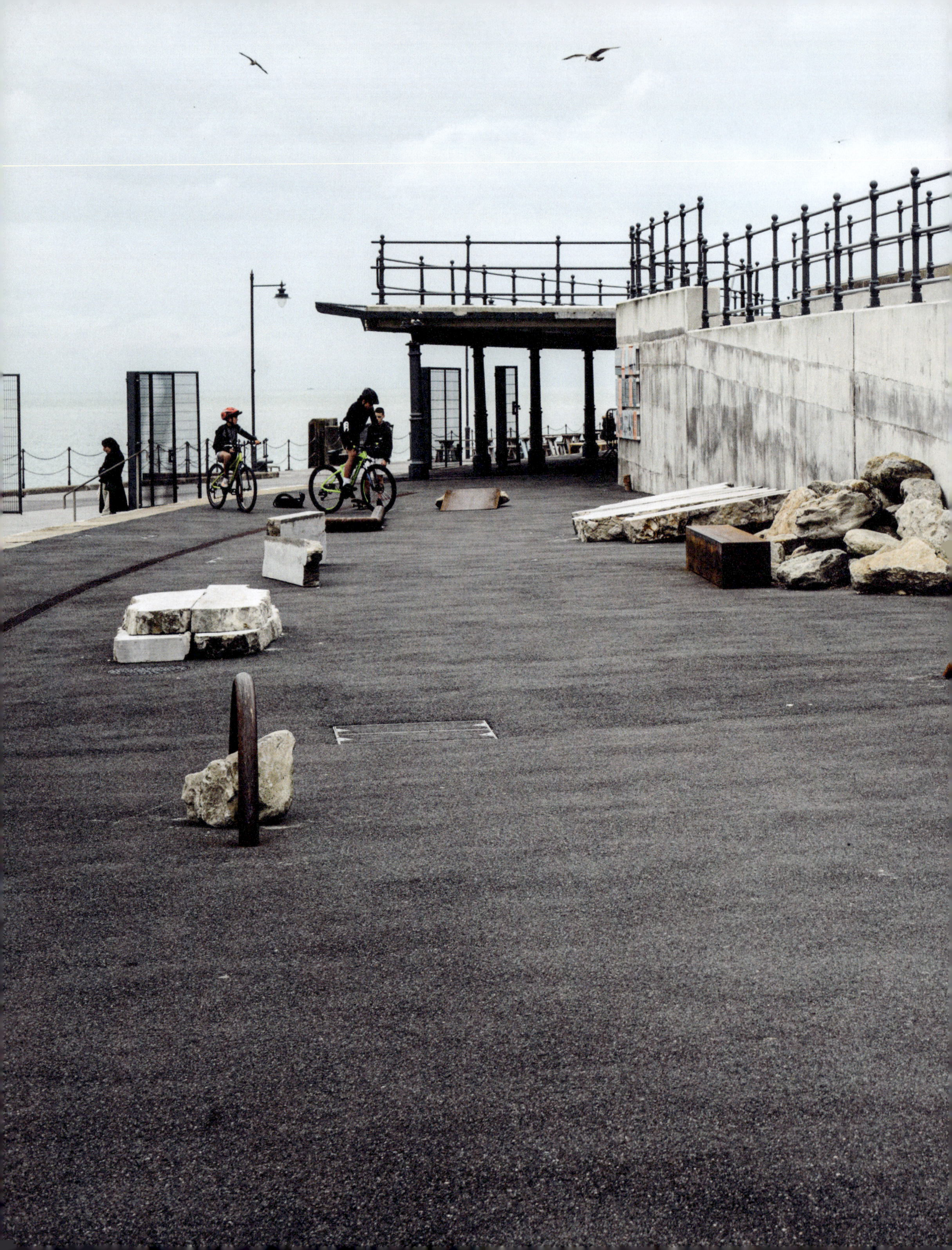

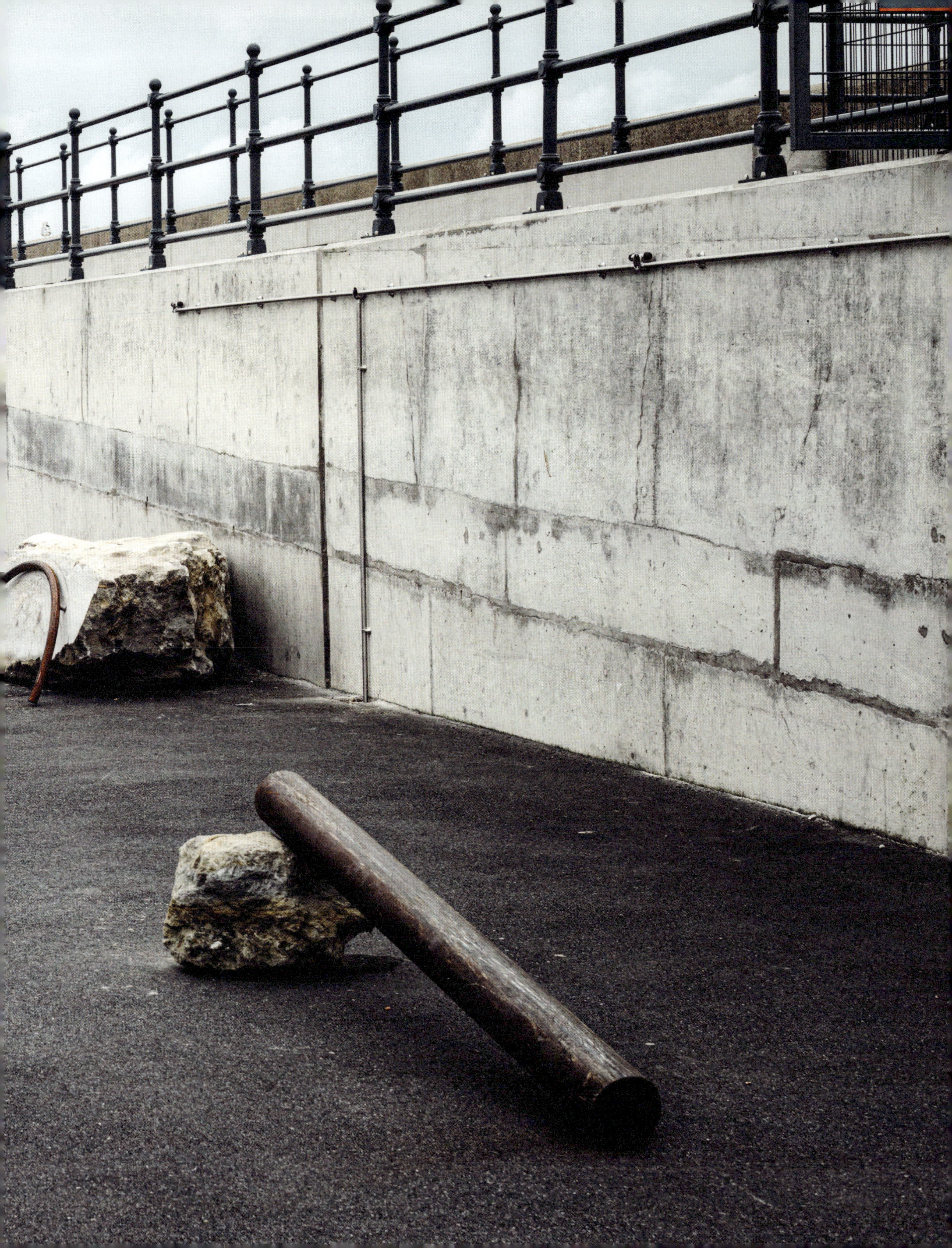

A hand-drawn illustration that Assemble posted on the Baltic Street Adventure Playground's website to show the dos and don'ts of 'anarchic play'.

The rules for play posted on the colourful boards Assemble designed for the playground gate.

a third boulder. Each of these pieces extended the moves the skaters could make there, while also becoming sculptures that transformed the metal posts and balustrades already on site into works of art. Skating Situations was so successful that it became a permanent part of the Folkestone harbour.

BALTIC STREET ADVENTURE PLAYGROUND

The most elaborate, and also the most invisible, public installation Assemble has constructed (and continues to contribute to) is the playground they established in the economically depressed neighbourhood of Dalmarnock in east Glasgow, Scotland. This project was, like many of the early commissions on which the group worked, the result of a large sporting event. In this case the 2014 Commonwealth Games. Local authorities saw the arrival of this international event as an opportunity to invest in Glasgow in a manner they felt would improve living conditions there, and invited proposals for public art projects that would further this aim.

Assemble were invited to tender by the curator Sarah McRory and commissioning body Create London, and went to the site to figure out if they could do something that would be more than just a visual adornment. In speaking with local inhabitants and community organizers, they heard that the only local playground was due for demolition and that no replacement was planned. There had been a football pitch, but this had also been demolished to make way for a coach park. As Amica Dall recalls: 'The enormous amount of demolition to make way for Commonwealth infrastructure had left loads of empty sites, which were bleak. Our first thought was to make this an opportunity for the local children to make something for themselves, after

Children being helped by a member of staff to play with a length of sewer tube.

so much had been taken away from them.' The team were introduced to playworkers Robert and later Alan Kennedy, who were working on zero-hour contracts and other organizations but who had little agency over their work; both were keen to work on something they could have more say in and with organizations that would better respect them as workers. They also had an idea for its placement: a former coalyard of a factory that had been bombed out, which was already in unofficial use by the children as one of the less dangerous sites in the area.

'We built on what we had learned from New Addington,' Dall adds. 'We wanted to construct the basic infrastructure that the children could build on over time. The idea was the children who occupied the space had agency over what happened there.' The team took Robert and some other Glasgow youth workers to London to visit various relevant projects, including adventure playgrounds. This idea, of a specific kind of environment (with its own international movement and association) that enables children to make up their own activities with skilled supervision and equipment, was appealing. 'The idea of risk was part of it,' Robert Kennedy points out. 'We want to make sure they can try and fail and learn from that.' To figure out how best to make such a place, Dall, Alice Edgerley and Paloma Strelitz together with the Kennedys studied existing examples around the UK – over time, the Baltic Street Adventure Playground grew to become a model for other adventure playgrounds.

BALTIC STREET ADVENTURE PLAYGROUND

Children playing in the newly finished playground.

The play structure near the centre of the playground was built by volunteers using scrap lumber. The shaped land caps a store of coal Assemble found on site.

Assemble and the Kennedys worked with a construction skills college to, first of all, clean up the rubble on site. They then shaped the site, undertaking extensive groundworks to make the site safe, creating a small hill at the far end of the yard, cutting back trees and installing fencing. Swings were hung from trees and, over the next five years, Assemble, the Kennedys and the children themselves built various wooden climbing structures. A small hideaway appeared, made out of cast-off material. Children made paths, climbed trees, secreted themselves in bushes and occasionally asked grown-ups to formalize possible jumping or hiding points they had devised.

Over time, the Playground's remit expanded. It became a community focal point, hosting formal and informal events. A vegetable garden appeared, which helped support a kitchen that serves food to young people and the wider community. The kitchen and offices were housed, in the manner of Blackhorse Workshop, in slightly modified modular prefabricated units. A social worker came to provide support to those in physical or psychological need. Farm animals including chickens and rabbits were slowly introduced.

Assemble took gradual steps back from the playground but they remain involved at board level. Visit the Baltic Street Adventure Playground today and it appears, above all, messy. That confusion comes from the ad hoc nature of most of the structures, made largely of found materials and by unskilled labour. It is also the result of the wear and tear

The playground in use; to the right, a small tree fort the children imagined and which the staff helped them build.

that the objects poking out of the well-trodden ground have endured. This is a continual construction and deconstruction site: a place of adventure, discovery, making and un-making. It is also where children can learn. They get to know their own bodies as they test their limits (during my visit an adult member of staff somehow always appeared, as if by magic, before a possibly dangerous fall, encouraging and catching the jumper), how to play and work with others and how to be in a group. They also come to care for their community, with some of the participants growing up to become volunteers.

The Baltic Street Adventure Playground site, which turned out to be an especially important asset during the COVID-19 lockdown, now serves a diversifying but stable community that has so far avoided gentrification. The playground has become a focal point and stabilizer, galvanizing social coherence in the few blocks around its loosely guarded perimeter through its activities. As such, it has become a good model of Assemble's brand of light architecture: an almost invisible form of design completely tied up both with the community it serves and with the site in which it appears. To find what look like the elements of traditional building or landscaping you have to look hard, but it is obvious that a coherent, well-used and joyful place emerged out of Assemble's process.

Play KX at King's Cross in London, where children turned part of Lewis Cubitt Square into a maze with shelters in the middle.

Assemble and free play expert Penny Wilson found the material in second-hand shops and helped children hang it according to drawings they made, which are visible on the ground.

THE VOICE OF CHILDREN

In 2016, Assemble documented what they learned during this process in a research project called The Voice of Children. With support from the British Council and private foundations, the members produced a collection of films shot in Glasgow, but also at similar sites in Japan, Spain and Mexico. They found and documented various degrees of child-built adventure playgrounds, as well as a wide range of activities on these sites. Most of all, having decided that 'most of the built environment inhibits children's play', at least until they learn to use it like the skaters in Folkestone did, they concentrated on how children played without any or only minimal adult intervention. The children became the performers of their own temporary structures, much as Assemble had been in their early work, and over time some of their activities, when they were repeated often enough and when adults assisted them, turned into reasons to have more lasting structures. 'We learned so much from that,' comments Dall, 'not just for Glasgow, but for what we do in general.'

PLAY KX

The Baltic Street Adventure Playground also led Assemble to design a number of other sites for children to gather and play. Some of them, like Play KX in King's Cross in central London, were ephemeral recurring events, while others such as The Brutalist Playground in Pimlico were exhibitions. The site for Play KX was the newly developed area north of Kings Cross railway station, where what had been a largely industrial zone has been replaced by new office and residential blocks. Assemble

The maze structure consisted of tying the fabric onto the existing trees and street furniture with rough knots.

Children were also free to use the material in other ways, such as for cloaks in their play.

were asked to activate the new zone's central area, Lewis Cubitt Square, in 2018. They teamed up with Penny Wilson, an expert on the kind of 'free play' that is possible at the Baltic Street Adventure Playground, to start an offshoot called Assemble Play. Together the group concentrated on 'loose parts', a term coined by artist and educator Simon Nicholson and defined by Penny as 'anything that can be moved around, carried, rolled, lifted, piled on top of one another, or combined to create interesting and novel structures and experiences'.

That ambition translated into basic building blocks of at least three kinds. Blue foam elements (produced by Imagination Playground, an organization that pioneered a loose parts playground equipment system and with which Wilson had been involved with) could be sat on, stacked into ladders and forts or even just joyfully thrown around. Fabric, mostly light and gauzy, was sourced from fabric stores and the children, with the help of a few adults, could hang it from strings to make scrims or more containers for play, or simply trail it along behind them like capes. And there was miscellaneous other material that the players and playworkers found on site, from sticks to pieces of cardboard.

The aim of this rather ephemeral playground was, according to Assemble, to create 'an environment where visiting children could play freely with behaviour that is freely chosen, personally directed, and intrinsically motivated'. Parents and other adults were meant to watch what the children came

The base of Ernő Goldfinger's Balfron Tower (1963) showing the playground he designed including a concrete slide.

up with, assisting them only when asked. The result was a not-very-designed environment that was still, given the context in which it took place, considerably cleaner than an adventure playground. The elements were stored away when not in use and, during inclement weather, the site moved to sheltered areas. While one source of inspiration could be attributed to a film Assemble made featuring a boy who turned a cardboard box he found into a secret hideaway and fort, what Assemble Play provided was considerably more like the basic building blocks of what you might call architecture.

THE BRUTALIST PLAYGROUND

Assemble found another method for disassembling and reassembling architecture in The Brutalist Playground, an installation recreating elements of playgrounds in three post-war housing estates in Pimlico, Poplar and Paddington in London. Each of the sites is part of a residential development from the 1960s or 1970s carried out at a large scale with forceful forms – a manner of designing that was criticized even at the time as being unhuman and oppressive, but that has since gained acceptance for its monumental forms and the often

A digital axonometric drawing of Assemble's proposal for the various elements that could make up The Brutalist Playground exhibition in different venues.

A digital planometric in which Assemble laid the elements out in the gallery space at RIBA.

expansive and open qualities of its public spaces. Assemble, in collaboration with artist Simon Terrill in a project commissioned by the Royal Institute of British Architects (RIBA) and staged at their gallery, set about adopting and adapting some of those forms to make them into places to perform play.

Assemble's installation took pieces from what remained of some of the original playgrounds on the sites, as well as adjacent elements, walls and even vents, recreating and abstracting them into rectangles, blocks and hexagons, as well as larger pieces: stairs, ramps, a tilted round disk and a raised lookout or hideaway area. Made out of lightweight reconstituted foam (the mixture creating colourful patterns on the surface), the pieces were strewn around the gallery while films, photographs and drawings of the estates were projected on the walls. Adults could enjoy the exhibition as an evocation of the essence of the geometries inherent in the original architecture, showing how the original architects had made structures that embodied the more joyous and experimental aspects of what they had built. Children, on the other hand, could just play, climbing on the structures and throwing the loose elements around. Here, Assemble's interest in how public space is formed, used and interpreted came together with their ability to take analysis and turn it into places of free play.

Assemble designed an abstracted version of a Jeep as one of the play elements. All the elements were made of reconstituted foam.

Top: A child plays on Assemble's version of the Balfron slide at the RIBA gallery.

Bottom: Assemble's version of the Brunel Estate in Westbourne Park (1984) designed my Michael Brown (1974). In the background is the montage of historic photography assembled by Simon Terrill.

The flying saucer, which recreated a concrete element from the playground at Churchill Gardens (1962) by Powell & Moya, installed in the S1 Artspace, a gallery space on the Park Hill estate in Sheffield.

▶

THE BRUTALIST PLAYGROUND   155

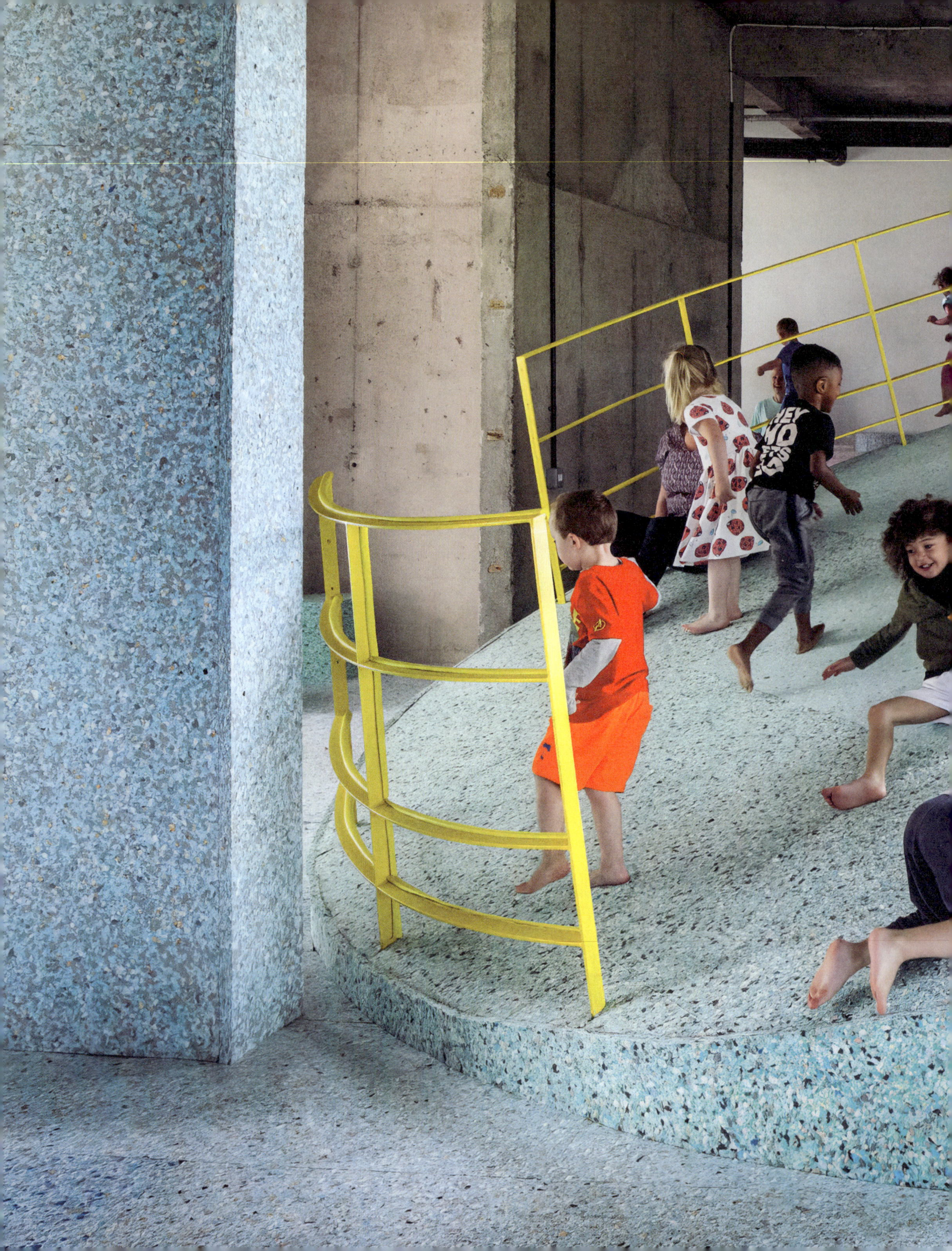

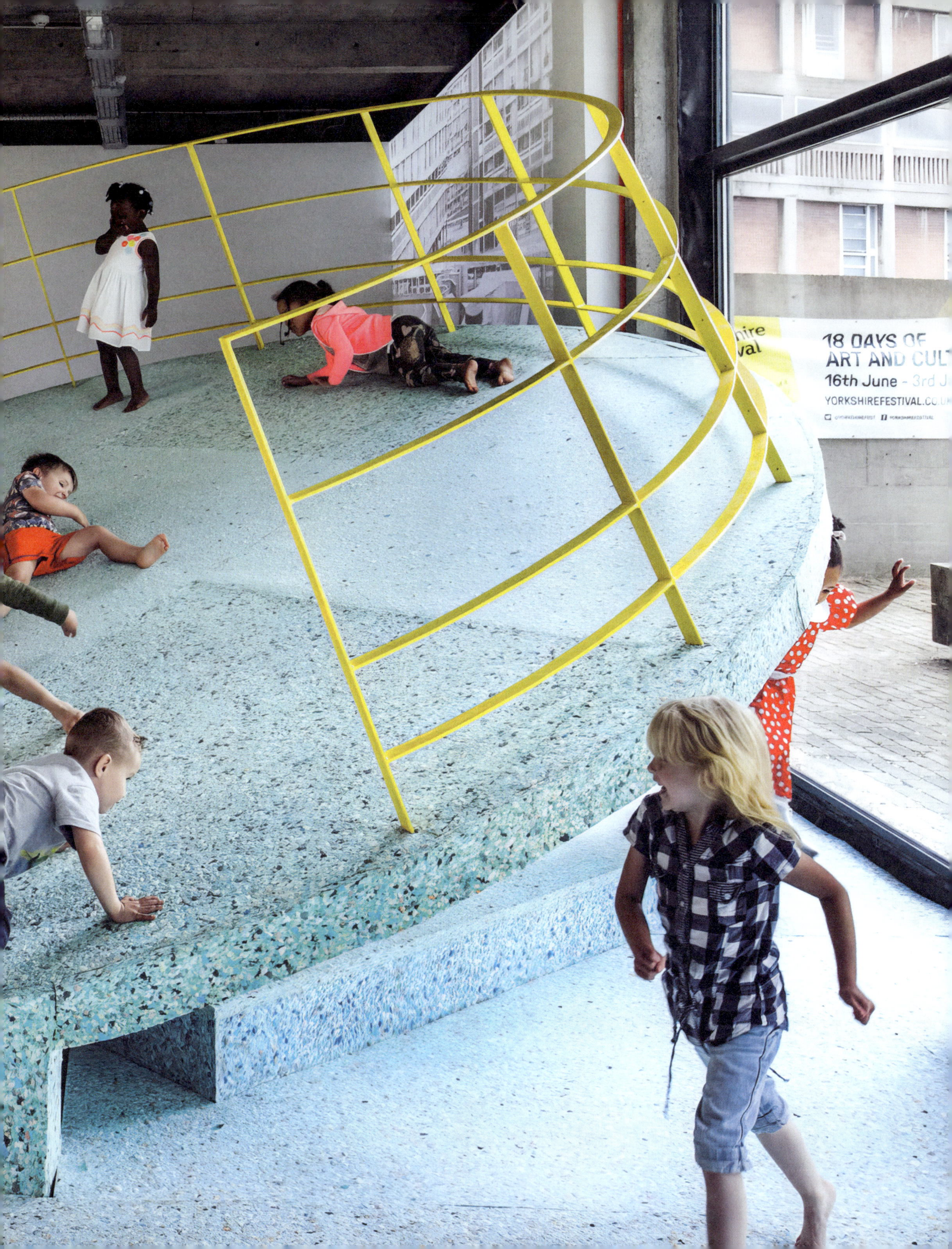
18 DAYS OF
16th June - 3rd
YORKSHIREFESTIVAL.CO.UK

Part of the S1 Artspace installation, with the original concrete tunnel rendered in reconstituted foam over a timber frame. A view of the original is visible in the projection above.

158

The exhibition installed at the The Edge arts centre in Bath. The original hexagons were meant to evoke the Giant's Causeway in Ireland. Here they were freely placed elements.

THE BRUTALIST PLAYGROUND

A digital axonometric drawing of Bramcote Park's two halves: one focused on play and openness and the other on enclosed nature.

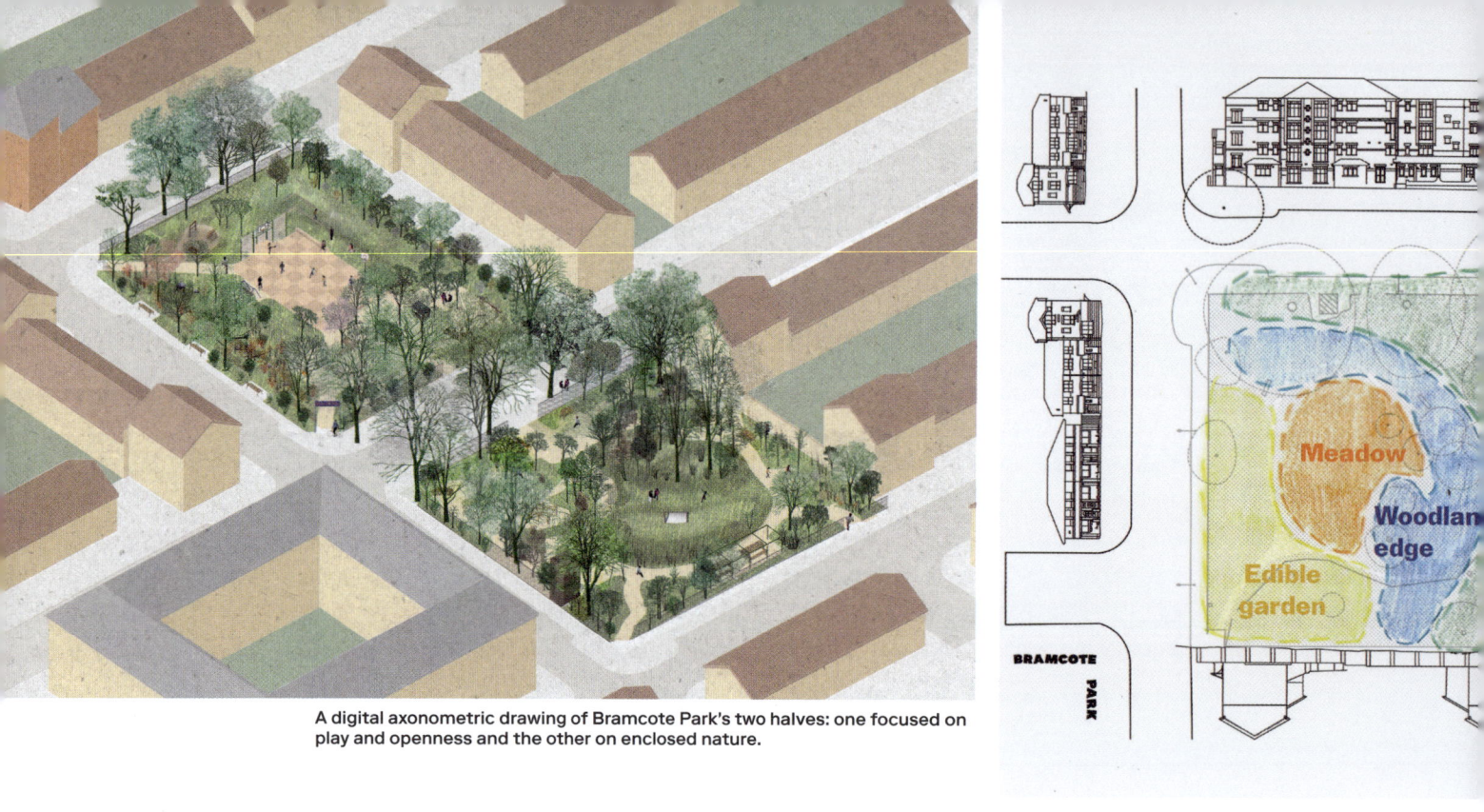

BRAMCOTE PARK

The most ambitious permanent public installation that combines many of the elements Assemble has developed over the last decade is currently underway. Located in South Bermondsey, London it is a commission the architects together with Local Works Studio obtained through their connection with that community in 2022. Called Bramcote Park, it is currently two different areas divided by a road. To the north is the 'play' part, with standard play equipment for children, a basketball court and an open field. To the south, the park is dedicated to nature, enclosed by tall trees and meant for relaxation. Its primary use, as is the case in most such facilities, is as a dog walking park. In talking to the local community through several exploration and design sessions, Assemble came to realize that the park did not need to be fundamentally rethought or redesigned, but called for an approach that would strengthen its most important features while addressing problems such as drainage, access and security.

Building on their experience in other similar situations, Assemble did more than talk with potential users. They organized community meetings and play events where children could explore different ways to use the park, and collected drawings by inhabitants showing what they thought Bramcote Park could be. Older people wanted to 'chat with friends by greenery', children wanted things such as 'just a big tyre to swing on' and everybody wanted to lessen the barrier formed by the bisecting street.

Assemble did, in the end, suggest a more thorough redesign of the area, dividing it into different zones

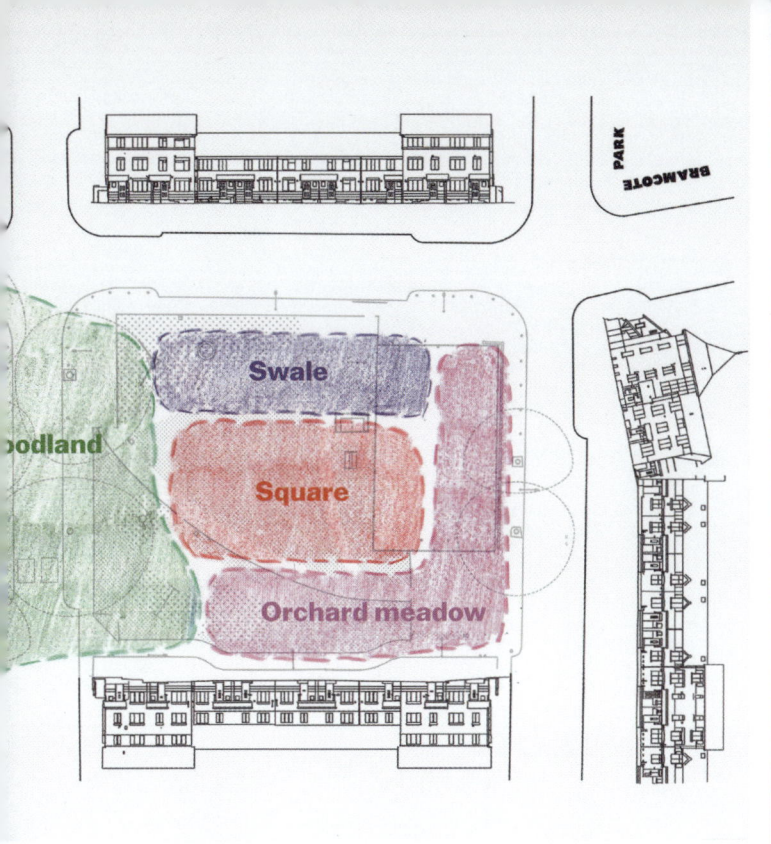

The zones Assemble envisioned in a sketch drawing, including an open square surrounded by meadow and swale, a woodland area with a wilder meadow and an edible garden.

A railing from the existing playground being adapted for use as part of a new play area.

including a cultivated garden, a meadow, an orchard and woodlands, as well as transition zones between these. They proposed specific plantings and patterns for paths and pavements but otherwise recommended leaving the possibilities as open as possible, in the manner of an adventure playground. They also suggested that local inhabitants could be trained in new skills on the site by helping with some of the construction, and foresaw working with local colleges and training venues as they had done at Blackhorse Workshop.

    The designers also made a long list of available materials in the park itself and in the vicinity that could be repurposed for the new park design. The strategy was an expansion of their formerly more ad hoc foraging techniques, in which they sought to catalogue items such as surplus broken play equipment, metal railings, top soil, seeming trash that could be recycled and other leftovers, as well as how they could be upcycled. They even suggested how existing asphalt on the playing field could be broken up and then reused in other areas of the new park.

    The final proposal is a miniature evocation of the landscape that might have existed before the area was developed into massive housing estates and industry. It also

A workshop Assemble Play organized on the site incorporated foam elements so participants could try out different forms of play that might be possible there.

provided areas open enough to play in an undirected manner, leaving the landscape and its furnishing to indicate how the space could be used. Assemble added only a few big gestures, such as a slide (a form of which the group is rather fond) and objects that recall the pieces they exhibited in The Brutalist Playground. Tables and seating would provide focal points.

Assemble continues to be fascinated by what they can do to shape public space in a way that promotes the activities they see as central to their own sense of self-definition: participation and collective work, performance and play. Unlike most public space design, where the emphasis is on an overall form or image, they prefer to work on the edges of things. They raise levels of planting minimally, defining separate areas and providing places to sit on or grind your skateboard. They focus on pavement, choosing materials that are already on site or in the neighbourhood. They strew around opportunities for play or performance, rather than organizing them in an overall pattern. Sometimes, as in the Baltic Street Adventure Playground, they do almost nothing, encouraging the actual users of the place to discover the possibilities and flesh those out themselves. At other times, as at Bramcote Park, they propose a fuller redesign, but always in episodes and parts.

What is just as important is that Assemble understand that their designs exist in time and in place. The site where they have worked the longest, Baltic Street Adventure Playground, has changed considerably over time, although you would have to look hard to understand where the actual

Children playing on site with various elements Assemble developed to encourage different uses.

The finished plan for the wilder part of Bramcote Park, including the layout of the play area, the meadow and the garden, as well as proposed tree sites.

design insertions were or now are. In Glasgow, they work as consultants and critics, and sometimes builders, but let the place happen over time. Many of their early designs that were intended to be permanent are barely visible anymore, as the ways of using a place such the Central Parade at New Addington have changed. By not investing more than the absolute necessary resources, they feel they have not wasted money or constricted future uses. Other sites were only tuned up for the short period that parties or performances took place in a square, such as in Hounslow.

      In this way, Assemble makes architecture public in a deep sense: it is made as much by the actions of its users as it is by anyone, and it changes through time, just as people do. Through limited interventions, Assemble allow inhabitants themselves to discover what brings them together and how they can utilize space to be a better version of themselves – whether that is a kid building a fort, a teenager skateboarding on a rock, an adult performing in a play or a pensioner talking on a bench in the shade.

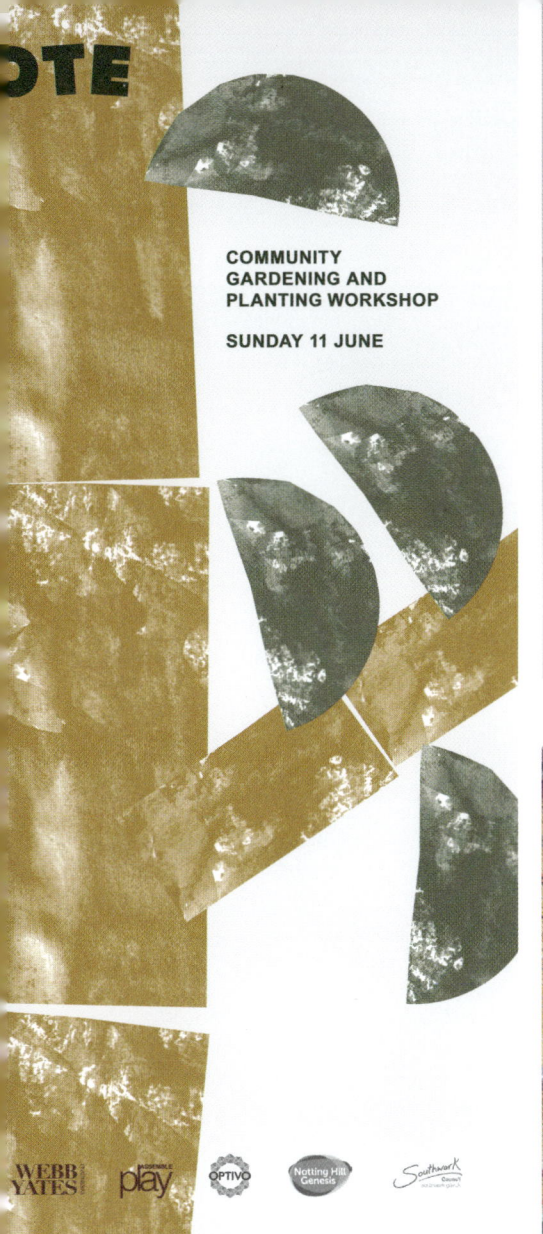

A poster Assemble made to advertise one of the workshops and planting events they organized as an integral part of the design process.

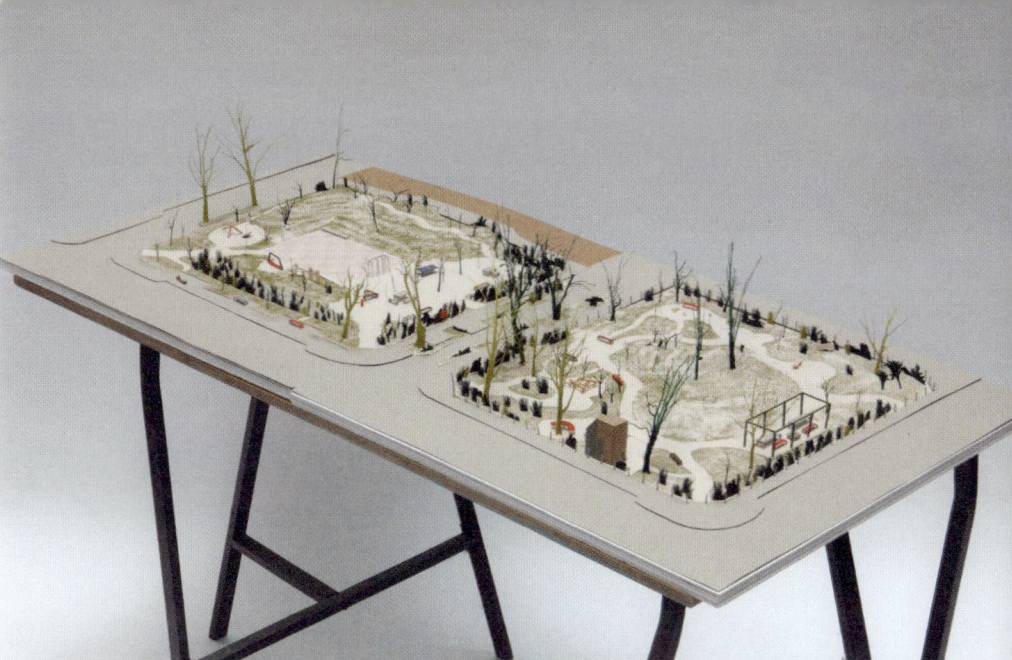

Top: Assemble made a site model to test out the different arrangements of the park.

Bottom: The north side of the park as Assemble encountered it with broken play equipment. Former railings and wing frames were used to create new play elements.

BRAMCOTE PARK

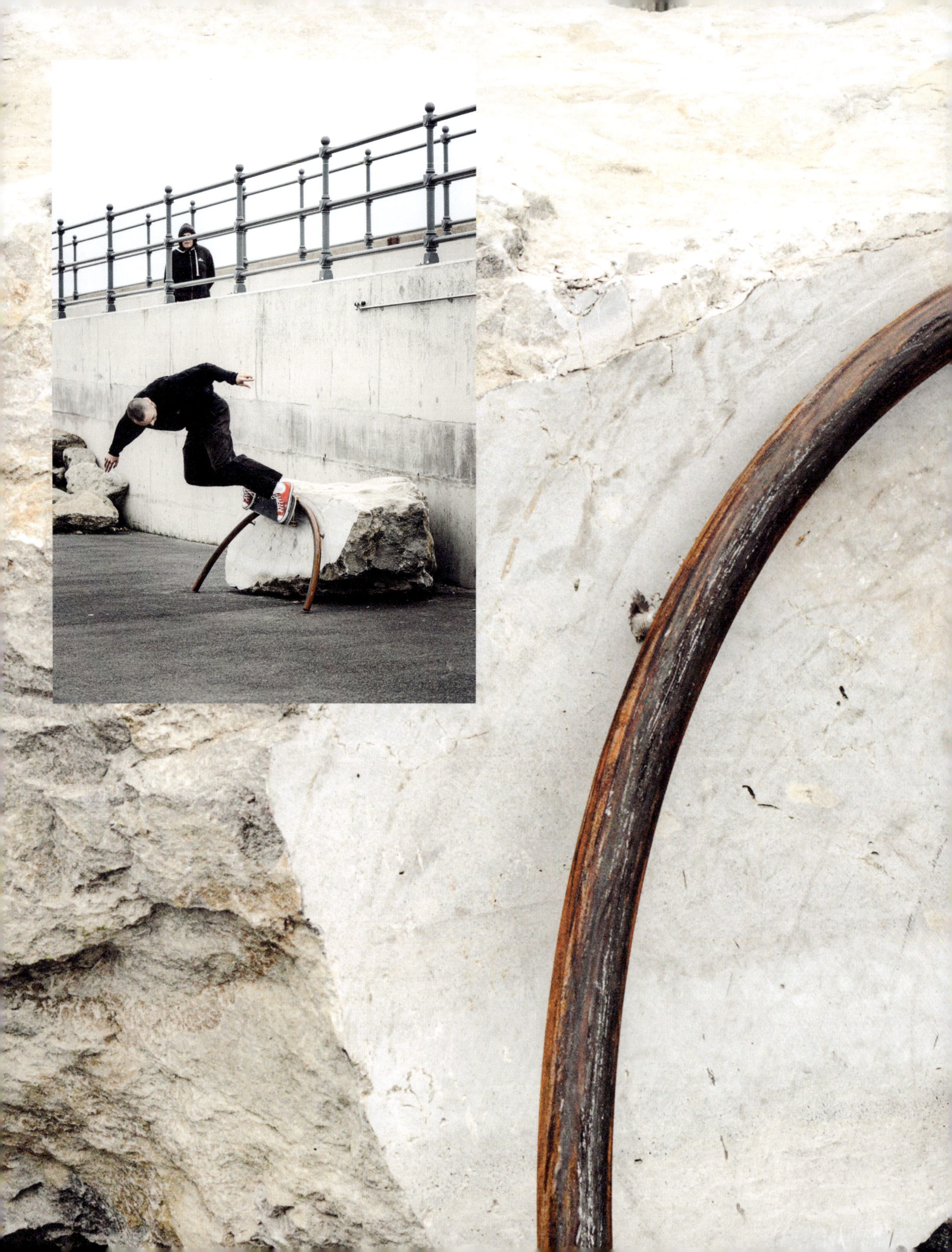

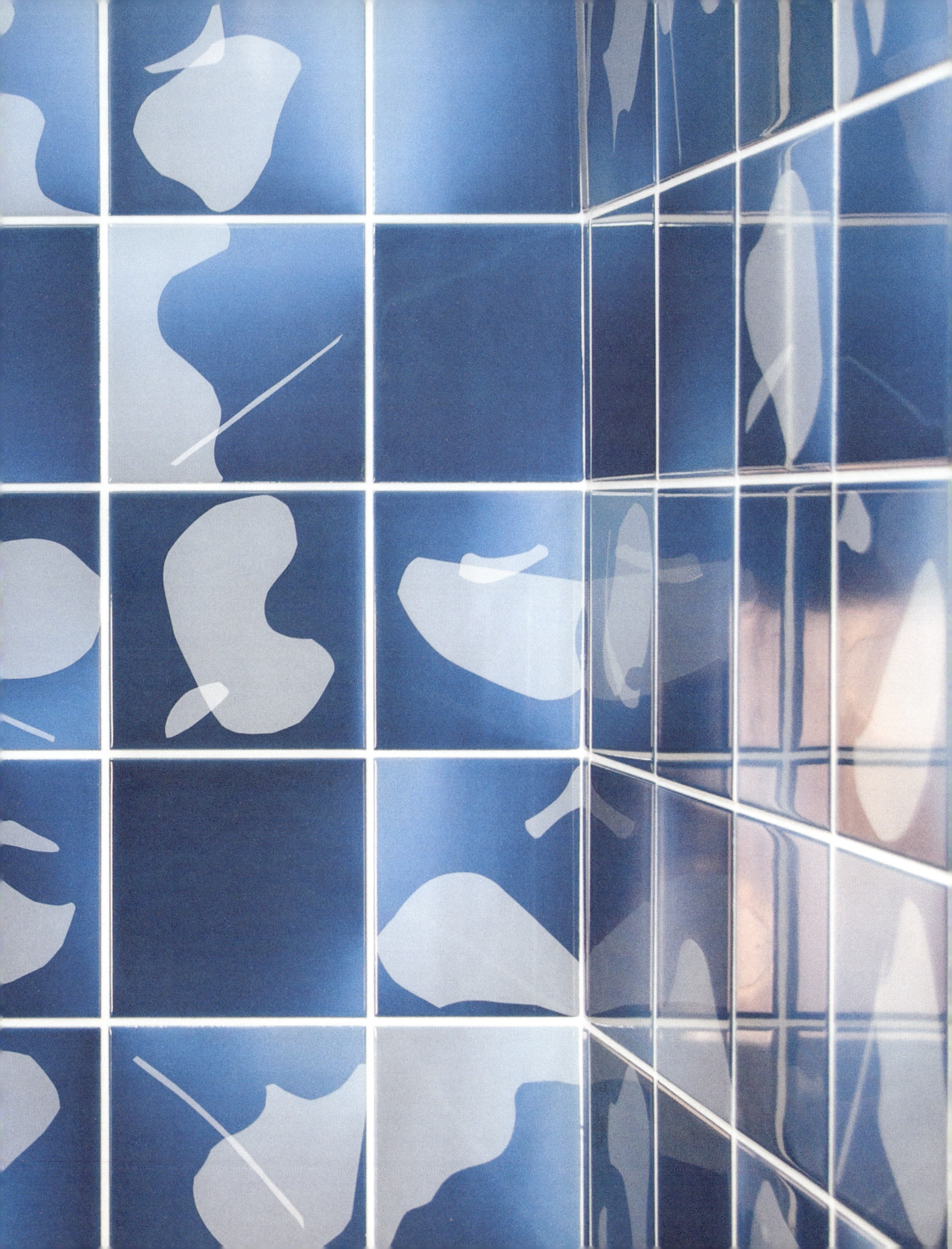

GRANBY WINTER GARDEN (See PG180)

4

Building Community

GRANBY FOUR STREETS

Many of Assemble's concerns with neighbourhood activism and community building through craft, reuse and event staging were brought together in a series of interventions, renovations, events and proposals for a working-class neighbourhood in Toxteth, Liverpool called Granby Four Streets. It also brought Assemble international recognition, including the UK's most prestigious art award, the Turner Prize. Eventually, the project encompassed the renovation of a number of houses, the creation of a winter garden that serves as a community hub, the establishment of a tile manufacturing facility and the tentative revitalization of part of the neighbourhood's commercial strip. A scheme for new houses to replace ones torn down by the local council has not yet materialized, but its design and the manner in which it was presented are among the most influential of Assemble's designs.

Above: The Winter Garden with its blue-painted steel reinforcement, new skylights, exposed brick walls, and whimsical chandelier by artist Nina Edge.

Top right: A drawing by Marie Jacotey of the Granby Four Streets proposal. The cut-away axonometric shows the community spaces and the new stores and buildings to be renovated are also visible.

Above: A drawing by Marie Jacotey of the installation of Granby Workshop fireplace elements in one of the houses.

169

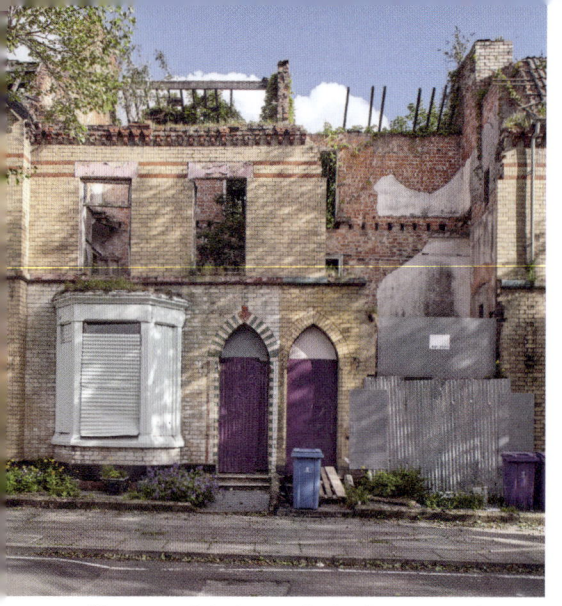

The state of the houses in the Granby Four Streets area ranged from inhabited to derelict before Assemble arrived.

A boarded-up house on which the local activists had expressed their determination to fight. The variety of brickwork in the area is also on display.

The area known as Granby Four Streets is in many ways typical of the inner-city areas developed during the Industrial Revolution to house workers who streamed into major cities all through the 19th and into the 20th century. One of the world's major trading centres in the 18th and 19th centuries, Liverpool had played an important role in the growth of the British Empire and was a major port for the mass movement of people, including both enslaved people and emigrants from northern Europe to America. The Granby Four Streets area, designed by the Welsh architect Richard Owens and built largely by Welsh workers, consists of terraced brick houses tightly packed together with small back gardens, and a small commercial strip leading to the Princes Park. At the beginning of the 20th century, cheap house prices and the area's proximity to the dockyards attracted merchant seamen, many from east and west Africa.[26] After the Second World War, Granby Four Streets became a popular destination with immigrants from the British Commonwealth; it became one of the UK's earliest multicultural neighbourhoods.

The active commercial area on Granby Street was a lively centre of trade and craft, but in the 1970s Britain's economic decline led to a severe downturn. Persistent unemployment and increasing racial discrimination displayed by the police force culminated in the Toxteth riots of 1981, part of a wider pattern of distrust that had led to the more well-known civil disturbances in Brixton three months earlier. Referred to as 'the uprising' by locals, the Toxteth riots led to at least one death

A digital drawing of the masterplan Assemble created to show the houses fixed up, as well as, in the foreground, the new build on Ducie Street they hoped to erect.

among protesters. In subsequent years and during the Thatcher regime the area lost most of its retail and community facilities, and became depopulated. In 2002, the UK government launched The Housing Market Renewal Initiative or Housing Market Renewal Pathfinders scheme, which proposed demolishing and rebuilding areas to renew failing housing markets; Granby Four Streets was identified as one such area. Thankfully, a core group of activists and residents were able to ward off the scheme and prevent the destruction of a still-loved neighbourhood.

First established as The Granby Residents Association (GRA) in 1993, the group had worked hard to prevent demolition attempts throughout the 1990s. It became clear that this neighbourhood could not rely on government redevelopment schemes to revitalize the area. In the mid-2000s, the remaining residents, led by a core group of women who had lived there since before the riots, began to work from their houses out, cleaning up their streets and adding planting. They agitated for more sensitive, small-scale, and – especially important to them – ethnically and economically mixed redevelopment. The GRA was disbanded in 2010, but was swiftly replaced by the Granby Four Streets Community Land Trust (CLT) in 2011. Such organizations are used by communities to band together

A drawing by Marie Jacotey of 49 Cairns Street as it would look after the renovation, with Granby Workshop tile used in several locations. The basement is used as storage for other renovations.

A drawing by Assemble illustrating how they could add some new wood trim and built-in furniture to an existing house.

to improve their public spaces and argue for investments and improvements in the housing stock.

Their activities attracted the attention of Xanthe Hamilton, a social activist working with the developer John Davey. Hamilton and Davey wanted to invest in (and obtain returns from) a new housing development, but they wanted to do it by helping to renovate an economically stressed and ethnically diverse neighbourhood in collaboration with the inhabitants, rather than imposing solutions from the outside. Hamilton was also aware of the work of Assemble; in 2013 she put the designers and the community organizers in touch with each other, and they began to discuss what architecture, design and planning could do in the Granby Four Streets area. She and Davey then founded 'social developer' Steinbeck Studio as an alternative mode of public/private partnership that would fulfil the same set of goals the Granby Four Streets community group espoused.

Ongoing conversations with local inhabitants, which included both the long-term residents advocating for change and more recent inhabitants, and opportunism eventually produced five different proposals: the renovation of houses on Cairns Street, which was where the core of the CLT was located (two leaders of the group – Eleanor Lee, resident since the 1970s, and Hazel Tilley, who has lived on the street since she was sixteen – were residents there); the creation of a winter

A renovated living room. The tile around the fireplace is by Granby Workshop.

Another view of the same living room, with the rebuilt and repainted staircase to the right.

garden in one of the abandoned or 'tinned up' houses; the founding of a workshop, modelled after some of the initiatives at Sugarhouse Studios and Blackhorse Workshop, to produce tiles for the renovation efforts and train local youth; the design of the new housing area; and the revitalization of Granby Street's commercial strip. Of these, the new housing area is the only one that to date has not been actualized, while new life on Granby Street is only sporadic. Ten houses were renovated on Cairns Street, the Granby Winter Garden is an active community hub and artist's site, and the Granby Workshop is producing tiles for applications around the world.

'Assemble saw the value of what we had achieved here and were trying to do,' recalls Lee, after recounting the long history of failed revitalization attempts by others. 'They didn't come with preconceptions, with a plan already worked out, or with any baggage. They saw the potential in the people here as much as in the place, and wanted to work with what we had and could do.' Their concentration, she continues, 'was on how to make the biggest impact with small reconstructions.' The group's interest was so strong that one of their original members, Lewis Jones, moved to Liverpool to live there and pursue a PhD in material research at the local university.

In another house, Assemble designed a Douglas fir partition wall, opening up the space.

10 HOUSES ON CAIRNS STREET

To implement the renovation of the Cairns Street houses, the CLT received a loan of £500,000 from Steinbeck Studio. They used the funds to bring the small rowhouses up to current safety and liveability standards, with much of the funds going into new wiring, plumbing, structural reinforcement and other invisible improvements. In addition, Assemble worked with inhabitants to open up some of the rooms to make them more spacious, removing walls and replacing them with porous dividers, and otherwise improving the homes' spatial characteristics within their constrained envelopes.

Assemble stripped the houses back to their bare brick walls and structure, but then, instead of stark new surfaces and materials that are alien to the original textures of the houses (more often than not, the cheapest option available to builders), the Cairns Street interiors have the sense of being versions of what they have always been, but with better space, light, surface coverings and infrastructure. Assemble achieved this largely by adding accents and new coverings such as tiles that they made at Sugarhouse Studios and later in the backyard of one of the finished houses.

As a result of this approach, it is difficult at first to see what the designers did when you walk into one of the Cairns Street projects. Then you notice the fireplaces – modern versions of those that were there before – the tiling, the quality of the light, and other subtle changes. Some of these are already buried by a decade of use, some of them are hidden in the structures' cores, but others are either evident or are points of pride of which the owners will make you aware.

An upstairs bedroom opened up into a loft. Assemble wanted to celebrate the chimney flue as a sculptural element.

Another partition wall acting as shelving and space divider. Assemble also provided a new door and floor.

10 HOUSES ON CAIRNS STREET

Granby Workshop launched a Kickstarter campaign to produce 'splatware': coloured clay plates.

The full range of products Granby Workshop developed for the Turner Prize Exhibition, including furniture Assemble designed. The terracotta lampshades were designed and made by ceramicist Lydia Hardwick.

GRANBY WORKSHOP

While working on the house renovations, Assemble developed an extension of their material and fabrication research they were doing at Sugarhouse Studios into what came to be called Granby Workshop. First located in the back garden of one of the houses being renovated, it later moved a few streets away, before finding its current home outside Granby Four Streets.

The bathrooms and kitchens of the ten renovated houses on Cairns Street use standard tiles decorated with coloured transfers at Sugarhouse, but these designs and processes would form the starting point of those produced at Granby Workshop. Drawing on the expertise of ceramicists and tile manufacturers with whom they consulted, Assemble then concentrated on finding ways to make tiles in standard formats and to industry specifications, but which also involved hand craft and invited randomness.

The workshop's encaustic tiles are made by randomly combining pieces of different coloured clays in a ram press under extreme pressure. The resulting tiles feature patterns that repeat and are, to a certain extent, standardized, but that also vary from piece to piece and produce moments of surprise. The workshop also produces terrazzo, including one called Granby Rock made from broken bricks, roof slates and other waste materials, and glazed ceramic tiles, as well as other interior items.

Smoke-fired ceramic cabinet handles made in a barbeque in the Granby Workshop courtyard.

The ram press Granby Workshop used to make the splatware by compressing different coloured clays into each other. ▶

GRANBY WORKSHOP 177

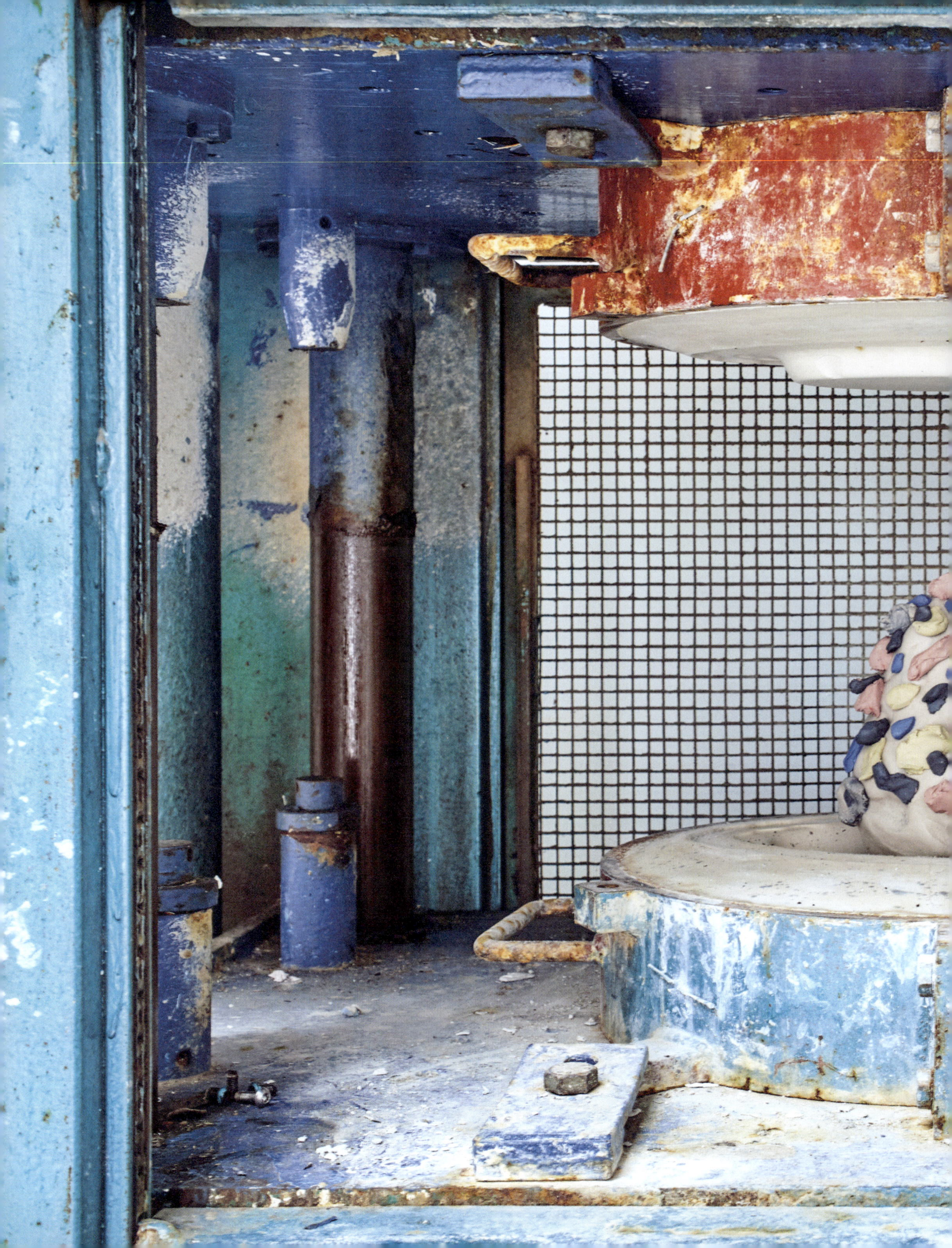

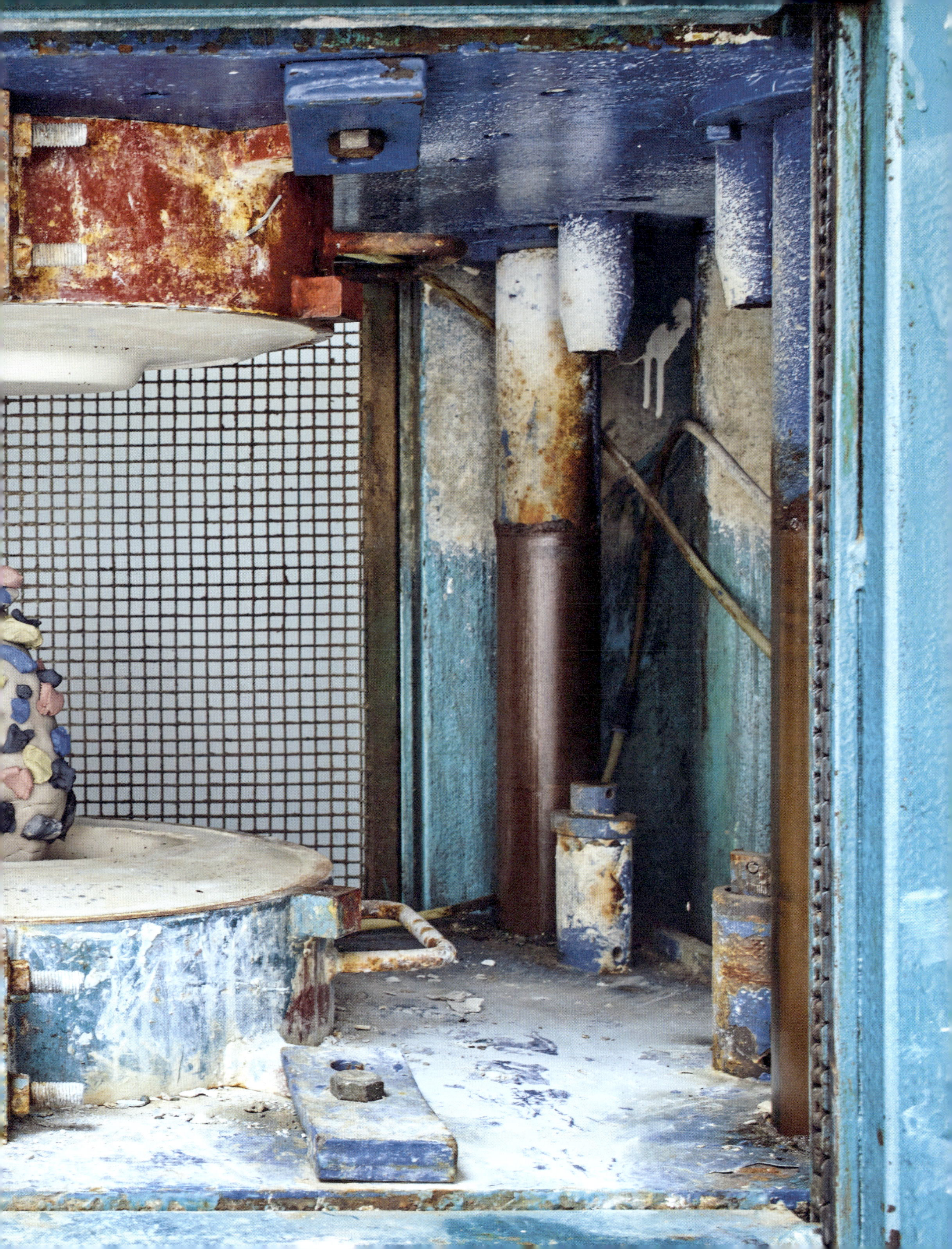

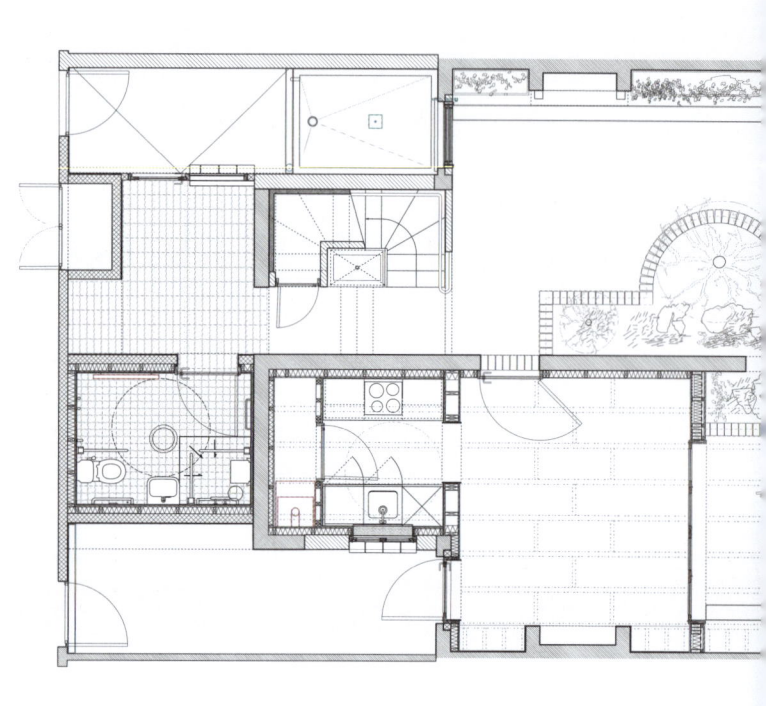

A selection of Granby Workshop wares assembled for a publicity shoot.

GRANBY WINTER GARDEN

The Granby Winter Garden is an altogether more dramatic intervention. Occupying the space of a house that was deemed beyond economically feasible to repair, it is mainly a large void. When you approach the house, you have little hint of what awaits you when you open the door and the space opens above and around you. After the tightly packed environment of Granby Four Streets, the explosion of space is astonishing. Assemble left only the front walls of the structure in place, reinforcing its bricks, stripped of any covering, with steel beams painted a colour that I have come to think of as Assemble Blue. Doors and other openings were reinforced with discreet concrete lintels. Tropical planting brings some of the luxury of the mansions just up the road from Toxteth that abut this working-class neighbourhood. It also recalls,

A model Assemble built of the garden in front of the to-be-renovated building.

An image of the Granby Winter Garden roof before construction.

A plan of the Granby Winter Garden. The two-storey space is to the top left, while the house at the bottom was renovated for support spaces.

says Lee, some of the landscapes that might be familiar to the immigrants from the Caribbean, South America and Africa who have recently moved into the area.

Small details such as new wood interior shutters and trim invite touch and continue the sense of a crafted space already established by the use of Granby Workshop tiles. In an adjacent area, Assemble left the wood joists, opening up the space while preserving a more intimate scale. Wooden bridges and balconies further tie the space together and to the adjacent house, which the project annexed for offices and other spaces that help the Granby Winter Garden's operation. The renovations to that neighbouring house are starker than in the residential projects on Cairns Street, reflecting the fact that this is a space for common use: classes, workshops and community meetings take place here, and there is a small apartment for visiting artists or activists.

In the Granby Winter Garden, Assemble produced the kind of impressive space (albeit at a relatively modest scale) in a permanent situation that architects often see as their core focus. The room has a sense of grandeur as it opens up under a skylight that takes up the full roof. The intricacy of the wood, tile and metal detailing, produced in collaboration with some of their fellow tenants at the Granby Workshop, gives the space a tactility and complexity that allows it to avoid the monumentality and abstraction commonly found in such places.

GRANBY WINTER GARDEN

A test panel for ceramic pieces in the garden at 49 Cairns Street, which Granby Workshop used as its first base.

A digital rendering by Assemble of how they envisioned the Granby Winter Garden.

The Granby Winter Garden was finished in 2019 and its design and construction ran in parallel with a larger scheme for both continuing the renovations and creating new housing. The plan for the renovations was to standardize the technique Assemble had developed on Cairns Street, concentrating on bringing houses up to code, maximizing their spatial possibilities and retaining their original character and (as much as possible) materials, while adding highly crafted surfaces or elements that would be made by an expanded Granby Workshop. The approach was to maximize the impact of the work by scaling up the crews and the production of the elements, while maintaining a focus on the specificity of each house. This was a departure from the usual method of renovating old terraced houses using all-new materials in a standardized manner. The designers and the CLT sought to show the developer and the council that they could renovate in a cost-effective manner by drawing on a local workforce and volunteers, while accepting the existing houses as much as possible. The goal was to move the area from being less than 35% occupied (in 2013, only 70 of the 200 houses were inhabited) to being fully used.

In addition, Assemble designed a complex of flats for an empty triangle of land at the confluence of Granby Street, Princes Avenue and Kingsley Road. They proposed buildings slightly higher than those present in the rest of Granby Four Streets, but which would abstract forms from and use facade materials similar to the existing structures. This would scale up the neighbourhood at its edge, where Princes Park begins, and form the public front for what were otherwise renovation projects. In addition, Assemble proposed infill buildings where houses were missing, with a particular aim of strengthening the streetfront on the commercial Granby Street. These buildings could make room for new enterprises but were also designed to accommodate pop-up and temporary occupation on adjacent lots.

An earlier digital drawing in which Assemble imagined a lighter structure and lusher foliage.

The Granby Winter Garden being used as a workshop.

The Granby Winter Garden under construction, with the blue-painted steel armature in place.

The grander scheme for Granby Four Streets would have applied Assemble's approach towards restoration and renovation to new construction. The project would have combined preservation with increased liveability and services, and encouraged the development of local skills to create building components that were specific to the area, but whose manufacturing could provide both training and economic opportunities. Unfortunately, Steinbeck Studio and the council failed to agree final terms and the deal fell through.

To this date, Assemble's residential designs have only been completed on Cairns Street. In 2020, the designers and the CLT also proposed a project for an empty lot at the corner of Cairns and Granby Streets. Called Fourth Corner, it would contain a cafe on the ground level with an apartment above, with the rental income supporting the CLT. Designed to respond to the gabled forms of many of the surrounding houses, while opening up its facade for commercial purposes, the building would be clad with tiles made out of recycled clay and produced at the Granby Workshop.

While the full scope of the Granby Four Streets scheme remains unrealized, the area is becoming increasingly occupied and well-tended. There are some signs of revitalization on Granby Street itself, although the COVID-19 crisis was devastating for many businesses there. The CLT continues to argue for more renovations and hopes to one day see the construction of the commercial projects. Jones and other members of Assemble continue to work with the CLT.

Left: The Granby Winter Garden during the beginning stages of its construction.

Right: An axonometric drawing to show the clients how the garden would look. Assemble illustrated the glass roof as well as the storage shelves in the rear of the building.

▶

GRANBY WINTER GARDEN

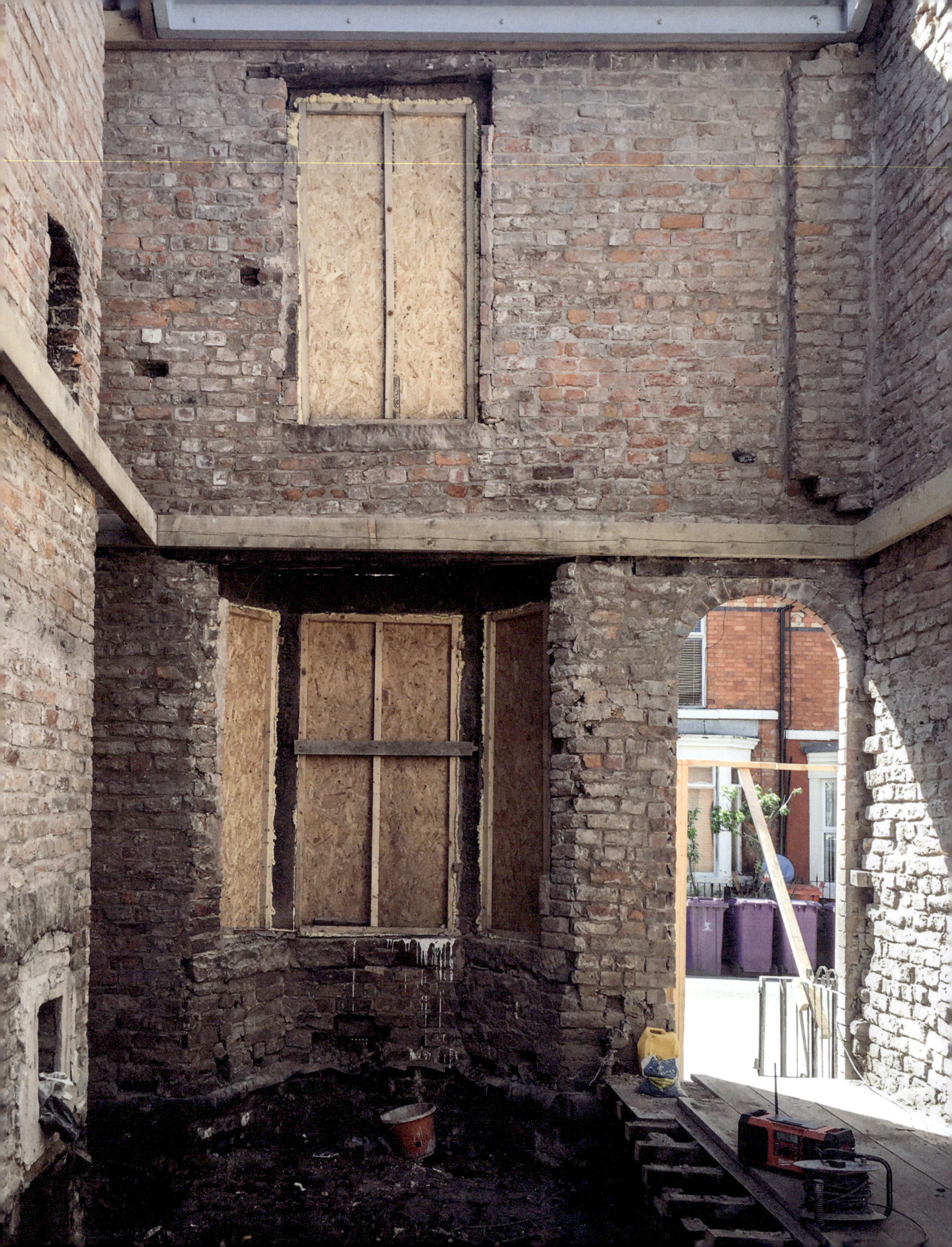

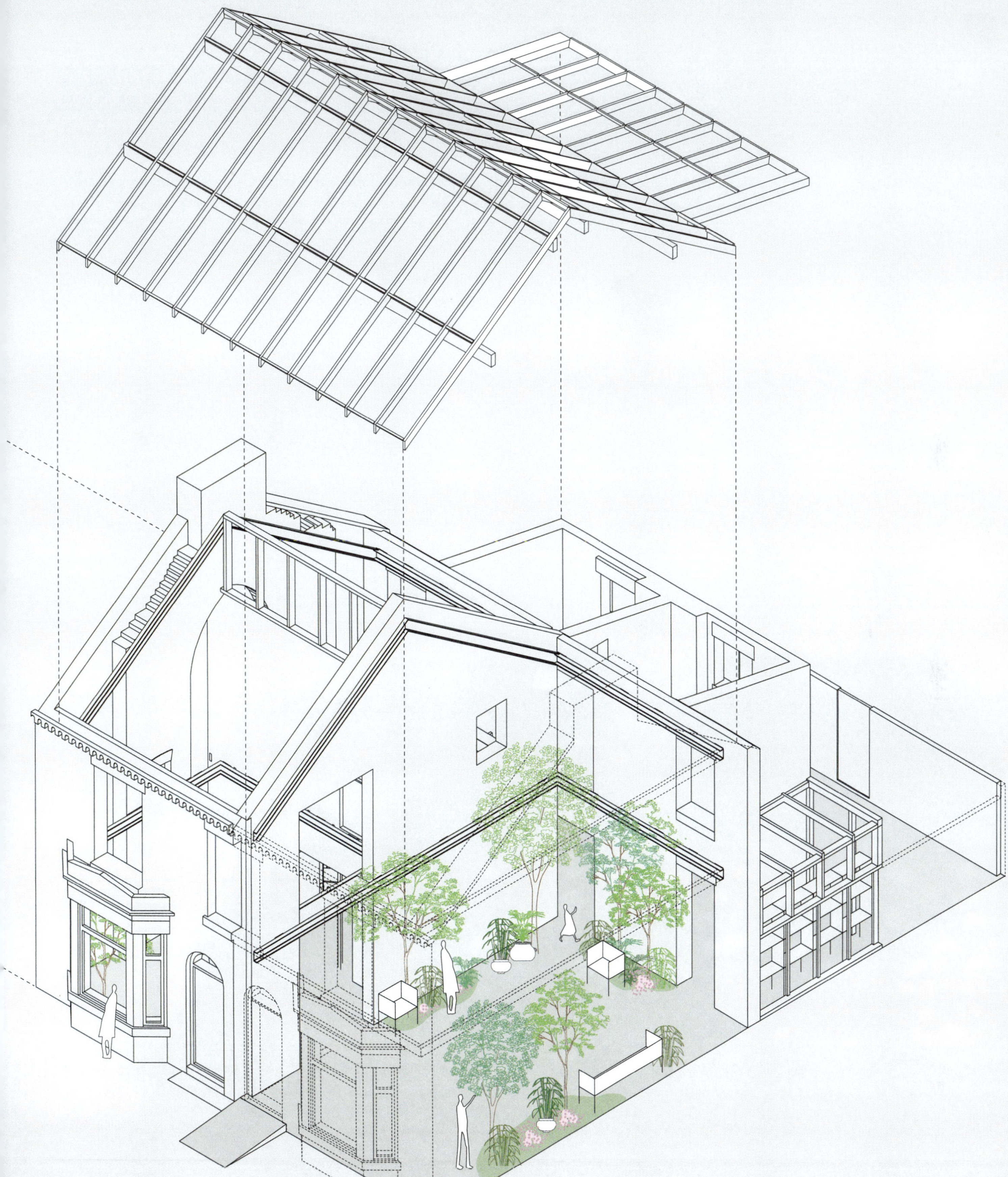

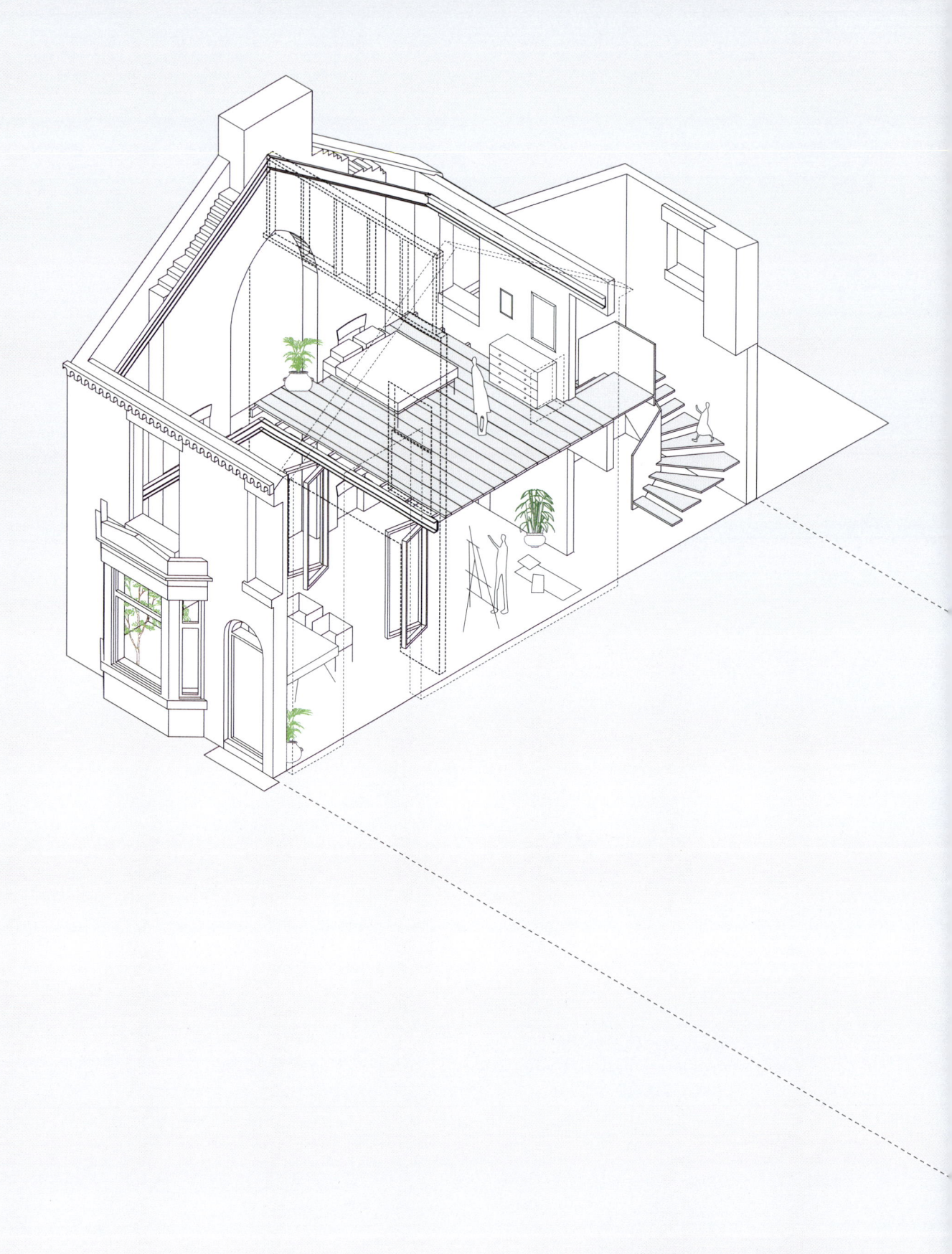

Above: Another axonometric detailing the workshop area in the adjacent house, as well as the bedroom for visiting artists above and the staircase Assemble originally proposed.

Right: The finished garden during one of the opening events. Assemble also specified the new concrete floor.

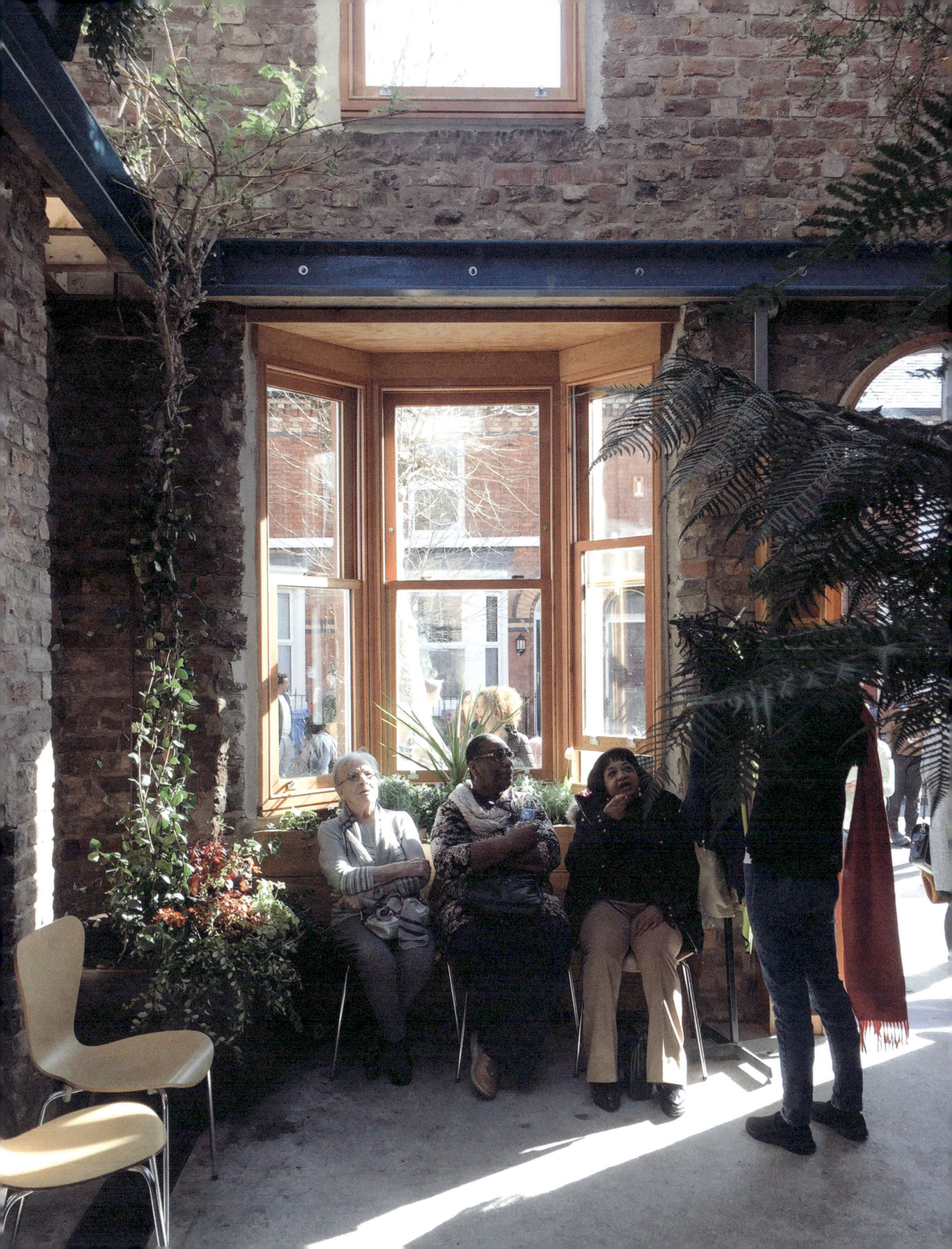

The rainwater tank, covered with Granby Workshop tiles, which Assemble installed in the rear of the garden.

Two of the pieces of furniture Assemble designed for the Granby Four Streets project.

Of great importance to both the neighbourhood and Assemble was the project's award of the Tate's Turner Prize in December 2015. The award brought with it a prize pot of £25,000, some of which Assemble used on the Granby Workshop, but more important was the amount of international recognition it brought to the designers and their work in Toxteth. The choice of Assemble was all the more remarkable as the Turner Prize was set up for artists working in the UK, not architects. By choosing Granby Four Streets and its designers, the jury recognized that this work was not just a technical achievement, but a form of cultural representation and empowerment.

In their jury report, which was read at the announcement by American rock band Sonic Youth's Kim Gordon, the jury stated of Assemble's work that 'they draw on long traditions of artistic and collective initiatives that experiment in art, design, and architecture. In doing so they offer alternative models to how societies can work'. While the choice outraged many artists and some art critics, it also showed how far the definition of art has come in recent decades and how important its social impact has become. The Turner Prize had already been awarded to makers working on what had until then been

A detail of Granby Winter Garden. Assemble had to reinforce the walls above the openings with concrete lintels. The new steel stair is visible to the right.

The shower at Granby Winter Garden, covered with encaustic tiles by Granby Workshop.

Looking from the upstairs bedroom across the two-storey space of the garden.

considered the edges of the field, such as performance, video and installation, and the choice of Assemble seemed to flow naturally from there. The award was also only the second time the prize had gone to a collective (the first was the duo Gilbert & George in 1986) and was the first handed out in Scotland, emphasizing the Tate's efforts to move beyond its London focus.

The attention that Assemble and, to a lesser extent, Granby Four Streets, received upon the award was tremendous, with the news carried not just by specialized art and architecture publications, but all the major British print and broadcast media and international organs like *The New York Times*. If The Cineroleum and some of Assemble's subsequent projects had made a more select audience aware of the group, now they came to a much wider public's attention. A few years later, the Turner Prize led directly to the group being elected to the Royal Academy of Arts as a collective – another breakthrough, both because of the members' ages and because of the supra-personal nature of the status.

GRANBY WINTER GARDEN

Visitors to the Granby Winter Garden admiring the landscaping designed by Assemble with garden designers Andrea Ku and Steven Perkins.

The Turner Prize award was also a recognition of a movement towards architecture as a means of recrafting communities, with an emphasis on tactical insertions, the staging of temporary events and structures, renovations and a blurring of the boundaries between activism, aesthetics and the making of things. That development also emphasized collectivity, both in the making team (extending from design through the physical craft) and in the way that the team worked with larger communities. It blurred the boundaries between art and architecture in the realm of installation, performance and activism. It also had its own aesthetics, based on craft traditions and focused on local materials, recognizable not only in its rough-hewn yet theatrical assemblage, but also in the manner in which the project was presented. In that sense the exhibition, which was also a workshop Assemble installed in the runup to the Prize, was as much what they were awarded for as their work in the field (see p. 280). All of this meant that the Turner Prize was recognizing the fact that Assemble had managed to coalesce the experiments in which their teachers, former employers and other designers, artists and activists around the world had been

A corner of the garden. The blue-painted steel beams reinforce the brick walls where Assemble took out the floor of the second storey.

Looking from the front of the garden to the rear. The stair to the upstairs area is visible in the middle.

engaging with for the two decades prior, not only at Granby Four Streets, but also in New Addington, Baltic Street Adventure Playground and the other community projects they had by then completed or were working on. They did not 'own' that approach, but they became its most visible and accomplished exponents. The kind of work that Markus Miessen and Shumon Basar had collected in *Did Someone Say Participate? An Atlas of Spatial Practice* and that was being created around the world now had a focal point (see Introduction).

The Turner Prize did lead to Assemble receiving more commissions, but they remained small-scale and in the social realm. This was partly because Assemble did not pursue the larger, more conventional projects that were offered to them as a result of all the publicity. At the same time, many potential clients realized that the group's working method was not economic or efficient in conventional situations.

The Stille Strasse concept exhibited at Berlin's Haus der Kulturen der Welt. The exterior is a 1:1 mockup of one of the space's potential subdivisions.

STILLE STRASSE

Assemble kept working on housing and community building issues, taking clients when they found them and found them to be sympathetic. One of their more remarkable ideas was produced for an exhibition called Wohnungsfrage (The Housing Question). Commissioned by the Haus der Kulturen der Welt (House of World Cultures – HKW) in Berlin, Germany, Assemble worked with an informal community centre in the city's Pankow district, Stille Strasse, to imagine a new model of housing for the area. Formed largely of elderly members of the community, Stille Strasse's main focus was the fundamental need for socializing and mutual support networks into old age and retirement. They were advocates for supported, self-determined living at all ages, and successfully campaigned to keep their meeting house in the face of local authority cuts by taking on the running themselves.

The resulting plan proposed an open concrete frame seven storeys tall. The first of these would house community activities, as well as a shared kitchen and shower block. Above that, each unit was to be divided into half. One side would be kitted out to allow for domestic occupation, with what Assemble called 'domestic windows and doors'. The other side would be left raw, 'like a garage'. The idea was that you could move into the residential space at a minimal cost. You would then self-build the apartment, using the garage as a workshop and storage space. Once you had filled out an area meant for living, you could take over the other half, or you could continue to use it as a workshop or office space. Heavy sound insulation built into partitions would minimize disruption of one side by the other and lifts were sized to accommodate building material and equipment, as were the oversized outdoor corridors running along the full length of each floor.

Over time, the downstairs area would lose its original communal areas, which could be converted to

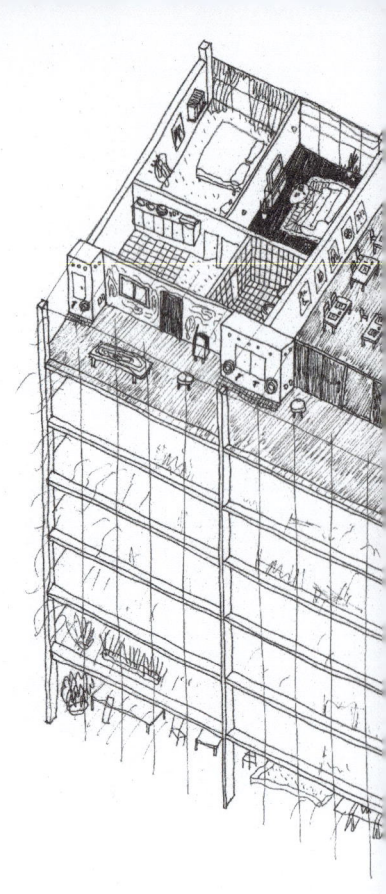

192

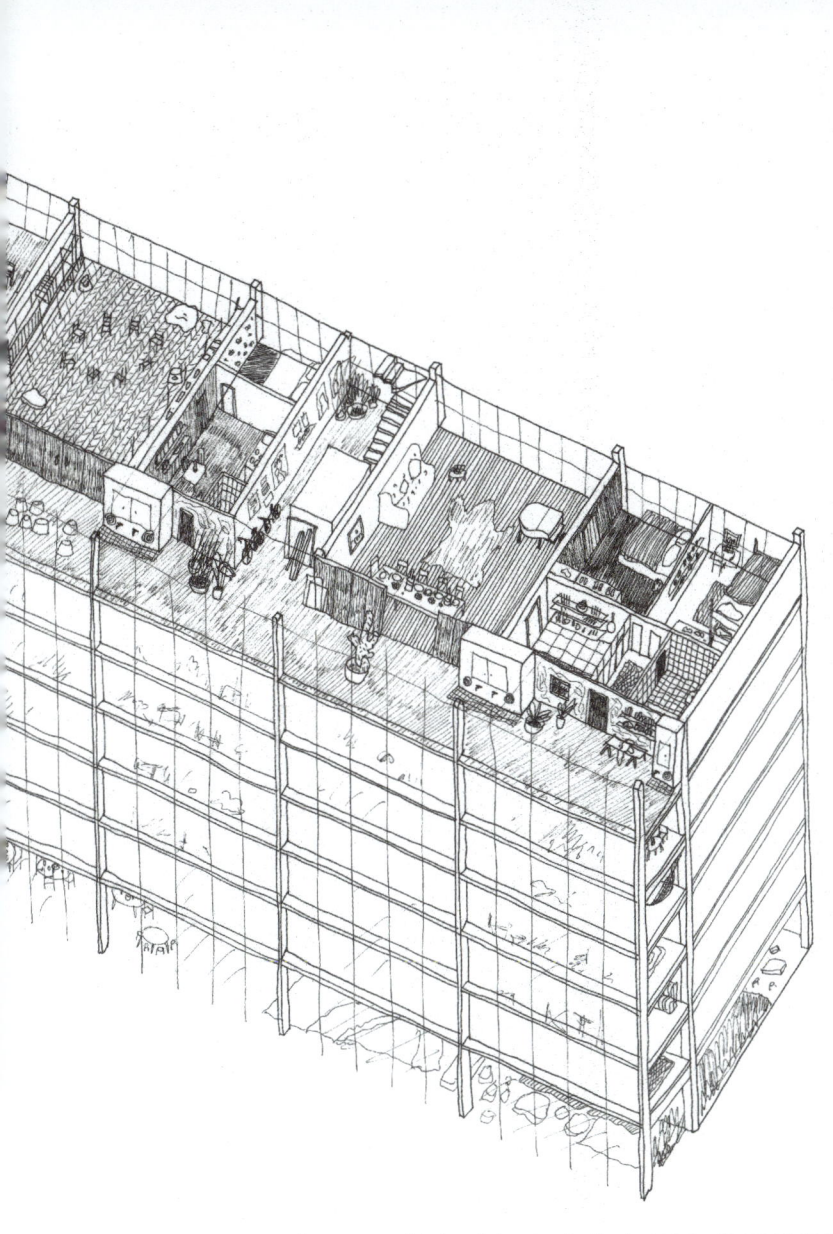

An axonometric hand drawing to illustrate how floors could be subdivided and used for living at either end, leaving an educational and community space in the centre.

Top: A view into the gallery installation that also exhibited the rough construction elements inhabitants could build out themselves.

Bottom: An overview of the gallery installation with its different proposed modes of occupation built out. Scale models were on exhibit within this framework.

functions that the inhabitants as well as the neighbourhood might need, such as a crèche or classrooms. If particular owners no longer needed all of their private space, they could give the portion they did not want back for communal use. A collective ownership structure was meant to resemble the open framework of the building itself. In a sense, Assemble saw Stille Strasse as an experiment in applying what they had learned in the Sugarhouse Studios and Blackhorse Workshop to a residential development, while helping to develop a new form of social and economic organization that could be implemented in community-building housing blocks. The drawings exhibited at HKW and the small book the institution produced to document the design showed the vivacity of the environment the designers envisioned, and began to show up in the work of students who followed the firm.

STILLE STRASSE

A digital axonometric drawing in which the space on the left is finished out as a community office, while the space on the right is awaiting completion as an apartment.

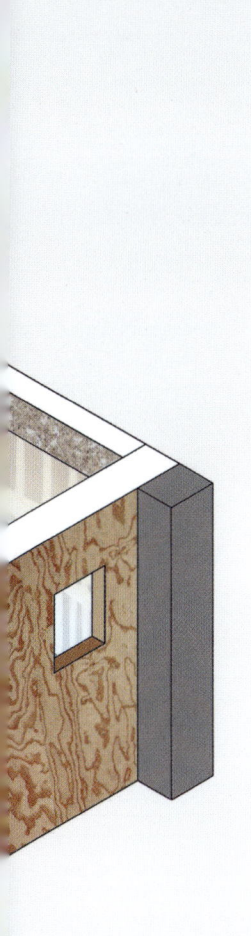

Teilwohnung

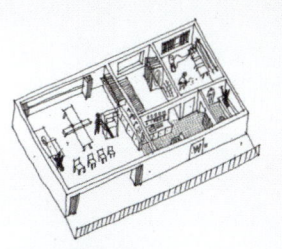

WHERE EVERY APARTMENT IS MADE OF TWO HALVES!

"In my view the most important aspect [of Teilwohnung] is that you can adapt your apartment to changes in your personal situation and with your family, without having to move out or sacrifice your private sphere, as would be the case if you sublet a room in a normal apartment."
- Stille Strasse member

Sweat equity saves money!

WORKSHOP and WINTER GARDEN INCLUDED!!!

~~EXTRA WIDE~~ elevator and winter garden corridor FOR YOU AND YOUR MATERIALS

HOUSE | GARAGE
A | B

OWNED — RENTED
SECURE — ADAPTABLE
PERSONAL — COLLECTIVE

+1 month
Moving in to the apartment, the tenants use the ground floor workshop to build furniture and partitions in their flat; with space 'B' used as storage and assembly area.

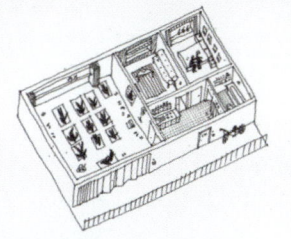

+2 years
A couple has transformed their Teilwohnung into a one bedroom flat, using part B to run occasional yoga classes and meditation sessions. They afford privacy, whilst running a community business.

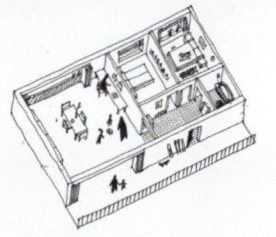

+10 years
The household has grown into a family unit, subsequently changing the housing arrangement to fit their needs. A accommodates two bedrooms, whilst B is a generous living room and play space.

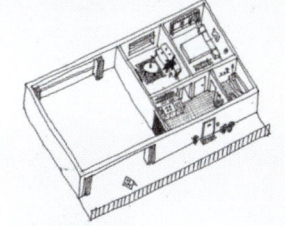

+30 years
As children grow up and leave home, less space is required. Part A is used again one bedroom flat, and B is returned to the cooperative in order to be rented out separately.

A and B parts make up a diverse apartment block. Neighbouring garages can be combined to make larger spaces for family events, work or education; whilst the houses can be split into two or one bedrooms. You can enjoy the privacy of your home or take part in communal activity.

Top: Assemble made this poster to illustrate how the housing would consist of both personal and shared space and would evolve over time.

Bottom: An axonometric sketch of what Stille Strasse could look like after it was fully built out and occupied for both private and communal uses.

STILLE STRASSE

A rendering of the proposed covered entrance between two of the houses on Bevington Road belonging to St Anne's College, discreetly built behind the existing boundary wall.

Assemble's proposal in collage. The outdoor space has been made accessible and new connecting pieces have been added. The building's exteriors have been largely left untouched.

ST ANNE'S COLLEGE

One residential project that is definitely going forwards is the renovation of a row of student housing for St Anne's College at Oxford University. Although much of the approach, as well as the fabric of the houses being renovated, is similar to Granby Four Streets, this is a very different socio-economic situation: the creation of dormitories for one of the most elite universities in the world. St Anne's College, however, is a bit of a newcomer to this tradition. It did not become a 'full constituent' of Oxford University until 1959, which meant it had to generally make do with buildings at the edge of the historic campus.

The buildings in question, therefore, have none of the glamour we associate with the university's historic quads. Built between 1867 and 1869 as semi-detached villas for families, they were repurposed as dormitories in the 1950s.[27] Over time, less-than-fortuitous renovations had stripped out whatever character the interiors retained, while access and egress were achieved by scrunching entryways and hallways in between the buildings. Referred to as 'the Bevs', after Bevington Road on which they are located, the structures also needed to be brought up to current structural and other codes.

Assemble was approached by the college's principal, Helen King, in 2018 as a direct result of her appraisal of the work they had done at Granby Four Streets. King saw

In an overall image of 'the Bevs' you can see their residential rhythm, which stands in contrast to the college's more institutional structures and which Assemble sought to preserve.

similarities with her situation, and sought a design that would preserve the Victorian buildings. What the designers found, recalls Holly Briggs, was 'messy buildings with great bones'. In conversations with King and other members of the community, Briggs and her collaborators found that the college had four main goals: 'care, embody history, wellbeing, and sustainability and environmental concerns'. The problem came with the conflicts among these goals: what made the students comfortable might not preserve the historic fabric, and might also conflict with what needed to be done to the buildings to reduce their energy use, as well as with the budget the college could provide.

Assemble's answer was, as Asia Zwierzchowska puts it, 'to make a lot of small things rather than one big thing'. The collective went into the project not just as community interlocutors, but also as forensic researchers with the aim of learning everything possible about the buildings, not only as they were first built, but as they were used and changed over time. They then worked with consultants to come up with ways to strengthen the underlying structure, to make structural repairs where necessary and to install an entirely new system of services. The aim was to keep these changes as invisible as possible while also reducing energy use.

What will be visible, however, is an array of interventions that attempts to turn the dormitory into something approaching a community, broken up into smaller pods according to the different entryways that each fed into what had been individual houses. New entryways will replace the ad hoc structures that had glued the Bevs together in the past; they will be made in timber with metal and glass screens, and each adjacent house will have its own colour scheme.

A scale model of the proposed new covered entrances joining two existing buildings for St. Anne's.

ST ANNE'S COLLEGE   197

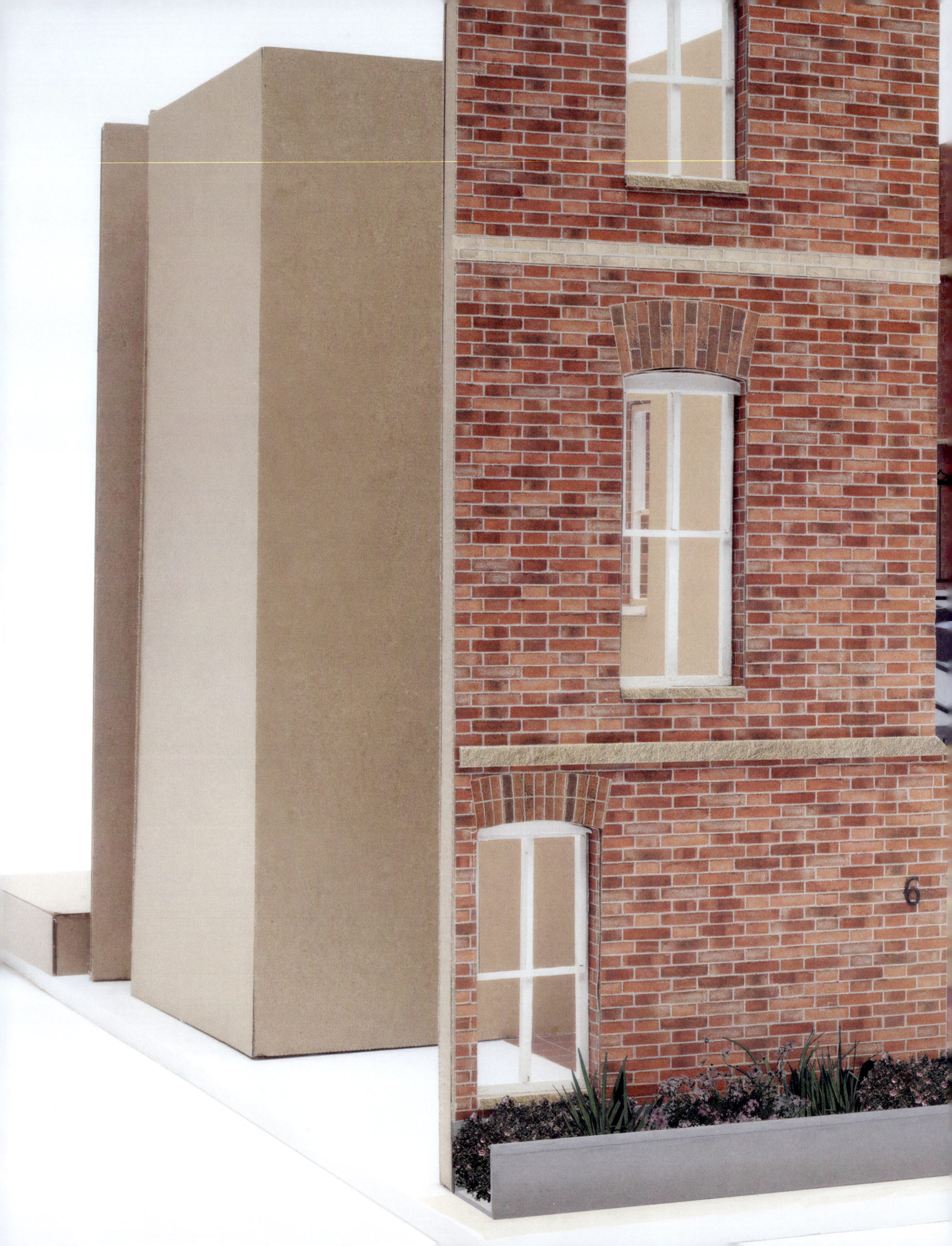
6

7

Assemble built a realistic physical model of their design, visible here and on the previous pages, to show how the new entrances would be inserted between the existing buildings.

Each of these small groupings will also share a kitchen Assemble have designed, says Briggs, 'to be a home away from home'. The aim, according to Briggs, is to create a 'domestic landscape' that places the students in the context of their shared collegiate experience. To fill out that landscape, Assemble and their collaborators have designed a 'family of furniture' that directly recalls the kinds of Victorian tables, chairs and dressers that might have originally populated the Bevs. In the designs, they become abstracted, hewn mainly from recycled materials, and at times decorated with the serially random patterns Assemble developed in places such as the Granby Workshop.

The St Anne's College project, which began construction in 2023, is by far the largest one Assemble has undertaken to date. Its budget, complexity and technical demands mean, says Briggs, 'that we had to take a leap of our own towards professionalism. It was a step up in scale from Goldsmiths (see p. 208) in talking with technical consultants, engineers, lawyers and VAT advisors on behalf of the college.' Though that might be a common situation for almost any architecture firm, for Assemble this implies that they are able to present themselves and operate as such an entity while preserving the collaborative, collective and loosely organized structure they had developed.

If Granby Four Streets marked the most complete embodiment of much of what Assemble wanted to achieve, it also showed the limits of what they could do in the manner they

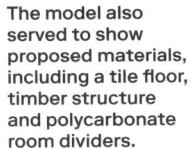

The model also served to show proposed materials, including a tile floor, timber structure and polycarbonate room dividers.

A digital rendering of one of the finished rooms. Assemble designed all the furniture, too, although not all of their proposals were used.

wanted to operate. The situation they encountered in Toxteth called for all the kinds of approaches Assemble believed were central to how architecture should be done. It came from the ground up, originating with inhabitants who were able to activate resources to make physical changes in their community. It focused on collaboration and volunteer activity to make that happen. The manner in which the work was carried out was minimal in both its scope and its design: Assemble did what was necessary where it could, rather than coming up with a grand scheme for the whole of Granby Four Streets, and then carried out the work without regard for how visible or noticeable the impact was to anyone other than the actual users and inhabitants. They used the project itself as a form of research and development in everything from how to navigate the complex politics of Liverpool, far away from their London base, to how to produce materials they could use in their designs in a cost-effective manner. Those materials were also directly related in look and manufacturing to the place where they were put in place, which helped them create educational and economic opportunities in Toxteth.

The Turner Prize recognized all of these qualities and let a whole new audience know about what Assemble did and how it approached architecture, making them a model for a future generation of designers and design activists. The prize also helped the Granby Four Streets CLT build some of what Assemble had envisioned directly, with members of Assemble, as usual,

ST ANNE'S COLLEGE

A digital sketch in which Assemble experimented with revealing existing timber floors, adding Granby Workshop fireplaces and using recycled timbers with light stains.

participating in that work. It also led, though perhaps not directly, to future commissions that kept the group going, even during the difficult period of the COVID-19 pandemic.

At the same time, the Turner Prize marked a turning point. For all of its scope and achievement, the Granby Four Streets project did not realize most of its overall aims: much of the area is still tinned up, the retail scene on Granby Street has not markedly improved and the new buildings were never constructed. The whole process makes evident how difficult working in this manner and in these kind of situations actually is. Rather than offering a breakthrough, the Turner Prize and the Granby Four Streets project reinforced both the validity of what Assemble was doing and the continued limits on their enterprise.

Those limits were made even more evident by the failure of any of the other housing experiments in which Assemble have engaged in subsequent years to be realized.

Assemble spent a great deal of time with students, faculty and staff, producing rough sketches along the way to test layouts and arrangements.

ST ANNE'S COLLEGE

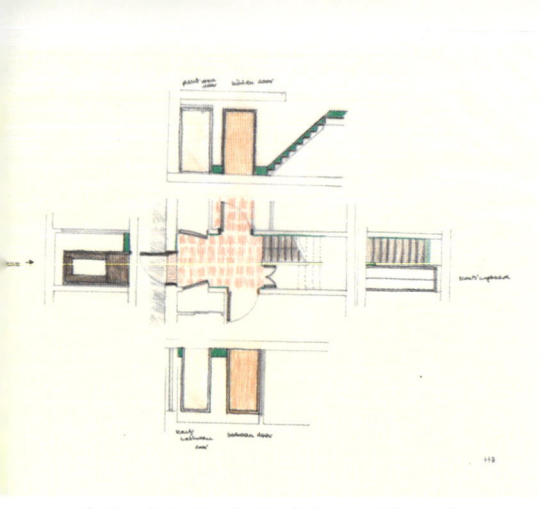

An 'exploded' or 'butterfly' view of the entrance proposal that shows its plan and surrounding walls simultaneously.

More of Assemble's hand-drawn sketches, which were produced during the collaborative design process.

Their daring experiment in rethinking housing, work and community proposed at Granby Four Streets and evident in subsequent projects such as the Dairy Road development and their analysis of the Hovinbyen area (see Chapter 7) remains on the drawing board. Those projects that are moving forwards, such as the Bevs for St Anne's College, necessitate a different kind of client and ask Assemble to operate in a more 'normal' manner. The project is also more conventional in that the designers have worked mainly with one person, King, and her team as students come and go. The result will also be dormitory rooms, which, for all their community aspects, have to be generic. Finally, it remains to be seen how much of Assemble's craft will survive the budgeting and construction processes. None of this means that there is anything wrong with what Assemble is trying to do. It only makes their achievements, humble as they may seem, all the more remarkable.

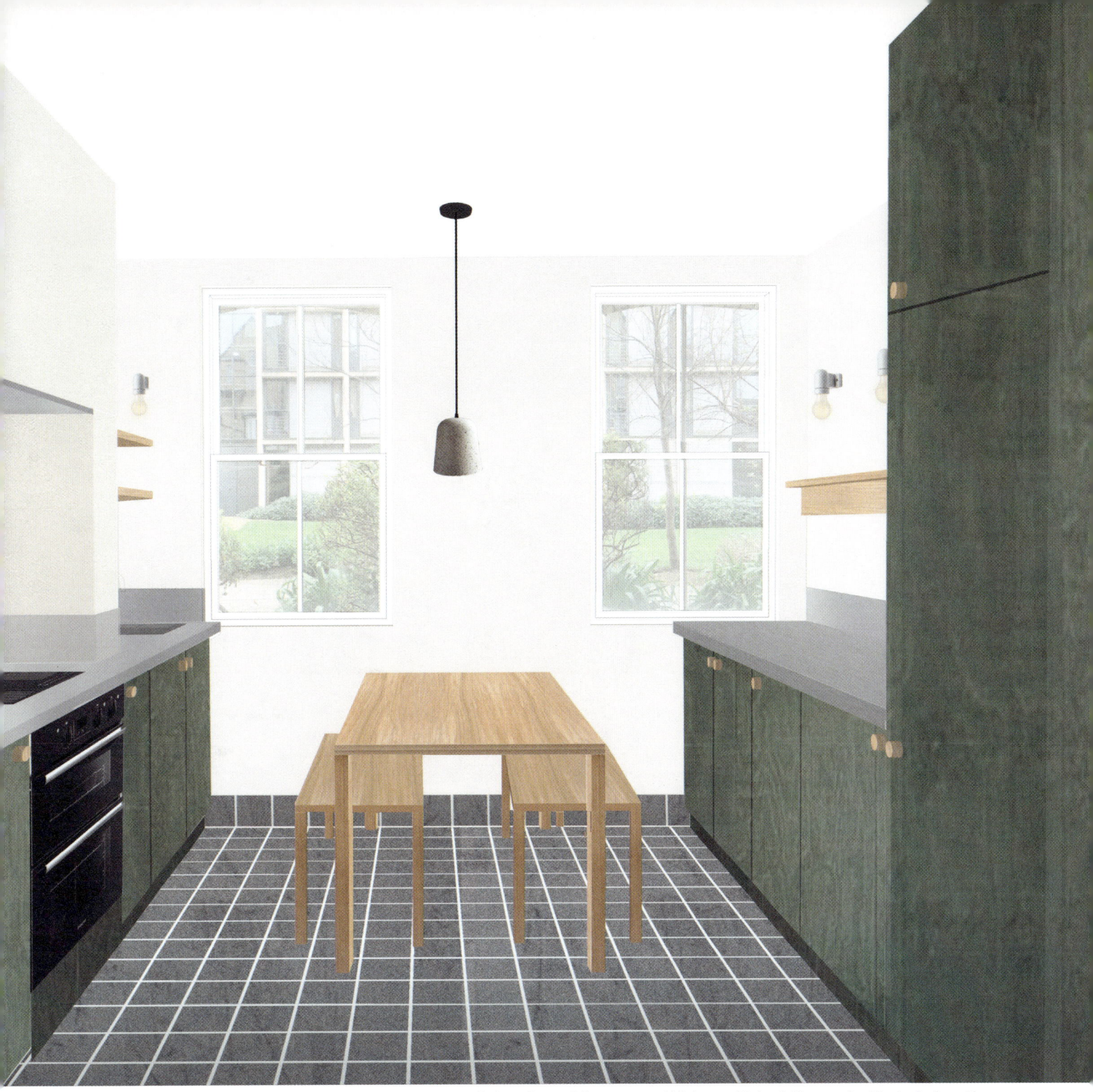

A computer rendering of one of the communal kitchens with furnishings and cabinets designed by Assemble out of rough and, where possible, recycled timbers.

ST ANNE'S COLLEGE

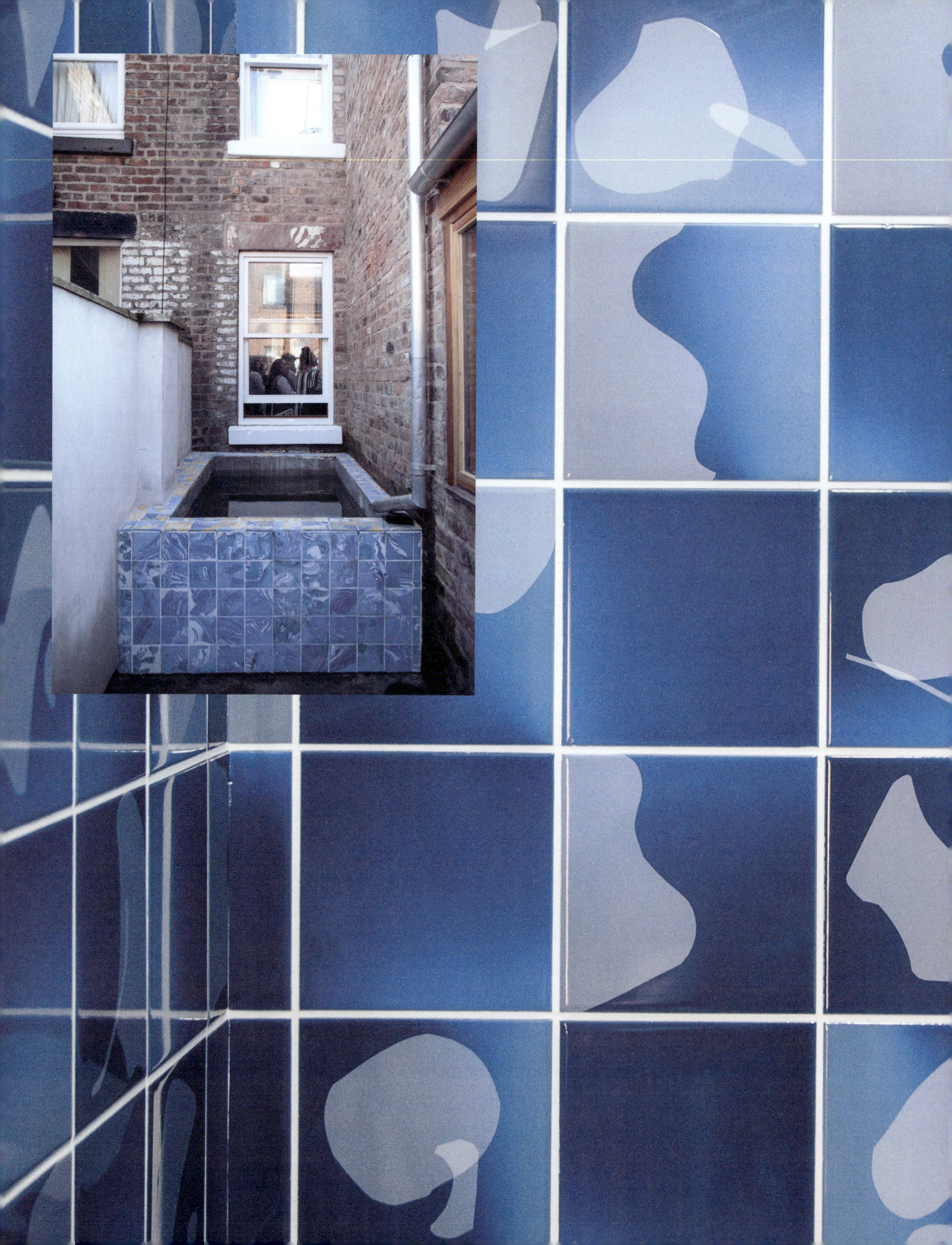

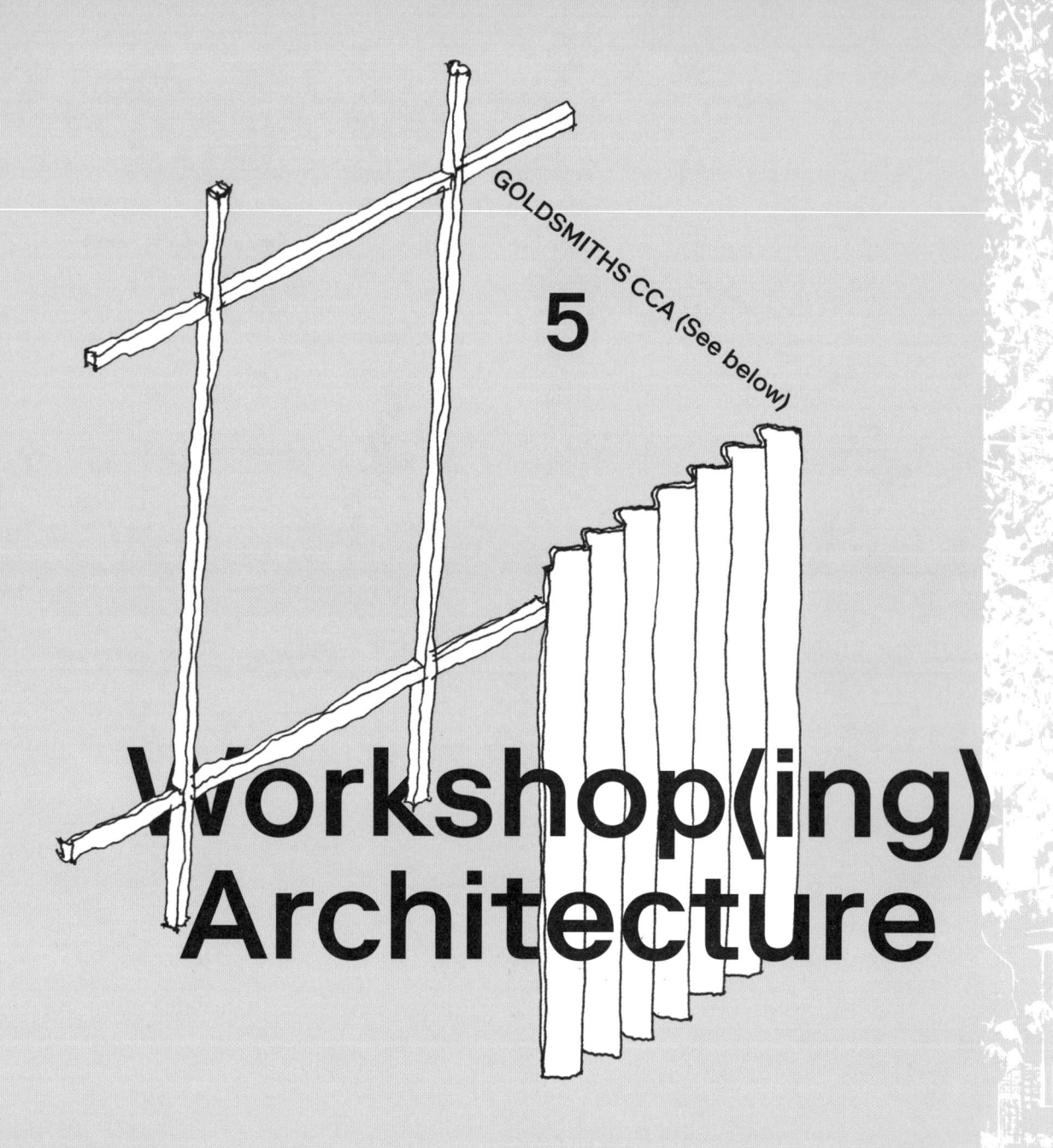

GOLDSMITHS CCA (See below)

5

Workshop(ing) Architecture

GOLDSMITHS CCA   If Granby Four Streets showed how Assemble could affect change in residential communities, their work for Goldsmiths College, University of London, exhibited their ability to do the same at an institutional level. Here they carried out the renovation of and addition to a former swimming pool on Laurie Grove, a road in New Cross in south London, into studios, galleries and offices for one of the most prestigious art schools in the UK. The manner in which they did this proved that they could carry out complex building projects, while retaining an emphasis on the importance of preserving and opening up the past as it is embodied in the human-made environment to exhibit and effectuate new creative and social possibilities.

Assemble obtained the commission for the transformation of the Laurie Grove Baths, built in 1898, through an open competition in 2017. In their proposal, they emphasized the importance of the facility, which had operated until 1991

A facade drawing of the same area, produced during Assemble's design process.

The new covered entrance to the Goldsmiths Centre for Contemporary Art (CCA). Above is a new gallery space. The designers figured out how to shape off-the-shelf fibre cement boards into the facade panels you see here.

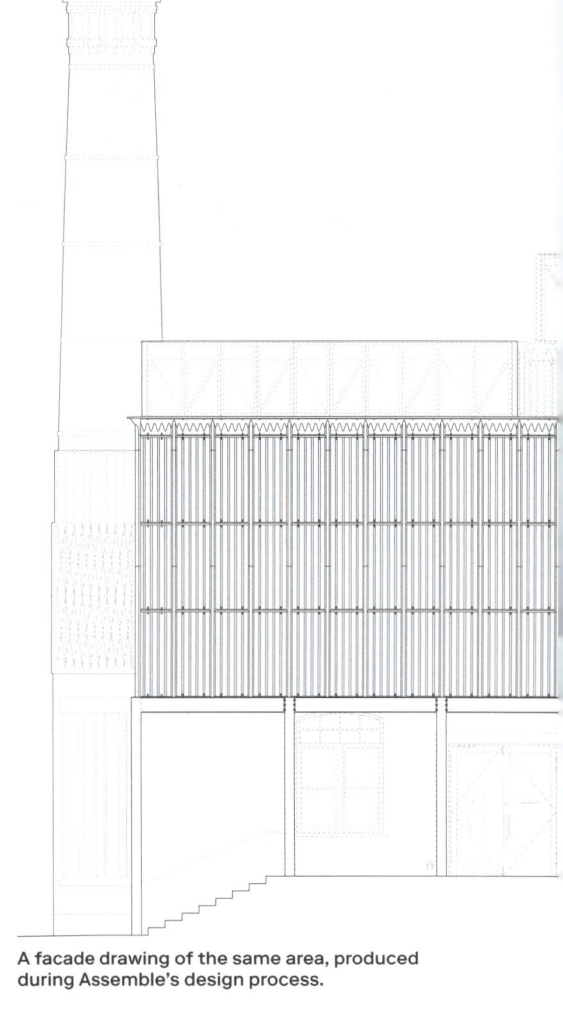

209

Assemble made a 1:33 scale model for the competition out of plywood and other material. This shows the side view, including the new areas to be built on top of the existing building.

as a resource for the local community. Not only had it provided recreational bathing opportunities, but it also offered laundry and personal bathing facilities when many homes did not have them.[28] The spaces ranged from the open expanse of the swimming pool through smaller-scale public function rooms to a rabbit's warren of offices and other support spaces. Even the underground areas, where the boilers and pipes were still located, exhibited some dramatic industrial grandeur.

Goldsmiths had already appropriated the swimming pool as studio spaces, and so Assemble concentrated on what had been the rear of the building complex: a three-storey utility block. They designed two substantial new volumes that formed the 'white cube' gallery spaces and which gave the school a public face into a new courtyard, which they had opened up between the baths and other structures the university owned. In their most dramatic move, they cut out the floor in the main block of what had been the baths' service building to create a double-height exhibition space.

'They simply understood what we needed and envisioned better than anyone,' recalls Richard Noble, the Head of the Art Department at Goldsmiths, of the competition choice. 'They showed how we could get the most out of the baths without losing the buildings and their history.' Assemble's renderings, which presented the new addition in a palette of soft colours rather than precise computer rendering – in the mode Assemble had by then perfected – certainly went a far way towards convincing the jury of the scheme's merits. The designers also built a fold-out model, which clarified how they proposed to make sense of the complex set of buildings, and exhibited the reuse of the spaces in a way that the jurors of the competition, which consisted of faculty, staff and outside consultants, could understand.

The commission proceeded relatively quickly, and the Goldsmiths Centre for Contemporary Art (CCA) was completed in 2018. The design process benefited from the

The model came apart to show the interior spaces Assemble was proposing to make out of the existing building and its additions.

A material board displaying Douglas fir samples stained with acetate, integrally coloured marble tiles, fibre cement and more.

fact that the school already knew what it wanted, having been through a constitutive consulting process before the commission, and had raised the funds for the building through an auction of pieces donated by alumni who had gone on to considerable success in the art world.

'It did mean that we had to become much more professional very quickly,' recalls Paloma Strelitz. The CCA project coincided with the work on Granby Four Streets and came after the awarding of the Turner Prize, during a period when Assemble were receiving quite a few inquiries and growing beyond their small original base. Several of the original members, including both Strelitz and Adam Willis, had come back to the organization after they had left to complete their education and internships, and thus a level of professional knowledge was now present in the organization. Moreover, Assemble had developed internal systems that allowed it to keep track of financial issues, while contracting out some of the other aspects of running a business. The original gang had continued to renew the group by recruiting new members once they had worked for Assemble for a period of two years and were accepted by the existing cohort. The management of Sugarhouse Studios provided a cushion of income and a domicile, while also giving them close ties with collaborators, several of whom they worked with on the CCA commission. 'Goldsmiths was the project where we showed we had grown up,' says Willis.

A 1:1 mockup of the striated fibre cement facade panel. The cornice was eliminated during design development.

It was also where Assemble, for the first time, created a permanent and public piece of new building. The two galleries, one with clerestory windows on three sides and one with a 'lantern' skylight, sit on top of a steel frame that forms a covered porch in front of the gallery's main entrance. This outdoor space acts as a social buffer where students, faculty and the public can mix, and also lifts the galleries up to be an object of contemplation. Assemble clad the lifted gallery block with corrugated cement board, a material that is usually employed as a roofing material in industrial situations. They developed an iron acetate stain at Sugarhouse Studios that gives the boards a greenish tint, similar in appearance to oxidized copper. The designers also intended the treatment to recall the appearance of the glazed tiles inside the bath areas. As an abstract block posed in the courtyard, the gallery building presents itself as a modern element that both recalls the history of formal gallery spaces in Western culture and abstracts out the volumes of the adjacent utility buildings. A block set on top of one of those brick structures, clad in metal panels stained a dark grey and festooned with strengthening crosses that mimic a pattern Assemble found inside

The mould for the chair Assemble designed and produced for the centre's cafe.

The finished passivated steel chair with its golden hue.

the boiler room, hides new mechanical equipment and acts as the tower to the galleries' four-square geometry.

Assemble also brought the materiality they developed for the outside of the building to the spaces inside it, by staining some of the metal doors and walls they found or added to recall the colours and patina of the exterior, and by designing furnishings with a similar aesthetic of a weathered, brick and slate, almost industrial, appearance. This includes bespoke furniture, some of which was put into production by their collaborator, design and fabrication firm Cake Industries. The cafe chair is made out of zinc that is only 1.5 mm (0.06 in) thick, which is attached to an equally minimal frame with five rivets. Assemble put the metal through a process that is usually part of the coating process for machinery and the result is an iridescent sheen. The reception desk, meanwhile, is faced with the same material as

The new gallery Assemble designed in the existing cast iron water tank. They cleaned up the space, adding windows, a new floor and a roof.

the exterior of the galleries, but stained red. The designers also used Granby Workshop tiles in some areas. Not all of their new interventions had such a strong patina, however. Where they created new railings and balustrades, they made simple metal structures painted the slate blue colour that has become part of their signature.

The insides of the new lobby and the block of galleries above it, as well as the staircase used to reach the upper spaces, are thoroughly modern environments with unadorned white walls and simple wood floors, while the detailing of the staircase is similarly straightforward. Here, Assemble showed their ability to detail and finish new spaces in the minimalist manner that had become prevalent in London with the work of architects such as David Chipperfield, and had been further developed by some of their teachers and influences, including Tom Emerson of 6a and Caruso St John. It has become their standard aesthetic when they create new public environments.

The spatial qualities of the galleries are equally simple. Well-composed and proportioned, the places for the display of art are tall and airy, with exposed trusses past which the clerestory or skylight light washes onto the walls. Where Assemble had to add walls – to divide the studios or to outfit some of the offices – they did so in a utilitarian manner and concentrated again on clean details and a sense of height.

For all the sophistication of the new elements, it is still the manner in which Assemble exposed and opened

A 1:20 model of the clerestory gallery above the centre's entrance. Assemble produced this model as part of the competition.

A 1:20 model of the two-storey space in the basement area in use for an art installation. Assemble produced this model as part of the competition.

up the existing interiors that gives the complex of buildings its character. This is especially true in the boiler rooms and support buildings in the back of the baths which, in a flip of the original situation, became the public part of the school. Here, Assemble exposed the existing brick wherever possible and, where they had to cover up the walls with new plaster, turned the pipes and ducts into visual reminders of the building's guts. Painted a dull grey, these and other mechanical elements became sculptural eye-catchers in the white-walled spaces.

 Assemble's most spectacular intervention was the creation of a double-height space in the middle of this back building, formed by simply removing the floor in one room. All of the public functions circulate around this new heart for the school's communal and public activity, which serves as a space for performances, lectures and gatherings, as well as for display. The upper half of this space is painted white, both to increase the sense of height that is central to the design, and to make it fit with the white-walled spaces around it.

 In the lower half of the space, however, partial pilasters and stub ends of joists remain as they were when the original construction was finished, and the designers left the finishing more or less as they found it too. This brings this part of the space into relation with the surrounding spaces on this

The finished clerestory gallery during an art exhibition.

The 'project space' Assemble created in the middle of the project by removing the ground floor. You can see the cafe through the door in the middle.

Another view of the project space. The designers left the different finishes of the walls as they found them. They constructed a new wall to the left and poured a new concrete floor.

Looking down into the project space to the left and towards the lobby area to the right. The bridge leads to the clerestory gallery. ▶

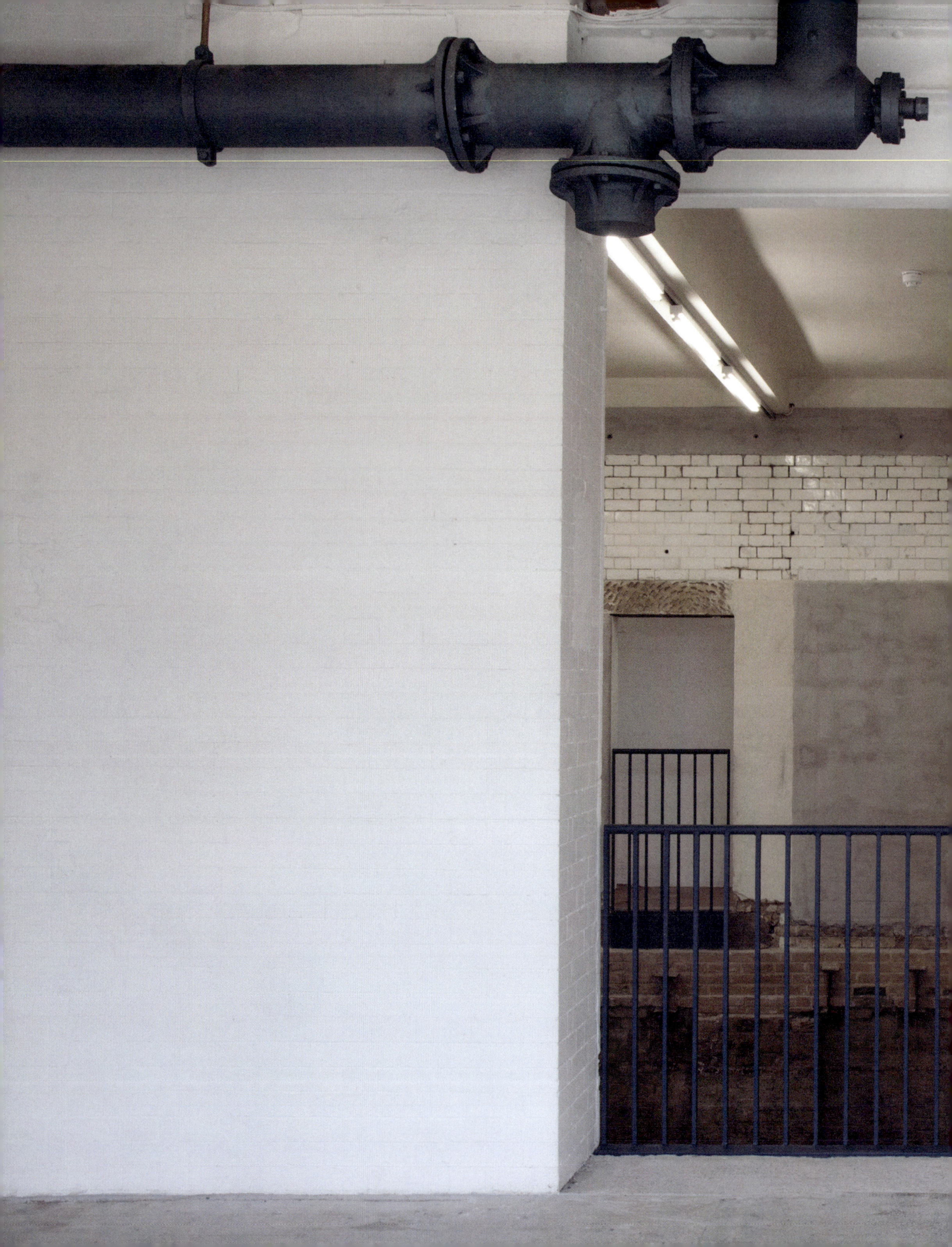

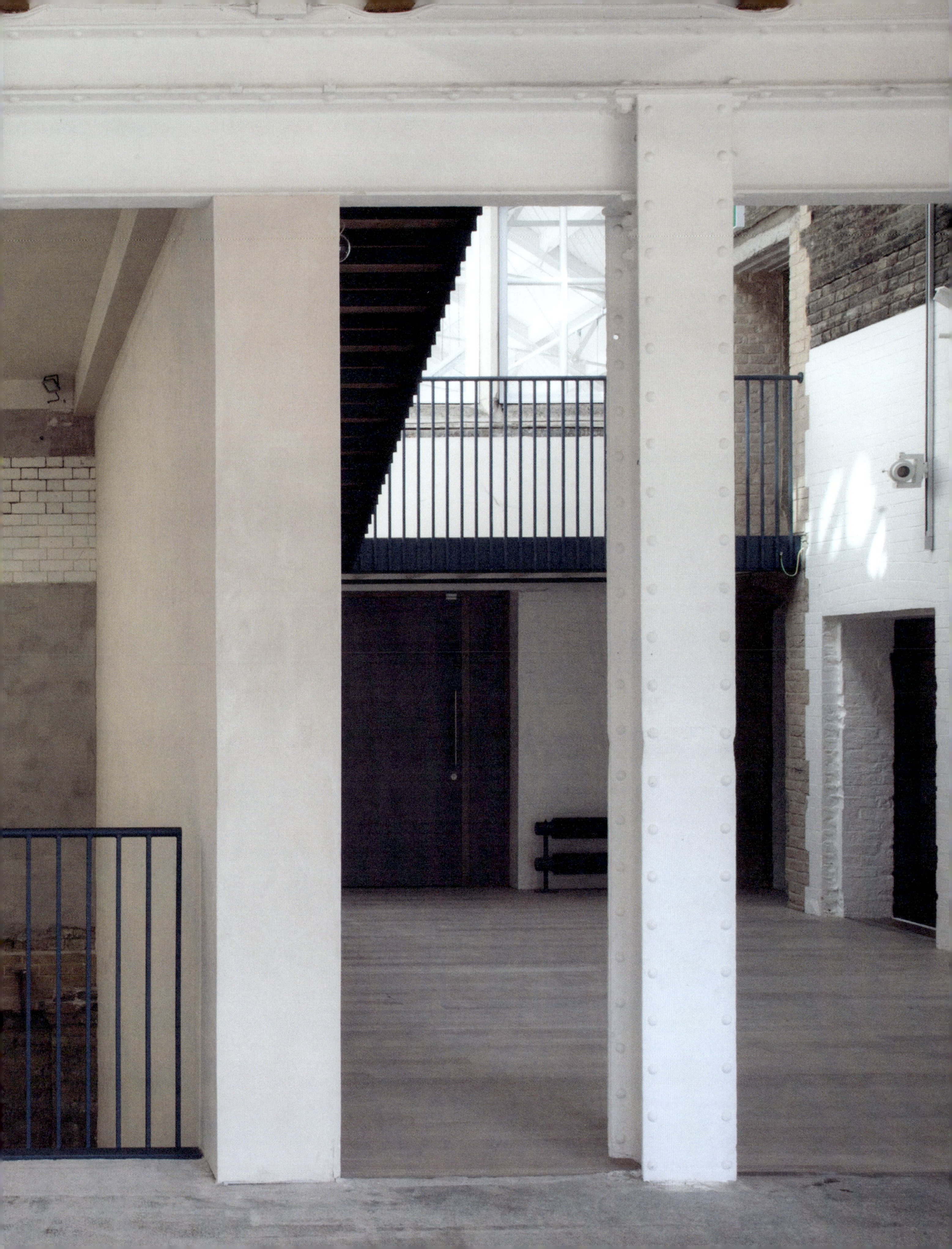

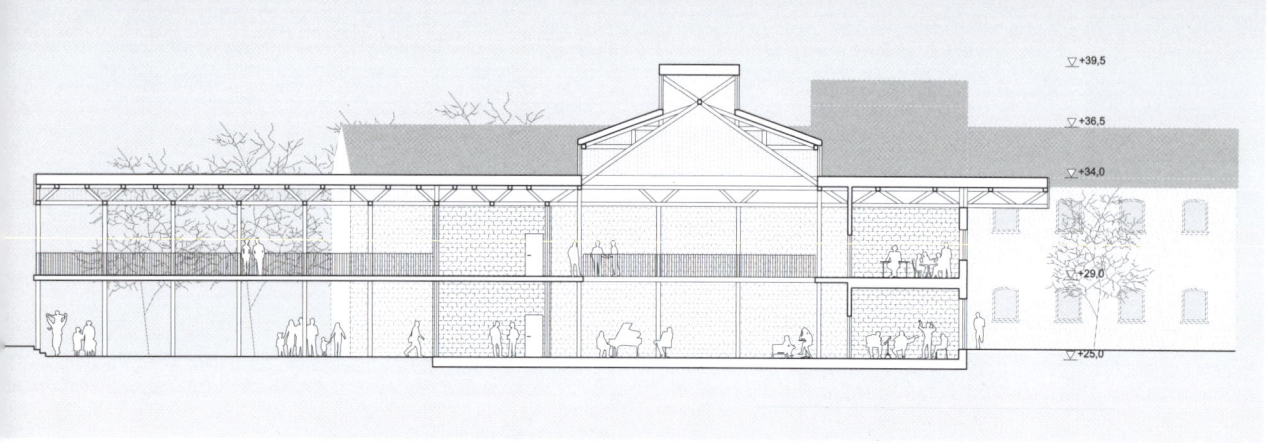

A section through Assemble and Czvek Rigby's competition entry for the Kunstacademie (Art Academy) in Zwevegem, Belgium. The double-height multi-use space is in the middle.

lower level, where the boiler rooms, narrow basement passages and other parts of the building's undercroft have been revealed, stabilized and made accessible. On this level, you enter into what remains of the bath's past, and its implements and textures not only become part of the architecture, but respond to the artworks the school places in these areas.

The CCA project has a sense of being an archaeological site, in which remains are treated as relics of great beauty and importance, even when their nature is mundane, while the new construction becomes a way to view, (literally) build on and open up that past. 'We wanted to be clear about what we knew, which is what we could see in the old building, and what we didn't know, which was the new element. That latter part is abstract and open, both to use and interpretation,' states Adam Willis. 'We enjoyed the labyrinthine quality, and the mystery of the baths,' adds Strelitz. 'We used it as a way to create something quite theatrical.' What ties the new and the old together, the designers believe, is craft: both the making of the new elements with their high-effect materials and colours, and the craft of opening up the old elements and combining them with the new ones. Says Strelitz: 'We understood this to be a cultural institution that used craft and aesthetics to give agency, and we wanted to continue that work in our design.'

CCA remains one of the most complex building projects Assemble has undertaken to date. It is also still used almost exactly as the designers and Noble envisioned it. As the building has been used, some of the new elements have also weathered, become scuffed up and even encrusted with artworks, which strengthens the ties between the new and the old.

Beginning CCA, Assemble have made the production of art spaces into a mainstay of what they do as architects. During the period when they were working on the project, they entered a few other competitions for arts and performance spaces, mainly in Europe.

220

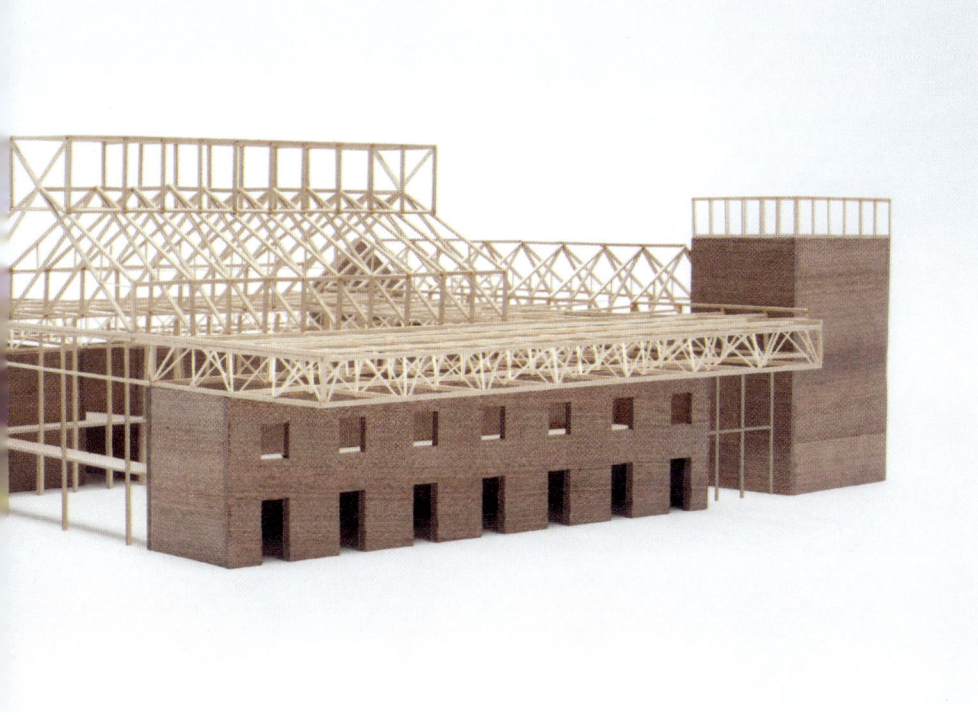

A 1:50 model of the design: Porotherm clay blocks supporting a lightweight timber structure.

Top: A rendering of the courtyard Assemble designed with Czvek Rigby. Four buildings would be connected by a timber structured walkway.

Bottom: A rendered perspective of the central space overlooking and opening up to the adjacent canal.

KUNSTACADEMIE ZWEVEGEM

The largest of these was a proposed addition to the Kunstacademie (Art Academy) in Zwevegem, Belgium, which they designed together with Brussels-based practice Czvek Rigby. There they used the remains of an old textile factory along a canal, adding new music and dance spaces to the studios that were already housed in the existing building, and combined the whole into a coherent complex. A central space took up the heart of the new structure, which the architects proposed building out of timber with a ribbed tile facade not dissimilar to the CCA. The double-height space, with its exposed rafters and wood columns, also drew on the design of Yardhouse, which they had completed a few years earlier. Although Czvek Rigby and Assemble won the competition in 2019, the new project was sadly abandoned by the client.

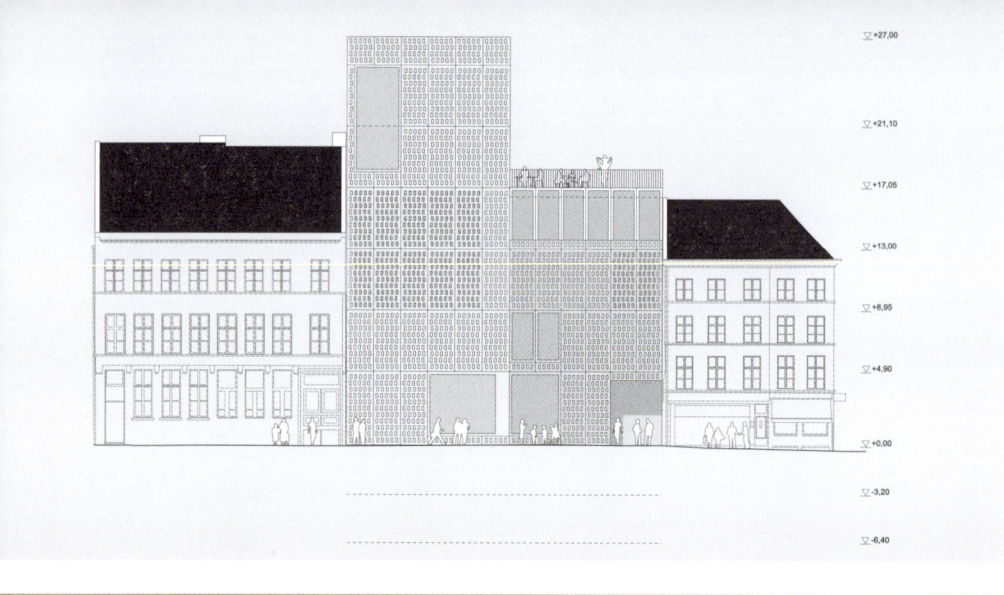

Top: An elevation drawing of Assemble's insertion into the Design Museum Gent viewed from Drabstraat.

Bottom: An inside perspective of the new space looking over the gallery and out into the city. The structure would be formed of Glulam timber beams with plywood sheets forming the walls.

DESIGN MUSEUM GENT

Czvek Rigby and Assemble were also shortlisted for an extension to and renovation of the Design Museum Gent in the same year that they won the Kunstacademie Zwevegem competition. The team proposed a wood structure to slot in between existing buildings, connecting existing galleries to each other and public areas.

Top: A 1:500 scale model of how the new wing would fit into the existing complex. The model was made with timber off-cuts and cast plaster, with the new addition highlighted in pink.

Bottom: Another competition model made at a larger scale showing the proposed facade detail.

A rendering of what the new building would look like on Drabstraat. The tiles were meant to be reflective, so they would shimmer from this angle.

DESIGN MUSEUM GENT

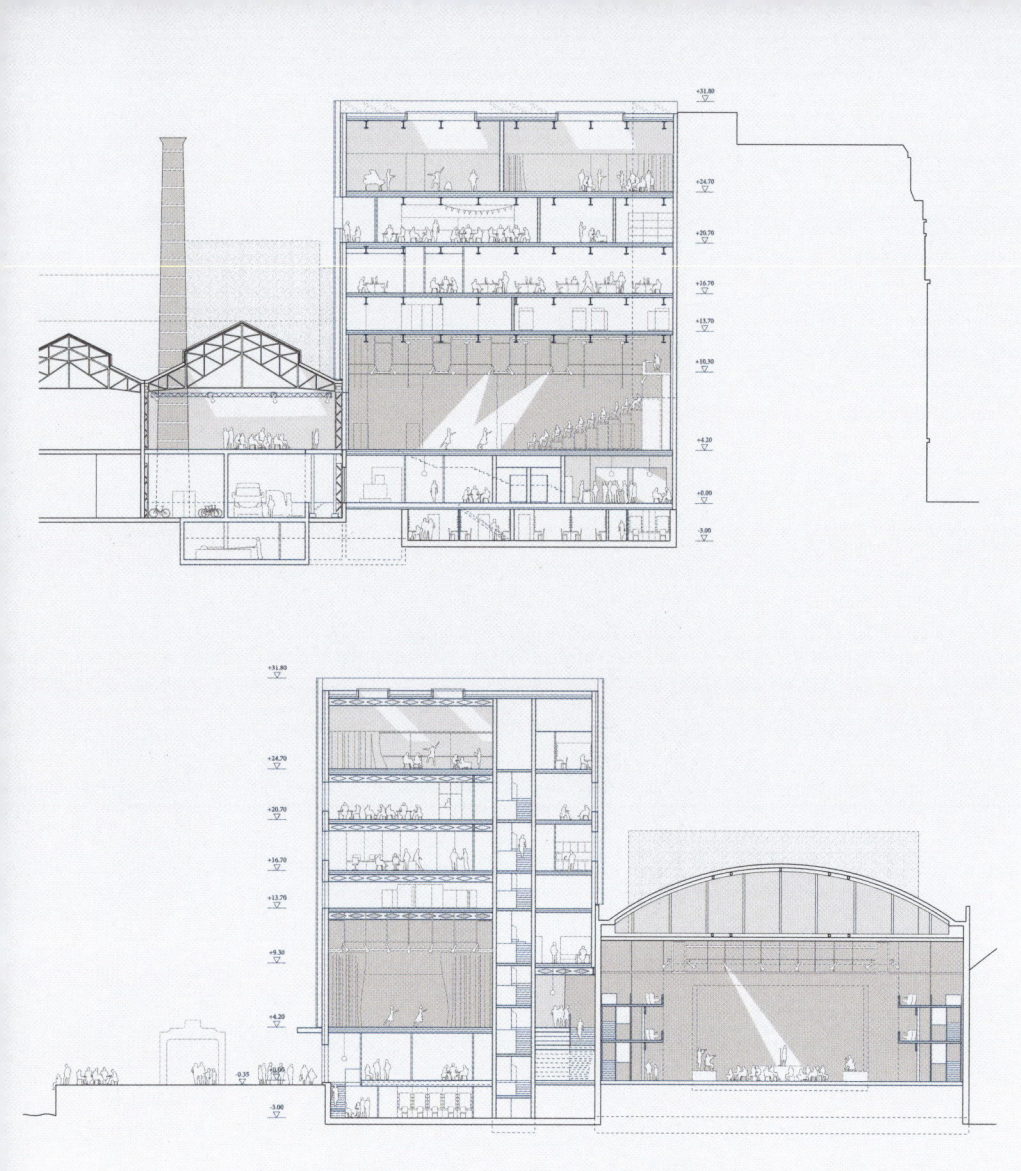

Above: A section through the new infill building Assemble proposed for the Kaaitheater in Brussels, with the reused industrial space to the left.

Top right: A 1:20 fragment model of the facade of the new building, highlighting the translucent glass Assemble wanted to use.

A detail of the 1:20 fragment model in production.

KAAITHEATER

Finally, the two firms came in second in another cultural commission for the redesign and addition to the Kaaitheater in Brussels. Here they proposed to first renovate the Art Deco-style theatre the troupe occupied, and then open up adjacent industrial spaces through a renovation that would treat the existing brick, concrete and equipment on site as part of a collage of old and new. The whole complex would then be unified by a new building the architects wanted to insert in such a manner as to create a maximum of flexibility and openness, while emphasizing the layering of existing and added elements.

224

Top: A 1:100 model of the new infill building.

Bottom: A view of the completed complex at night. The original theatre is visible to the right; the industrial space can be seen to the left.

KAAITHEATER 225

+21.98
3 Roof

+19.31
2 Second Floor

+16.70
1 First Floor

±14.08
0 Ground

An elevation drawing of Bill Brown Creative Workshops on Storey's Way. The entrance is past the low wall to the left.

BILL BROWN CREATIVE WORKSHOPS

In 2016, Assemble was asked to design a new home for the Bill Brown Creative Workshops, a facility where the students at Churchill College, Cambridge University, could experiment with digital technologies. The project reuses a former oil tank storage space. Assemble proposed a new wooden shell within this existing brick building, as well as opening up the walls and ceiling with apertures to allow light and air to penetrate. The project would have conflated several qualities they had explored at CCA, but is currently awaiting funding.

During this period, however, Assemble were able to design a series of workshops for art and fabrication in existing buildings that have since been completed: the Kamikatz Brewery on Shikoku Island in Japan (2017); the Material Institute in New Orleans, Louisiana, USA (2018); the Fabric Floor in Brixton, London (2019); the D. H. Chen Foundation Gallery in Hong Kong (2019); and Atelier LUMA in Arles, France (2023). Apart from Fabric Floor, these were projects far from Assemble's home territory, confronting them with new cultures and material regimes to which they had to respond.

A 1:10 model of the 7-metre-high (23-ft) central exhibition space. A Douglas fir structure would contain light funnels. Part of the structure at the top would remain visible, the bottom part of the walls would be plastered with a lime render.

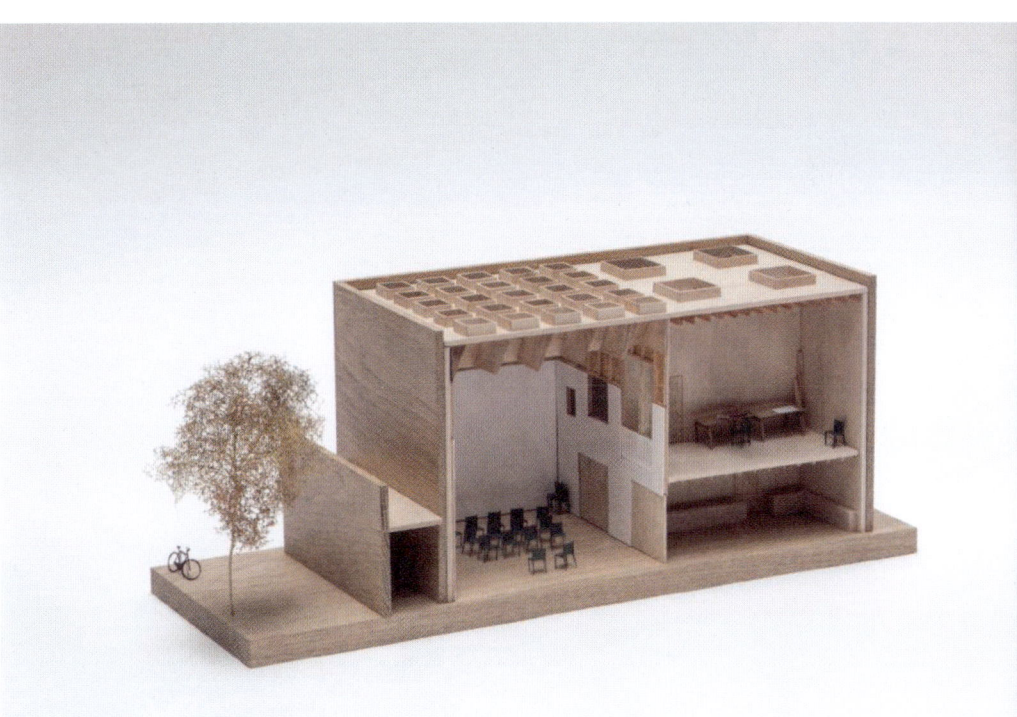

Top: A model fragment in which each room was built at 1:10 scale so that they could be photographed and studied intensely. The structure of the roof and the skylights are also separated out.

Bottom: A sectional model at 1:10 scale showing the main space, the workshop space and studio above to the rear and the entrance to the front.

The existing space after the oil tanks were removed but before construction started.

A 1:10 model of the doorway looking into the gallery.

The roof of the main space with its skylights and the window from the upstairs as built.

BILL BROWN CREATIVE WORKSHOPS

Assemble's drawing of the new tasting room at Kamikatz Brewery as it would be seen approaching from the valley below. It was made during Assemble's first residence there for the client.

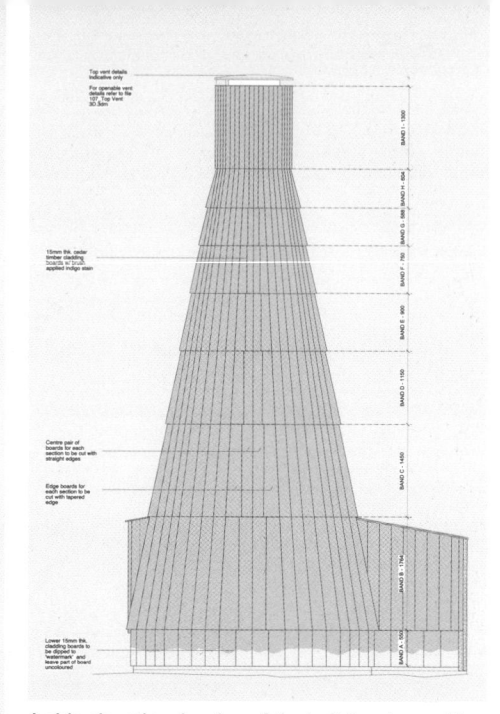

A side elevation drawing of the building Assemble made during the design development phase. Assemble wanted to make the tasting room into a sign.

KAMIKATZ BREWERY

The first of these, the Kamikatz Brewery, is not strictly speaking a workshop, but it is a place of manufacturing – a former sawmill that the Rise & Win brewing company had converted for their purposes. Located in Kamikatsu, a village of less than two thousand people on Shikoku Island in Japan, the company mainly uses the corrugated metal shacks as they were found, with minimal improvements. Assemble developed a plan for the better utilization and eventual expansion of those buildings, and added a tasting room where the public could experience the small facility and sample the sake made there.

The new tasting room is a wood-framed tower rising up as a marker for the new activity taking place. Members of Assemble immersed themselves, not so much in the needs or desires of the community this time, but in local manufacturing and craft techniques. Based on that research, they designed the tower as a twisted version of a pagoda structure, its structural members spiralling upwards in the manner of a baroque 'monkey ladder' that minimized the amount of material used. They clad the tower with cedar wood they sourced from the forest surrounding the brewery.

The fixtures within the tasting room were all produced by local craftspeople, with whom the Assemble members consulted before they started the project. These include ceramic vessels that were made from local clay and

Assemble's hand-drawn section through the tasting room. The fire pit warms the space. The insulation below the local cedar boards is Firmacell board. The entrance is to the right.

Top: Stools being made in the workshop of local carpenter and sculptor Nobiru San.

Bottom: The hands of the local indigo dyers called Buasiou. They provided this pigment, usually reserved for expensive clothes, for Assemble to use on the tasting room's exterior.

then dyed using traditional techniques, including one that repurposed yeast waste produced during the brewing of the local sake. Japan has a long tradition in both these and other crafts that has emphasized the way in which humble materials can be enriched through minimal but highly skilled interventions of glaze, figuration or pattern. In recent years, new technology has allowed artisans to experiment even further, and the Assemble members who collaborated on this project confessed that they went to the country at least in part to learn from these developments.

KAMIKATZ BREWERY

508
04/05/06

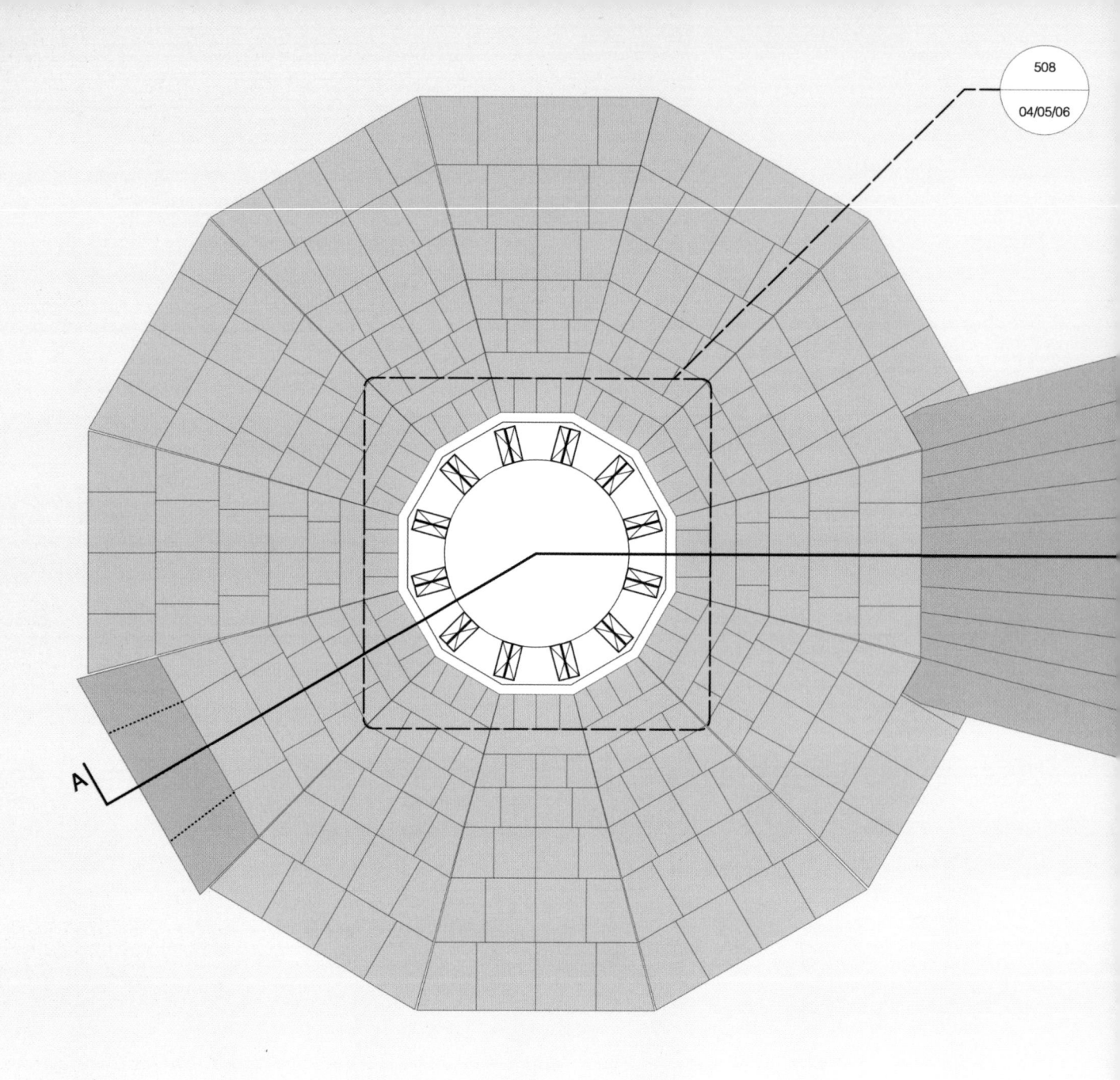

A

A computer section through the top of the tower. It cuts through the timber frame and the pattern of cedar panels below. The skylight in the middle is operable.

A view looking to the top of the finished tasting room. The structure was designed by engineers Structure Workshop in the UK and then handed to local collaborators. It is meant to withstand typhoons.

The fire pit was made by a local, Mr Nakamura, together with Assemble. Made of earth, it strengthens the more it's used.

A view through the entrance into the tasting room. A concrete floor turned out to be necessary to support the torqued structure.

The dyed cedar shingle planks become smaller the higher up they go, both because of the diminishment of surface and to make the tower look taller when seen from below.

KAMIKATZ BREWERY

Another view of the tasting room, looking back down towards the valley.

A view of the finished tasting room from the same perspective as the drawing on page 230. The adjacent structure is a repurposed timber shed that the brewery converted for its operations.

Pottery Assemble members made in the UK and brought with them for use at the brewery in their second residence. The glazing was produced by taking the hot ceramics out of the kiln and dipping them in the liquid yeast of beer waste.

The tasting room to the left and the timber shed used by the brewery to the right.

KAMIKATZ BREWERY

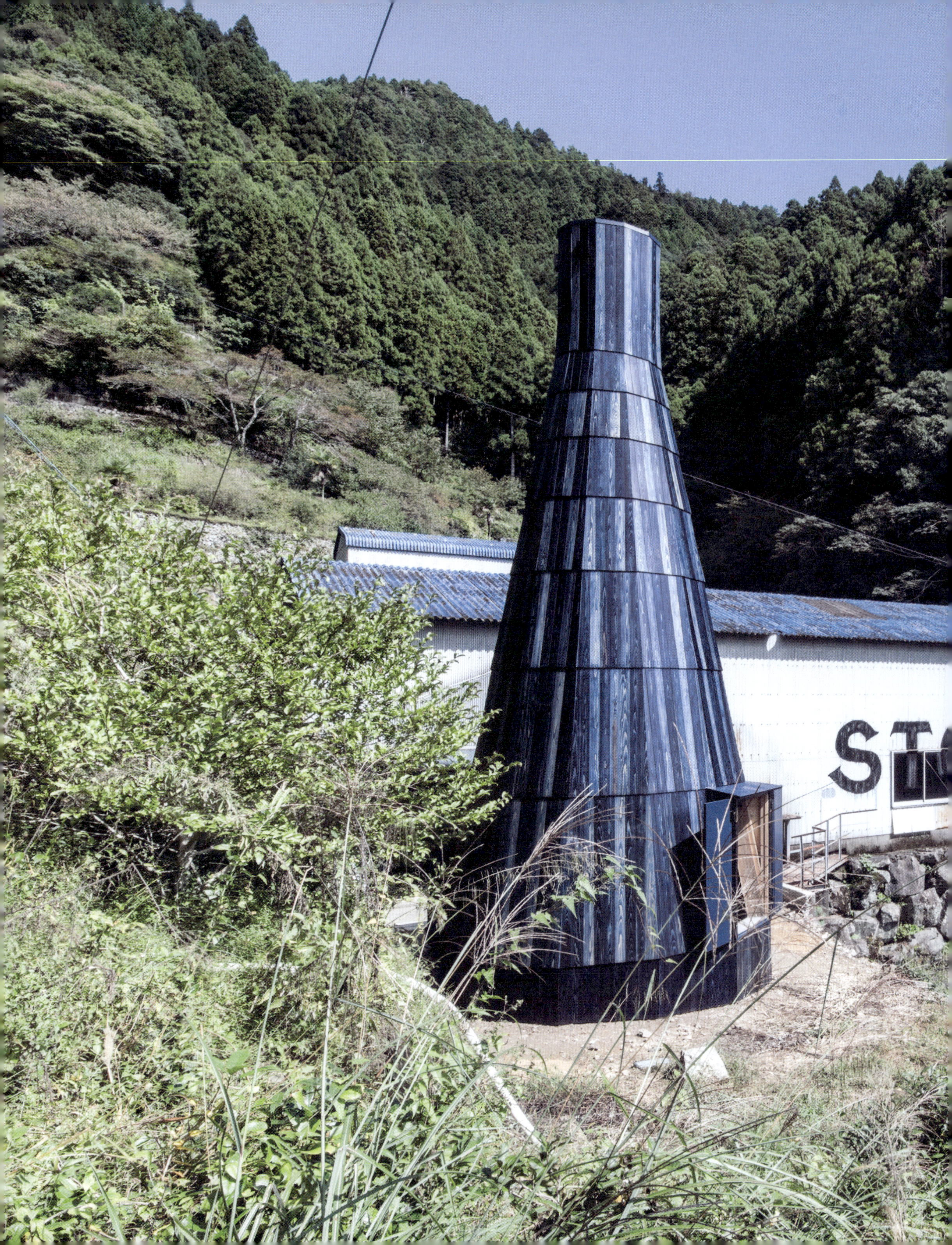

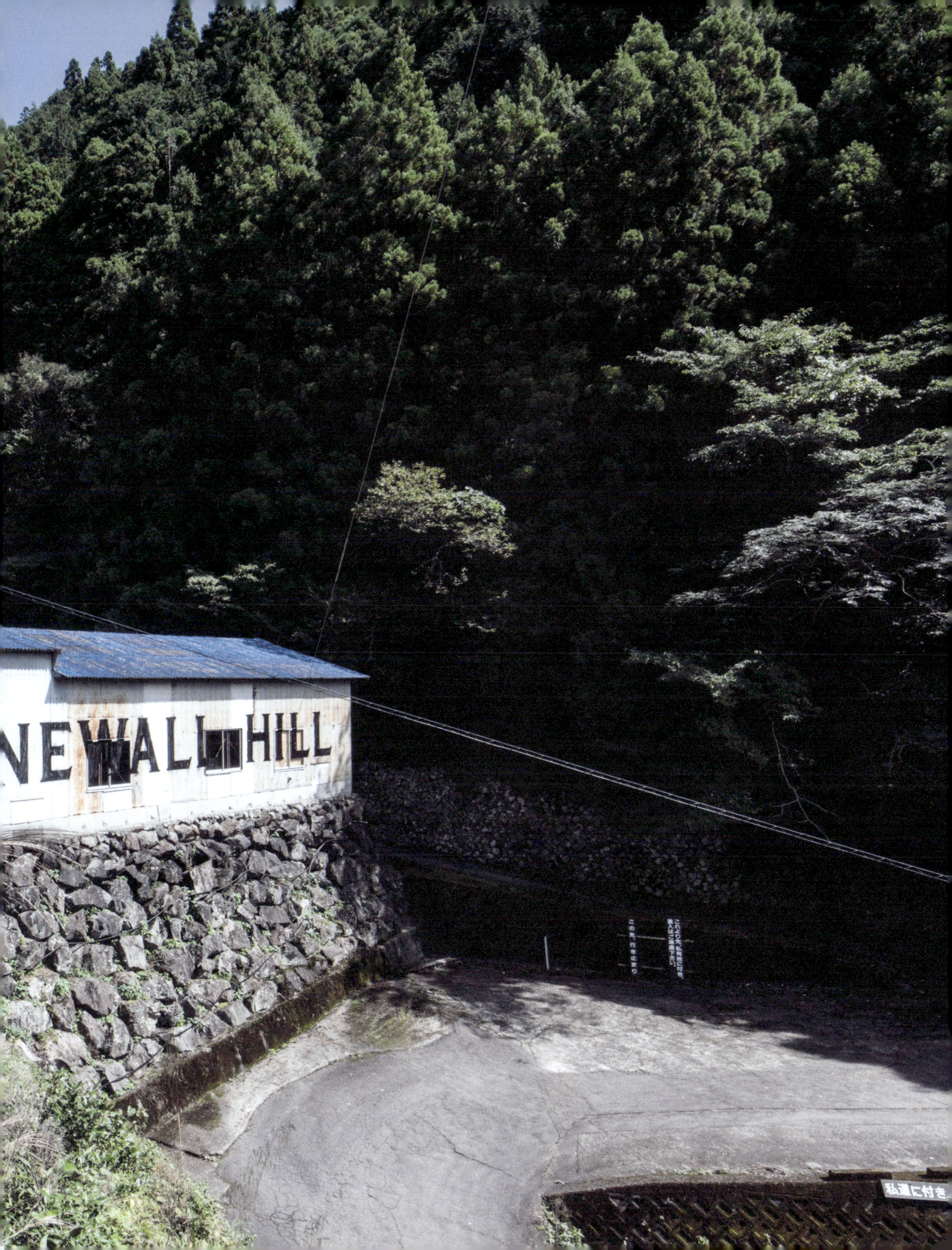
NEWALL HILL
私道に付き

Assemble cut a hole through the existing space at the Material Institute to create access to a courtyard and let in light, leaving the opening rough and unfinished.

MATERIAL INSTITUTE

Textiles are the main focus of the Material Institute in New Orleans, Louisiana, in the USA. The organization is an independent institution located in St. Roch, part of the historic heart of the city's Black community, north-east of the French Quarter. The Institute came about through the work of Kirsha Kaechele, an artist, performer and curator who had lived in the area at the beginning of the millennium. In the aftermath of Hurricane Katrina, she initiated several community-building and strengthening efforts, including a productive garden. After she moved to Australia in 2010 and subsequently married David Walsh, an Australian businessman who had founded the Museum of Old and New Art (MONA) in Tasmania, she often returned to visit and work in New Orleans, looking to found a school that would draw on local arts and craft traditions. She found Assemble and asked them to design a new structure for the proposed institution. While Kaechele was developing the institution, she worked with Assemble to turn a former car repair shop and adjacent lot into an incubator for the activities that would lead to the deployment of the full curriculum of the school. In particular, the team wanted to build on the traditions of making that came out of both the mixed African (and in particular Yoruba), Creole and Caribbean legacies in the city and the elaborate Black Masking Indian suits made annually for the Mardi Gras parade and other social events and rituals.

Assemble member Maria Lisogorskaya went to New Orleans and was impressed by both the energy of the staff involved with the nascent organization, which at that time had no name or clear structure, and the skills she found on site. As a result of the visit, Assemble took on the task of consulting with local makers, designers and members of the community to first figure out exactly what was needed to focus and renew New

The sewing atelier at the Institute, furnished with mainly recycled furniture and equipment.

The Corten steel stairway (previously a pink stairway) connecting the workshop to an adjacent space used for support functions.

Orleans' fabric traditions, and then what the structure of such an effort would need to be. While this kind of exploration was their normal mode of operation, in this case they formalized it into a relationship in which Assemble was responsible for articulating and then helping to start the organization and its curriculum. Assemble had by this time realized that they had developed the expertise necessary to do this kind of work, and have since entered into similar agreements with other such organizations.

What Assemble proposed and MONA funded was a set of courses with a goal, as Lisogorskaya explained to the architecture and design website *Dezeen*, to 'provide space, tools and professional guidance to those who would not have access to those opportunities elsewhere'. She saw it first and foremost as a place 'where students are able to express themselves in a creative and professional way, and are supported to gain financial independence through their craft'. As a model, Assemble and Kaechele both looked towards Black Mountain College, an independent and experimental art school that attracted artists, designers and theoreticians to its site in North Carolina during the 1930s and 1940s.

Assemble accepted the single-storey, concrete block building much as they found it. They had to add some structural elements and clean up surfaces, but their biggest design intervention was to open up three large holes in the exterior surfaces, persuading the contractors to stop once the rough openings had been made. They filled in the openings within these jagged edges with clear panes of glass to create

MATERIAL INSTITUTE

Students using the handloom to weave fabrics.

windows and doors that sport plantings at their base. They also added a small exterior staircase to the adjacent building they incorporated into the Institute and painted it pink. Beyond a few other acts of cleaning and painting, for which they used a palette of colours that recall New Orleans (including dusty green in one part of the ceiling and dull orange for steel beams), they left the space open. Sewing machines, a clothes press, rows of desks and a few mirrors propped against the wall provide the remainder of the Institute's décor.

      In its few years of operation, the Material Institute has come to fully inhabit the space, offering classes and training to local students, some of whom have gone on to obtain formal degrees in fashion, while others use the skills to work in local businesses. The Institute hosts raucous fashion shows that have become community focal points in the manner of the pop-up events Assemble likes to organize. The Institute is also a venue for live music events that range from classical performances of music by Maurice Ravel to appearances by local DJs and rappers. Assemble has worked with local artists to explore new ways of manipulating fabric that combine machine and hand crafting. The rough appearance of the space, with its emphasis on the visible act of opening up and clearing out, emphasizes the idea that anything is possible in this creative place. Lisogorskaya continues to participate in workshops and provide curricular advice. MONA runs a garden and music department as well as the Material Institute and still hopes to build the full new school by further developing its curriculum and activities, partially necessitating the use of adjacent buildings the institution owns.

The Institute builds on local traditions of fabric and costume design that use a great deal of sewn-on decorative elements.

Dress patterns hang in the main space. You can see the mark where Assemble cut out an existing floor to create a taller space.

Dyed fabrics on a stepladder in the courtyard. In the background you can see how Assemble removed a wall to create an outdoor shelter in the courtyard.

244

Top: Students watching a performance at the Institute. They are wearing clothes of their own design and fabrication.

Bottom: One of the elaborate Black Masking Indian suits the students made at the Institute.

The hole from the Institute into the courtyard and the street. Assemble also removed the concrete in front and planted a garden.

MATERIAL INSTITUTE 245

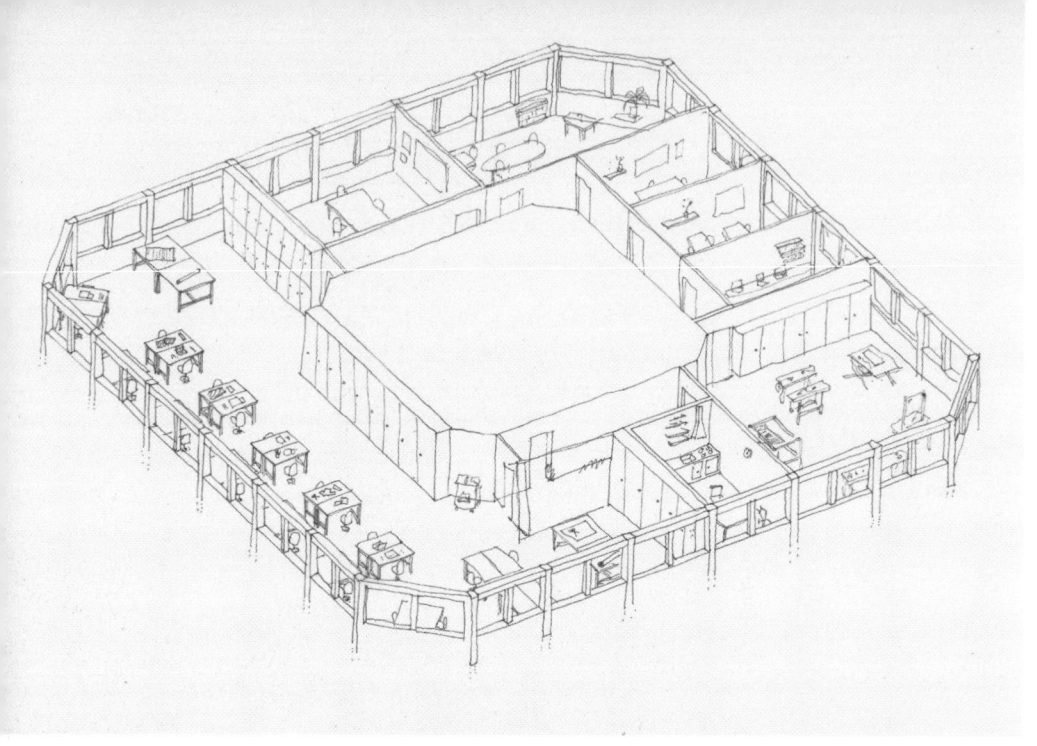

An axonometric sketch of Fabric Floor, with the rest of the building on top of this area cut away to show the division of the space into an array of workshops and communal areas.

FABRIC FLOOR

Mirroring the work in New Orleans, in 2019 Assemble converted one storey of a 1960s-era office building in Brixton, London into a workshop called Fabric Floor. Here they took out all of the material that had covered the floor, ceilings and walls, exposing the concrete and other raw materials underneath. They then divided the space into private offices and studios, as well as central, communal work areas, using the plywood partitions they had also used at Sugarhouse Studios and Blackhorse Workshop. The building and workshop are managed by 3Space, a charity that designs, builds and manages affordable spaces that act as incubators supporting local craft, entrepreneurship and activism, with funding from Lambeth Council. The council provided the equipment necessary for the workshop, and members of Assemble return regularly to teach and give advice.

A sketch of how the large communal space can be used, with furniture designed by Assemble and built at Sugarhouse Studios Bermondsey.

Top: The space as Assemble encountered it. They removed all the existing furniture and the floor and ceiling coverings.

Bottom: The Fabric Floor under construction, showing how Assemble stripped it down to a bare state and added new timber floors.

FABRIC FLOOR

A sewing station with a spectacular view of London.

Top: A board of different logos and dyes with which the Fabric Floor's users experimented.

Bottom: A shirt designed by another of the Fabric Floor's users.

The communal office area serving the Fabric Floor.

FABRIC FLOOR 249

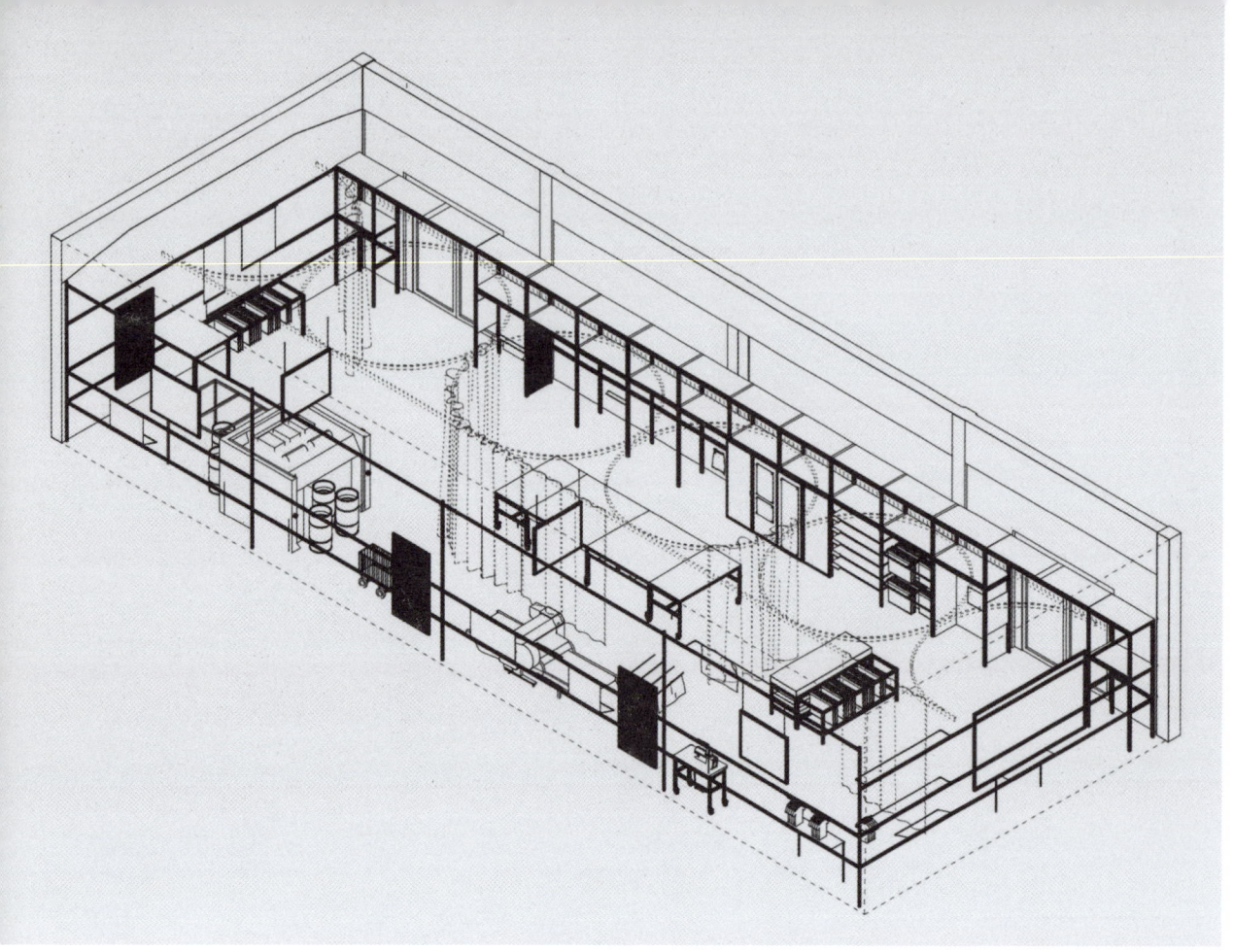

A digital axonometric drawing of the D. H. Chen Foundation Gallery. The extruded aluminium scaffolding system rings the floor, providing storage. Curtains within their perimeter can create separate spaces.

D. H. CHEN FOUNDATION GALLERY

The D. H. Chen Foundation Gallery in Hong Kong is also devoted to fabrics, but from a different perspective. Funded by the eponymous organization, founded in 1970 by Dr Din Hwa Chen, a local industrialist and philanthropist, the gallery is part of the Centre for Heritage, Arts & Textile (CHAT), a museum located in a spinning factory that had been a central part of Chen's operations in the Tsuen Wan area of Hong Kong. CHAT focuses on the history of local garments and production techniques, and the emphasis in this gallery is on how fabric is transformed: various spinning, pressing and weaving implements are on display, along with samples of what was produced on site.

Unlike the rest of CHAT, the gallery Assemble designed leaves the industrial bones of the mill exposed. Within that space, an extruded aluminium profile system that acts as scaffolding for cases and display gives the curators the ability to show, store and work with materials. CHAT holds classes here that show how textiles were and can be sewn or otherwise manipulated to make clothing or coverings, and Assemble worked to have the furnishings they designed show off how they were made by accentuating their components and how they are assembled.

A detail of the storage system, showing some of the many samples the foundation makes available for students and visitors.

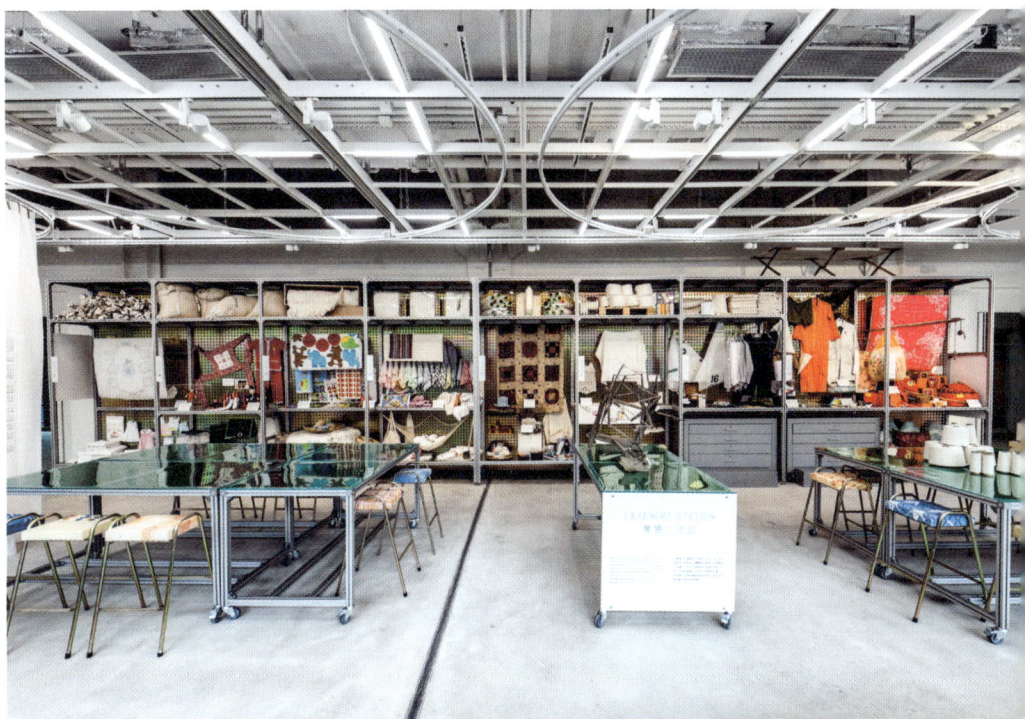

Top: One of the operable curtains. This one also acts as a sign at the entrance of the gallery.

Bottom: A view of the main space with the scaffolding storage system at the back. You can see the curtain rails at the top and the workshop tables in the foreground.

D. H. CHEN FOUNDATION GALLERY

Top: Children play with knotted sculptures in the gallery.

Bottom: Along the walls, Assemble created displays that highlight D. H. Chen's company history. They also show some of the original sewing and fabrication machinery.

252

Looking down the length of the gallery; the storage wall is to the left, the displays to the right, and the space has been opened up without any curtains suspended from the rails.

D. H. CHEN FOUNDATION GALLERY

2. Raw Earth Brick

Assemble made a series of sketches to show how they hoped to use locally mined materials to create structures within the old shed building they were renovating for LUMA.

ATELIER LUMA

The most elaborate of the workshops Assemble has designed is for LUMA, a foundation in Arles, France, with a mission to combine the display and production of contemporary art with design, sustainable agriculture and the economic rejuvenation of the Camargue area. Initiated and funded by the Swiss philanthropist Maja Hoffmann, who had grown up partially in the area while her father (co-founder of the World Wildlife Fund) set up a research facility, LUMA took over a former rail depot and repair yard on the edge of the UNESCO-protected Roman-era centre of the city in 2013.

The focal point of the 11-hectare (27-acre) LUMA campus is a twelve-storey set of intertwined, metal-clad towers that twist their way out of the ground designed by architect Frank Gehry. Most of the other industrial sheds on the campus, which house galleries and workshops as well as ancillary spaces, have been renovated by the American architect Annabelle Selldorf, in a manner that opens and cleans up the buildings with a minimal palette of new materials and forms.

In 2019, Assemble, along with the Belgian firm BC Architects, who have a hybrid practice that mixes design, teaching and material research, began working with Atelier LUMA on the design of their new workspace. Headed by Jan Boelen, a Belgian curator and educator, Atelier LUMA brings together scientists, designers and material experts to figure out how what is left over from the productive uses of the River

Chaining, Laminated Timber
Lintel, Laminated Timber
Beam, Laminated Timber
Structural Wall, Raw Earth Brick
Balustrade, Wood
Reinforcement Beam, Steel

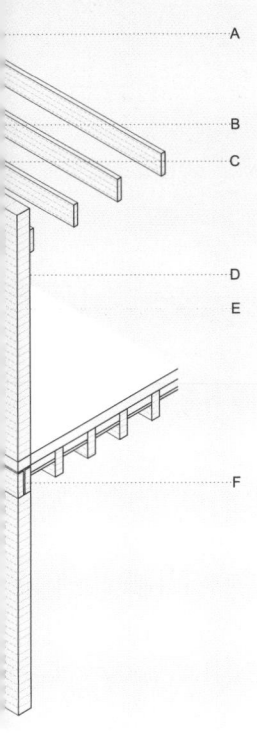

8. Indigo Wood Stain

A. Staining, Indigo Dye
B. Railing, Metal
C. Floor, Wood
D. Structure, Wood
E. Footing, Metal

A digital axonometric Assemble produced with BC Architects to show how they would combine laminated timber and earth bricks to create the gallery.

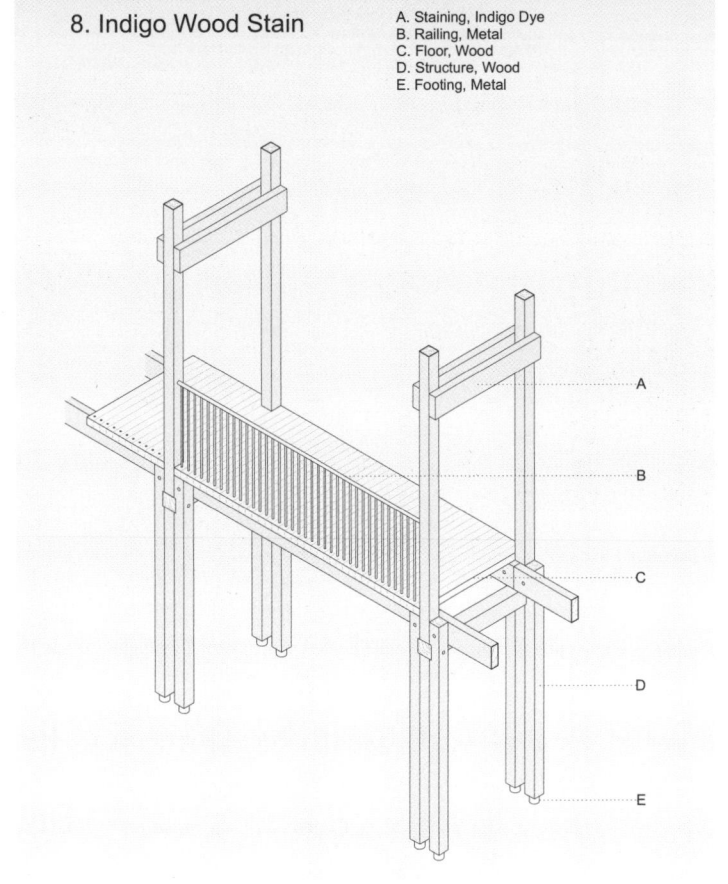

Another digital axonometric drawing concentrating on the wood construction.

Assemble's model of the whole Atelier LUMA project, seen from above with the roof removed so that the various spaces inside are visible.

Rhône delta can be repurposed for construction. The former electric workshop where Hoffmann foresaw the Atelier building was largely a ruin; she wanted the design to highlight how agricultural waste and locally available dirt or clay could be used to create new buildings. The Atelier was thus meant to be a workshop that would use its own construction as a test case for research and development of such materials.

In Arles, Assemble not only met with the team of BC Architects and Atelier LUMA employees that was already in place doing research at LUMA, but also accompanied them on trips to fields and factories in the surrounding areas. The design of the Atelier then proceeded through a series of interactive workshops in which the testing of these materials as building blocks was as much part of the design process as considerations of spatial organization or structure.

The first level of design Assemble had to engage in was figuring out how to stabilize and insulate the structure. That meant replacing the tiles on the roof and adding insulation to the building, and they took care to mimic the original form while opening up the existing skylights to bathe the interior with light. They used the salvaged tiles from what was left of the original roof covering as part of the aggregate for a new terrazzo floor.

ATELIER LUMA

Near the town of Vallabrix where Assemble mined some of the material for its pigments. It shows the distinctive red colouring of the local soil.

An early stage compression test conducted by BC Architects of different clays the designers wanted to use in the project.

Within this building, which was finished on the outside using the lime technique common in the area, Assemble constructed a secondary structure made out of timber with rice straw insulation. These new walls help insulate the building's thick stone envelope, and shape a series of functional spaces within the open volume. The central one of these – as in most of the workshops Assemble have designed – is a two-storey, light-filled and open room. It is intended for exhibitions, but also acts as a core for the array of offices, laboratories and workshops that line it on all sides. Wood lintels frame the openings but there are few other visible details. The design of this new structure is minimal and monolithic, emphasizing the connection not just to the industrial nature of the campus, but to the architecture of heavy, shade-giving walls that define Arles' historic character.

To articulate the simple framework, Assemble concentrated on developing fixtures that tried out new ways of upcycling agricultural waste. Door handles were made out of a product derived from local salt. Wall and acoustical panels were produced by pressing together what remained of sunflowers after their seeds were harvested. Some of the tiles used local clay and were co-developed by BC Architects and LUMA, while also building on the techniques Assemble had developed at the Granby Workshop. LUMA investigated algae plastic and paints. Algae is also used to filter the wastewater in the building. Salt that LUMA obtained from evaporative ponds in the Camargue, and which had already been used on the inside of the Gehry building, was also put to use here. Overall, more

A similar test on local stones to determine how they could be used.

than twenty materials made from the leftovers of the area's agricultural industry helped build the Atelier.

Many of the test samples for the construction, along with the materials and results of current experiments, are on display in a long, two-storey gallery that runs the full length of one of the building's long facades. Here Assemble designed a framework in their favourite blue (here produced with local indigo) to support balconies of unpainted timber pieces. In the rear, a completely open and raw space is outfitted to be used for lectures and conferences, but also for performances.

What Assemble did at LUMA was to show an alternative to either the kind of expressive new building that Gehry is so good at designing, or the kind of reactive Minimalism in which most of Selldorf's renovations on the campus were carried out. While Gehry's work points the way to a shiny future where decomposed building blocks are stacked and twirled into something resolutely new, the highly refined Selldorf designs seek to inhabit the old only in the most respectful manner.

The Atelier, on the other hand, goes back to basics, both formally and materially. It accepts and accentuates the buildings as they were, leaving their raw nature on view as much as possible. It then inserts forms that are resolutely new

Materials being tested at a local workshop, with samples of the different lime and plaster wall coverings the group explored using.

The finished facade uses chunky fragments of the ceramic tile from the old roof to create a course render.

and abstract, but builds them out of the very stuff that makes up the local landscape. The new forms appear primitive because of their lack of detailing – no cornices or base boards on the walls, no mouldings anywhere – but directly refer to the stone walls of Arles. Within that framework, the designers have worked to make the spaces as simple, open and flexible as possible, while at the same time giving them a strong character that belies the messiness of the workshops they house. The small details of door handles, wall boards and tiles, along with the terrazzo tile and the rammed earth walls, together shape that atmosphere of being both new and ancient, and act as visible reminders of the ingenuity at work within the spaces.

What makes all of this cohere is the maturity of Assemble's design vision. Having worked for over a decade as a more or less stable team, and having gained experience on a wide variety of projects, the architects were able not only to coordinate and produce a larger structure, but also to carry out the design with a sense of proportion and a sequencing of rooms that makes everything seem larger and more generous than it really is – a quality that also lies at the heart of Gehry's best designs.

The techniques that Assemble and Atelier LUMA came up with and continue to perfect can be used in other applications. The concentration now is on how these

The new galvanized door to the Atelier that allows access of larger material and equipment.

A view into the main two-storey space at the heart of Atelier LUMA.

▶

ATELIER LUMA 259

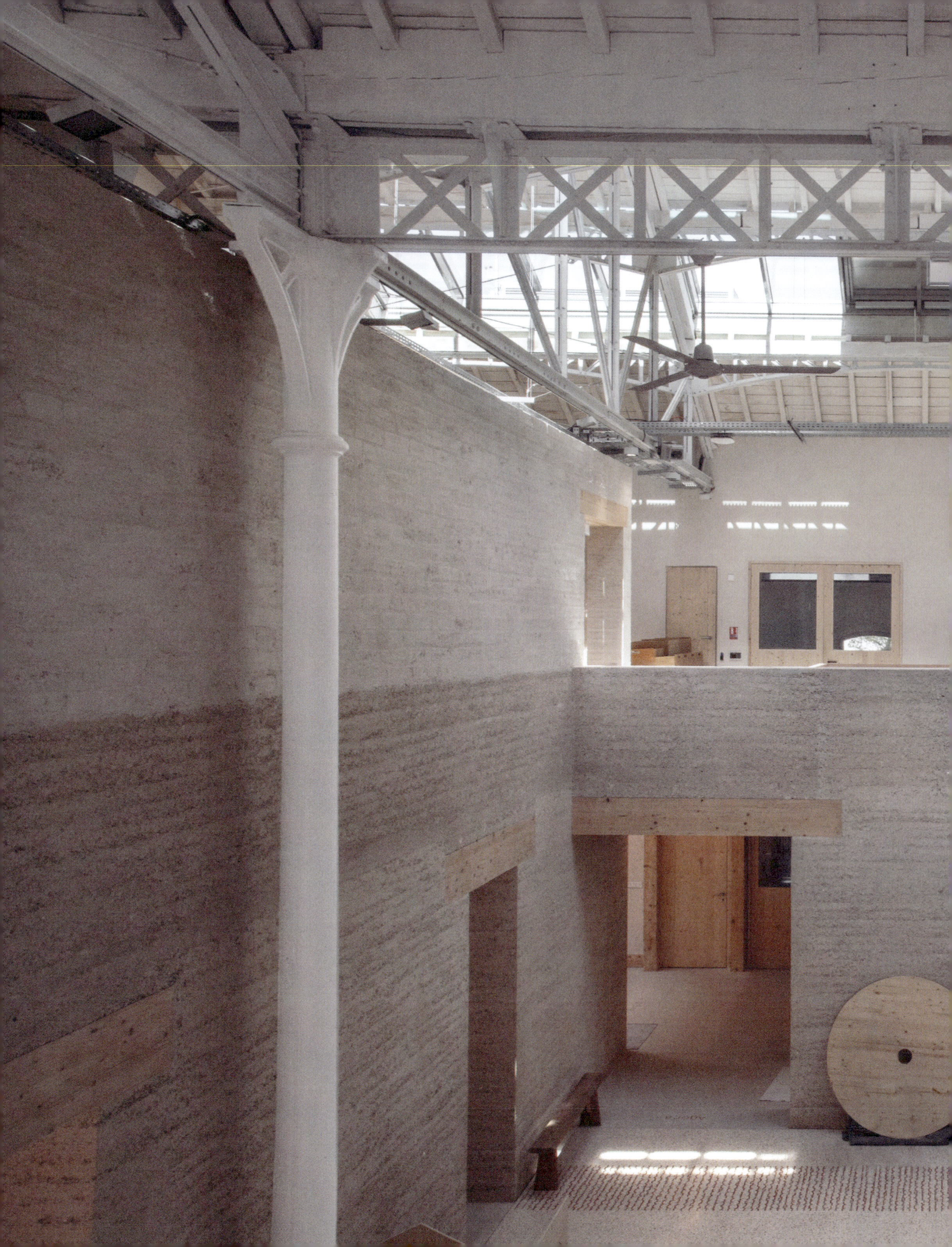

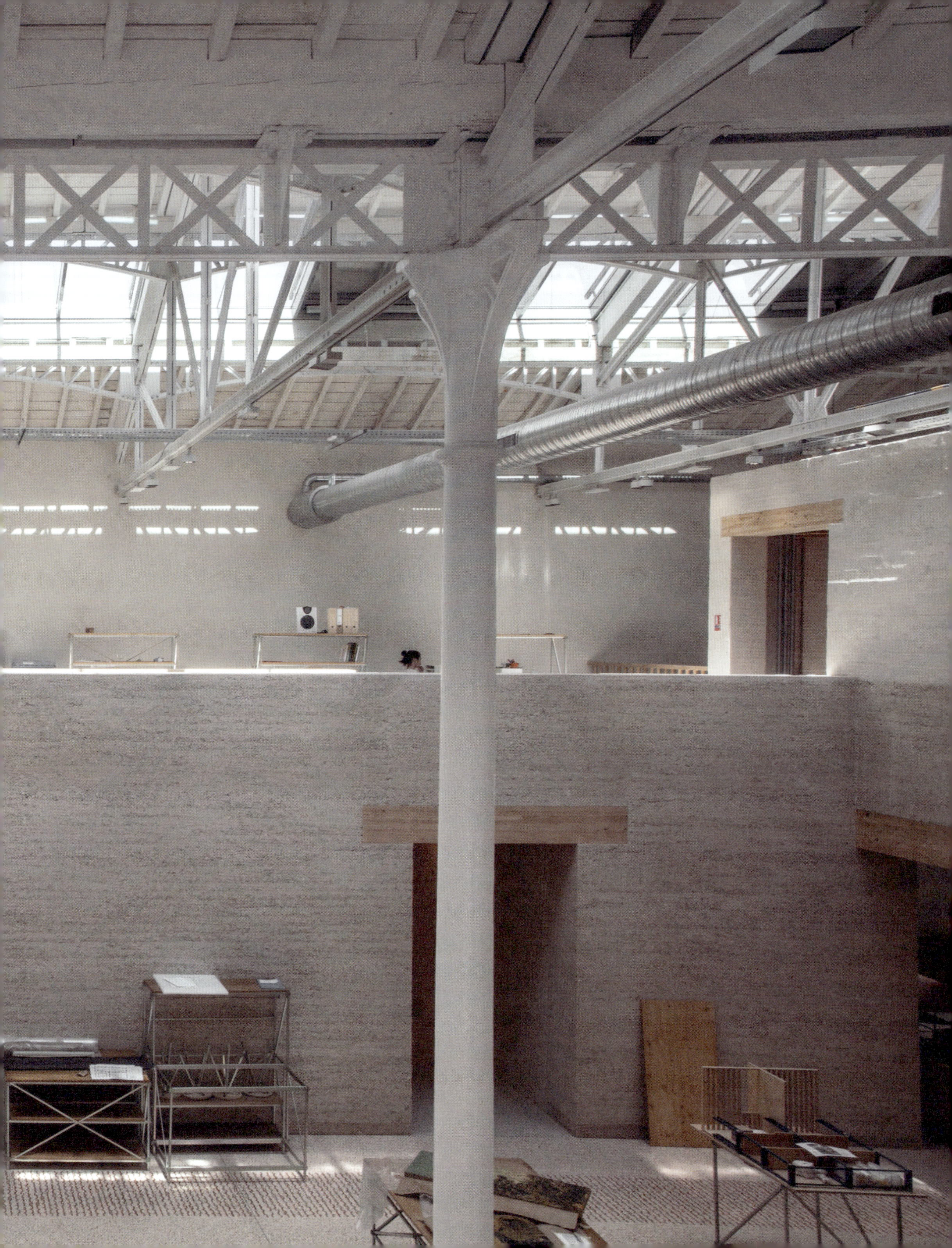

The timber structure in the gallery space creates a mezzanine level with workshops below.

The Atelier's new floor is a terrazzo that includes crushed pieces of the original roof tiles.

experiments can be scaled up, and the conundrum the organization is facing is much the same as what Assemble has confronted as they have grown: how to take an artisanal and experimental mode of making and develop it to work in a manner that accepts the economic and social realities in which Atelier LUMA and Assemble are both operating.

Top: A view across the mezzanine of the main space in which the compressed earth walls are visible along with the reclad roof.

Bottom: One of the offices, with the walls rendered in a local clay rubble and the new timber ceiling exposed.

ATELIER LUMA

Assemble designed a light shaded pergola for one of the outside walls. The planting is by planting designer Piet Oudolf.

The Atelier gallery with its timber structure to the right. Assemble dyed the structural members of this element using local plant material.

The main, double-height space in use as a gallery exhibiting the design of the Atelier. Assemble added wood timbers to frame openings both in the existing structure and the new walls.

ATELIER LUMA 265

Clay slip being poured into Armitage Shanks' toilet moulds to make miniature plaster models at Sugarhouse Studios Bermondsey; a way for Assemble to test different ways of marbling the material.

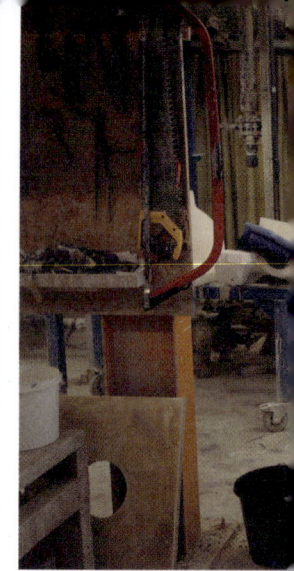

ARMITAGE SHANKS The designers had already made other forays in that direction. In 2017, they visited the toilet manufacturer Armitage Shanks and were invited to work with their moulds. Assemble took what they learned back to their workshop and came up with versions of the item that incorporated the marbling methods developed at Yardhouse and Granby Workshop.

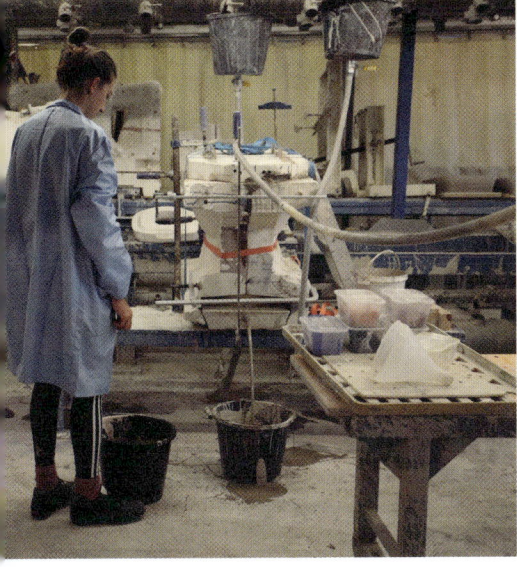

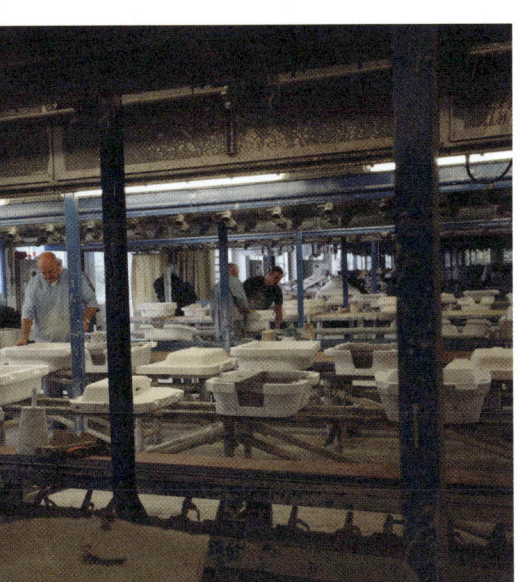

Top: Collaborator Isabel Farchy casting toilets using bench moulds at the Armitage Shanks factory.

Bottom: A broader view of the factory with workers checking finished toilets.

Top: Clay being poured into a mould at the factory to test materials.

Bottom: Assemble then attempted to build a full-scale toilet at Sugarhouse Studios Bermondsey based on their experiments.

ARMITAGE SHANKS

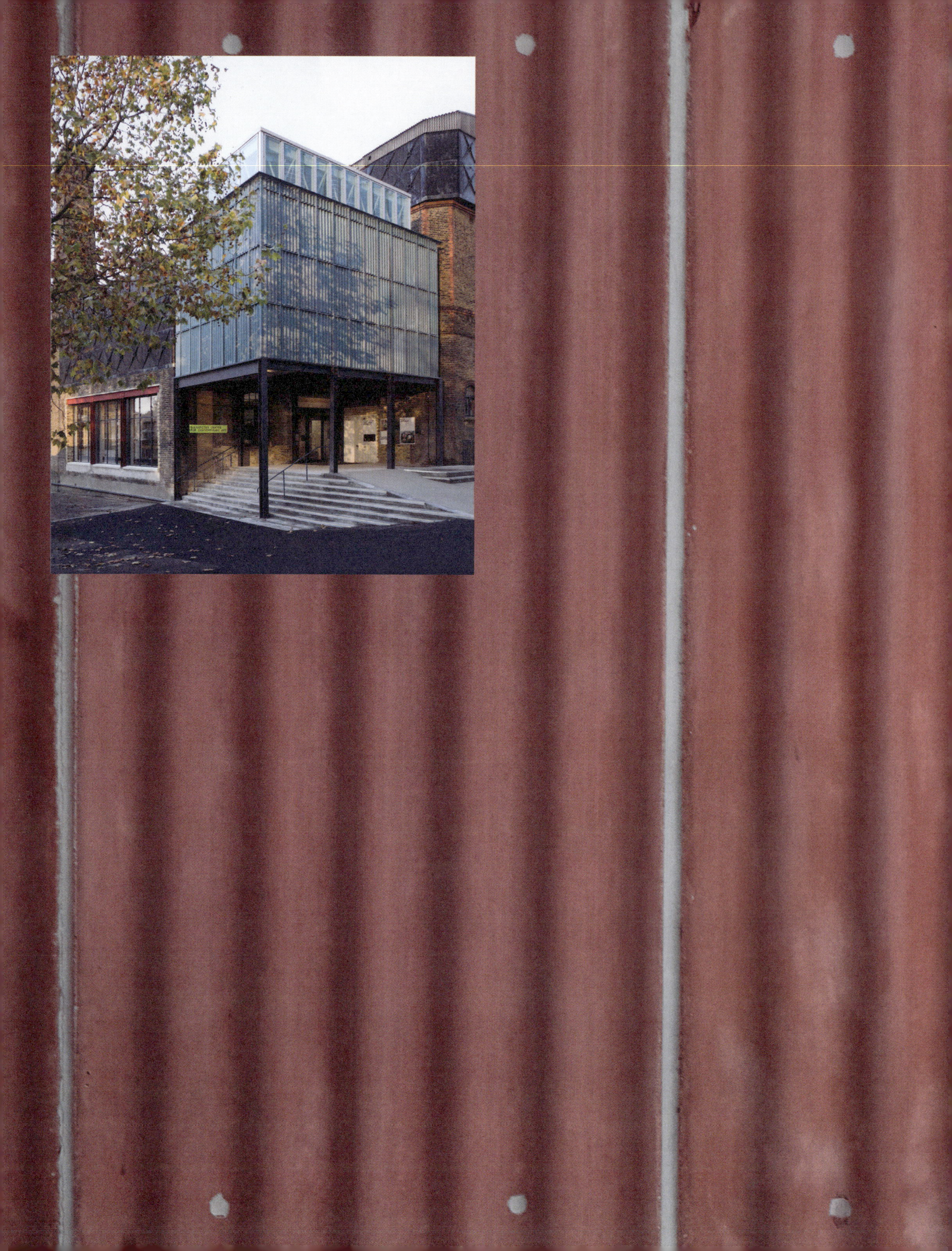

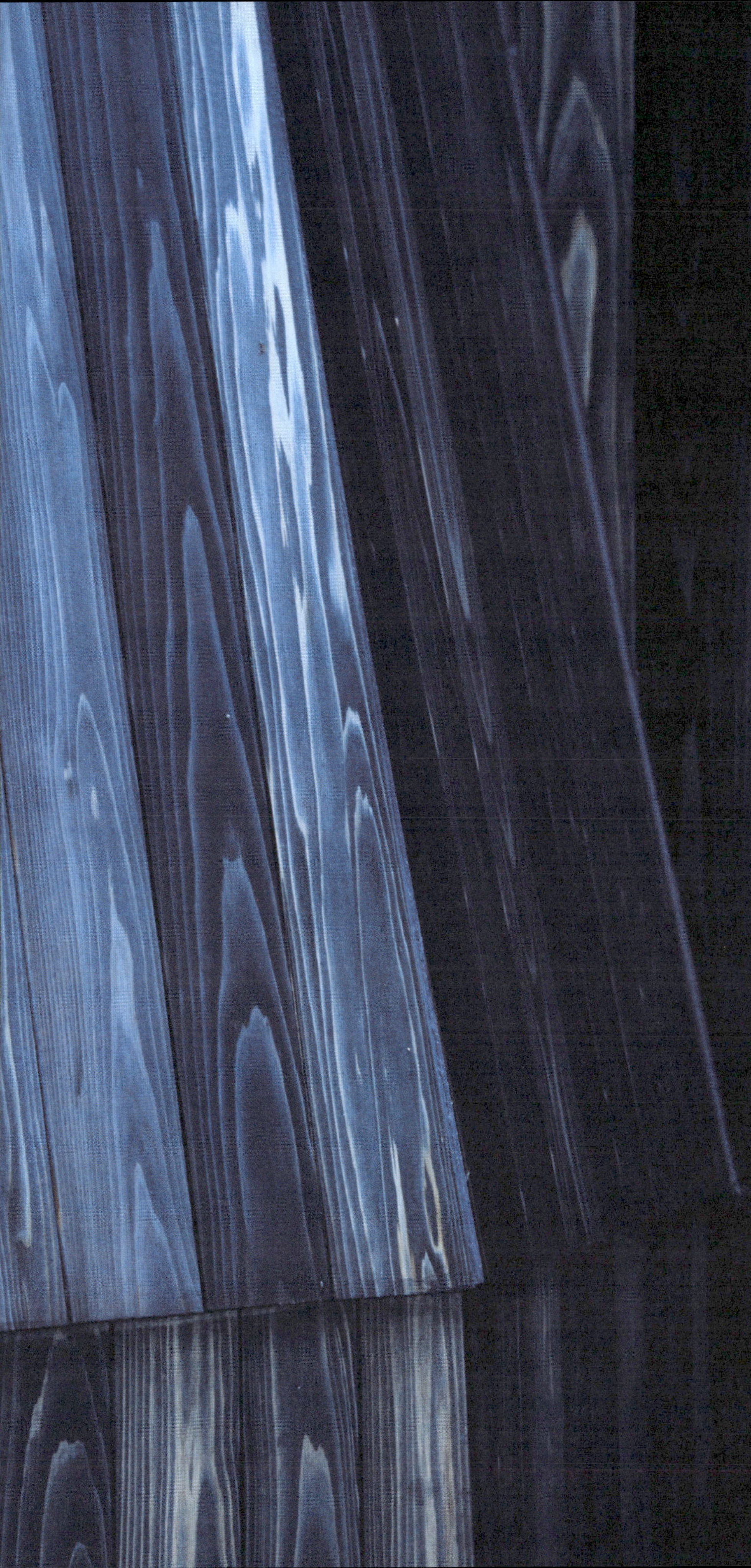

TRIANGLE CHAIRS (See PG276)

6

Showing Off

From the very beginning of its practice, Assemble has seen its task as activating change for communities through actions in the built environment. They have done so through their work on the design of buildings and environments, though, as the preceding will have made clear, they have done so sparingly. They have also created installations that resemble and have been awarded as works of art, participated in performances, done research and development in collaboration with both experts and inhabitants of their project areas, and increasingly worked at the level of processes, acting as institutional change agents and even initiators, more than as designers. Weaving itself through much of this activity has been their interest in a kind of critical show-and-tell in the form of exhibitions, which in turn has led to a line of standalone showcases of both their own and other people's work.

The strong concentration on exhibitions, of which the group has curated, co-curated or designed over twenty so far, also comes out of their initial strategy of architecture

The Lina Bo Bardi: Together exhibition in Paris – see page 274.

For a retrospective exhibition of Assemble's projects at Architecturzentrum Wien (Vienna Architecture Centre – see page 286), Assemble showed the tiles they made for Yardhouse at Sugarhouse Studios Stratford, along with a full-scale section of the OTOProjects wall.

271

The Lina Bo Bardi: Together exhibition as it was installed at ArkDes museum in Stockholm.

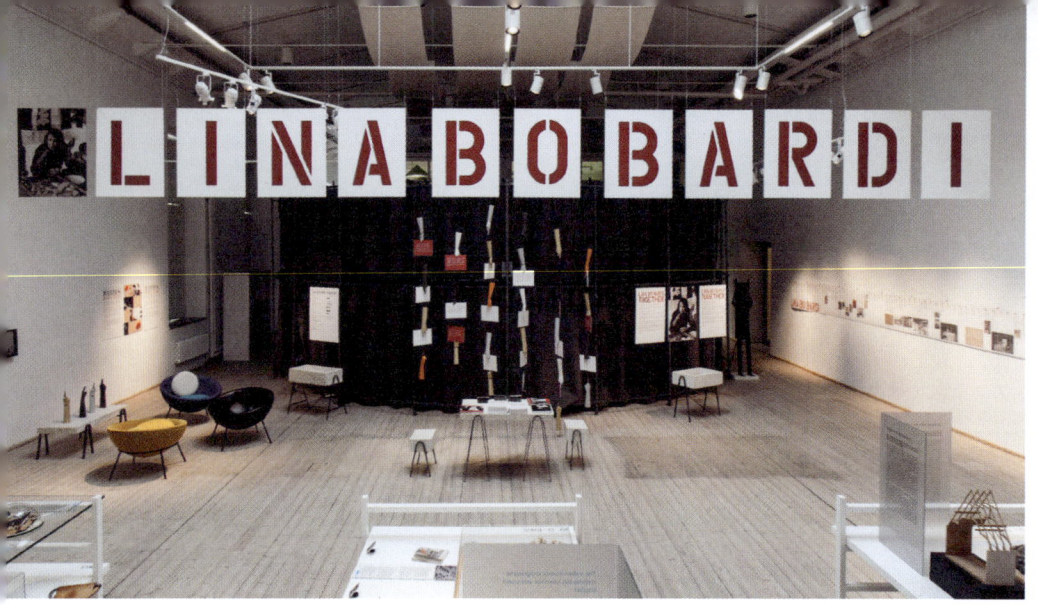

The exhibition on show at the Deutsches Architektur Zentrum (German Architecture Centre – DAZ) in Berlin.

in a theatrical mode. Their first impulse, when they were still students at Cambridge University, was to put on a show, both to exhibit their own craft and creativity, and to enliven and celebrate what they were putting on display. They made stages for human performance and play, finding ways that their forms and colours could afford different forms of action and interaction among audience and performers. Along the way, they often blurred the lines between those two.

Over time, the loose group of aspiring architects became a more formal grouping that began to resemble an architecture firm, but never quite became one. Instead, it has remained a team that collectively chooses projects both for the way they draw on their acquired skills and knowledge, and for the impact they can have in communities. In that process, they have found that exhibiting art, architecture, furniture or other products of human making is an extension of their early theatrical acts. The exhibits let them enact projects within an institutional framework, borrowing the walls, floors and ceiling of the buildings in which the shows take place. They also rely on the ability of the museum or other organization to draw attention and visitors while giving the displays the curatorial rigour and cultural weight that such monuments to and of culture bring with them. In other words, Assemble draw on the long history of exhibitions to create architecture that both shows off and explains within a framework in which it will find a receptive audience.

They are not the only design collective that does this. A comparison with the Belgian design collective Rotor is illuminating, as they are perhaps the closest analogue to what Assemble is doing. A collaboration among architects, activists and historians, the group has been around for roughly the same amount of time as Assemble, and has curated, designed and produced displays, engaged in research, and undertaken design projects. A similar path has been taken by such entities as the slightly older group

Experimenting with casting the 'papercrete' display cases designed for the exhibition.

Some of Assemble's sketches for the exhibition's display cases.

Crimson Historians & Urbanists in Rotterdam, the Netherlands, and by architect Teddy Cruz in the USA.

The movement towards design firms making exhibitions, however, was part of the broadening of the architecture discipline around the turn of the century. It was heralded by the research and development work of the Dutch firm OMA during the 1990s, but its proximate cause was the realization by many architects that the process of building had become so complex, and so restricted by social, economic and regulatory codes, that it was difficult to effect the kind of critical change they hoped for in permanent structures. Architects also began to notice the effect that artists had been achieving, since the 1970s, through the creation of site-specific installations and by recasting themselves as activists. During the 1990s, many artists began working increasingly in the realm of architecture. At the same time that Assemble was moving towards a more open interpretation of what it meant to be an architect, for instance, artists Theaster Gates (who trained in urban design) and Tyree Guyton, both based in the USA, were essentially acting as architects while also exhibiting their work on site and in other venues. The Albanian artist Edi Rama, after becoming mayor of the capital city Tirana in 2000 and then President of Albania in 2013, treated first the city and then the country like the largest open air architecture exhibition in the world, commissioning installations and interventions – like painting whole blocks of buildings – that drastically changed his country.

Assemble picked up on these trends and, more interestingly, adapted some of those radical endeavours to more traditional environments. Perhaps their training at an elite university had something to do with that, but they also soon realized that by fitting their work into museums, galleries and art fairs, they could have a great deal of impact with limited means. By now the group has developed a strong specialization in what you might think of as traditional exhibition design, although their work here always has a critical edge.

The cast concrete furniture Assemble designed to display some of the work was meant to evoke Lina Bo Bardi's own designs.

The Lina Bo Bardi: Together exhibition installed at Arcam in Amsterdam.

LINA BO BARDI: TOGETHER

The project that first brought Assemble into this area was an exhibition of the work of the Brazilian architect Lina Bo Bardi that they were asked to design right when they were starting out in 2011. The project was initiated by the independent curator Noemí Blager, who had become fascinated not only by the quality of Bo Bardi's work – an expressive Modernism often existing within or emerging from existing buildings – and the fact that she was a rare successful woman architect in the period immediately after the Second World War, but also by the fact that she extended her work into collaborations with craftspeople and was a political activist as well.

Blager had already decided to work with the architect and artist Madelon Vriesendorp, who had been one of OMA's co-founders, and reached out to the architecture critic Rowan Moore to find architects who could help her further develop the project. Moore recommended Assemble based on The Cineroleum and Folly for a Flyover, the only projects they had completed at the time.

'This exhibition really opened up a whole new field for us,' recalls Jane Hall. 'I had heard of Bo Bardi, but so little was known about her at the time. She wound up being the subject of my PhD dissertation.' 'It became our testing ground for materials and forms, where we were free to experiment, but were inspired by what she had already done,' adds Joe Halligan. 'I just found them to be terribly intelligent, and playful at the same time,' says Blager. 'It turned out be exactly what the project needed.'

Blager had envisioned the exhibition as a travelling show, with the first venue in London in 2012 at the British Council gallery. Eventually, Assemble designed versions for Vienna, Basel, Paris, Stockholm, Amsterdam, Berlin, Milan, Treviso, Chicago, Miami and São Paulo. At every stop they used

To contain the films and slides that were shown as part of the Bo Bardi exhibition, Assemble designed a curtain made out of a corrugated sheet installed here at the British Council gallery in London.

The exhibition installed at the Graham Foundation in Chicago.

some of the same material, but also created new furniture and display elements. Films commissioned by Blager from artist and filmmaker Tapio Snellman were projected onto the exhibition's most striking elements: curving screens whose shapes evoked some of Bo Bardi's more playful gestures. Assemble also created rectangular dividers on which the public could see photographs the curator commissioned from Ioana Marinescu.

Vriesendorp added her own sculptures, inspired by Bo Bardi, and Assemble organized all of these elements into a flexible arrangement that could be adapted at each venue. While the original layout was organic in its shape and defined by curtains along the edges, for instance, the display in Paris showed the material in a rectangular space and the one in Stockholm in a circle. The felt curtains were hung in pleats from a combination of either an edited scaffolding system or wall brackets that could be attached to the floor, ceiling or wall of almost every space in which the exhibition unfolded. They could also be left out where they were not necessary.

The other major elements Assemble contributed were display tables and boxes that they cast using a kind of concrete called 'snowcrete', based on a lightweight and whitish cement, to which they added a vermiculite aggregate and then hand-hammered to give it a rough surface. These were held up with splayed metal legs, which also supported display panels for the commissioned photographs and drawing reproductions. Assemble also designed and fabricated lightweight furniture for visitors to sit on, along with placing some of Bo Bardi's own chairs in the exhibition. 'It was incredible to see them react to and take on what Bo Bardi had designed,' says Blager, 'and then even better to see them figure out how to actually make it themselves.' Most of the pieces were fabricated either on site or at Sugarhouse Studios. Vriesendorp also collaborated with children in a workshop in Brazil to make some of the objects on display.

LINA BO BARDI: TOGETHER

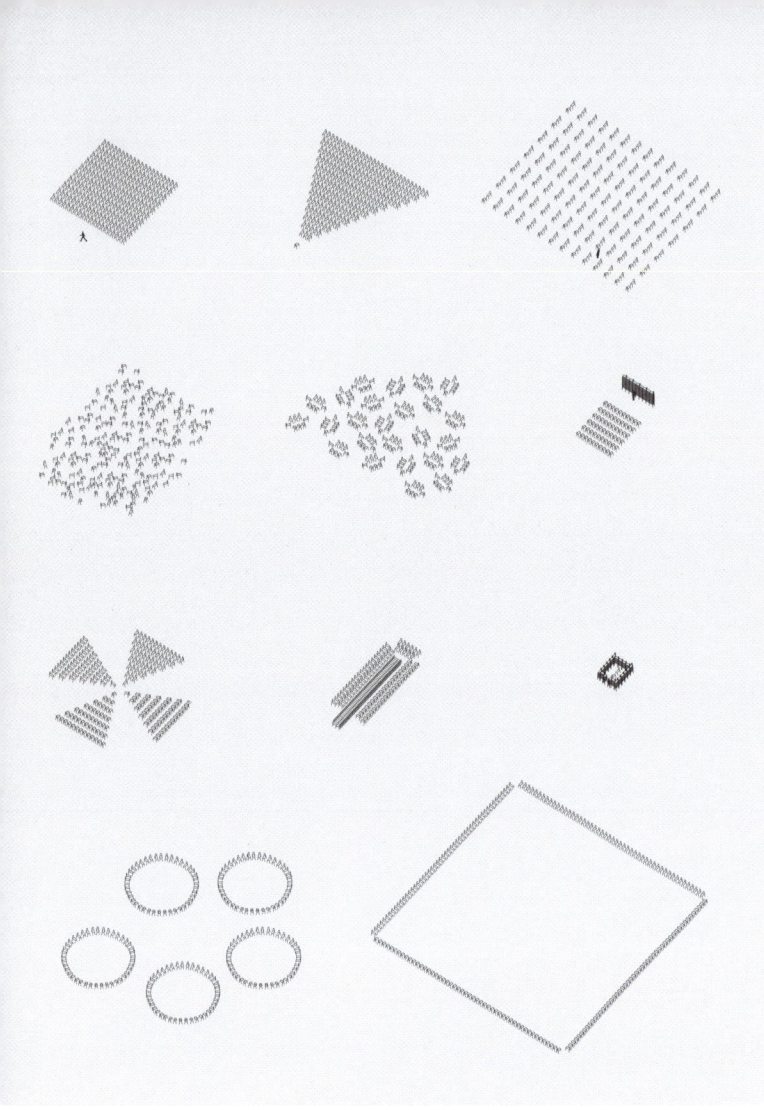

A digital drawing to show how the Triangle Chairs could be arranged in configurations for different social situations and gatherings.

Top: Fabricating the metal structure at Sugarhouse Studios Stratford.

Bottom: The chair's basic structure was designed for ease of fabrication and stacking.

TRIANGLE CHAIRS

The work on the Bo Bardi exhibition led Assemble not only towards other display projects, but also to making furniture that could be used for other purposes. Their Triangle Chairs, produced in 2012 for Clerkenwell Design Week, were part of that research. The modular, triangular metal chairs and tables, made at Sugarhouse Studios, were meant to be arranged or even stacked however organizers and users wanted, creating social situations when they were aggregated and singular objects when used by themselves. The plywood seat and back were supported by a metal structure and powder-coated in three different colours so that a variety of colour patterns developed when they were used in groups.

276

The finished, but uncoated chairs at Sugarhouse Studios Stratford, awaiting their final finish.

Top: The chairs' geometry meant that they could be arranged to create smaller and larger social groupings, here in relation to an existing park bench.

Bottom: When not in more formal use, the chairs can be pulled up or away for individual purposes.

TRIANGLE CHAIRS

A spalt wood table made for the Harrow Lowlands project – see p. 280.

Stackable chair designed for Harrow Lowlands featuring recycled tree trunks for the seat.

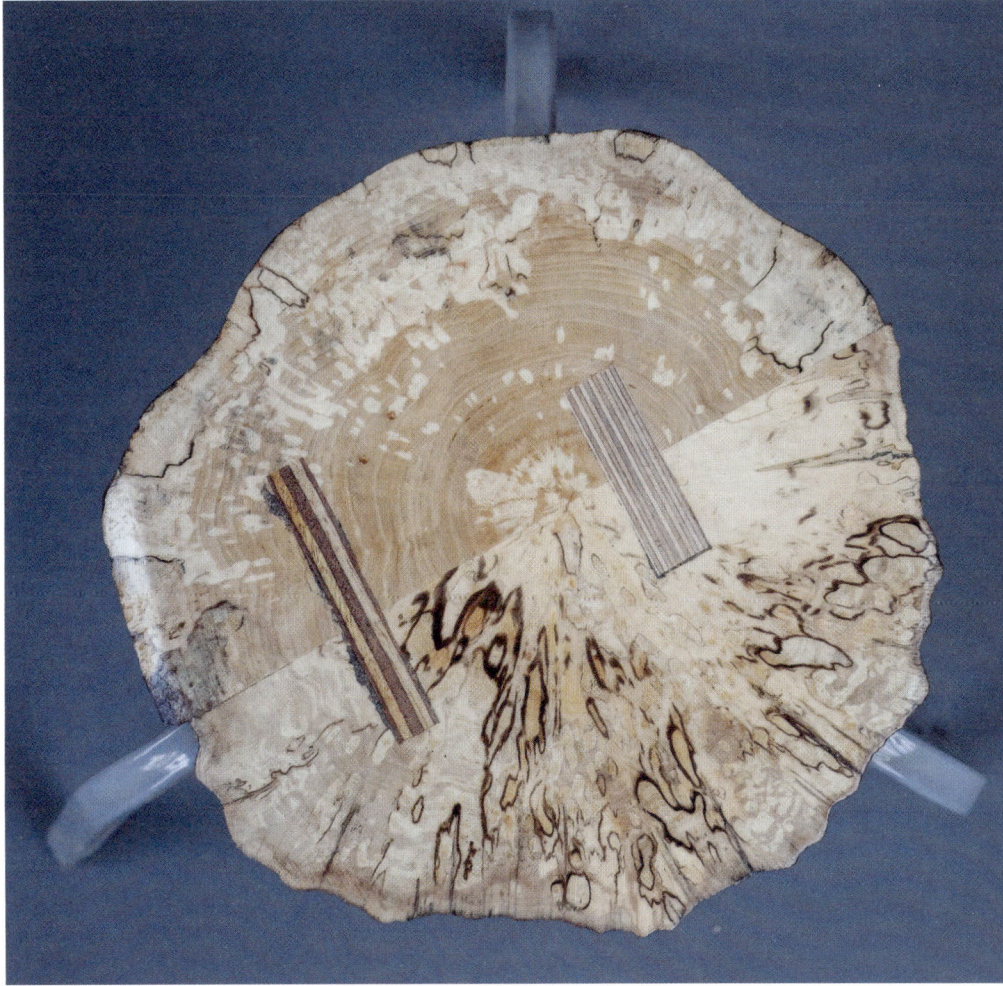

Top: The tree trunk chairs arranged around a table with a found metal base, painted and with added decoration, and a top of recycled timber.

Bottom: A view of the tree trunk stool from above.

TRIANGLE CHAIRS

279

Soft play objects Assemble designed for Harrow Lowlands in the shape of food.

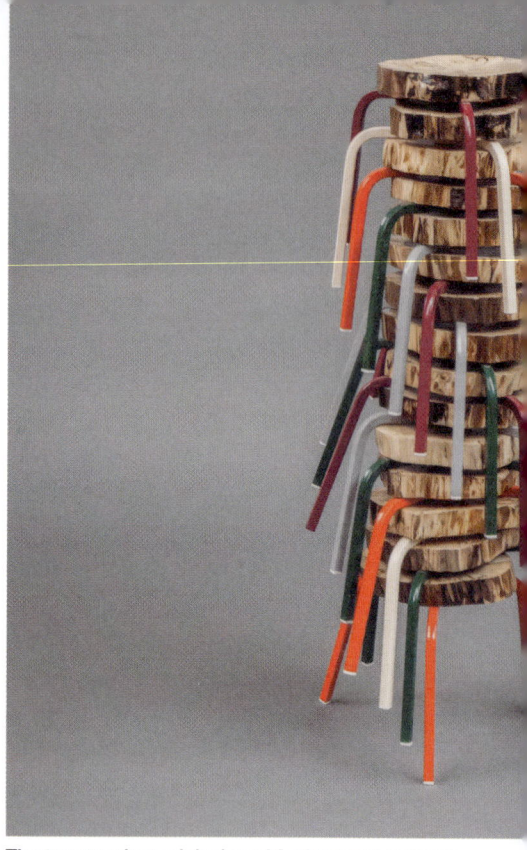

The tree trunk stool designed for Harrow Lowlands were also stackable.

HARROW LOWLANDS

This experiment led to the furniture Assemble designed for the Lowlands Recreation Ground in Harrow, north-west London. Assemble used pieces of tree trunks that had been culled from nearby Epping Forest, combining disparate parts to increase the variety in their patterns, and attached them to metal supports they designed and built at Sugarhouse Studios.

TURNER PRIZE EXHIBITION

The exhibition that brought the most amount of attention, however, was the showroom they created for the Turner Prize Exhibition in 2015. The Turner Prize process involves inviting the shortlisted nominees for the award to create a display of their own work. The 2015 exhibition was the first one the Tate put on in Scotland and took place in an arts venue called Tramway in Glasgow. In this post-industrial space, rather than showing their drawings and models for Granby Four Streets, Assemble built a full-scale model of the shell of one of Granby Four Streets' terraced houses, thus bringing the scale and arrangement of the project inside. The space was finished in a pinkish plaster that was left rough, so that it evoked the brick walls of the project site. Rough wooden furniture, both to display items and to serve as seating, was made out of recycled timber.

In addition, Assemble together with Granby Workshop and external consultants designed products that

A Granby Rock terrazzo mantelpiece for a fireplace being finished in the backyard of one of the houses on Cairns Street.

could later be both employed on site at Granby Four Streets and manufactured for use on other projects. Breaking two standard rules of museum exhibitions, Assemble and their collaborators continued to develop the twenty-seven different products during the run of the show, so that the display was never quite finished, and offered them for sale on a pre-order basis through a catalogue that doubled as a record of their entry.

    The pieces on view included various versions and try-outs of the Granby Workshop tiles, as well as examples of the marbled terrazzo fireplaces they were creating. Plates and other crockery showed how these techniques could be extended to objects of everyday use. Carved newel posts were placed on the wall, both in a straight line and in a diagonal that showed how they could march up the side of a staircase. Assemble also worked with textile artists to develop what could become curtains or other fabric inserts. Samples, bits and pieces of raw material, and failed tests took their place along with the finished projects on display.

    The approach worked on an immediate level, both in terms of securing Assemble the Turner Prize itself, and in obtaining enough orders for the Granby Workshop tiles to formally launch that enterprise. But it also thought big, demonstrating many different ways in which exhibitions can go beyond the usual, white-walled displays of isolated and precious works of art. Within the Tramway space, the designers created a home for their work, and then invited visitors to share that space, as well as their fascinations, research and ways of making. They extended the collection to include products made by others, expanding the notion of who is the creator of a work of art. By blurring the

A detail of Assemble's contribution to the Turner Prize Exhibition at the arts venue Tramway in Glasgow. You can see samples of Granby Workshop tiles, pottery and fireplaces.

boundaries between house and gallery, art and commerce, making and showing, and individual and collective effort, they opened up the museum exhibition structure.

Their approach was not without precedents. If the Turner Prize Exhibition resembled anything it was the kind of period rooms created in many museums in the Western world between the end of the 19th century and the Second World War. These carefully crafted time capsules showed art, artisanal products and architectural elements in an integrated manner. Though most museums abandoned them because of the way they created an often literal barrier between viewers and the display, the period rooms did offer an alternative to the silos of painting, sculpture, craft and architecture that still define most museum organizations. They also showed that art in its broader sense could be a reflection of daily life, not just a record of great deeds or people.

The Tramway exhibit also resembled a furniture or antiques show, its disparate objects stacked together without a clear organizing principle beyond showing off their potential uses to people who might want to integrate them into their lives. Finally, the exhibition showcased a resurgent interest in heavily patterned, shaped and coloured craft, recalling the Arts & Crafts tradition as it was embodied in sites such as the Red House in south-east London, designed by Philip Webb and William Morris, who also designed the interiors and textiles today perhaps most closely associated with the British department store, Liberty.

A view into the exhibition's central space, including some furniture and lamps Assemble also designed for the Granby Four Streets project.

TURNER PRIZE EXHIBITION

283

Top: Furniture designer Robin Day working on a prototype of one of his chairs.

Bottom: An arch that was erected for Queen Victoria's visit to Hughenden Manor in High Wycombe in 1877, which provided inspiration for Assemble's design of the Robin Day exhibition.

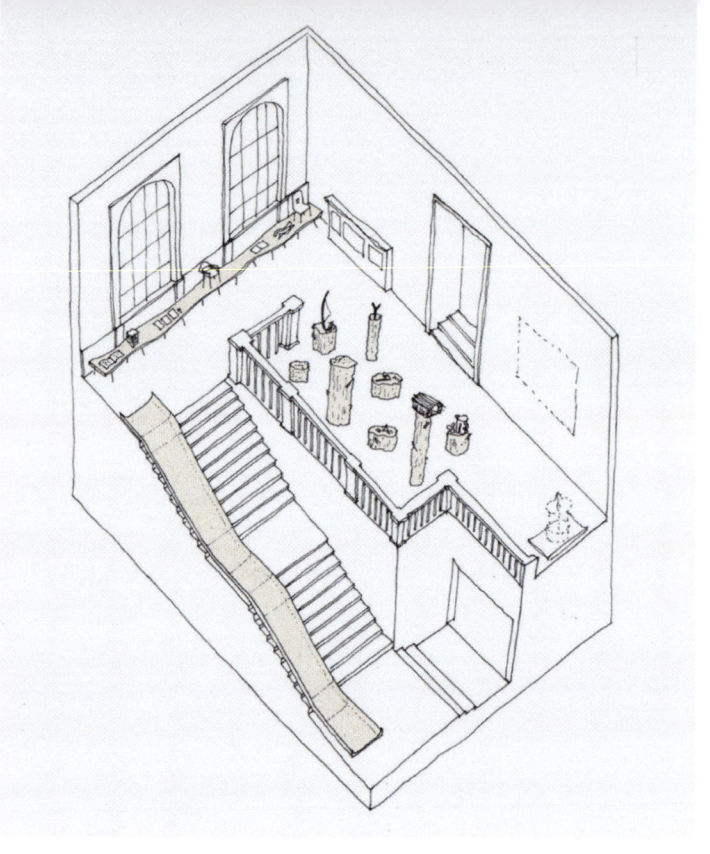

Top: A sketch for the layout of the exhibition at the Victoria & Albert Museum (V&A) in London.

Bottom: Assemble envisioned a series of thin podiums that some objects could straddle, although the curators did not allow this in the end.

ROBIN DAY

All of these historic precedents fed a project that was intended as a social activator as well as a form of communication to a wider public, and which itself became a generator for further Assemble projects. In a direct way, it led curators at museums to the team, and several commissions of exhibitions of a more standard sort came out of the Turner Prize Exhibition. The first of these was mounted in 2016 at the Victoria & Albert Museum (V&A) in London of the work of the furniture designer Robin Day. This was a small and, for Assemble, quite simple display. Highlighting Day's inventiveness with wood, which he used to produce chairs and other everyday objects, Assemble's constructions consisted of wood pedestals at different heights, so that the objects were removed from their association with regular social situations and were elevated in a manner that allowed all their joinery and detailing to be studied.

Day's chairs were raised on pedestals so that their construction was more visible.

Top: Day's archival materials displayed on tables.

Bottom: Differing heights of the wood pedestals create contrasting views of Day's designs.

ROBIN DAY

The sequined sign for the How We Build exhibition recalled Assemble's adaptation of a technique they observed around Sugarhouse Studios Stratford for one of their first signs.

HOW WE BUILD

Much more elaborate, but in many ways also rather conventional, was Assemble's first full retrospective exhibition, How We Build, which they mounted at the Architecturzentrum Wien (Vienna Architecture Centre) in Austria in 2017. Assemble built and curated the display, which consisted largely of 1:1 replicas of elements of their buildings. In addition, they brought samples of some of the pieces they had built, including tests for the fireplaces at Granby Four Streets, a reconstructed part of the exterior wall at Yardhouse, the wall of OTOProjects and the pleated fabric screen for the Bo Bardi exhibition.

At the same time, a pavilion designed by students at a local technical university where two members of the team were teaching at the time was built in the courtyard of the institution, which is housed in a former imperial stables. Using bricks from the local Wienerberger factory, the students made an aedicula by dry stacking the building elements and strapping them together to form four posts. The back and front areas and the whole top were filled in, with spaces between the blocks increasing vertically as the structure grew, to lighten its appearance and weight. More strapped bricks formed the bases for slats of wood, creating benches and chairs placed both on and next to the low stage. Intended for both formal and informal gatherings, the construction evoked such designs as Folly for a Flyover, but here in a blocky form that responded to the stripped-down neoclassical forms all around.

Top: Hand-printed fabrics contained a small display of samples from Granby Workshop.

Bottom: The exhibition featured many photographs of Assemble's work, as well as one of the Granby Workshop fireplace surrounds.

A recreation of the original Tyvek curtain from The Cineroleum, along with a fragment of the cinema's neon sign, a replica of the schedule board and proposals for usher uniforms that didn't materialize.

HOW WE BUILD

287

The workshop at A/D/O as Assemble envisioned it in an early design sketch they showed to the client.

Top: The courtyard in the Brooklyn warehouse area before Assemble went to work.

Bottom: The wooden structure for the wall, recalling that of Yardhouse at Sugarhouse Studios Stratford.

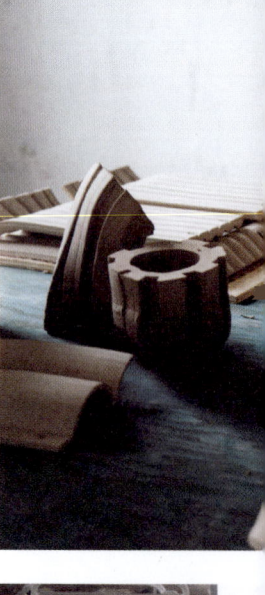

A FACTORY AS IT MIGHT BE

Assemble offered an alternative to such standard exhibitions in their installation of the same year at A/D/O, a now-shuttered co-working and art workshop in the Greenpoint district of Brooklyn, New York, USA founded by the automative brand MINI. Instead of bringing their products to the USA, the group set up shop there, turning one of the courtyards of the warehouse complex into what they called A Factory As It Might Be. They covered the space with an off-the-shelf metal structure, leaving one end open, and brought in clay, extruders, a kiln and a host of implements with which to make ceramics. Assemble also provided samples of their own experiments with clay.

Working with artists Will Shannon, Mollie Anna King and Niamh Riordan, Assemble set about experimenting with the properties of local clay, producing vessels, forms and tiles. As they had the most amount of experience with the latter, the workshop soon gravitated towards the production of ceramics, and the volunteers and Assemble members together came up with a mould that let them produce standard tiles in white and blue that were slightly kinked at the bottom to fit over each other. The group then erected a wall of these elements in a manner that mimicked what Assemble had done at Yardhouse, but with a tighter configuration of the pieces. While most of the equipment was returned to the Granby Workshop after it was used, some members of the workshop continued their experiments.

Top: Some of the ceramic experiments Assemble produced in the workshop for the cladding of the courtyard wall.

Bottom: A collection of one of these ceramic experiments in different shapes and geometries waiting to be fired.

Top: Assemble built a nozzle for an extruder that produced variegated shaped clay that they then cut into individual pieces.

Bottom: Some of the ceramic pieces after they had been fired with different glazes to create marble effects.

The tile-clad wall at A Factory as It Might Be. ▶

A FACTORY AS IT MIGHT BE

289

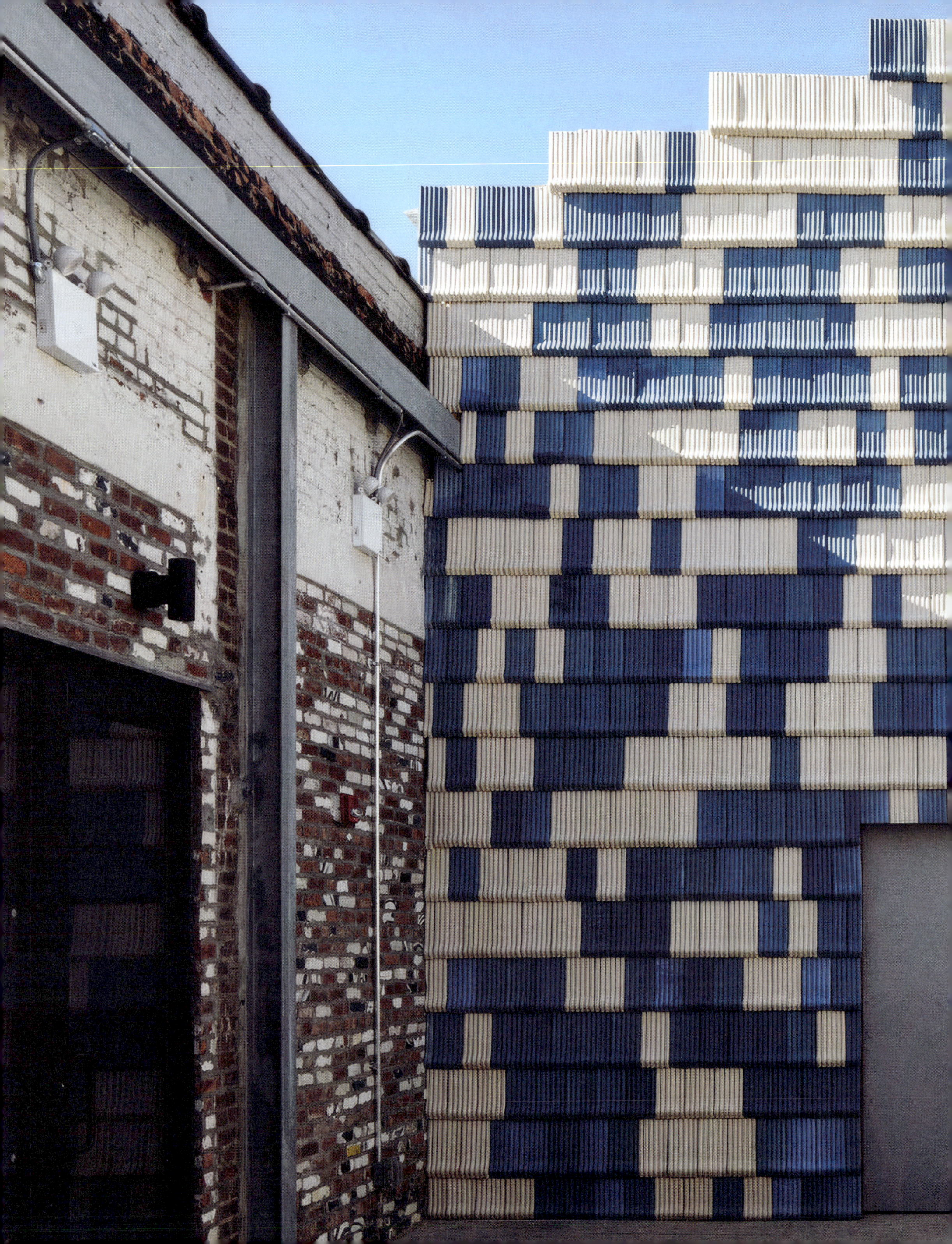

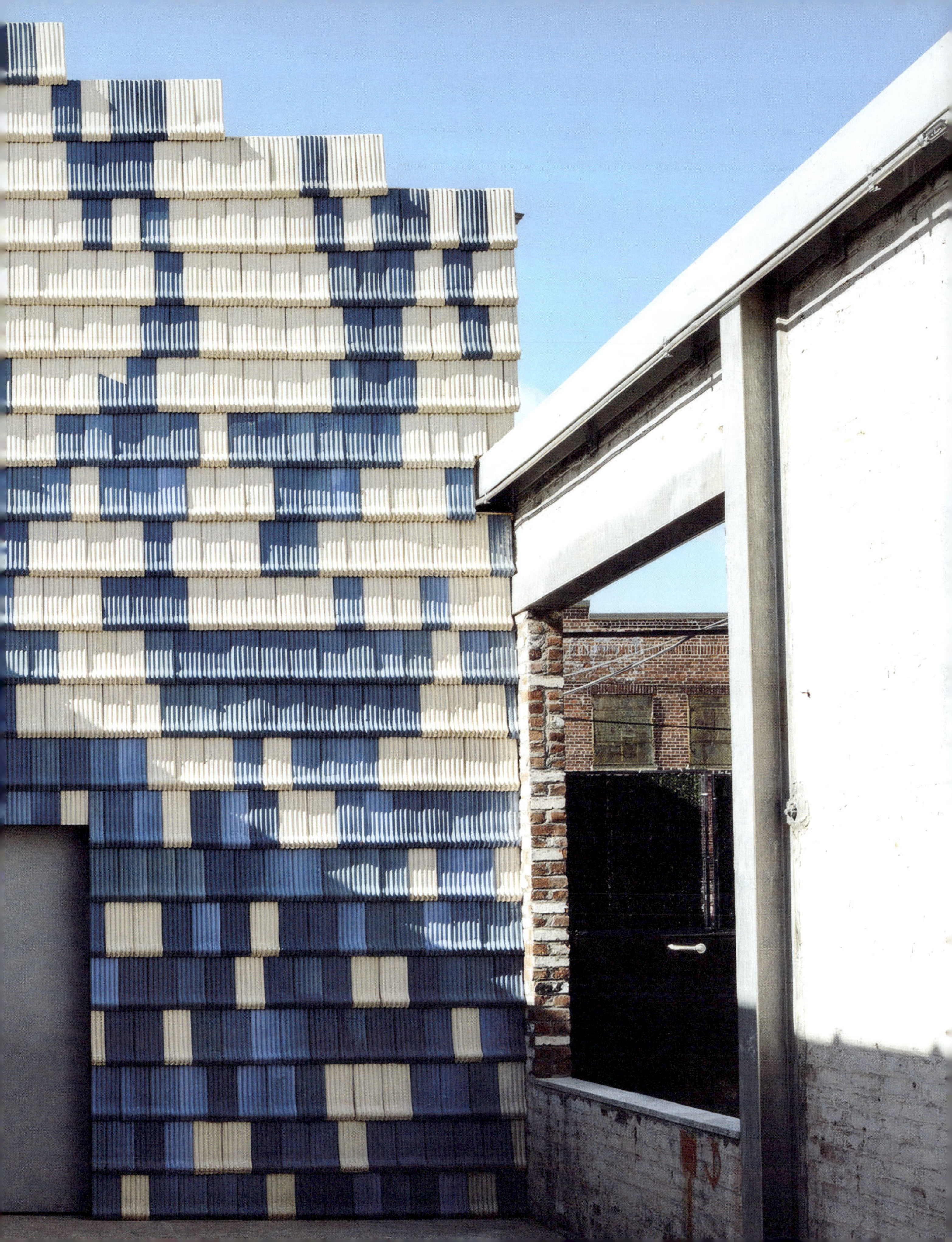

For the tile floor of The Factory Floor, the team mixed a turquoise pigment into the clay to make a block that would then be mixed to create a marble effect; this was done in an industrial workshop. The process was finished at Granby Workshop.

THE FACTORY FLOOR

In 2018, Assemble took the experiments in which they had engaged at Granby Workshop and pushed them further to produce The Factory Floor, their entry into that year's Venice Biennale of Architecture in Italy. They had been working with mixing different clays at a very high pressure to create swirling, cloudy patterns that they called 'splatware'. For the Venice project, they developed that method, using a 60-tonne hydraulic press to create encaustic tiles whose complex colours were mixed throughout the body of the pieces, rather than being applied as glazes.

Eight thousand tiles were produced at the Granby Workshop in Liverpool and then transported to Venice, where Assemble laid them on the floor of the Chini Room of the Central Pavilion in the Biennale's Giardini area. As this octagonal room is the main introductory space for this central display building, the tiles became highly visible, showing off Assemble's craft and design.

Top & bottom: Two angles of the finished tile floor with colours designed chosen to mirror the Chini Room's ceiling.

The floor installed in the Central Pavilion. Assemble also designed and built the Douglas fir benches with Steve Cook of Workshop East. On the wall is the Granby Workshop manifesto.

THE FACTORY FLOOR

Top: A hand-drawn plan Assemble created to show how the pools of the Laguna Viva would evoke the tidal lagoons of the Po River delta.

Bottom: A painting by the artist Eleanor May Watson envisioning the atmosphere the garden could evoke.

LAGUNA VIVA

After the Biennale closed, Assemble moved most of the tiles across Venice to the Palazzo delle Zattere, which was being converted into a new arts venue by the V-A-C Foundation according to a masterplan that Assemble had helped articulate in 2017. Working with environmental scientist and founder of We Are Here Venice, Jane da Mosta, alongside botanists and designers, they designed and built tile-covered salt-water tanks that showed how the area's marshes filter and manage water. Local plants were arranged to evoke the variety of environments in the Venetian Lagoon. Pathways and seating areas, also covered with the Granby Workshop tiles, provided a meandering landscape from which one could either admire this artificial version of the wider world outside the Palazzo's gate, or merely shelter from Venice's hubbub.

A view of the Palazzo Delle Zattere with the newly tiled garden and planted tanks (Assemble did not design the furniture).

A detail of how coloured tiles came together to create a variegated pattern.

LAGUNA VIVA

A view from the courtyard garden to the adjacent canal. The tile in this area was chosen to harmonize with the colour of the existing stucco-covered wall.

Looking down from the surrounding palazzo at the garden in use as a cafe with a formalized version of the lagoon referenced in the raised planters.

LAGUNA VIVA 297

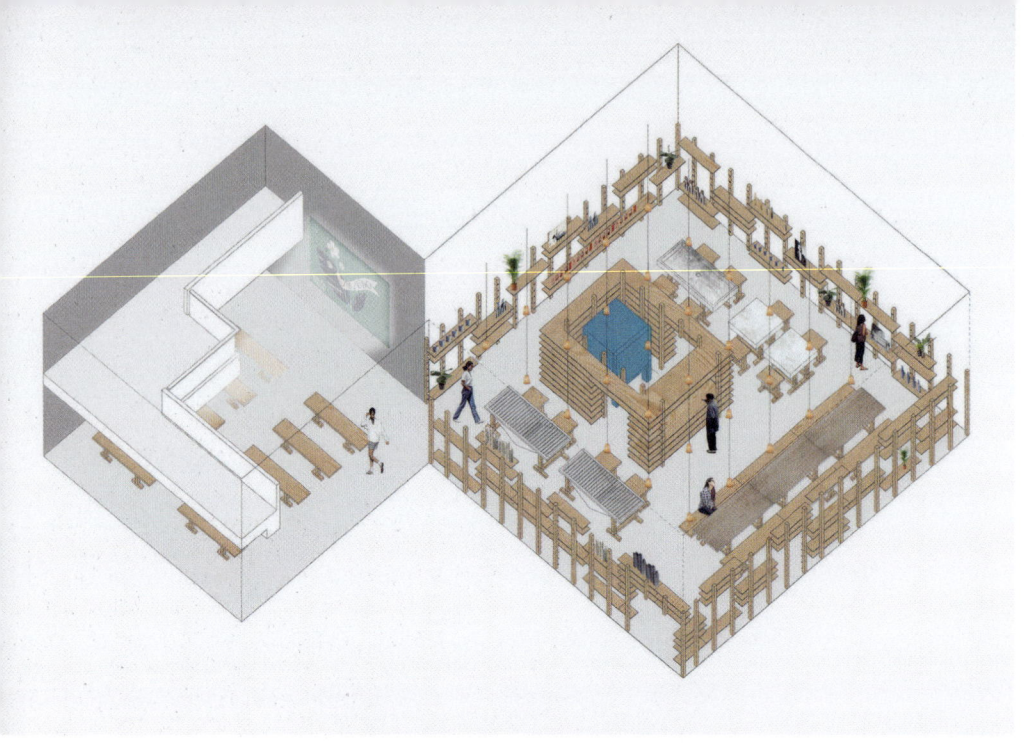

A digital drawing in which Assemble explained how the display system would work at The Rules of Production exhibition. The axonometric also shows their outfitting of an adjacent classroom.

After the full complement of ceramics had been designed, produced and brought back to the gallery, it filled the shelves and tables.

THE RULES OF PRODUCTION

The following year, Assemble continued the development of Granby Workshop tiles in an exhibition at Shiseido Gallery in Tokyo, Japan called The Rules of Production. To start the installation, they designed and built wooden shelves, tables and benches, and brought in some samples of ceramics they had previously produced, transforming the gallery into a working ceramics studio. In the first two weeks, the designers worked with the master ceramicist Minoru Suzuki to produce slip-casting forms and learn the traditions and nature of Japanese ceramics. This workshop produced a set of vessels, which were then fired in Suzuki's kiln and brought back to the gallery to display. The objects had varied surfaces that were the result both of where they had been placed in the kiln and how much fly ash mixed in with the ceramics in the process.

Assemble called the results Stacked Bottles, and the mould system was used back in the UK at Granby Workshop to produce new products, which were launched during London Craft Week.

Top: The production of the vases in molds by Assemble's local collaborators.

Bottom: The finished vases and bowls waiting to be fired. Their variegated texture, which came during firing, is not yet apparent.

THE RULES OF PRODUCTION

Top: The firing of the ceramics in Minoru Suzuki's kilns.

Bottom: The finished ceramics at the kiln, with their different finishes now evident. Different glazes also distinguished some of the pieces.

300

Mapped out sections of a Tufting Gun Tapestries sculpture on hessian stretched over a timber frame at the Material Institute.

A textile ready to be dyed with cochineal and hibiscus, hung in the Material Institute courtyard to test scale.

TUFTING GUN TAPESTRIES

A similar approach to workshops, collective experimentation with local volunteers and students, and then sales, became a mainstay of the Material Institute in New Orleans. Working with the Institute students, in 2019 Assemble mounted Tufting Gun Tapestries, a display and workshop for the Chicago Architecture Biennial (CAB) in Chicago, Illinois, USA that sought to learn from traditional carpet-making techniques. Taking apart the weft and weave of those most ancient core objects of craft, Assemble and their team (which included the Institute's founding teachers Big Chief Demond Melancon and Norma Hedrick as well as composer Duval Timothy) pulled apart the planes, extended them and then draped them around various parts of the Institute. They used traditional dyeing techniques but in more abstract patterns than was common, and made use of the eponymous tufting gun, which automates the process of interweaving yarn into stretched garments. The results, which changed over time as this was both an exhibition and active workshop, created spaces that brought to mind the heavily carpeted interiors of the traditional homes in the Middle East.

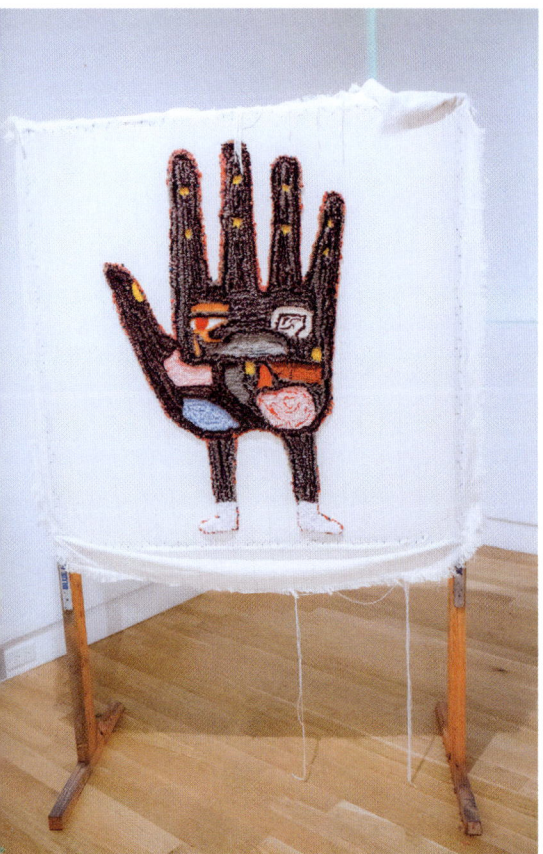

Top: Material Institute student work displayed at the Logan Center for the Arts as part of the Chicago Architecture Biennial in 2019.

Bottom: Another example of student work from the Material Institute displayed in Chicago.

Top: Photographs taken by Granby Four Streets resident Sumuyya Khader that were part of the Ways of Listening exhibition.

Bottom: Jesmonite sculptures children at Baltic Street Playground made in collaboration with artist Lauren Gault.

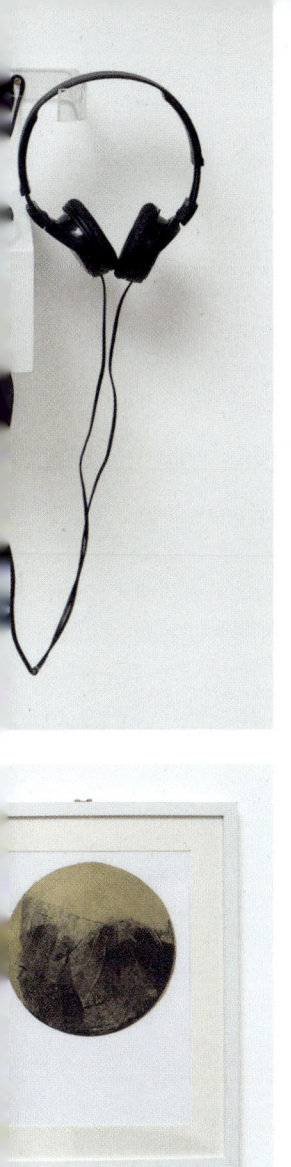

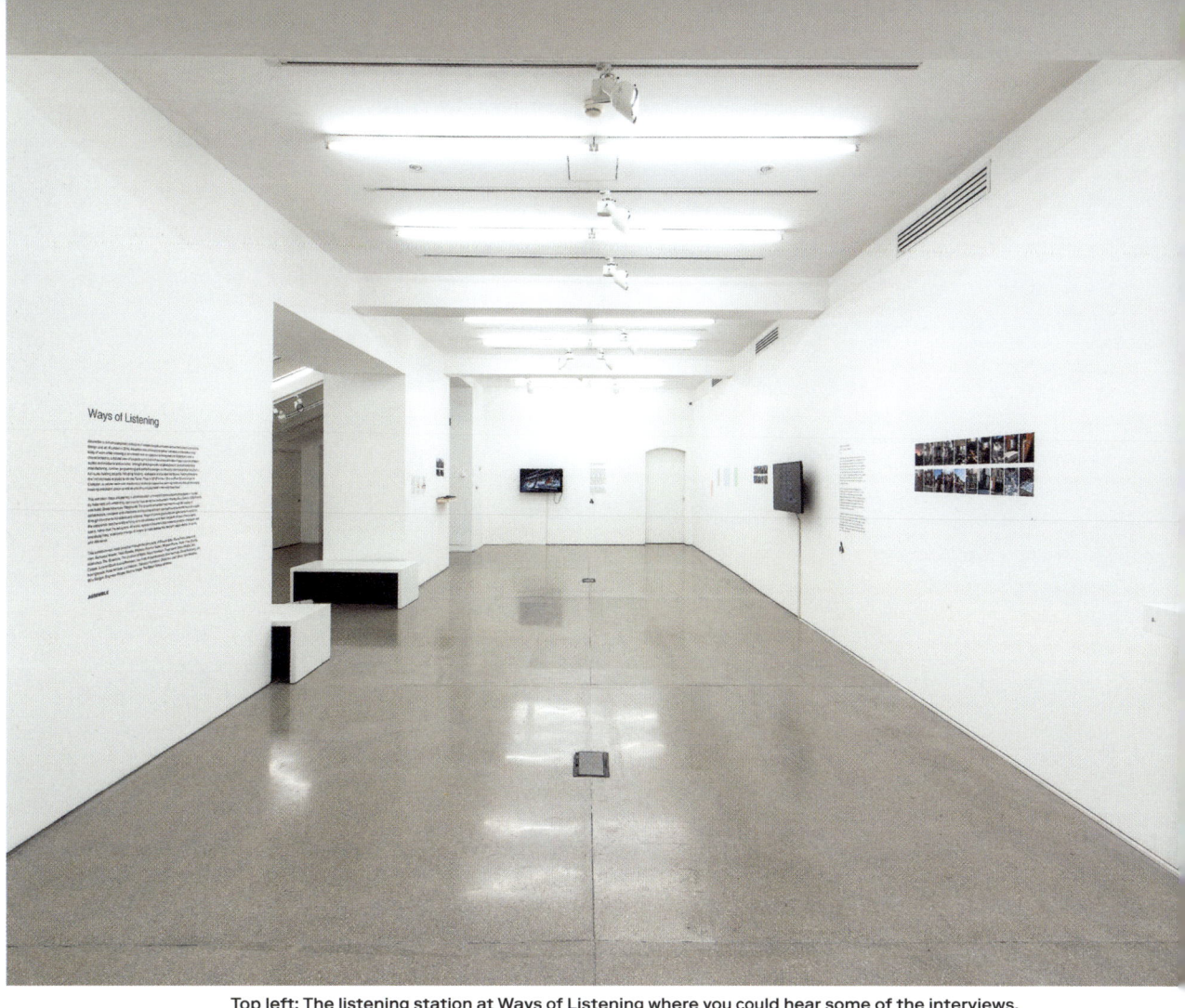

Top left: The listening station at Ways of Listening where you could hear some of the interviews.

Bottom left: The exhibition also featured Mapping the Margins, a work by Jacqueline F. Kerr, who participated in the first Granby Four Streets workshop, and an untitled work by the Granby Four Streets resident Vicki Opomu.

Above: An overview of the exhibition, showing the listening stations and photographs of some of those Assemble interviewed.

WAYS OF LISTENING

Assemble's most radical continuation of their work in exhibition format may have been the display they created in 2018 for the British School at Rome in Italy, Ways of Listening. Here they built almost nothing and showed just as little. A few drawings and photographs were placed on the gallery's white-painted walls, but the main content of the show came from interviews Assemble members conducted with collaborators and users of OTOProjects, the Baltic Street Adventure Playground and Granby Four Streets. Visitors would put on headsets hanging on the walls and find themselves aurally immersed in the rather vivid and gritty environments these places presented, even as they remained physically in a completely abstract and neutral environment.

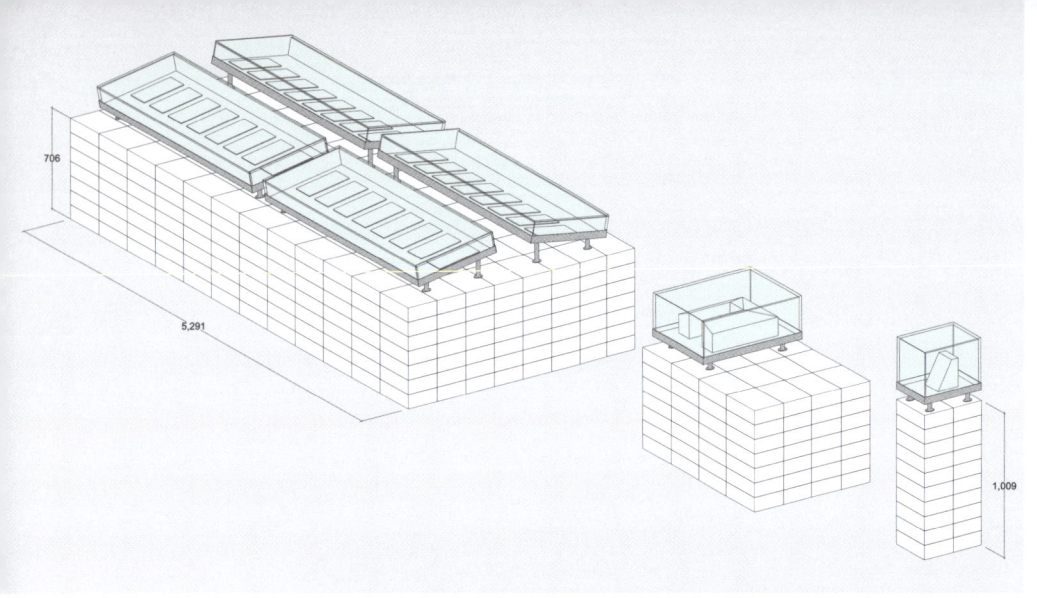

A digital axonometric of the display case Assemble designed to house the notebooks and models at the Charlotte Perriand: Design Museum exhibition. Bespoke powder-coated steel vitrines sat on top of calcium silicate blocks.

CHARLOTTE PERRIAND: DESIGN MUSEUM

Continuing the work they had done on the Bo Bardi and Day exhibitions, in 2021 Assemble designed an exhibition of the work of the French architect and furniture designer Charlotte Perriand at The Design Museum in London. While most of the exhibition consisted of conventional material, including drawings, photographs and examples of Perriand's work, Assemble sought to give these pieces a context more sympathetic with the designer's aesthetics. Walls were painted in saturated colours and instead of traditional pedestals, they dry stacked calcium silicate blocks to elevate the design objects. These blocks were designed so that the next exhibition could reuse the pieces in different configurations.

In their research, Assemble found that Perriand liked to show her furniture in carefully staged ensembles. In collaboration with the exhibition's curators, the designers assembled a series of set-piece rooms – modernist, stripped-down versions of the period room they had created at Tramway for the Turner Prize Exhibition – in which the pieces were placed as Perriand had arranged them. They then made these spaces visible through large picture windows. The effect was to show Perriand's work not just in isolation, but as she thought of it: part of a set of continually changing spatial arrangements.

Top: A 1:1 scale mockup of the block, testing arrangements at the fabricators' workshop.

Bottom: A stool by artist and designer Faye Toogood on top of found concrete blocks. This was part of Assemble's testing of ideas for the exhibition at Sugarhouse Studios Bermondsey.

Top: The central room of the Charlotte Perriand display at The Design Museum. Furniture from across Perriand's career is visible in the foreground.

Bottom: The room devoted to Perriand's early work, including her collaborations with architect Le Corbusier, was painted blue.

CHARLOTTE PERRIAND: DESIGN MUSEUM

A view into Assemble's recreation of one of Perriand's apartment designs. The vivid colours refer to those found in her modular furniture.

Pictured here is a found stone Perriand treated as a sculpture. You can also see her organic furniture and photographs she took of other found objects.

The recreation of Perriand's design for the Salon d'Automne in Paris in 1929.

CHARLOTTE PERRIAND: DESIGN MUSEUM

A sample of different stains that could be used on the larch display panels.

Drawings of the Being Human exhibition at the Wellcome Collection in which Assemble illustrate the proposed layout.

BEING HUMAN

The most permanent – and expensive – foray into exhibition design Assemble have produced to date is Being Human, a suite of display spaces at the Wellcome Collection in London in 2019. Fifty works of art addressed themes central to the Collection, including infection, genetics, the relation between mind and body and the influence of the environment on our corporeal and mental health.

Being Human thus functions as an introduction to the Collection's changing displays – educational spaces focused on health and human wellness – as well as to the collection of medicine-related objects visitors can find there. The Being Human gallery is also meant to be a contemplative place where visitors can begin to concentrate on the body and its representations. Assemble opened up windows to let natural light in, laid down a wood floor and installed dividing walls, which they built out of larch panels painted vivid colours, to create the exhibition's sequence. They used cross-laminated timber (CLT), a material made out of wooden planks and usually

Assemble built a model to experiment with different layouts and display methods. In this version, the plinths and panels consist of stack timber.

A display piece embedded in a larch panel stained a mint green colour.

A detail of the neon sign designed by artist Jochem Holz for the exhibition.

utilized for structural members, to create the display and seating furniture, sanding down this usually not very expressive material to reveal its components and grain.

The result is the Assemble display that may have been seen by more people than any of their other works (the Wellcome Collection draws over half a million visitors a year), but is also their most elegant and reserved exhibition. Though their attention to craft and environmental sustainability, as well as on the needs of different communities (they worked closely with differently abled groups in the design process) is on full display, the result is a subdued and recognizable set of spaces.

What Assemble have been able to do in designing exhibitions for over a decade is to create a way to show off both their own work and the traditions in which they feel comfortable. They have highlighted the work of Bo Bardi, Day and Perriand, but also that of traditional ceramicists in Japan, woodworkers in various countries, and weavers and Black Masking Indian suit makers in New Orleans. A strong example of the latter was the exhibition they organized about Black Masking Indian culture at the Material Institute in 2019 (part of which later travelled to the Victoria & Albert Museum in London). Here, they collaborated with local artists who create the costumes for Mardi Gras and other celebrations. In this manner, they have made it clear that they see themselves extending the Arts & Crafts tradition that seeks to enable larger and less economically secure groups of people to make beautiful things. That production can, in turn, become an economic asset for communities. Assemble have

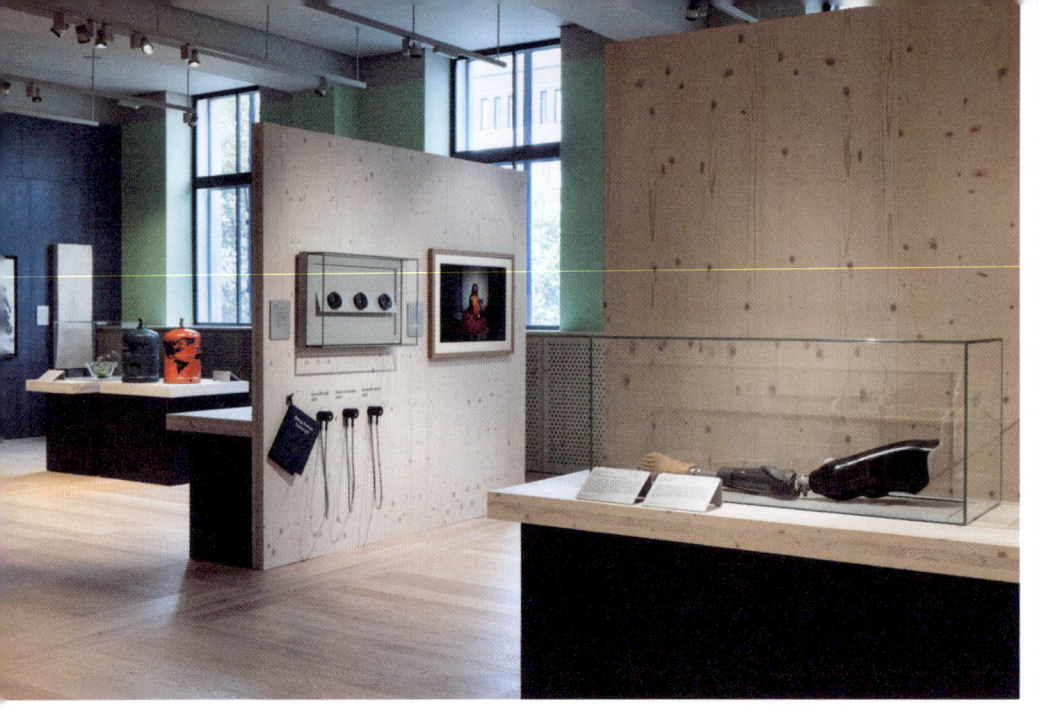

Looking into the main exhibition space. Some of the cross-laminated panels were left with a clear stain and the bases were painted black to make them visually recede.

not just posited their ideas and shown examples of it, but they have also turned opportunities in which they were asked to display their own work into workshops where a broader Arts & Crafts notion that includes a wide variety of media and makers from different cultures can become reality.

THE SYMPATHY OF THINGS

Along the way, Assemble have helped open up the notion of what exhibitions are. Making and showing, enshrining and selling, and display and object have mixed through each other in Assemble's exhibition work, creating overall environments that are also a continuation of their early concentration on temporary installations and theatrical spaces. They have continued those efforts in other media as well, producing a two-part radio documentary for the BBC in 2018 called The Sympathy of Things that explores how objects are and could be made. For Assemble, architecture and design is indeed the assembling of material, people, skills, knowledge and equipment into a process of discovery that they hope will open up new ways of working and being in our society.

The main exhibition sign as it is visible from the entrance lobby of the Wellcome Collection.

Assemble also made the exhibition furniture out of cross-laminated timber.

THE SYMPATHY OF THINGS

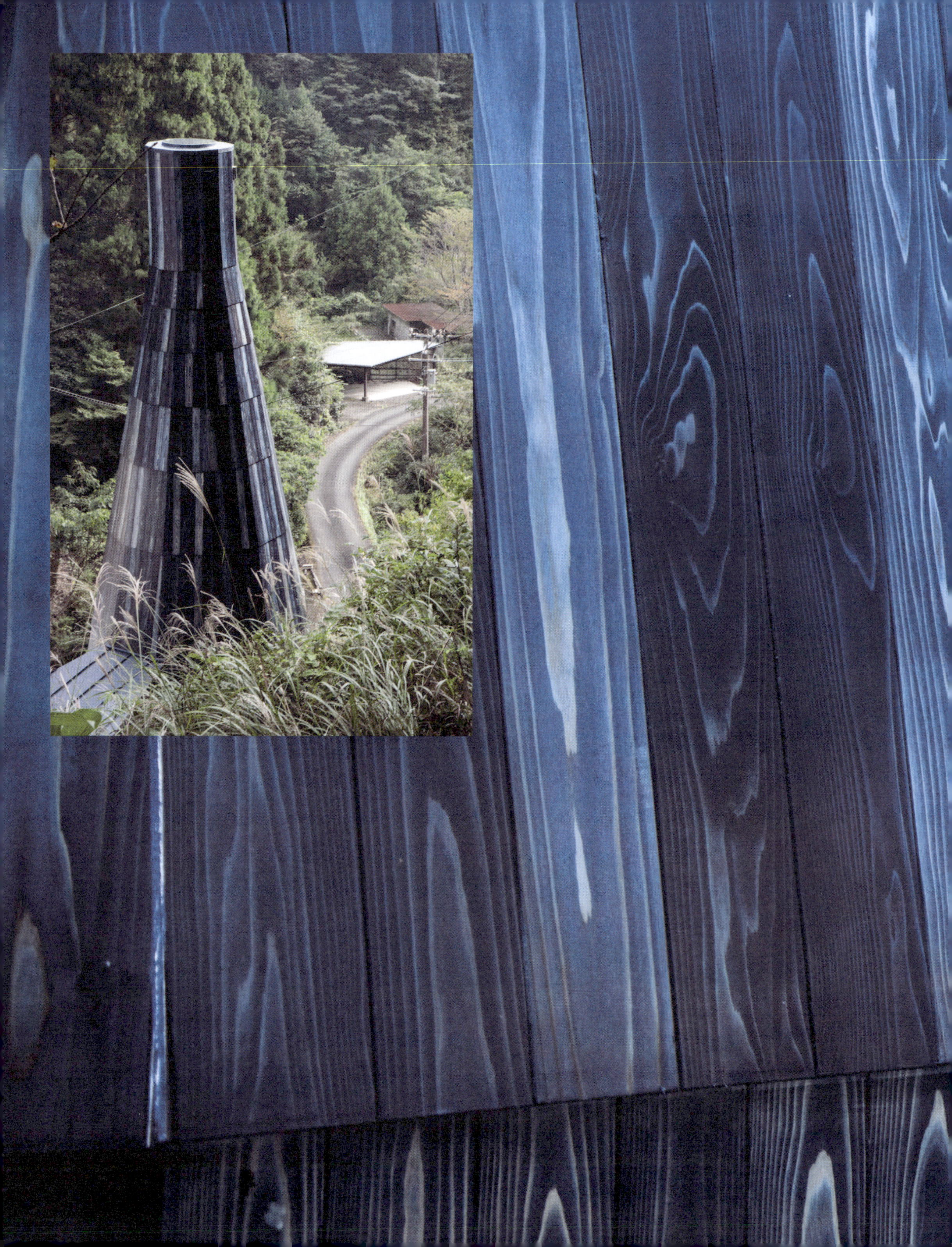

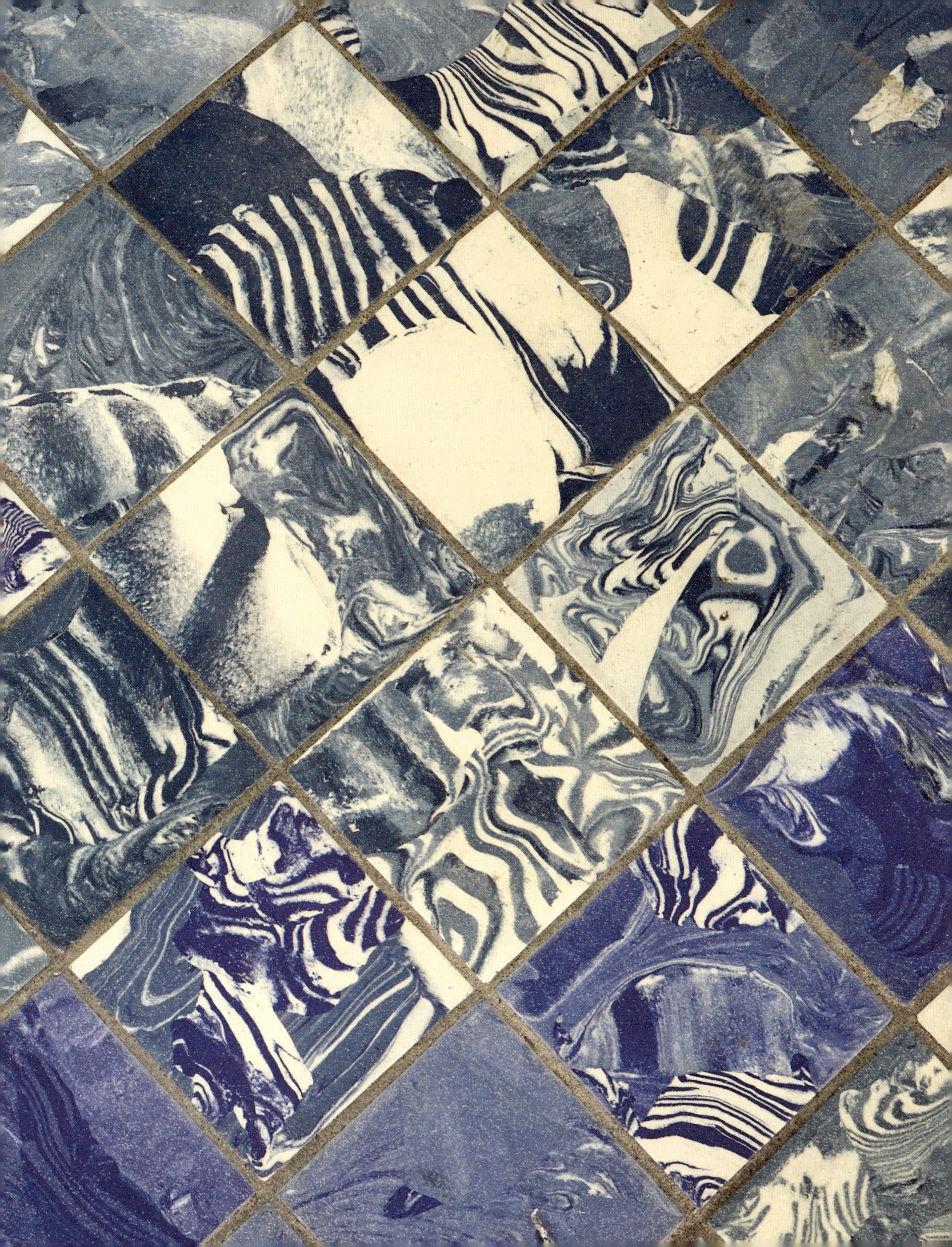

7
Still Assembling

TOTTERIDGE ACADEMY QUAD (See P330)

In the time that Assemble has been operating, they have evolved from a band of students coming together to put on a show in a former petrol station to an office providing not just architecture services, but also exhibition, furniture and object designs. They advise and offer strategic planning consultations to nonprofits, and have started workshops around the world: Sugarhouse Studios, Blackhorse Workshop, Granby Workshop, Material Institute and Fabric Floor. The group runs several facilities, including Sugarhouse and Domeview Yard, where makers operate, often in collaboration with each other and with Assemble. The group is a collective member of the Royal Academy of Arts in an arrangement the august institution had not used before. Assemble members teach, conduct workshops and lecture around the world. Even this book itself, in the assembling of their projects and the various perspectives on what they have achieved, is a formalization of what Assemble has become as an active force in architecture and the community in which it operates.

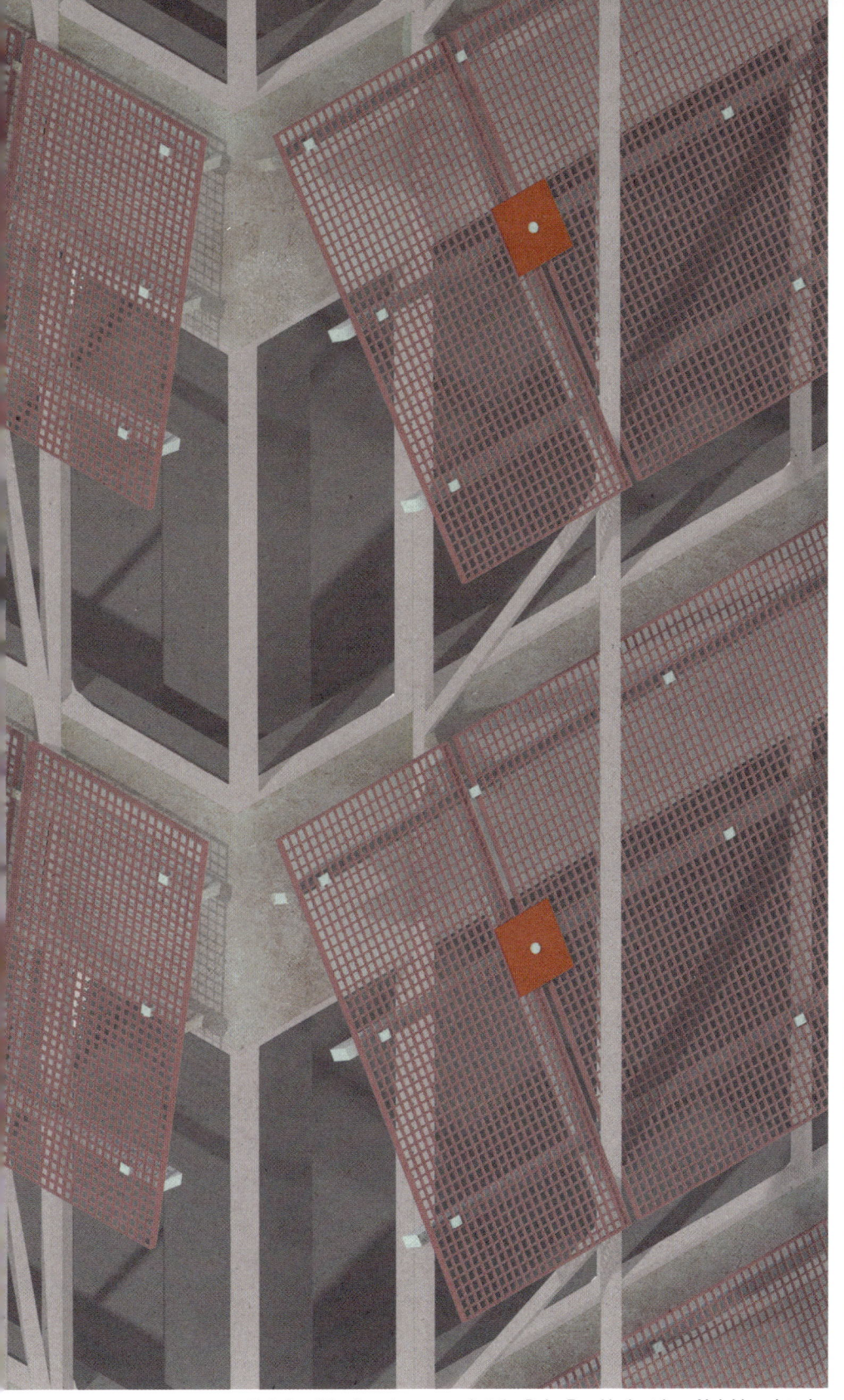

Details of the facade proposal at the Dairy Road Industrious Neighbourhood project by design studio and collaborators JAM.

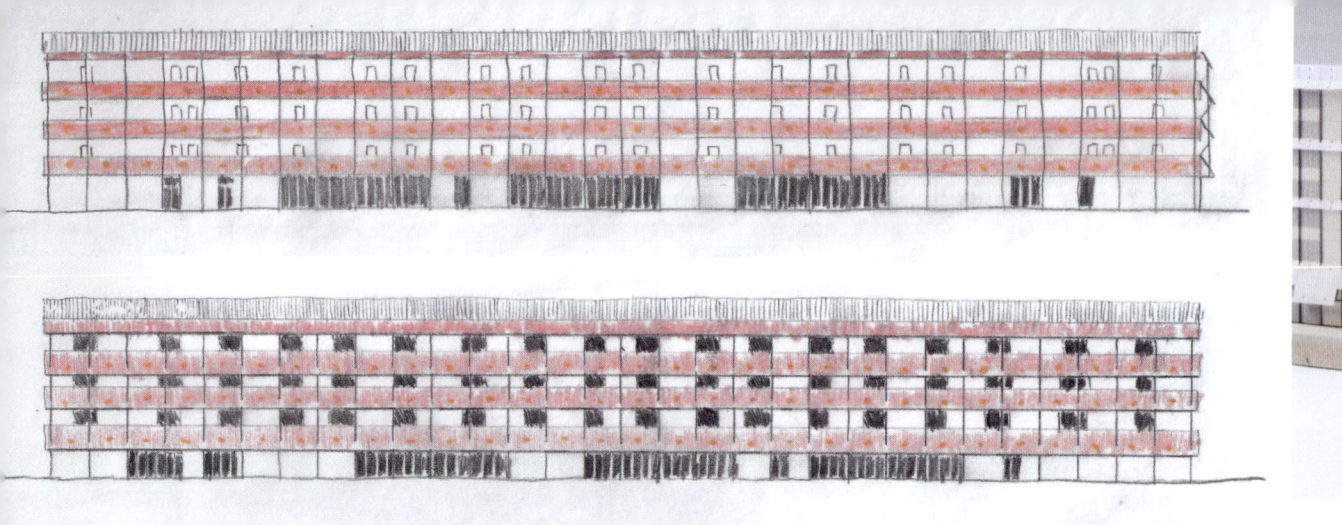

A design sketch by JAM of a typical facade. The ribbons of windows and infill panels were meant to evoke the generic office buildings of the post-war era.

The question now is what will become of Assemble. It is rare for an ad hoc group of this type to not only formalize itself, but to then keep going over an extended number of years. Even rarer is the fact that the group still operates roughly how it was started, as an organization where decisions are made collectively, pay scales are generally close to equal, and where projects are pursued not for fees, but for how well the group believes they can be critical activators for social change in their communities. Assemble has managed to do this in London, with its extremely high costs – causing them to move their Sugarhouse Studios base three times – and in a professional framework in which the pressure to become a more 'normal' architecture office is baked into its disciplinary culture.

Now the original members that came together in 2011 are entering into something close to middle age. They have commitments beyond Sugarhouse Studios, from families to teaching and other professional positions. Some of the original members have left and the memories of the first acts of architecture are fading. The collective will have to figure out how they can maintain their loose, collaborative structure with new people as interns, associates and members. They will have to do so in a landscape in which operating tactically is becoming, because of both real estate and construction costs, increasingly difficult. Whereas the post-recession landscape in which they started allowed for some inventive interventions, and funding sources related to the Olympic Games and other urban revitalization projects gave them a start, that environment has now become much more rationalized and without many obvious sources of funding.

Assemble thus not only has many side gigs, so to speak, but also operates in other cities, countries and situations where they can act in the manner they think is right. Recently, however, even those opportunities have seemed more difficult to obtain. Partially that is because many firms have sprung up in recent years who have learned from and even emulate Assemble. They are not – nor were they ever – the only group with experience in a hybrid practice between architecture, making, art and tactical services, not only in London, but in other cities around the world.

In a model made by Assemble, the metal awnings proposed for the buildings are visible over the striped facade.

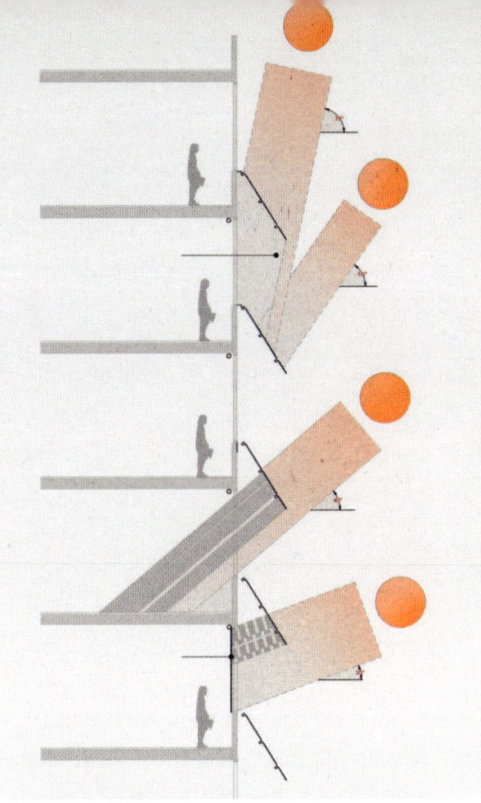

A diagram by JAM showing the awnings, which were designed with input from environmental engineers Ritchie+Daffin to allow for views out while providing shading at the hottest times of day and year.

While that means their mode of action is more recognizable to potential clients, they have also bred their own competition by training several cohorts of former employees who have gone on to start their own ventures. In addition, the ever-tightening budgetary and code restrictions that constrict architecture – and any public installation – make their particular mode of design ever more difficult, even as they have learned how to translate those tactics into more standard commissions. For all these reasons, it is unlikely that the group can keep going the way they have. It seems clear that Assemble will have to continue to adapt.

Two recent projects indicate ways in which they could evolve. They represent extreme opposites, but also both embody many aspects of what has made Assemble successful. The first of these, a masterplan for the Dairy Road development in Canberra, Australia, involves an upscaling of their activity that moves it closer to urban planning. The second, House of Annetta in Spitalfields, east London, moves it further towards social activism and cultural planning.

DAIRY ROAD INDUSTRIOUS NEIGHBOURHOOD

The masterplan for what Assemble has dubbed the Dairy Road Industrious Neighbourhood is the largest and most ambitious project they have undertaken to date. The plan foresees the construction of over 100,000 square metres (over one million square feet) of new and repurposed industrial and workshop spaces. The site, on the messy edge of Canberra, Australia's capital, is adjacent to the wetlands around a tributary to the Molonglo River, a sewage treatment plant, a highway and a railroad line. The project was initiated by a local developer group calling itself Molonglo after the river, which is part of the controlled watershed around which Canberra was successfully planned in the 20th century. The children of the original owner, who had founded the firm in 1964, began searching for more socially and environmentally active ways to develop. The scheme seeks to take advantage of both a global and local rise in demand for generic warehouse space, while also looking to preserve and enhance low-scale local production and other facilities.

DAIRY ROAD INDUSTRIOUS NEIGHBOURHOOD

A digital rendering of how two of the buildings might appear in the relatively flat terrain of the site.

The ground floors of the buildings were intended to house commercial and community functions, and their corners were designed to open up to adjacent terraces.

When Assemble was approached to look at this site in 2019, they were wary of creating such a large plan in what was largely a vacuum. After visiting Canberra, realizing the complexities of the local situation and being inspired by Molonglo's fervour for socially and environmentally sustainable development, they were intrigued and turned to historic models to inspire them in their designs. In particular, they looked at the documentation of sparse landscapes and industrial and agricultural structures by American photographer David Plowden in the middle of the 20th century. They also looked to the work Finnish architect Alvar Aalto had done at Sunila, a scheme on the estuary of River Kymi in Finland, comprising a pulp mill and residential buildings. In both, they found stripped-down forms in landscapes marked by a mix of agricultural and industrial production and the remains of small-scale occupation – similar to the situation they found at the Dairy Road site.

As usual, in reacting to these conditions, the designers did not only propose buildings. Working alongside the British architect David Chipperfield, whom Molonglo commissioned at the same time to develop a large housing estate that forms part of the Dairy Road project, Assemble first prioritized the preservation of the small industrial sheds on site, which contained such varied enterprises as workshops, a nursery, a brewery, an organic food store and a cafe. Their work also involved strategies to not only retain these existing tenants and attract new ones, but also to position the Dairy Road project as something akin to the workshops they created at Sugarhouse Studios and Blackhorse Workshop – the latter having been inspired, after all, by the appearance of cooperative making spaces such as the Men's Sheds in Australia several decades earlier.

Their idea, which the developers embraced, was to see if such complexes could both be enlarged and envisioned as newly built structures on the edge of, rather than in the middle of, an urban environment. The subtitle they gave the endeavour, 'an industrious neighbourhood', indicates their ambition in that direction. 'We were most interested in encouraging a culture of production at many scales,' says James Binning. 'Our idea was to make use of a very basic approach to building at scale that harnessed the economy of pre-cast

The buildings' interiors were meant to be flexible and adaptable, and were to be finished in the simplest and most durable materials possible.

concrete, which is a kind of local vernacular, practically universal in new construction in Canberra. The aim in accepting those limitations is to build space that is cheap enough to meet the needs of the kinds of productive, industrious activities that make up the adjacent areas that are really mixed.'

In order to create this kind of inexpensive and flexible space, Assemble accepted the need for standard construction methods for the new buildings on site, concentrating instead on their placement to meet the goals of environmental responsiveness, activating the local maker community and working with the local industrial vernacular, and on developing a facade system that could be deployed across the development in an economical manner. They also collaborated with landscape architects and environmental specialists to find ways to not only preserve but enhance and expand the adjacent wetlands, while fingering green areas throughout the project. Assemble then placed ten new blocks so as to create a small neighbourhood defined by streets and common squares, envisioning larger blocks at the corners. They also preserved three existing buildings.

Each of the ten new buildings will be covered with vertical fins and stripes, with metal awnings and light shelves picking up on and extending them in a horizontal direction. In many ways, these facade divisions are an extension of the division of building faces into continuous lengths of windows alternating with opaque bands that were the standard mode in which office buildings were designed during or after the Second World War, so that the buildings respond to the kind of vernacular of such small office structures on the outskirts of Canberra. Here the motifs will be carried out in shades of soft reds, greens, blues and whites that help to de-emphasize the structure's mass. Molonglo envisions working with future tenants to specify those hues and the nature of the bands and extensions so that the overall complex remains coherent, while each building has its own identity.

A digital drawing illustrating the overall view of the project layout.

▶

DAIRY ROAD INDUSTRIOUS NEIGHBOURHOOD

319

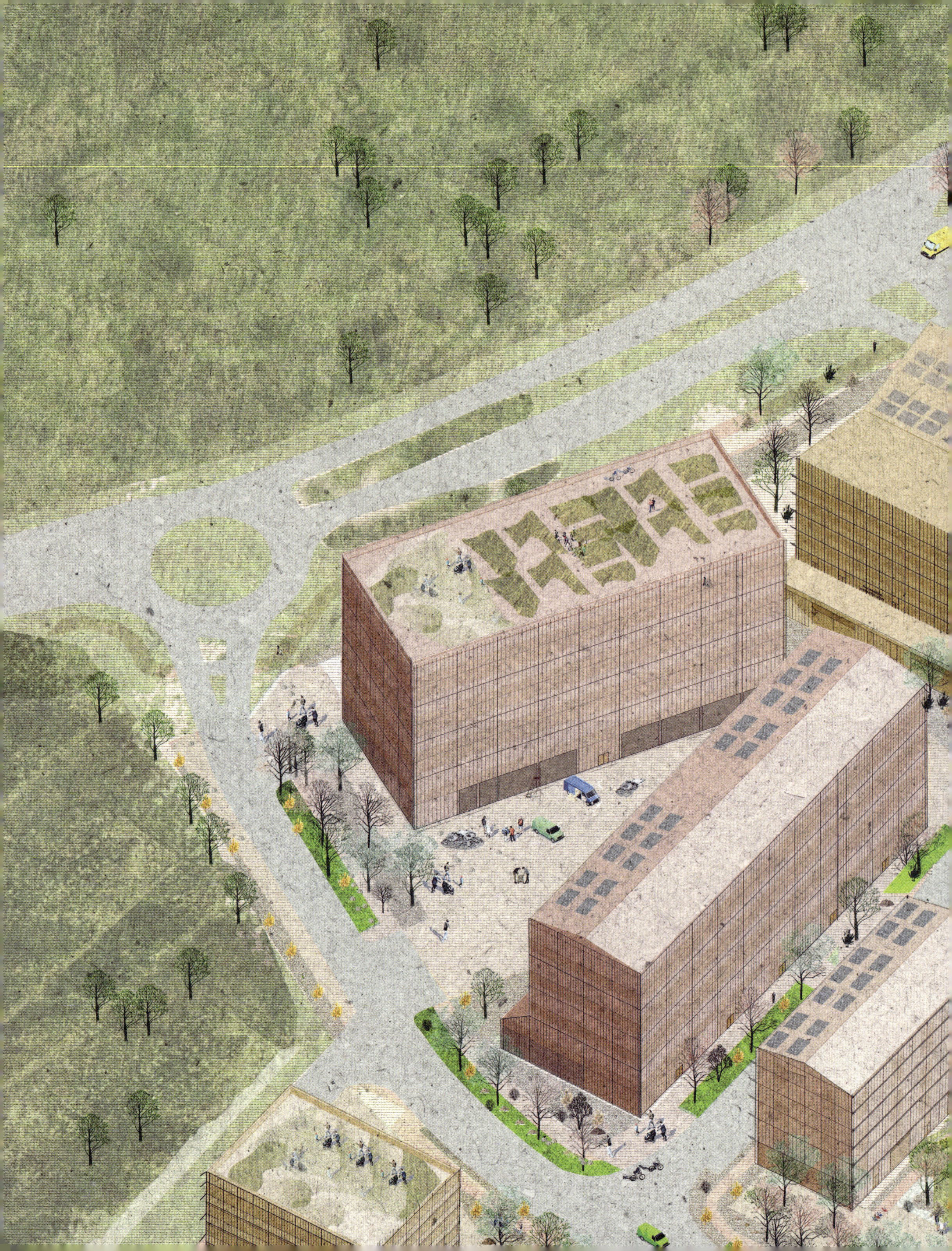

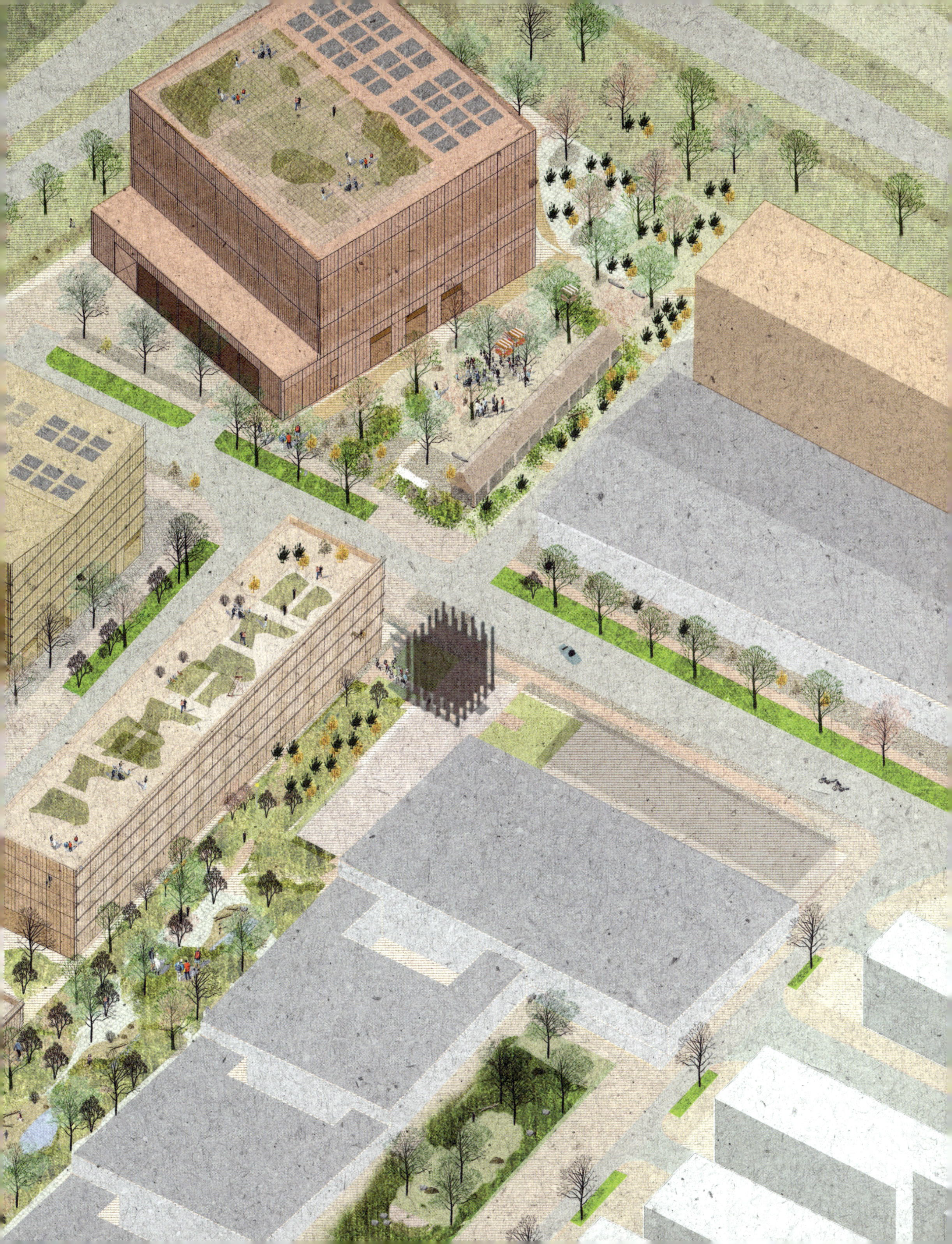

The interior of Annetta Pedretti's house after she had passed away, with both her art and personal belongings remaining.

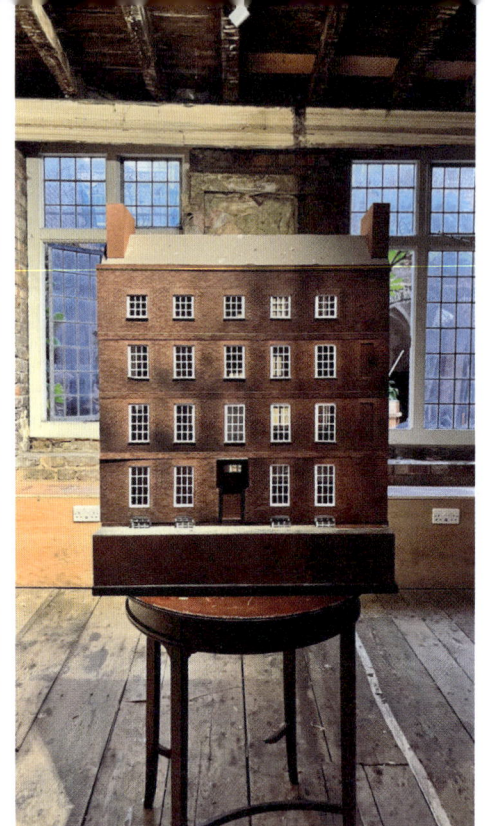

A model gifted to the project by Save Brick Lane campaigner Jill Wilson, used by Assemble to iterate designs with different communities in the house.

HOUSE OF ANNETTA

At the other end of the spectrum from the Dairy Road project is Assemble's involvement with the House of Annetta in Spitalfields, east London. This ongoing renovation of a house into a 'social centre and platform for practicing systems change' has been spearheaded by one of the group's original members, Fran Edgerley, who has left Assemble to devote themselves three days a week to the institution's development.

The project is the result of the donation of the building by the family of the Swiss artist, architect, theoretician and activist Annetta Pedretti to the Edith Maryon Foundation upon her death in 2018. Pedretti had lived in the house since 1980, when Spitalfields was a socially and economically troubled neighbourhood. Her family had hoped that the foundation, which works to remove land from speculation in order to support affordable housing, neighbourhood or community building, and the integration of arts into these efforts, would preserve her art and continue its principles there while making the house available for housing and community activities.[29]

The foundation found Assemble in 2019 and contracted them at a very early stage to assess what possibility the structure had in these directions. When Edgerley and member Louis Schulz visited, they found a building that was in need of serious repairs, but which also housed a large collection of Pedretti's artefacts and the remains of what had been a site for lively discussions, collaborations and art events. The Assemble members became fascinated by the artist's research into

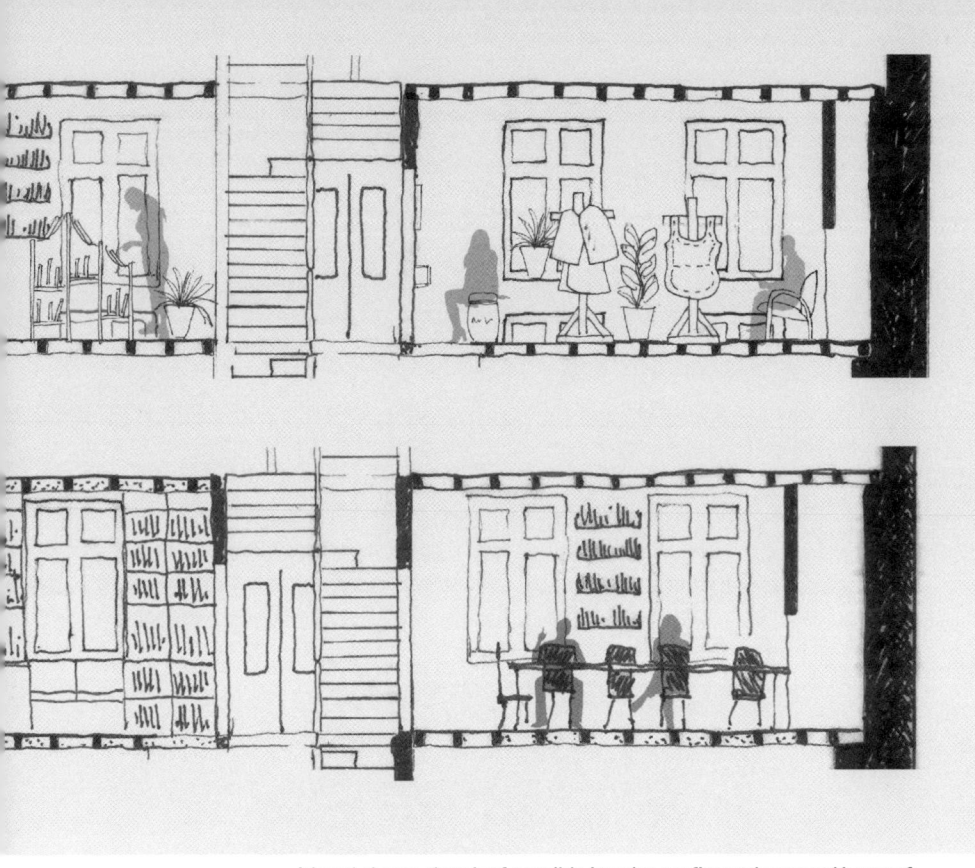

A hand-drawn sketch of possible interior outfits and uses at House of Annetta, emphasizing the possibilities for working, studying and meeting.

cybernetics as the basis for art, architecture and life in general. They also found Pedretti's neighbourhood activism and feminism to be a strong inspiration for their own work.

To assess what was possible, Assemble made a proposal to the Edith Maryon Foundation that they would evaluate not only the existing structure and what repairs it needed, along with sketching out the spatial possibilities it might afford, but would also create a mission and vision for a proposed institution to be housed there, a financial and fundraising plan and other outlines for the site's strategic development. Assemble eventually proposed what has now become the House of Annetta, and Edgerley left Assemble to head its efforts in 2022. Since then, Assemble has been working with Edgerley and architectural worker and artist Aska Welford, now as clients, as they work with inhabitants of the local neighbourhood and potential users, as well as a wider network of activists. They are also looking to articulate how the organization and its design can respond to the intense gentrification pressures on the area.

The physical efforts in Spitalfields involved repairs and interventions to infrastructure similar to the work they had performed on the houses on Cairns Street in Liverpool. Assemble also initiated repairs on the infrastructure, learning from similar work they had performed on the houses on Cairns Street in Liverpool. They now envision finishing some of the spaces with some of the crafted materials they have developed, as well as with more locally produced artefacts and surfaces.

A design sketch of the whole house exploring further uses and activities.

Floorplans of a typical floor at House of Annetta drawn by architecture students in Takero Shimazaki's unit at London Metropolitan University.

HOUSE OF ANNETTA

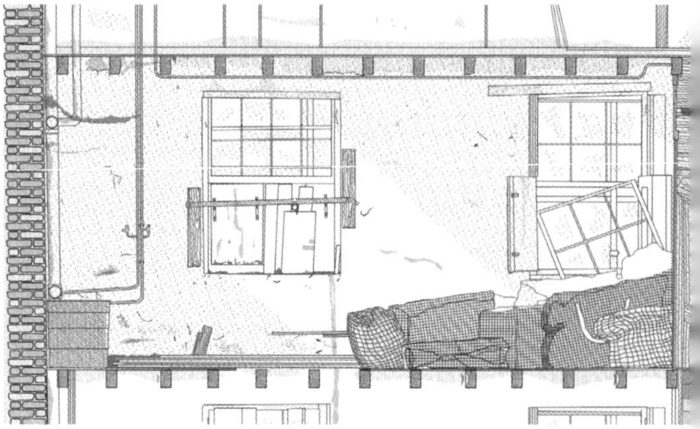

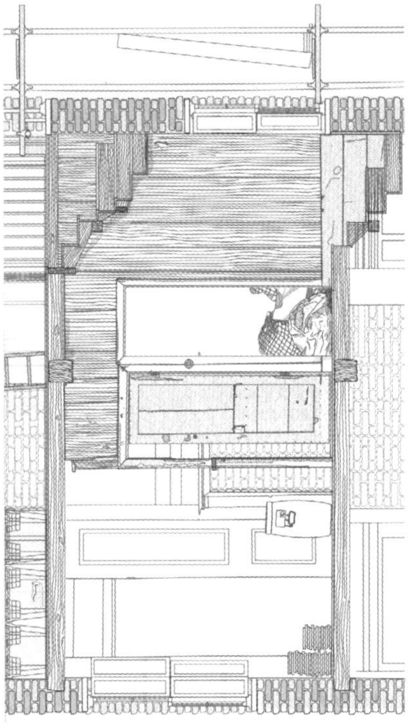

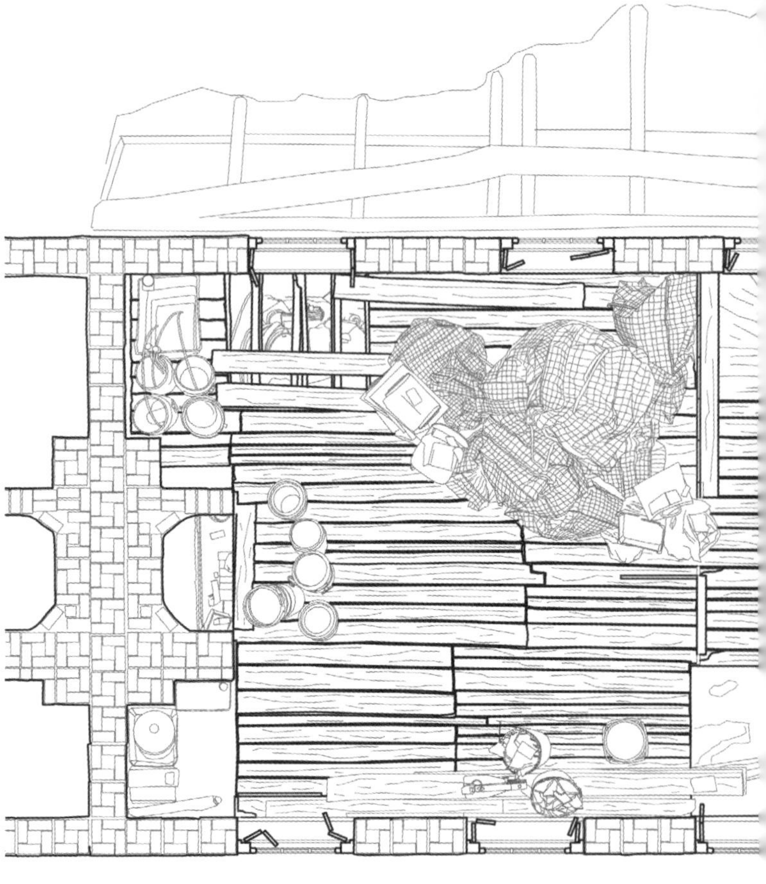

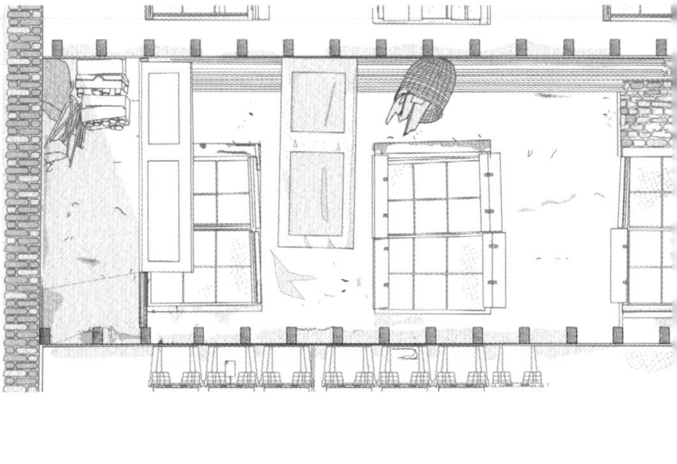

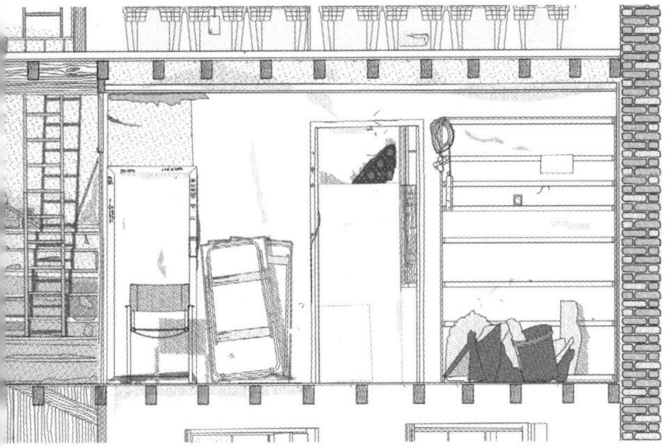

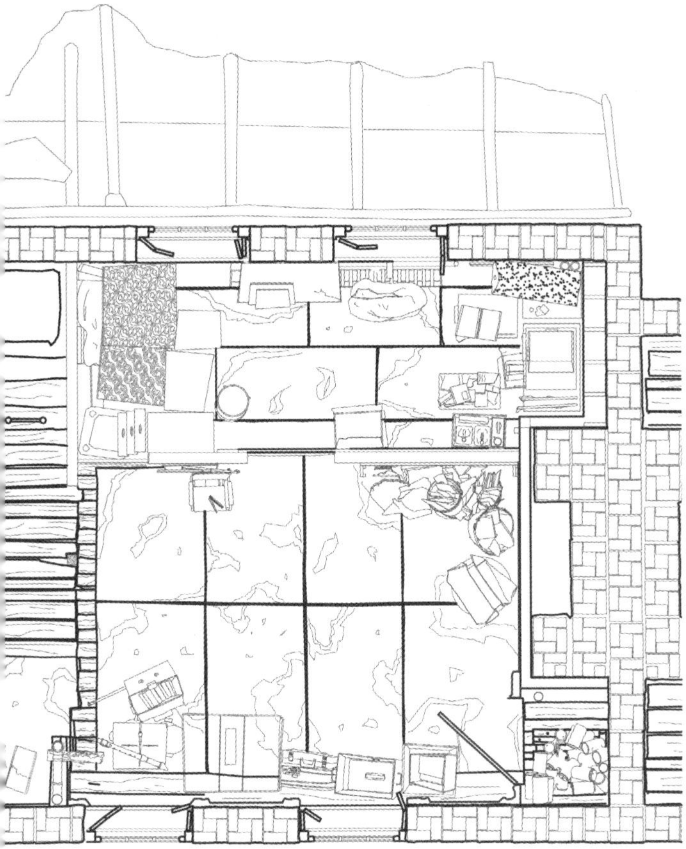

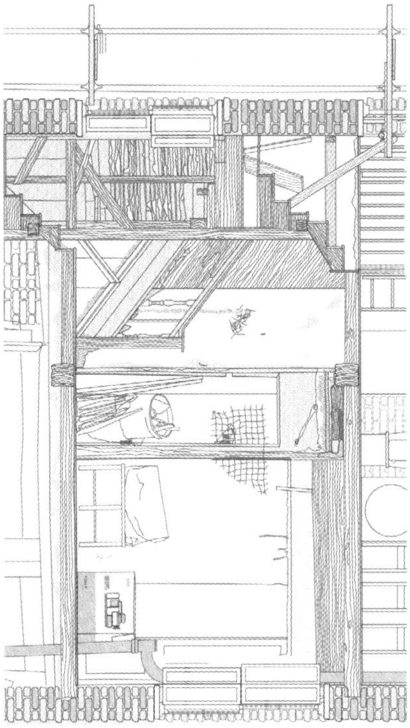

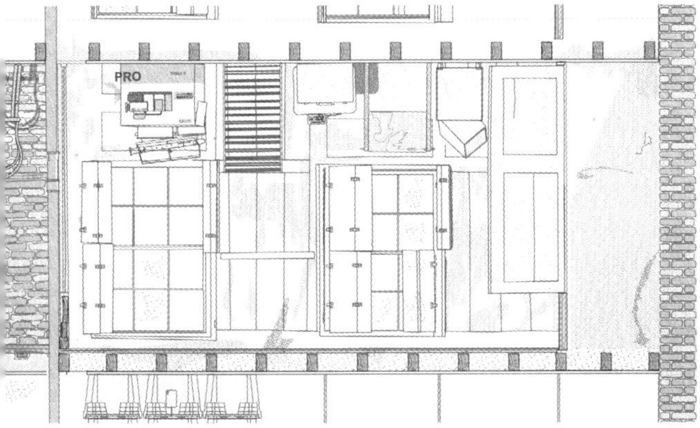
PRO

A workshop held with community groups in House of Annetta to discuss the brief and ambition for the project.

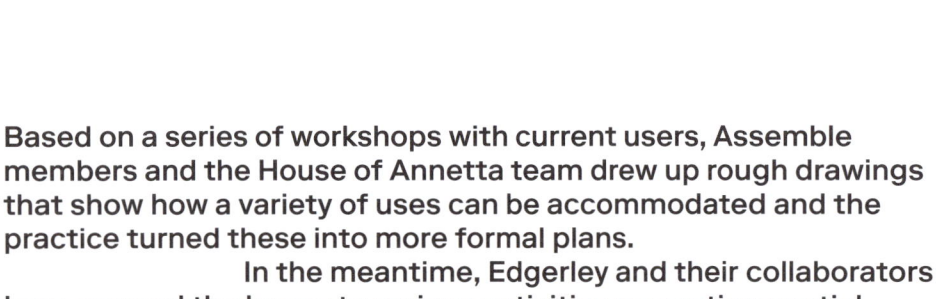

The House opened its doors to neighbours and artists, inviting them to come in, explore, participate and suggest future directions the building could take.

Based on a series of workshops with current users, Assemble members and the House of Annetta team drew up rough drawings that show how a variety of uses can be accommodated and the practice turned these into more formal plans.

In the meantime, Edgerley and their collaborators have opened the house to various activities promoting spatial justice, and in particular efforts to counter Spitalfields' gentrification. They have also hosted exhibitions of Pedretti's art, encouraged discussions about cybernetics and made the house into a 'sanctuary' for people with non-traditional ideas and modes of life. 'We are not going to finish it out in the traditional sense,' says Edgerley. 'We are concentrating on what motivates and shelters people, what brings them together, and what we invest in architecture will be absolutely minimal.' That also means leaving in place as much as possible of what was revealed when the walls, ceilings and floors were stripped down, so that the history and materiality of the house remains present, and to create a sense of openness, roughness and a lack of structure. The house is now a lively, if very much unfinished, site for exhibitions, discussions and performances.

Top: Assemble cleaned up and renovated some of the spaces, allowing the patina of the original house to remain and filling the space with found and donated furniture.

Bottom: Annetta had removed most of the 19th and 20th century additions to the house, in some cases leaving only the studs in place as a screen and structural support.

HOUSE OF ANNETTA 327

As part of the Open School East programme, associate artist Moira Moin transformed the living room of the Open School East building. The space was stripped and redecorated. The riso print images in the background were produced by her associates.

In the library space, the visual artist Daniel Norie placed these books as a site-specific collage.

OPEN SCHOOL EAST

Assemble was part of a similar effort in 2021 at a Grade II-listed townhouse in Margate, home to Open School East, a free art school that had moved there in 2020. They were invited as visiting artists to develop the curriculum, resulting in 'Who Cares', which started from the notion of preserving and restoring the house, and aimed to develop infrastructure that would make it easier for the artists to both work alone and in collaboration with each other. They termed their physical interventions 'a culture of repair', localizing what new elements they added as much as possible, making them in collaboration with potential users and finding ways to have the interventions both reveal their own making and bring out aspects of the existing building. Small pebbles, for instance, dot the cleaned-up staircase and also become rough drawer pulls in the kitchen.

The House of Annetta shows Assemble using its skills not just in building, but planning for non-profit, community- and craft-oriented organizations. The group has become a kind of bottom-up version of the urban consultancies that some larger architecture firms have evolved to be. Instead of proposing urban interventions in the mode of the late Richard Rogers or the Dutch firm OMA, or acting as organizational consultants like Rem Koolhaas of OMA, or like firms specializing in areas such as architect selection, such as Cooper Eckstut in the USA or Malcolm Reading in the UK, they work directly with small, activist groups to make them effective and sustainable. This is in itself a relatively new model for architects, and while other firms also work in this mode, such as designers Urban-Think Tank and ZUS, Assemble distinguishes itself by not always making a building or built urban intervention the core of their efforts.

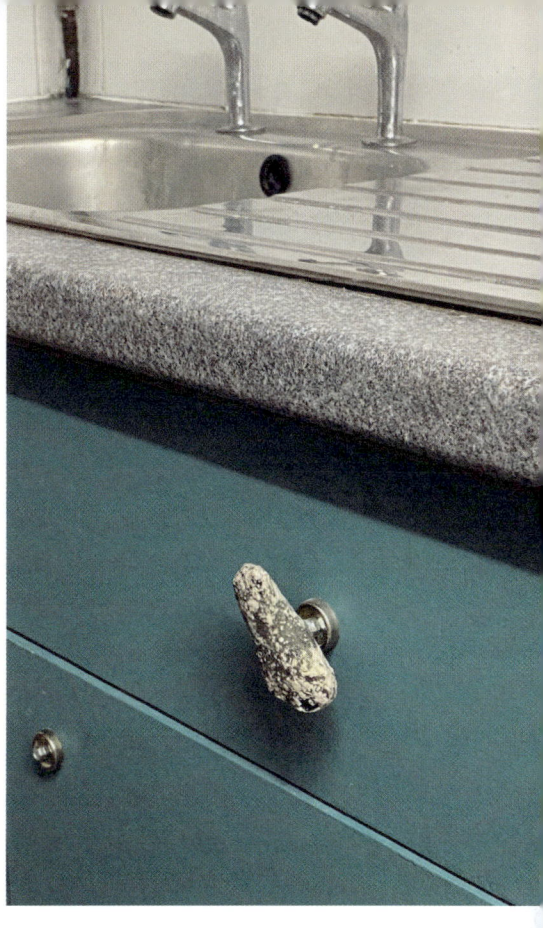

Top: A table assembled by Daniel Norie out of scrap wood.

Bottom: A student-made collage.

Top: Students repurposed elements such as found stones as drawer pulls in the kitchen.

Bottom: Cement fragments found in the school's garden became part of the students' experiments in terrazzo.

OPEN SCHOOL EAST 329

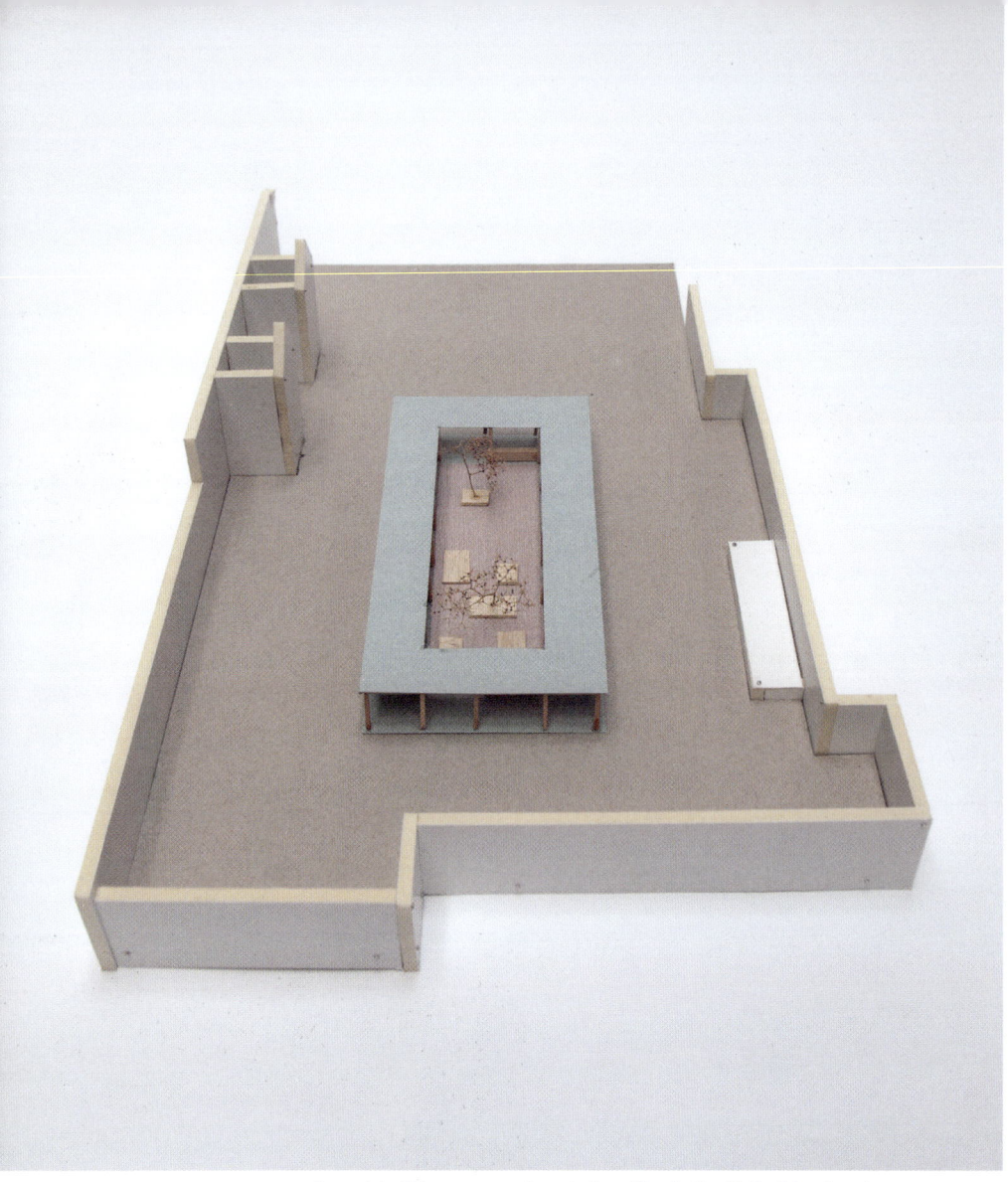

A model of the proposed central pavilion in the Totteridge Academy courtyard, seen from above.

The construction of the pavilion out of steel poles topped with a corrugated metal roof.

TOTTERIDGE ACADEMY QUAD

Assemble does not work exclusively for activist groups. A good example of their efforts outside of this core is their continued involvement with the Totteridge Academy. This is a new secondary school in Barnet on London's northern fringe. In 2018, Assemble met with students and faculty of this institution, which serves a racially and economically mixed group of students, to figure out how to activate the school's site. The students wanted a quiet outdoor space in addition to the sports fields the school already had. Together with the pupils, the group designed a simple scaffolding structure supporting a corrugated metal roof with low concrete block walls to be used for seating around a newly planted garden.

Top: Students planting the school garden in the planters Assemble designed.
Bottom: Another view of the planting activities in which the shading roof of the pavilion is visible.

TOTTERIDGE ACADEMY QUAD 331

The centre of the pavilion does not have a roof, creating a cloistered garden at the heart of the school.

Students walking in the shade of the pavilion. Assemble also poured a concrete base, and the planters are made from concrete blocks.

TOTTERIDGE ACADEMY QUAD

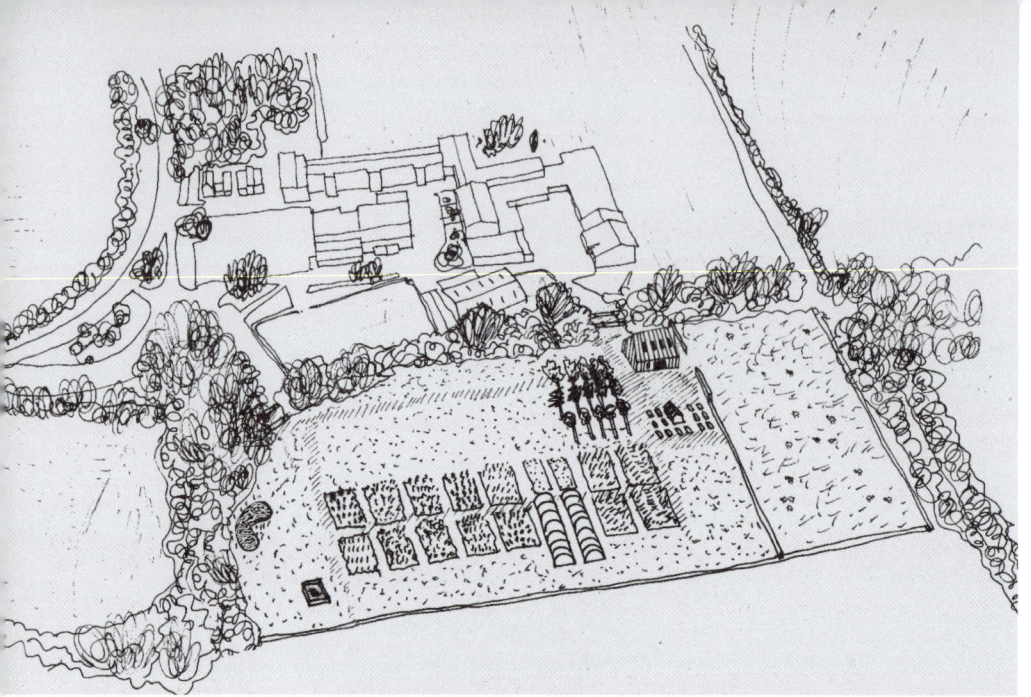

A sketch design for how the different gardens and planting areas could be laid out at GROW Totteridge Farm.

GROW TOTTERIDGE FARM

At the same time, the former British TV presenter George Lamb agreed a partnership with the school to set up the agroecological farm, GROW, on the 2.5-hectare (6-acre) site adjacent to the school, with the vision that it could become a place where students can learn and practice agriculture. Assemble again collaborated with the students to develop a plan for the venture, and then worked with them on the actual planning and planting of the farm. They have also proposed small built structures that can be implanted over time.

With Assemble extending its efforts in such widely different directions and at such disparate scales, it would be easy to think that the group does not have a coherent plan for what it is or wants to become. To a certain extent, they do not. They hold regular open discussion sessions as well as more long-term retreats, but they eschew the kind of strategic business planning in which other firms engage. They remain, both in their actions and in their own constitution, tactical. They do, however, have core ideas and values that come out in

A rendering of how the farm will appear once it is fully completed and grown out. The school is visible at the top.

Looking into the completed farm from the tool shed Assemble proposed, with students both working in and enjoying the gardens.

the projects, and which also help them decide which projects they should pursue. Those are the subjects of their internal discussions and are further honed by their teaching and writing activities. Jane Hall, for instance, authored *Breaking Ground*, a survey of architecture designed by women from 1900 onwards, which was published in 2019.

One place where they have clearly articulated what they believe in and want to achieve with their labour is in a report they produced as part of a consultancy in Norway. The project catalogue contains not only their specific analysis of and proposals for a neighbourhood outside of Oslo, but also manifesto-like statements on what they think that architecture in a broad sense can do to activate community and improve the settings in which groupings of people can thrive. The project and the catalogue serve as a clear statement of what Assemble has learned and what they believe they can and should do.

GROW TOTTERIDGE FARM

A digital rendering of how the farm might appear when in full bloom.

The farm will also have sheep and other livestock that will form part of its ecosystem.

GROW TOTTERIDGE FARM

Students from Totteridge Academy about to start work on the farm.

Top: Marking the different plants, flowers and herbs for planting.

Bottom: Totteridge Academy students showing off their soil-covered hands.

A student marking one of the pots to indicate what it contains.

The farm has chickens that the students help to care for.

GROW TOTTERIDGE FARM 339

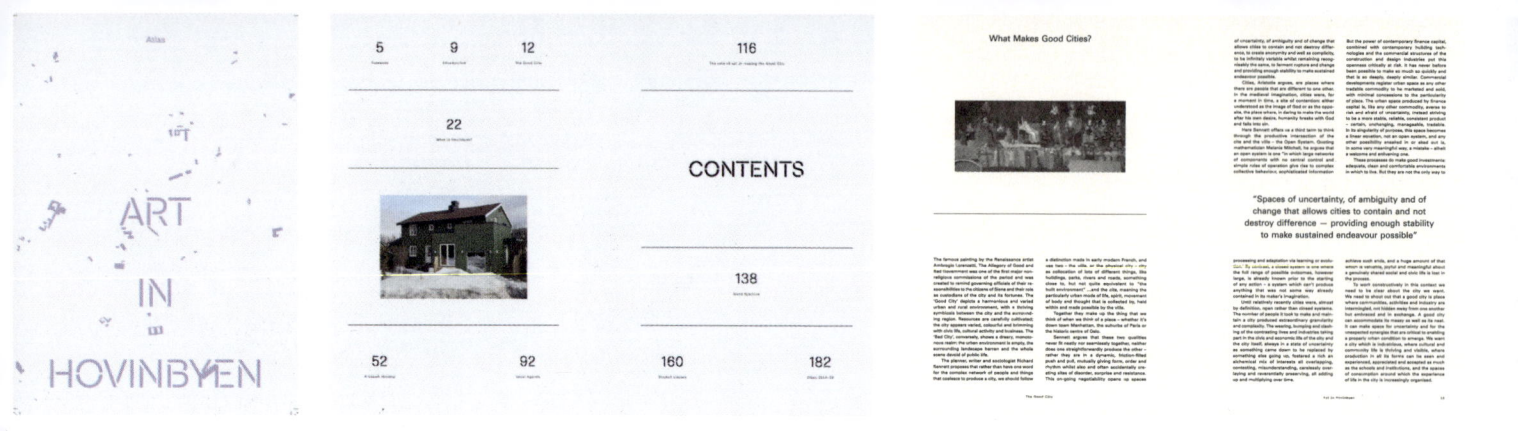

ART IN HOVINBYEN

On the outskirts of Oslo in Norway, Assemble have acted as analysts, planners and curators for a large-scale programme for art in the public spaces of the Hovinbyen community. This large, planned suburb, built in the 1970s and 1980s, has undergone social transformations not unlike those that occurred on Granby Four Streets many decades ago, as large groups of immigrants have moved into the housing blocks.[30] The area has for a long time been perceived as isolated and out of the way, and almost a decade ago the government realized it needed to upgrade housing and facilities in a manner that would respond to the changing demographics of the area, to the realities of urban sprawl, and to the need to strengthen the area's physical and social infrastructure. A small amount of the investment that will make this possible was intended for arts projects, and the Norwegian arts funding organization KORO contacted Assemble to come up with a way to do so that would avoid the usual 'plunk art' that is usually the result of such programmes.

After the extensive effort of exploration and community discussion that is core to everything they do, Assemble then declined to provide the 'art plan' that KORO expected. Instead, they noted that 'art practice is a powerful tool for improving situations, building on and building up imaginative capacity and collective energy', and defined their work as 'prepar[ing] the ground for artists to begin work on projects in Hovinbyen that demonstrate this'. The report they produced in 2020 to accomplish this goal, Art in Hovinbyen (self-published by Assemble with KORO), also serves as their most complete statement of architecture theory:

> A good city can accommodate its messy as well its neat. We want a city which is industrious, where cultural and community life is thriving and visible, where production in all its forms can be seen and experienced, appreciated, and accepted as much as the schools and institutions and the spaces of consumption around which the experience of life in the city is increasingly organized.[31]

Assemble make the point that such messiness is not only a fact of life in Hovinbyen and similar city-edge neighbourhoods, but an important part of what makes it a diverse and fluid place open to different people and activities. However, both real estate developers and social planners tend to concentrate on cleaning up and regularizing places that are actually in continual flux.

340

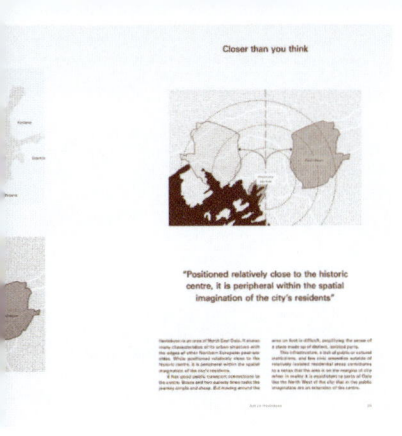

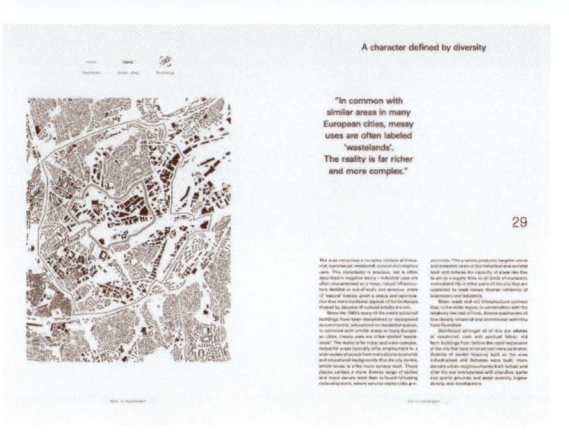

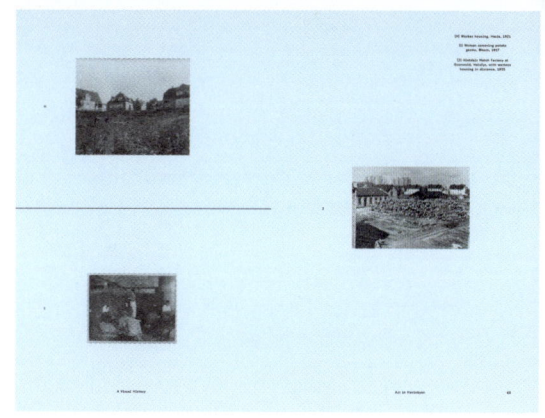

Pages from the report Art in Hovinbyen, published in collaboration with KORO.

Instead, Assemble says: 'The challenge is to realize the area as a varied tapestry of urban fabric that is open, sustaining, and enables civic, cultural and social organizations to add up to a rich, holistic experience.' They then go on to define ways to strengthen this dynamic character and establish a sense of place that will sustain the mix and 'respect the strangeness' of the residential, natural, commercial and industrial area. They go on to argue for the creation of better shared public spaces designed to mix people not only of different economic groups, but also of varied ages. Around these open areas, improved housing and other renovated and new buildings could arise.

Assemble's definitions of what make a good city and how it can be extended and strengthened are in some ways obvious, but also challenge existing notions of architecture and planning. The core notions include: 'The City as a tool, not an artifact', 'Networks, not hierarchies', 'Context, not concept' and 'Infrastructural, not institutional'. The emphasis is thus on the reality of the built version of communities as active, unfinished and continually changing but very real things within and upon which we must operate to make them more sustainable, open and attractive. The work to be done has to itself occur collaboratively, Assemble points out – in Hovinbyen, but by implication, in general. Designers who come in should be aware of their privileges and otherness, and proceed not with ideas that they bring from the outside, but from material experimentation and spatial exploration on site. This means 'Working in the margins' both of what is economically and physically possible, and of communities that either have few of their own resources or are under threat of redevelopment. It is exactly in such fraught situations that Assemble's tactics are most needed and can flourish.

As far as Assemble is concerned, such efforts could be carried out in any number of modes or styles by good architects. What is key to this tactic's success is to understand the history, the natural and human-made landscape, and the fact of continual economic and demographic flux as well as the actual structure and character of Hovinbyen. The way to make that knowledge present and active, then, is through art projects. Assemble proposed that the local community groups, KORO and the project's outside funders create not individual commissions, but a 'network of projects' that would form a 'cultural infrastructure'. This would develop in collaboration with artists, who would also be encouraged to work together and become a 'mosaic' rather than a plan.

The Hovinbyen project is currently being developed locally with Assemble's continued involvement. More important than the nature of the actual results is, in this case, the analysis and proposition the group made in developing their idea of a mosaic of art. The idea that architecture is a way of learning about, analyzing and understanding a physical and social community, whether through data or through art, photography, narratives and discussions, is at the core of everything they do. This process then usually (but not always) leads to either an event or a set of material or spatial experiments.

The reality is that this often means that no permanent building results. Partially it is because Assemble gives themselves, as they conclude in the book, 'Permission to fail', realizing that that is the nature of an experimental mode of working in the margins. It is also the inevitable result of the immense social and economic pressures that confront them as they eschew working with standard property developers designing houses or office buildings for those with means, or housing institutions central to state or culture. Assemble's history is marked by more failures than successes – but the same can be said of the portfolios of most architecture offices.

It is often difficult to find what Assemble has achieved. Much of their work is temporary. Much of it takes the form of social processes. Much of it consists of material or object development. Much of it therefore is or becomes invisible. That means that the result of their work is as much the drawings, photographs, models and writings they produce as it is a final built product. Though they did not invent the ideas or modes with which they work, Assemble has been central to opening up the discipline of architecture as an agent for social change and community development while also becoming a model for both internal and external collaboration. That means understanding architecture not as a service, as most national professional organizations and laws define it, and not as purely focused on the production of new, standalone buildings. It means redefining what architects do for an unstable global society riven by social conflicts and facing imminent self-destruction, and facing those vast problems with the skills, knowledge and tactics proper to architecture, but not defined solely by the act of building.

A visit to an Assemble project often puts you in a messy situation. So does a trip to their Sugarhouse Studios home. You will not find the traditional beauty of architecture embodied in any finished or stable form. What you will experience is the assembly of the building blocks for a better, more sustainable, more just and more beautiful world.

The variegated colour tile wall at Yardhouse at Sugarhouse Studios Stratford.

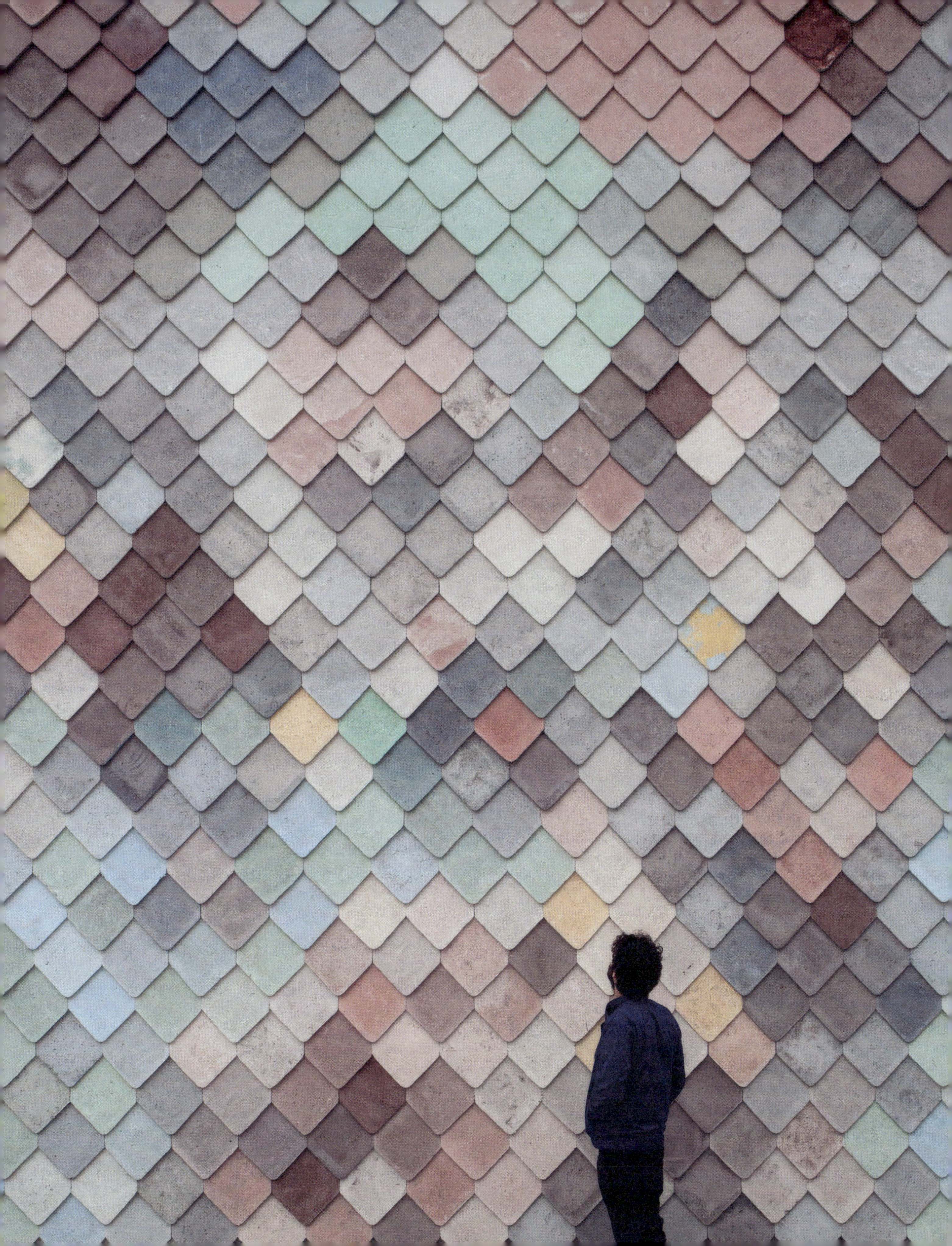

ASSEMBLE MEMBERS

Below is a non-exhaustive list of Assemble members and people who have been part of an Assemble company, past and present

Assemble Design
Seyi Adelekun, Mary Anderson, Farrokh Aman, Jenine Baptiste, Astrid Bois d'Enghien, Joe Bibbey, James Binning, Holly Briggs, Naomi Credé, Sofia Deria, Amica Dall, Alice Edgerley, Frances Edgerley, Anthony Engi Meacock, Irgel Enkhsaikhan, Mark Gavigan, Angus Goodwin, Jane Hall, Joe Halligan, Antonia Halse, Lauren Harbord, Eleanor Hedley, Amy Grounsell, Harry Johnson, Lewis Jones, Karim Khelil, Owen Lacey, Mat Leung, Yibeijia Li, Maria Lisogorskaya, Amelia Mashhoudy, Alex McLean, Inés Miño Izquierdo, Bushra Mohamed, Ikesha Patrick, Amy Perkins, Joe Ridley, Anna Russell, Felix Sagar, Amrit Sandhu, Jordan Sashov, Louis Schulz, Giles Smith, Kaye Song, Paloma Strelitz, Jaymi Sudra, Mariia Suprun, Valeria Szegal, Bushra Tellisi, Audrey Thomas-Hayes, Emily Wickham, Adam Willis, Penny Wilson, Ali Zine, Asia Zwierzchowska.

Sugarhouse Studios
Jenine Baptiste, Lauren Harbord, Inés Miño Izquierdo, Ikesha Patrick

House of Annetta
Sofia Deria, Hugo Fer, Emma Leslie, Yibeijia Li, Hester Moriarty-Thompson, Saif Osmani, Claire Louise Staunton, Tati food canteen (Oitij-jo), Imani Qamar, LION

Assemble Play
Kwaku Adjei, Cristina Birle, Kerri Anne Burton, Charlie Caplan Wilson, Cezzi Cezara Misca, Laura Cortes, Panda Rose Gavin, Emily Gillings-Peck, Neville Hayes, Sioned Hughes, Zareen Islam, Guillermo Lloret Fariña, Christian O'Mahony, Jess Mehan, Chris Roberts, Jake Stevens, Joe Stevens, Penny Wilson, Milly Wood, Eloise Wu, Kevin Yoon

Granby Workshop
Lanty Ball, Evelyn Broderick, Paddy Brown, Jacob Chan, Becky Christian, Jade Crompton, Takiyah Daly, Paula Frew, Lydia Hardwick, Anna Johnston, Jacqueline Kerr, Mollie Anna King, Sumuyya Khader, Sufea Mohamad Noor, Salma Noor, Vicky Opomu, Niamh Riordan, Mohammed Saad, Sagar Sharma, Will Shannon, Ines Suarez de Puga

IMAGE CREDITS

Abbreviations are: T = top; B = bottom; L = left; R = right; C = centre; TL = top left; TR = top right; BL = bottom left; BR = bottom right; TC = top centre; BC = bottom centre

2, 6L: Assemble; 6–7C: Photo Maurice Savage/Alamy; 7R: Mole Architects/Photo David Butler; 8L, 8–9C: Photo William Morris Gallery, Walthamstow; 9R: Alison and Peter Smithson, Hunstanton School, Norfolk, 1949-54; 10L, 10C: Photo Dale Hickman; 10–11C: Smithson Family Collection; 11C, 11R, 12L, 12C: Photo Dale Hickman; 12–13C: Sergison Bates/Sba; 13C: Tony Fretton Architects/Photo Lorenzo Elbaz; 13R: Tony Fretton Architects/Photo Martin Charles; 14L: Smithson Family Collection; 14–15C: Sergison Bates/Photo Stijn Bollaert; 15R: Sergison Bates/Photo Karin Borghouts; 16L: Caruso St John Architects/Photo © Russell McDowell, 1990; 16–17C, 17R: Caruso St John Architects/Photo © Roger Spetz, 1992; 18L: Richard Wentworth, London, England 1976. Making Do and Getting By, 1976. Unique photographic prints, 48 x 107 (18 7/8 x 42 1/8). © Richard Wentworth; Courtesy Lisson Gallery; 18–19C: Richard Wentworth, South West France, 2007, 2007. Unique colour photograph, 29.7 x 42 (11 3/4 x 16 1/2). © Richard Wentworth; Courtesy Lisson Gallery; 19R: Richard Wentworth, Nicosia, 2001. Unique colour photograph, 28.8 x 19 (11 3/8 x 7 1/2). © Richard Wentworth; Courtesy Lisson Gallery; 20L, 20C: Photo David Grandorge; 20–21C, 21R: Photo 6a architects; 22, 23, 25L: Morley von Sternberg; 25R, 26L, 26C, 26–27C; 27R: Assemble; 28L: Morley von Sternberg; 28–29C, 29R: Assemble; 30L: Alexander McLean; 30–31C: Morley von Sternberg; 31R: Assemble; 32–33: Morley von Sternberg; 34: Assemble; 35R, 36L, 36–37C, 39: Morley von Sternberg; 37R, 38L, 40L, 40–41C, 41R, 42L, 43, 44L, 44–45C, 45T, 45B, 46L, 46–47C: Assemble; 47R: David Grandorge; 48L: Assemble; 48–49C: Morley von Sternberg; 49R: David Vintiner; 50L: Assemble; 51: David Vintiner; 52–53: Lewis Jones; 54L, 54–55T, 54–55B, 55R: Assemble; 56L, 57, 58, 59R, 60–61: Jim Stephenson; 62L, 62–63T, 62–63B, 63R, 64L, 64–65C, 65T, 65B, 66L, 67TL, 67BL, 67R, 68L, 68–69C, 69R, 70TL, 70BL: Assemble; 70R, 71C, 71R, 72L, 72–73, 74–75: Jim Stephenson; 76L, 76C: Assemble; 76–77C, 77R, 78L, 79, 80L, 80–81C, 81R: Jeroen Verrecht; 82L, 82C: Morley von Sternberg; 83, 85L, 85R, 86L, 86–87T, 86–87B, 87R: Assemble; 88L: Philipp Ebeling; 88–89C: Assemble; 89R, 90L: Philipp Ebeling; 90–91C, 91R, 92: Assemble; 93TR, 93BR: Philipp Ebeling; 94L, 94–95C, 95R, 96L, 96–97C, 97TR: Assemble; 97BR: Philipp Ebeling; 98L, 98–99C: Assemble; 99R, 100L: Charlotte Swinburn; 100–101C: Assemble; 101R, 102L: Charlotte Swinburn, 102–103C, 103R: Assemble; 104L, 104–105C: Ben Quinton; 105R: Assemble; 106L, 106–107T, 106–107B, 107C, 108, 109R: Ben Quinton; 110L, 111L, 111R, 112L: Assemble; 112–113C, 113R: Hannah Thual; 114L, 114–115C: Takeshi Hayatsu; 115R, 116L: Assemble; 116–117C, 117R: Hannah Thual; 118L: Jim Stephenson; 118–119C: Hannah Thual; 119R, 120–121, 122L, 123L, 123TR, 123BR, 124: Jim Stephenson; 125: Rich West; 127L: Assemble; 127R: Linus Kraemer; 128L, 128R, 129L, 130L, 131L, 131R, 132L, 132–133C, 133TC, 133BC, 133R, 134L, 134R: Assemble; 135C, 135R: Benedict Johnson; 136L: Assemble; 136–137C: Guy Archard; 137R, 138–139, 140TL, 140BL, 140C, 140–141C: Assemble; 141R: Rich West; 142TL, 142BL: Thierry Bal; 142–143C, 143R, 144–145: Rich West; 146L, 146R, 147L, 148L, 148R, 149R, 150L, 150R, 151C, 151R: Assemble; 152L: Simon Terrill; 152–153C, 153R: Assemble; 154, 155TR, 155BR, 156–157, 158L, 159: S1 Artspace; 160L, 160–161C, 161R, 162L, 163, 164L, 164–165C, 165TR: Assemble; 165BR: Agnese Sanvito; 166: Rich West; 167, 169L: Assemble; 169TR, 169BR: Marie Jacotey; 170L, 170C, 171: Assemble; 172L: Marie Jacotey; 172–173C, 173C, 173R, 174L, 174–175C, 175R, 176L, 176–177C, 177R, 178–179, 180L, 180–181C, 181C, 181R, 182L, 182C, 182–183C, 183C, 183R, 184, 185, 186, 187, 188L, 188C, 188–189C, 189C, 189R, 190L, 190–191C, 191R, 192L, 192–193C, 193TR, 193BR, 194, 195TR, 195BR, 196L, 196R, 197, 198–199, 200L, 200–201C, 201R, 202L, 203, 204L, 204C, 205, 206, 207, 209L, 209R, 210L, 210–211C, 211R, 212L, 212–213C, 213R, 214L, 214–215C, 215R, 216L, 216–217C, 217R, 218–219: Assemble; 220L, 221L, 221TR, 221BR, 222TL, 222BL, 222–223T, 222–223B, 223R: Assemble & Czvek Rigby; 224L, 224–225TC, 224–225C, 225TR, 225BR, 226L, 226–227C, 227TR, 227BR, 228L, 228–229C, 229R, 230L, 230C, 230–231C, 231TR, 231BR, 232, 233R: Assemble; 234L, 234–235C, 235R: Patrick (K brewery); 236L, 236–237C, 237R, 238–239, 240L, 240–241C, 241R, 242L, 242–243C, 243R: Assemble; 244L: Duval Timothy; 244–245C: Kelly Colley; 245TR, 245BR: Kewon Hunter; 246L, 246–247C, 247TR, 247BR, 248TL, 248BL, 248–249C, 249R, 250L: Assemble; 250–251C, 251TR, 251BR, 252TL, 252BL, 253: Lusher Photography; 254L, 254–255C, 255C, 255R, 256L, 256R, 257R: Assemble; 258L, 258R, 259R: Schnepp Renou; 260–261: Assemble; 262L: Assemble; 262R, 263TR: Schnepp Renou; 263BR, 264L: Assemble; 265L, 266L, 266–267T, 266–267B, 267TR, 267BR, 268, 269, 271L, 271R, 272L, 272R, 273C, 273R, 274L, 274C: Assemble; 274–275C: Ioana Marinescu; 275R, 276L, 276TC, 276BC, 276–277C, 277R, 277BR, 278L, 278–279C, 279TR, 279BR, 280L, 280–281C, 281R, 282L, 283, 284TC, 284BC, 284–285TC, 284–285BC, 285R, 286L, 286–287TC, 286–287BC, 287R, 288L, 288TC, 288BC: Assemble; 288–289TC, 288–289BC: Sam Nixon; 289TR, 289BR, 290–291, 292L, 292–293TC, 292–293BC, 293R, 294TL: Assemble; 294BL: Eleanor May Watson; 294–295C: Marco Cappelletti, 295R, 296L: Assemble; 297: Marco Franceschin; 298TL, 298–299C, 299TR, 299BR, 300TL, 300BL: Assemble; 300–301C, 301R: Duval Timothy; 302TL, 302BL: Sarah Elizabeth Larson; 302TC, 302BC, 302–303TC, 302–303BC, 303R, 304L, 304–305TC, 304–305BC: Assemble; 305TR, 305BR, 306L, 306–307C, 307R: Lewis Ronald; 308L, 308C, 308–309C: Assemble; 309C, 309R: Thomas Adank; 310L: Steven Pocock; 310–311C, 311R: Thomas Adank; 312, 313: Assemble; 315L, 315R: JAM; 316L, 316–317C: Assemble; 317R: JAM; 318L, 318–319C, 319R, 320–321, 322L, 322C, 322–323C, 323R: Assemble; 324–325: Students of Takero Shimizaki, London Metropolitan University; 326L, 326–327C, 327TR, 327BR, 328L, 328–329C, 329TC, 329BC, 329TR, 329BR, 330L, 330–331C, 331TR, 331BR, 332L, 333, 334L, 334–335C, 335R, 336, 337R, 338L, 338–339TC, 338–339BC, 339C, 339R, 340–341, 343: Assemble.

PROJECT DIRECTORY

The Cineroleum
Clerkenwell, London, UK 2010

Folly for a Flyover
Hackney Wick, London, UK 2011

Sugarhouse Studios Stratford
Stratford, London, UK 2011

Theatre on the Fly
Chichester, UK 2012

Lina Bo Bardi: Together
Various 2012-2016

Make, Don't Make Do
Stratford, London, UK 2012

Triangle Chairs
Clerkenwell, London, UK 2012

Big Slide
Stratford, London, UK 2012

OTOProjects
Dalston, London UK 2012-2013

New Addington
New Addington, London, UK 2013

Barkingside
Barking, London, UK 2013

Durham Wharf
Hammersmith, London, UK
2013 - Ongoing

Granby Four Streets
Liverpool, UK 2013 - Ongoing

Yardhouse
Stratford, London, UK 2014

Harrow Lowlands
Harrow, London, UK 2014

The Playing Field
Southampton, UK 2014

The School of Narrative Dance
Rome, Italy 2014

Bell Square Pavillion
Hounslow, London, UK
2014 - Unbuilt

Blackhorse Workshop
Walthamstow, London, UK 2014

Baltic Street Adventure Playground
Glasgow, UK 2014

Stille Strasse
Berlin, Germany 2015

Turner Prize Exhibition
Glasgow, UK 2015

The Brutalist Playground
Various 2015

Chicken Town
Tottenham, London, UK 2015

Granby Workshop
Liverpool, UK 2015

10 Houses on Cairns Street
Liverpool, UK 2015

The Voice of Children
Venice, Italy 2016

Robin Day
South Kensington, London, UK 2016

Granby Winter Garden
Liverpool, UK 2017-2019

Sugarhouse Studios Bermondsey
Bermondsey, London, UK
2017-2023

Kamikatz Brewery
Shikoku Island, Japan 2017

How We Build
Vienna, Austria 2017

Poppenbüttel Community Centre
Hamburg, Germany
Competition: 2017

A Factory of As It Might Be
New York City, NY, USA 2017

Art On The Underground
Seven Sisters, London, UK 2017

Blackhorse Yard
Walthamstow, London, UK 2017

Armitage Shanks
Rugeley, UK 2017

Horst Festival
Holsbeek, Belgium 2017

Calverley Old Hall
Calverley, UK Competition: 2017

Ways of Listening
Rome, Italy 2018

Material Institute
New Orleans, LA, USA 2018

The Factory Floor
Venice, Italy 2018

Goldsmiths CCA
New Cross, London, UK 2018

The Sympathy of Things
Radio documentary 2018

Play KX
King's Cross, London, UK 2018

Assemble Play
Various, London, UK 2018

Laguna Viva
Venice, Italy 2018

Fabric Floor
Brixton, London, UK
2019 - Ongoing

D. H. Chen Foundation Gallery
Hong Kong, China 2019

The Rules of Production
Tokyo, Japan 2019

Kunstacademie Zwevegem
Zwevegem, Belgium
Competition: 2019

Totteridge Academy Quad
Barnet, London, UK 2019

Being Human
Euston, London, UK 2018

Tufting Gun Tapestries
Chicago, IL, USA 2019

GROW Totteridge Farm
Barnet, London, UK
2019 - Unbuilt

Design Museum Gent
Ghent, Belgium
Competition: 2019

Bridport Housing
Bridport, UK 2019 - Unbuilt

Kaaitheater
Brussels, Belgium
Competition: 2019

Black Masking Culture
South Kensington, London, UK
2019

St Anne's College
Oxford, UK 2019 - Ongoing

Domeview Yard
North Greenwich, London, UK
2019 - Ongoing

House of Annetta
Spitalfields, London, UK
2019 - Ongoing

The Place We Imagine
Toronto, Canada
and Nottingham, UK 2019-2022

Atelier LUMA
Arles, France 2019-2023

Fourth Corner
Liverpool, UK 2020 - Ongoing

Dairy Road Industrious
Neighbourhood Masterplan
Canberra, Australia
2020 - Ongoing

Skating Situations
Folkestone, UK 2020-2021

Charlotte Perriand:
Design Museum
South Kensington, London, UK
2020-2021

The Making Room
Dundee, UK 2021

ThreeSixty
Barking, London, UK 2021-2022

Bill Brown Creative Workshops
Cambridge, UK 2021-2024

Open School East
Margate, UK 2021

Mu.ZEE
Oostende, Belgium
2021 - Ongoing

Earth Core Family at
Valerie Traan
Brussels, Belgium 2021

Broadridge
Devon, UK 2021-2023

The Blue
Bermondsey, London, UK 2022

Dreamachine
Various 2022

Building 13, Dairy Road
Industrious Neighbourhood
Canberra, Australia
2022 - Ongoing

Churchill Road
Cambridge, UK
Competition: 2022

Bramcote Park
South Bermondsey, London, UK
2022 - Ongoing

Campo Winterthur
Winterthur, Switzerland
Competition: 2023

Fleeting Forest
King's Cross, London, UK 2023

Siegen Architecture School
Arles, France Competition: 2023

Play Works
Twickenham, London, UK 2024

Barry Flanagan
Summer Exhibition
Spitalfields, London, UK 2024

Gwanju Hanok
Seoul, South Korea 2024

Royal Academy
Summer Exhibition
Piccadilly, London, UK 2024

ENDNOTES

1	Andrew Saint, 'The Cambridge School of Architecture: A Brief History', University of Cambridge, School of Architecture: https://www.arct.cam.ac.uk/aboutthedepartment/aboutthedepthome, accessed 24 Jan 2024.
2	I am grateful to Professor Joseph Bedford, who has written extensively on British architecture history of the recent era, for this background information.
3	Conversation with Irénée Scalbert, 7 Jul 2023.
4	J. M. Richards, *The Castles on the Ground: The Anatomy of the Suburb,* London, 1973, p. 32.
5	Alison and Peter Smithson, *The Charged Void: Architecture*, New York, 2001.
6	cf. Tony Fretton, *Tony Fretton Architects: Buildings and Their Territories*, Basel, 2013.
7	cf. Irina Davidovici, Dirk Somers, Martin Steinmann, *Sergison Bates architects: Buildings*, Lucerne, 2014.
8	Adam Caruso, Peter St John, *Caruso St John: Collected Works Volume 1 1990–2005*, London, 2014, pp. 13-15.
9	Ibid.
10	Conversation with Irénée Scalbert, 4 Jul. 2023.
11	Irénée Scalbert, 6a architects, *Never Modern,* Zürich, 2013.
12	Ibid., p. 38.
13	Ibid., p. 106.
14	Conversation with Irénée Scalbert, 4 Jul. 2023.
15	Conversation with Joseph Bedford, 25 Jul. 2023.
16	Markus Miessen and Shumon Basar, *Did Someone Say Participate?: An Atlas of Spatial Practice,* Cambridge, MA, 2006.
17	Alfredo Brillembourg and Hubert Klumpner, *The Architect and the City: Ideology, Idealism, and Pragmatism*, Berlin, 2021, pp. 60-63.
18	Many of these tactics were collected and analyzed by the London-based critic Justin McGuirk, who not only wrote about them for local publications, but also collected them into his 2014 book *Radical Cities*. See: Justin McGuirk, *Radical Cities: Across Latin America in Search of a New Architecture,* London and New York City, NY, 2015.
19	Miessen and Basar, *Did Someone Say Participate?,* p. 23.
20	Ibid.
21	Ibid., p. 286.
22	Tschumi used the phrase to describe many of his projects throughout the 1990s, ranging from his designs for the Parc de la Villette (1982–98) to the arts center at Le Fresnoy (1991–97). See: Bernard Tschumi, *Event-Cities,* Cambridge, MA, 1994.
23	Anthony Giddens, *Modernity and Self Identity: Self and Society in the Late Modern Age*, (Palo Alto, CA, 1991)
24	See: https://en.wikipedia.org/wiki/New_Addington, accessed 31 Jan 25.
25	Ruth Bloomfield, 'A meteor storm: Anti-parking boulders which cost £7,000 spark fury', the *Evening Standard*, 16 Oct. 2012: https://www.standard.co.uk/news/london/a-meteor-storm-antiparking-boulders-which-cost-ps7-000-spark-fury-8212824.html, accessed 24 Jan 2025.
26	Andy Beckett cited in Ian Jack, 'Promised You a Miracle: UK 80-82 by Andy Beckett review – how today's Britain was born in the early 80s' the *Guardian*, (5 Sep. 2015): https://www.theguardian.com/books/2015/sep/05/pomised-you-a-miracle-uk-80-82-andy-beckett-review, accessed 24 Jan 2025.
27	Duncan Jones, 'St Giles Road', *Bevington Road*, St Anne's College, University of Oxford: <https://www.st-annes.ox.ac.uk/life-here/library/blog/bevington/, accesed 30 Jan 25.
28	Professor Tim Crook, 'The Artesian Well of Contemporary Art- Laurie Grove Baths', *Goldsmiths History Project*, Goldsmiths University of London: https://sites.gold.ac.uk/goldsmithshistory/the-artesian-well-of-contemporary-art-laurie-grove-baths/, accessed 30 Jan 25.
29	See: https://maryon.ch/en/edith-maryon-foundation/, accessed 5 Feb 25.
30	'Strategy for the transformation of the fringe in Hovinbyen', URBACT, (Spring 2018): https://urbact.eu/sites/default/files/2023-03/oslo_gebundeld.pdf, accessed 4 Feb 25.
31	Assemble, *Art in Hovinbyen*, (29 Sep. 2022): https://issuu.com/kul43/docs/art_in_hovinbyen_atlas_lowres, accessed 24 Jan 25.

INDEX

6a (Architects) 15–17, 20, 21, 110, 214
    Cowan Court, Churchill College 17
    Raven Row Gallery 16, 20
10 Houses on Cairns Street 172, 173, 174–175, 176, 181, 182, 183, 281, 323
11th century 86
18th century 88, 170
19th century 8, 10, 86, 88, 113, 170, 282
20th century 9, 17, 88, 170, 317, 318, 327

A
Aalto, Alvar 318
Adjaye, David 8, 15
A/D/O 288
A New Direction 134
Architectural Association 18
Architekturzentrum Wien (see also Vienna Architecture Centre) 271, 286
Armitage Shanks 266–267
Art Deco 224
Art in Hovinbyen 340–343
Art on the Underground 134–139
Arts & Crafts 8, 10, 18, 282, 309, 310
Arup 25, 31
Ashbee, C. R. 8
Assemble Play 151, 152, 162
Atelier Bow Wow 100
Atelier LUMA 226, 254–265

B
Baltic Street Adventure Playground 146–149, 150, 151, 162, 191, 303
Barbican Centre 40, 41, 63
Basar, Shumon 19, 20, 191
BC Architects 254–257
Bedford, Joseph 18
Being Human exhibition 308–310
Bell Square Pavilion 132–133, 134, 135
Beuys, Joseph 14
Bidgood, Juliet 41
Big Slide 66–67
Bill Brown Creative Workshops 226–229
Binning, James 35, 70, 89, 110, 129, 130, 132, 318
Blackhorse Workshop 89, 103–110, 111, 116, 148, 161, 173, 193, 246, 314, 318
Black Masking Indian suits 240, 245
Black Mountain College 241
Blager, Noemí 274–275
Blue, The 112–123, 141
Bo Bardi, Lina 271, 272, 274–275, 286, 304, 309

Boelen, Jan 254
Bramcote Park 112, 160–165
Briggs, Holly 197, 200
British Council 150, 274, 275
Brown, Michael 155
    Brunel Estate 155
Brutalist Playground, The 150, 152–159, 162
Buasio 231
Building Crafts College 89

C
Cafe OTO 62, 64
Cake Industries 213
Cambridge School of Architecture 7
Cambridge University 6, 7, 8, 15, 17, 18, 21, 26, 129, 226, 272
Caruso, Adam 13
Caruso St John 8, 14, 16, 17, 46, 214
    Pleasant Place Doctors' Surgery 14, 16
    Stable, The 14, 16–17
    Studio House 14
Centre for Heritage, Arts & Textile (CHAT) 250
Charlotte Perriand: Design Museum 304–307
Chen, Dr Din Hwa 250
Chicago Architecture Biennial (CAB) 301, 302
Chipperfield, David 12, 214, 318
Cinema Museum, The 36
Cineroleum, The 6, 24–39, 47, 48, 54, 56, 89, 115, 117, 189, 274, 287
Clarke, Katherine 41
clay 114, 136, 176, 183, 221, 230, 255, 256, 263, 266, 267, 288, 292
Commonwealth Games 146
Cook, Sir Peter 15
Cook, Steve 293
Cooper Eckstut 328
COVID-19 149, 183, 202
Crawshaw, Alison 129
Creasey, Ken 31
Create London 40, 146
Crimson Historians & Urbanists 100, 273
Cruz, Teddy 273
Czvek Rigby 220, 221, 222, 224

D
Dairy Road Industrious Neighbourhood 315, 317–321
Dall, Amica 36, 146–147, 150

Davey, John 172
Day, Robin 284–285
Day-Lewis, Daniel 104
Deconstructivism 13
Design Museum Gent 222–223
Design Museum, The (London) 304–307
Deutsches Architektur Zentrum (see also German Architecture Centre/DAZ) 271–272
D. H. Chen Foundation Gallery 111, 226, 250–253
Domeview Yard 110–111, 314
Dougherty, Dale 104

E
East London School of Furniture Making 100
Edge, Nina 169
Edge, The 159
Edgerley, Alice 31, 34, 49, 147
Edgerley, Fran 49, 322–323, 326
Edith Maryon Foundation 322, 323
Emerson, Tom 15, 17, 18, 214
Europa (graphic design studio) 104–105
Expedition Engineering 62
EXYZT 18, 26–27
    Southwark Lido project 26, 38

F
Fabric Floor 226, 246–249, 314
Factory as it Might Be, The 288–291
Factory Floor, The 292–293
Farchy, Isabel 266–267
Farrell, Terry 135
Featherboard 65
Fior, Liza 41
Flints Theatrical Chandlers 31
Floyd-Maclean, William 118
foam 57, 68, 151, 153, 154, 158, 162
Folkestone Triennale 140
Folly for a Flyover 6, 26, 39, 40–53, 115, 133, 274, 286
Formica 27, 37
Fretton, Tony 8, 11–13, 15
    Lisson Gallery 12, 13
    Molenplein housing project 12

G
Gates, Theaster 273
Gauld, Lauren 302
Gavigan, Mark 140, 142
Gehry, Frank 254, 256–258

349

gentrification 18, 21, 88, 111, 115, 116, 149, 323, 326
German Architecture Centre (*see also* Deutsches Architektur Zentrum/DAZ) 271–272
geotextile 54–56
Giant's Causeway, The 159
Giddens, Anthony 77
Gilbert & George 189
Goffman, Erving 77
Goldfinger, Ernő 152
    Balfron Tower 152
Goldsmiths Centre for Contemporary Art (CCA) 86, 208–220, 221, 226
Gordon, Kim 188
Graham Foundation, The 275
Granby Four Streets 168–173, 176, 180, 182, 183, 188, 189, 191, 196, 200, 201, 202, 204, 208, 211, 280, 281, 283, 286, 302, 303, 340
Granby Four Streets Community Land Trust (CLT) 171, 172, 174, 182, 183, 201
Granby Residents Association, The (GRA) 171
Granby Winter Garden 173, 180–191
Granby Workshop 119, 123, 169, 172–173, 176–179, 180–183, 188–189, 202, 214, 256, 266, 280–282, 287–288, 292–294, 298, 314
GROW Totteridge Farm 334–339
Guyton, Tyree 273

H
Hadid, Zaha 31
Hall, Jane 30, 34, 35, 103, 111, 274, 335
Halligan, Joe 35, 110, 274
Hamilton, Xanthe 172
Hardwick, Lydia 176
Hargreaves Associates (now Hargreaves Jones) 88
Harrow Lowlands 278–279, 280–281
Haus der Kulturen der Welt (House of World Cultures/HKW) 192–193
Haworth Tompkins 54
Hayatsu Architects 112, 114
Hedrick, Norma 301
Hoare, Tim 54
Hoffmann, Maja 254, 255
Hoggart, Richard 8
Holz, Jochem 309
Horst Castle 76
Horst Arts and Music Festival 76–81
House of Annetta 317, 322–327, 328
How We Build 286–287

I
Industrial Revolution 8, 170

J
Jacobs, Jane 18
Jacotey, Maria 169, 172
JAM 315–317
Jencks, Charles 134
Jones, Lewis 30, 40, 98, 173, 183

K
Kaaitheater 224–225
Kaechele, Kirsha 240–241
Kamikatz Brewery 226, 230–239
Kennedy, Alan and Robert 147–148
Kentish Ragstone 140–141
Kerr, Jacqueline F. 303
Khader, Sumuyya 302
King, Helen 196–197, 204
King, Mollie Anna 94, 288
Koolhaas, Rem 328
KORO 340–341
Kraemer, Linus 127
Ku, Andrea 190
Kunstacademie Zwevegem 220–221, 222

L
Lacey, Owen 30
Laguna Viva 294–297
Lamb, George 334
Laurie Grove Baths 208
Le Corbusier 305
Ledwich, Anna 54
Lee, Eleanor 172–173, 181
Lee Navigation 40
Leslie, Emma 89, 119
Lewis Cubitt Square 150, 151
Lina Bo Bardi: Together 271, 272, 274–275
Lisogorskaya, Maria 26, 35, 100, 103, 111, 116, 128, 131, 132, 240, 241, 242
Local Works Studio 160
London Craft Week 298
London Festival of Architecture 26
London Film Festival 36, 86
London Legacy Development Corporation (LLDC) 40, 86, 89

M
Mackintosh, Charles Rennie 46
MacNamara, Eva 62
Make, Don't Make Do 102–103, 115, 131
Marinescu, Ioana 275
marquetry 27, 37
Material Institute 111, 226, 240–245, 301, 302, 309, 315
MAXXI museum 68–69
Melancon, Big Chief Demond 301
McRory, Sarah 146

MDF 29, 55
Men's Sheds 103
Merton Abbey 8
Miessen, Markus 19, 20, 191
Minimalism 12, 13, 15, 257
Modernism 9, 134, 274
Moin, Moira 328
Mole Architects 7
Moore, Rowan 37, 274
Morris, William 8, 282
muf 40–41, 44, 48, 100, 110, 129
Museum of Old and New Art (MONA) 240–242
Muzio, Sara 26

N
National Theatre (London) 31
neo-vernacular 8, 12
New Addington 126–132, 134, 135, 140, 141, 147, 164, 191
New Art Centre 27
Nicholson, Simon 151
NL Architects 41
    A8ernA 41
Noble, Richard 210, 220
Norie, Daniel 328, 329
Nuffield Theatre 70

O
O2 110
Oakley, Michael 54
Olivier, Laurence 54
Olympic Games 40, 42, 86, 88, 94, 316
Olympic Park (Queen Elizabeth) 44, 88
OMA 273, 274, 328
Open School East 328–329
Opomu, Vicki 303
OTOProjects 62–65, 271
Oudolf, Piet 264
Outer London Fund 128
Outram, James 135
Owens, Richard 170

P
Pedretti, Annetta 322–327
Perkins, Amy 46
Perkins, Steven 190
Perriand, Charlotte 304–307, 309
Pevsner, Nikolaus 9
Pimlott, Mark 15
Playing Field, The 70–75, 76, 95, 115, 161
Play KX 150–152
Plowden, David 318
plywood 41, 63–65, 66, 68, 71, 91, 106, 210, 222, 246, 276

polycarbonate 63, 201
Powell & Moya 54, 155
    Chichester Festival Theatre 54–61
    Churchill Gardens 155
Postmodernism 13, 135
Practice Architecture 27, 41
    Big Bench 27
    Frank's Cafe 27, 38
    Yard Theatre 27
Prytherch, Joe 105

Q
R
Rama, Edi 273
Ravel, Maurice 242
Raw, Matthew 134, 135
Reading, Malcolm 328
recycled materials 17, 35, 36, 42, 46, 54, 57, 59, 71, 84, 95, 99, 114, 116, 161, 168, 183, 200, 202, 205, 210, 241, 279, 280, 304
Royal Institute of British Architects (RIBA) 153, 155
Richards, J. M. 7, 9, 10
Riordan, Niamh 288
Rise & Win 230
Ritchie+Daffin 317
Robin Day exhibition 284–285
Rogers, Richard 328
Rossi, Aldo 13
Rotor 272
Royal Academy of Arts 189, 314
Rules of Production, The 298–300
Ruskin, John 8

S
S1 Artspace 155, 158
San, Nobiru 231
Save Brick Lane 322
Scalbert, Irénée 8, 15, 16, 18
Schroder, Ingrid 18
School of Narrative Dance 68–69
Schulz, Louis 322
Second World War 8, 62, 128, 170, 274, 282, 319
Selldorf, Annabelle 254, 255
Senatore, Marinella 68
Sennett, Richard 18
Sergison Bates 8, 11–13, 15
    Cadix harbour building 13, 15
    Hampstead mansion block 12
Sergison, Jonathan 12
Shannon, Will 288
Shimazaki, Takero 323
Shonfield, Kath 41

Skating Situations 140–146
Smith, Giles 6
Smithson, Alison and Peter 8–14, 16, 18–19
    Appliance House 11
    Golden Lane Estate 10–11, 14
    House of the Future 11
    Hunstanton Secondary Modern School 9–11
    Robin Hood Gardens 11–12
Smithson, Robert 14
Snellman, Tapio 275
Snowman, Joe 142–143
Sonic Youth 188
South London Gallery (6a) 17
Spatial Agency 18
'spatial practitioners' 20
St Anne's College 196–205
Steane, Mary Ann 8
Steinbeck Studio 172, 174, 183
Stille Strasse 192–195
Stinsensqueeze 112–113, 119
Stirling, James 135
St John, Peter 13
Stratford Rising Festival 66
Strelitz, Paloma 30, 34, 147, 211, 220
Structure Workshop engineers 71, 233
Studio Dekka 30
Sugar House Island 89, 98, 100, 102–103
Sugarhouse Studios 112, 115–116, 173–174, 176, 193, 211–212, 246, 275, 280, 286, 288, 314, 316, 318, 342
    Bermondsey 98–101, 102–103, 110, 118–119, 135, 247, 266–267, 304
    Stratford 84–93, 94, 103, 110, 271, 276–277, 342–343
Sugden House 11
Suzuki, Minoru 298, 300
Sympathy of Things, The 310–311

T
Tate Museum 46, 280
Team X 19
Terrill, Simon 153, 155
Theatre on the Fly 54–59, 66, 76, 115
Theatre Royal Stratford East 66
Thomas, Sean 105
Tilley, Hazel 172
Tillmans, Wolfgang 16
Timothy, Duval 301
Torre David 20
Totteridge Academy Quad 330–333
Triangle Chairs 276–279
Tschumi, Bernard 38

Tufting Gun Tapestries 300–301
Turner Prize 160, 188–191, 201, 202, 211
Turner Prize Exhibition 176, 280–283, 284, 304
Tyvek 25, 26, 287

U
'urban acupuncture' 69, 100
Urban-Think Tank 19, 100, 328

V
Vastint 86
Venice Biennale of Architecture 41, 292
Venturi, Robert 13, 135
vernacular 7, 9, 10, 11, 12, 13, 15, 19, 20, 131, 134, 319
Vesely, Dalibor 7
Victoria & Albert Museum (V&A) 284, 309
Vienna Architecture Centre (*see also* Architekturzentrum Wien) 271, 286
Voice of Children, The 150
Vriesendorp, Madelon 274–275

W
Wainwright, Oliver 100
Walsh, David 240
Warden, Harriet 105
Watermans 133
Watson, Eleanor May 294
Ways of Listening 302–303
Webb, Philip 282
Welford, Aska 323
Wellcome Collection 308–309, 311
Wentworth, Richard 15, 16, 18–19,
West 8 (landscape architects) 41
    Carrascoplein 41
Whisperers, The 15, 17, 18, 21
Williams, Raymond 8, 9, 16
Willis, Adam 211, 220,
Wilson, Jill 322
Wilson, Penny 150–151
Woolf, Jonathan 15
Workshop East 89, 106, 293

X
Y
Yardhouse 89, 94–97, 221, 266, 271, 286, 288, 342–343

Z
ZUS 100, 328
Zwierzchowska, Asia 197

Front cover, clockwise from top left: 10 Houses on Cairns Street © Assemble, Horst Festival © Jeroen Verrecht, Goldsmiths CCA © Assemble, Folly for a Flyover © David Vintiner, Yardhouse ©Assemble, Kamikatz Brewery © Assemble, The Cineroleum ©Assemble, A Factory As It Might Be © Assemble

Back cover: Illustrations © Assemble

First published in the United Kingdom in 2025 by Thames & Hudson Ltd, 6–24 Britannia Street, London WC1X 9JD

First published in the United States of America in 2025 by Thames & Hudson Inc., 500 Fifth Avenue, New York, New York 10110

Assemble © 2025 Thames & Hudson Ltd, London

Text © 2025 Aaron Betsky

All images © 2025 Assemble unless otherwise indicated

Designed by thonik

All Rights Reserved. No part of this publication may be reproduced or transmitted in any form or by any means, electronic or mechanical, including photocopy, recording or any other information storage and retrieval system, without prior permission in writing from the publisher.

EU Authorized Representative: Interart S.A.R.L.
19 rue Charles Auray, 93500 Pantin, Paris, France
productsafety@thameshudson.co.uk
interart.fr

A CIP catalogue record for this book is available from the British Library

Library of Congress Control Number 2024935637

ISBN 978-0-500-02700-4
01

Printed and bound in China by Toppan Leefung Printing Limited

The author would like to thank all the members of Assemble and their clients for their collaboration, and Lucas Dietrich, Augusta Pownall and Rachel Hughes at Thames & Hudson for their astute guidance in this project. In addition, Joseph Bedford, Irénée Scalbert and Ingrid Schroder provided valuable insights, and the author is grateful to Robert White for his hospitality in London. This book was partially made possible by travel funding provided by Virginia Tech University.

Aaron Betsky is a critic and teacher living in Philadelphia. He has held numerous academic and museum positions around the world and directed the 11th Venice International Biennale of Architecture. Betsky is the author of over twenty books, including *50 Lessons to Learn from Frank Lloyd Wright*, *Architecture Matters* and *The Monster Leviathan: Anarchitecture*.

Assemble is a multi-disciplinary collective working across architecture, design and art. Founded in 2010 to undertake a single self-built project, Assemble has since delivered a diverse and award-winning body of work, while retaining a democratic and co-operative working method that enables built, social and research-based work at a variety of scales, both making things and making things happen.

Be the first to know about our new releases, exclusive content and author events by visiting
thamesandhudson.com
thamesandhudsonusa.com
thamesandhudson.com.au